The Mac® OS X Command Line
Unix Under the Hood

Kirk McElhearn

SYBEX®

San Francisco   London

Associate Publisher: Joel Fugazzotto

Acquisitions Editor: Elizabeth Peterson

Developmental Editors: Heather O'Connor, Brianne Agatep

Production Editor: Elizabeth Campbell

Technical Editor: James Bucanek

Copyeditor: Suzanne Goraj

Compositor: Laurie Stewart, Happenstance Type-O-Rama

Graphic Illustrator: Jeffrey Wilson, Happenstance Type-O-Rama

Proofreaders: Nancy Riddiough, Ian Golder

Indexer: Nancy Guenther

Book Designer: Judy Fung

Cover Designer and Illustrator: Richard Miller, Calyx Design

Library of Congress Card Number: 2004109302

ISBN: 0-7821-4354-7

Manufactured in the United States of America

10 9 8 7 6 5 4 3 2

Acknowledgments

If you bother reading this page, you are probably aware that writing a book like this is not an individual effort. While my name goes on the cover, many people were involved at different steps of the project to produce this book. It's important to give these people the kudos they deserve for supporting me and helping make this book as good is possible. Naturally, any weaknesses remain my responsibility, but many of the good parts of the book result from ideas, collaboration, and feedback from others.

Every book begins with an idea, and when an author believes in an idea, he or she needs to then convince a publisher that it is worthy of their time and investment. The first person who took this idea and helped me make it coherent was my agent, Neil Salkind, who has provided me with unfailing support over the years. Thanks to Neil, as well as to all the other people at Studio B who help manage contracts and other details.

Next, the fine people at Sybex came into the picture. First I want to thank Joel Fugazzotto, associate publisher, and Elizabeth Peterson, acquisitions editor, who believed in this project and carried it through to its final form.

Sybex's excellent production department made this book look nice: Elizabeth Campbell managed the book's production, keeping me on schedule and watching over the rest of the team at Sybex. Brianne Agatep took control of the nitty-gritty, until she decided to leave to enlarge her family, when Heather O'Connor grabbed the reins and insured that everything went smoothly. The wonderful team of Suzanne Goraj, Nancy Riddiough, and Ian Golder, copyeditor and proofreaders, made me look good by fixing my mistakes and correcting my typos.

Books aren't finished when an author completes his manuscript. One of the most important members of this team was James Bucanek, who is the best technical editor I've had the fortune to work with. James's understanding of Unix and the Mac is astounding, and the details he pointed out, both by e-mail and in many audio chats via iChat, helped ensure the accuracy of this book. However, any errors or omissions that remain are naturally my responsibility.

Thanks to Adam Engst not only for writing the Foreword to this book, but also for publishing excerpts of the book in TidBITS (www.tidbits.com). Thanks also to Scholle Sawyer McFarland for finding this interesting enough to publish an excerpt in *Macworld* magazine just after publication.

Thanks to Mike Bombich for his permission to adapt tips on cloning a Mac OS X startup volume.

Special thanks to Mark Willan, who provided a friendly ear on the telephone as this project progressed, and whose ideas and opinions were very helpful. Thanks also to Philippe Devallois and Stéphane Sudre for their assistance above and beyond the call of duty.

Thanks to the members of the X-Unix mailing list (www.themacintoshguy.com/lists/X.html), who often gave useful advice and shared their knowledge, and thanks to Eric Prentice, The Macintosh Guy, for hosting the list. Special thanks to Paul Dubois, Victor Eijkhout, Scott Kramer, Eugene Lee and William Magill, whose advice has been very helpful.

Thanks also to Rob Griffiths of Mac OS X Hints (www.macosxhints.com), who has provided valuable input during many discussions over iChat, and has maintained one of the most useful Web sites for Mac OS X power users.

Thanks to Steve Jobs for making Mac OS X interesting, by building it on a Unix foundation, and giving Mac users a chance to discover the command line.

Thanks to Marie-France, who read and commented on the entire manuscript, even though she knows nothing about using the command line, and suggested hundreds of changes throughout. And thanks to Perceval for making life fun.

I'd also like to thank the unsung heroes of the book channel: all the booksellers who live to share their enthusiasm for the books they love, and who help readers discover the book they need. And a final thought for all the trees that gave their lives for this book; in this day of computers and the Internet, printed books are still the best way to provide information, and it is important to realize that each page comes from a tree.

This book was written on an 800 Mhz G3 iBook, then on a 933 Mhz G4 iBook, using Terminal, iTerm, Microsoft Word, SnapzPro, and Photoshop Elements (as well as lots of Terminal commands). iTunes and my iPod provided a soundtrack, and music by Bill Evans, Brad Mehldau, the Grateful Dead, Leftover Salmon, moe, the Durutti Column, Iron & Wine, Bach, Schubert, and many others kept me going.

The view of the French Alps from my office window provided welcome respite as I reflected on some of the stickier issues.

Check out my blog Kirkville (`www.mcelhearn.com`) for more about using the command line with Mac OS X, and for more about my other books. If you have any comments on this book or suggestions for future editions, you can contact me at `kirk@mcelhearn.com`.

Foreword

When Apple first started talking about how Mac OS X would be based on a notoriously powerful and unfriendly Unix core, many long-time Macintosh devotees cringed with fear. Would the Mac's ease of use be compromised with the need to work on an obscure command line?

Happily, although Apple stuck with their plans to base Mac OS X on Unix, they also remained true to the Macintosh ethic of keeping it easy to use. The Unix command line is there, but it's stashed away in a back cupboard, accessible only via the Terminal program Apple provides. Converts to the cult of Macintosh from Unix use the command line all the time, and many of those who swore they'd never touch it have grudgingly given it a try when given a command to paste into Terminal.

The power of those occasional commands from friends, like "Here, just run this command to delete that file the Finder can't trash." were like a taste of the forbidden fruit. Was it possible to do stuff—cool stuff, even—from the command line that wasn't possible from the Mac's graphical interface? For many Mac users, it became clear that the command line could be a useful adjunct to the Finder and Apple's other utilities, and to view it as anything other than a potentially useful tool was merely spiteful.

But there's a big difference, it turns out, between accepting that the command line could have some utility, and internalizing enough of the cryptic commands that they could be used quickly at appropriate times. The command line and the Mac's graphical interface are both languages for communicating with the Macintosh, and those of who understood the graphical lingo needed a translator to make sense of inscrutable commands like `ls`, `rm`, `mv`, and so on.

That's where Kirk McElhearn steps in. You may not realize this, but he's a translator, a real one, who translates documents from French to English when he's not writing books or articles. Being a good translator requires a certain mindset, an understanding of what the words in one language mean, since it's meaning that must come through in a translation, not merely the results of a lookup table that finds matching words (if you don't believe me, try one of the online translation sites, like Alta Vista's Babelfish, for truly amusing results).

Kirk clearly understands what it is to be a Macintosh user, and he also has a strong grasp on the many and varied Unix commands (all little programs in their own right). But rather than just list them out, like so many other beginning Unix books, Kirk introduces them in the context of using a Macintosh, making sure to mention any Macintosh-specific details that are relevant, and generally making you feel at home.

Whether you'll end up using the command line enough to memorize all these commands isn't really important. What doesn't matter is that you'll know that the command line is a useful Macintosh tool that's at your disposal, and thanks to Kirk's efforts in these pages, you'll never be at a loss for the Unix command that will solve your particular problem.

—Adam Engst
Publisher of TidBITS (`www.tidbits.com`)

Contents at a Glance

See What's on the Command Line

Command	Page

Contents

Introduction

When I bought my first computer in 1991—a PowerBook 100—I chose a Macintosh because it ran an operating system I was familiar with, but, most of all, because it was easy to use. I had worked with computers before that, from using punch cards in computer math classes in Jamaica High School, in New York City, in the 1970s, to using terminals connected to an IBM mainframe when I worked for an actuarial consulting firm. I had seen how computers worked, and didn't like what I saw. I didn't want, for my first personal computer, to have to learn arcane codes and commands, and especially to spend my time typing—something at which, back then, I was not very proficient.

In 1991, I was working in a bookstore that had a couple of Macs, and I used them to create flyers, book lists, and other documents. I found the point-and-click interface so easy to use that I thought I would never want to work any other way.

Until Apple released Mac OS X.

The marriage of a Unix-based foundation and an attractive graphical user interface was something I hadn't expected. Here was the best of both worlds. I could point and click to my heart's content, but I could also muck around with what was under the hood. For between my PowerBook 100 and the release of Mac OS X, I had developed a fair amount of experience with various Linux distributions, and was no longer allergic to typing commands.

While I didn't want to use the command line all the time, I did appreciate that this minimalist interface gave me access to things that windows and icons couldn't touch. In some ways it was like when I used ResEdit to hack the system under previous versions of Mac OS. Now, with the command line in Mac OS X, I could not only find plenty of things to fiddle with, but I could also use the power of the command-line tools included with this system.

Mac OS X is a marriage of two types of operating systems: on the one hand, it is an extension of previous versions of Mac OS, and in spite of the novelty of the Aqua interface and brushed-metal windows, is not very different from what came before. But under the hood, everything is new. The Unix underpinnings of Mac OS X are based on Darwin, Apple's open-source foundation. Darwin is a full implementation of BSD Unix derived from the original 4.4BSD-Lite2 Open Source distribution. In addition to the many new (for Mac OS) technologies this offers—such as pre-emptive multitasking, symmetric multiprocessing, support for multiple file systems, and protected memory—one of the main advantages of this choice is that it makes Mac OS X rock-solid.

For a lot of long-time Mac users, the availability of the command line comes as a surprise. Many people began using Macs the way I did, out of a desire to have computers that were easy to use. Most Mac users will never see the command-line interface; it's only visible if you go looking for it. But if you've started reading this book, you're like me—you're interested in the power of the command-line tools and the flexibility they offer in managing your Mac.

Mac OS X and FreeBSD

Mac OS X is a revolutionary operating system in many ways. While it contains many technologies that are available in other operating systems, it brings the power and reliability of Unix to the desktop. In fact, Mac OS X is the best-selling desktop Unix system ever, even though many users never see its Unix foundation. This in itself is commendable; Apple has managed to put such a pretty face on top of this foundation that users don't need to know what's under the hood. Also, it's the first Unix-based system that can run both command-line tools and a wide range of consumer and business productivity, graphics, and game software.

Mac OS X is based on FreeBSD, one of many Unix operating systems. It is one of two main branches of Unix: BSD is the Berkeley Software Distribution (so named because it was developed at the University of California—Berkeley); the other is the System V branch. Both of these operating systems are different from Linux, which is actually a kernel wrapped in one of many distributions, though there are numerous similarities between Unix and Linux systems. In fact, Linux users with strong command-line experience will find Mac OS X easy to adapt to. Some of the key system functions are radically different, but the majority of the commands are similar, and they'll find the same shells they are used to using on their favorite Linux distributions.

As I said above, Mac OS X does a good job of hiding its Unix-based foundation. Many of the essential system files are not normally visible in the Finder, so users who don't need to know about them will never see them. But with the command line and Terminal—the application you use to interact with the command line—you can see all these files, edit them, and configure your Mac in ways you can't from the Aqua interface.

Nothing but Text

The main focus of a command-line system is text: everything is displayed as text. Files, folders, and applications all display as lines of text in Terminal windows. This is less visually stimulating than windows, menus, and icons, but it can save a lot of time for many tasks.

What may seem daunting if you're discovering the command line for the first time is the vast number of commands available. Not only are there hundreds of commands, but most of them have options, sometimes dozens of them. To give you a hand with this rich toolkit, all Unix-based systems—Mac OS X included—offer extensive help files that you can call up instantly so you can find out what the different commands do.

Using the command line does involve memory, though. You need to memorize commands and their functions. But this is much easier than it seems. You don't need to make lists or flashcards, but you learn by doing; as you progress, you'll begin to recall what the different commands do. Some of the commands may seem to have cryptic names, but these short names result from economy: when using the command line it is best to type as little as possible. You'll soon learn that the `cp` command means copy, the `ls` command means list, and the `rm` command means remove.

Who this Book Is For

The best way to start learning the command line is to jump into it. I've written this book for Mac users like myself who want to dig under the hood but who don't want to sweat too much. I've tried to present real-world examples for every command, and I've structured the book so it progresses from the basics to more complex tasks.

Among other things, I'm a translator, and have also been a teacher of English as a foreign language. Because of this, I have approached presenting the command line as a language. Learning a new language can be an intimidating experience, but if you move ahead in small steps you'll find that, before long, you can attain fluency. What you need most is practice. Learn the commands from my examples then try them out in other contexts.

This is not to say that I've neglected more advanced users in this book. While no book can be everything to everyone, I've tried to be sensitive to the needs of users with experience on other Unix-based operating systems. Whenever necessary, I point out differences in concept and usage between Mac OS X and "standard" Unix systems. While there are not a great many differences, they are most obvious in areas such as user and group management, which are radically different under Mac OS X than other Unix systems.

Using this Book

There are two ways to use this book. The first, for those unfamiliar with the command line, is to read through it sequentially, with your Mac in front of you and a Terminal window open. If you've never used the command line before, read through Chapter 1, *A Guided Tour of the Command Line*, which is a simple tutorial that will help you become comfortable with typing commands on your Mac. Then go through the next few chapters to learn how to navigate the file system, move and copy files, find files, view and edit text, and more. After you've read through these chapters and learned the fundamental commands, you're ready to move on to the more advanced chapters, which cover such things as users, groups, and permissions; networking; and system maintenance and management.

If you already have some command-line experience, you'll probably not want to read the earliest chapters, but you may find in this introductory material some differences between the Unix-based system you are familiar with and Mac OS X. The later chapters, which focus on more advanced topics, will certainly be of interest to you and again you'll discover many differences, albeit small, between your favorite flavor of Unix and the Mac.

Here's an overview of the chapters and what they cover:

- Chapter 1, *A Guided Tour of the Command Line*, is a simple, step-by-step tutorial for users who have never worked on the command line. If you are approaching the command line for the first time, take a few minutes to work through this tutorial with a Terminal window open, typing the commands it presents, so you can become familiar with a text-based interface.

- Chapter 2, *Using Terminal*, talks about Apple's Terminal application, included with Mac OS X, and tells you how to work with it and configure it. This application is your gateway to the command line, and it's a good idea to understand what it offers and how you can customize it.

- Chapter 3, *Getting Help while in Terminal*, tells you all about getting help for the many commands you use in Terminal, and how to access the thousands of pages of documentation on your Mac.

- Chapter 4, *Navigating the File System*, shows you how to move around on your Mac, how to list files, and how to get information on your files.

- Chapter 5, *Working with Files and Directories*, shows you how to carry out these essential actions from the command line.

- Chapter 6, *Saving Time on the Command Line*, explains how to use the built-in features of Terminal and your selected shell to make your work on the command line faster and easier.

- Chapter 7, *Finding Files, Directories, and Everything Else*, shows you how to find just about anything on your Mac using the command line.

- Chapter 8, *Viewing Files*, tells you how to view text files from the command line.

- Chapter 9, *Editing Text*, examines command-line text editors, and talks about how you can integrate graphical text editors with the command line.

- Chapter 10, *Printing*, looks at printing and managing printers from the command line.

- Chapter 11, *Compressing, Decompressing, and Archiving Files*, tells you about the many commands that accomplish these tasks.

- Chapter 12, *Working with Users, Groups, and Permissions*, presents the important concepts of users, groups, and permissions, tells you how permissions work, and explains how to manage users and groups from the command line.

- Chapter 13, *Using the Network*, looks at managing Mac OS X network functions from the command line, connecting to other computers from Terminal, and using the Internet.

- Chapter 14, *Managing Programs and Processes*, examines command-line tools to manage the programs running on your Mac.

- Chapter 15, *System Maintenance from the Command Line*, looks at the many tools used to maintain and manage Mac OS X from the command line.

- Chapter 16, *Configuring the Shell*, tells you how to configure the `bash` or `tcsh` shell to suit your needs.

When writing this book, I was confronted with the difficulty of presenting a vast amount of material in a somewhat progressive order. Many key Unix concepts—filenames and paths, wildcards, input and output redirection, regular expressions, and more—could fit in almost any chapter, because they apply to many different commands. Since these recurring concepts transcend any kind of chapter-oriented breakdown, I decided to give each of them their own short chapters that I call *interludes*. While these interludes are loosely related to the chapters that precede them, they focus on precise concepts that apply across the board. Especially if you are a new user, you'll want to come back to these interludes from time to time as your command-line expertise grows, to delve deeper into their subjects. Some of them are about specific tasks or commands—the interludes about the **open** and **sudo** commands, for example—and others about concepts that you can't do without—this is the case for the basic rules of filenames and paths, wildcards, or regular expressions.

Here's an overview of the Interludes and what they cover:

♦ Interlude 1, *Command Syntax* (follows Chapter 2), presents the essential concept of what order the different parts of commands must follow. Commands are like language, with rules describing their word order—to compose commands correctly, you need to know the basics of their syntax.

♦ Interlude 2, *Names & Paths* (follows Chapter 3), presents the notions of filenames and file paths.

♦ Interlude 3, *Redirecting Input & Output* (follows Chapter 4), tells you how to send command output to files and other commands, and how to send input into commands from files and other commands.

♦ Interlude 4, *Cloning your Mac OS X Startup Volume* (follows Chapter 5), explains how to make a bootable backup of your Mac OS X startup volume using command-line tools.

♦ Interlude 5, *The Versatile* open *Command* (follows Chapter 6), tells you all about the **open** command, a tool that is specific to Mac OS X, and that offers a bridge between the command line and the Finder.

♦ Interlude 6, *Wildcards & Globbing* (follows Chapter 7), looks at how the shell uses wildcards, and how wildcards can save you time when running certain commands.

♦ Interlude 7, *Using* sudo (follows Chapter 12), looks at the **sudo** command, which lets you perform tasks that require special authorization.

♦ Interlude 8, *Using the Developer Tools* (follows Chapter 15), looks at the command-line tools included with the Mac OS X Developer Tools.

♦ Interlude 9, *Automating Commands* (follows Chapter 16), looks at various ways to run commands automatically.

What this Book Isn't

No book can be everything to everyone, and this book is no exception. It is not intended to be an exhaustive inventory of the command-line tools available for Mac OS X. When I began writing this book I started from a simple premise: this book covers what's in the box, and with some very tiny exceptions, only what's in the box. There are thousands of programs out there that you can download and install to use with Terminal, but it seemed logical to limit this book to what is included with Mac OS X.

For this reason, also, my examples cover the **bash** shell, which Apple has chosen as the default shell for Mac OS X 10.3, or Panther. But since Apple only made **bash** the default shell starting with Panther, I also cover the **tcsh** shell, which was the default in previous versions of Mac OS X. If you have previous Unix experience and are used to using another shell, you can probably use it right away: Mac OS X Panther includes other popular shells, such as csh and zsh. But if you are familiar with a different shell, you probably know how to configure it already. For additional information, see the man pages for the specific shells.

While I can't cover every command accessible from Terminal—and there are hundreds—I try to cover the most important commands, the ones that everyone needs to know about. Many general Unix books cover more commands, but cover them less thoroughly. In my opinion, it is best to get a solid grounding in the basics before delving deeply into the myriad tools available.

One thing you won't find in this book is any command-line zealotry; I won't ever suggest that the command line is the best way to use a computer. In fact, I'll often suggest the opposite. While I use the command line, and actually enjoy doing so, I see no reason to eschew the GUI if the latter is more efficient. For this reason, I often use graphical text editors, for example, rather than command-line text editors. The command line is a tool for me, one of the many tools available on Mac OS X. As with any good toolkit, you shouldn't use the same tool all the time. There are many times when the command line is more efficient and, especially, more effective, but there are far more times when the GUI is the way to go.

Typographical Conventions

Unlike the other Macintosh books I've written, this one is mostly about text. For this reason, there are very few screen shots in this book. With the exception of Chapter 2, *Using Terminal*, and a few other locations, this is all text, nothing but text. It is therefore important to present a few typographical conventions.

When you use the command line, you have both input and output: input is what you type in Terminal, and output is what commands return and Terminal displays. When you type in Terminal, you always type after the *prompt*, which, for the bash shell, is the $ character (if you're using the tcsh shell, the prompt character is %). For example, if you are in your home directory and want to move to your Documents directory, you type this command:

```
$ cd Documents
```

You never type the $ character, but type everything that follows. At the end of the line, you press Return or Enter to execute the command. Each time I give an example of a command, the line is shown as above, with the prompt character. To distinguish between your input and the command output, the line you type is in bold. Here's an example:

```
$ ls ~
Desktop    Library  Music     Public
Documents  Movies   Pictures  Sites
```

The above command lists the contents of my home directory. When I type the ls command, this command returns the two lines of text below it.

Also, whenever I refer to a command in the body text of the book, I put its name in a monospace font. The same is true for any output I refer to.

System Requirements

To use this book you need any Mac running Mac OS X. One of the beauties of the command line is that, at least with the commands I present in this book, you'll rarely tax your processor; text, by its very nature, demands few resources, and even the slowest Mac that can run OS X is sufficient. If you start compiling software from the command line, this changes; you can spend hours waiting for code to compile.

To use the command line, you must have installed the BSD Subsystem when you installed Mac OS X. If you didn't do so, you can run the installer and update your system. Click the Customize button in the installer to choose this. Also, you'll want to install the Developer Tools to access some of the commands that Apple includes only with this part of the installation. There aren't many command-line tools in the Developer Tools, but some of them are very useful and are specific to the Mac. If you're short on disk space, don't install the Developer Tool documentation—it takes up several hundred megabytes.

You'll need an administrator account to do many of the tasks and run many of the commands in this book. You're already an administrator if you are the only user of your Mac. For users working on shared Macs, or on networks in companies or schools, if you don't have an administrator account there are many commands you simply cannot access. If you have any doubts, ask your system administrator.

Some of the commands, especially in Chapter 13, *Using the Network*, require network access either to the Internet or to other computers on a local network. If you have a standalone Mac, don't worry; you won't need to use commands that involve local networking, but you can still use those that access the Internet.

Finally, you'll need a good amount of curiosity and a bit of perseverance. The command line is different from what you may be used to, and while I do my best to make sure you can learn this new language in a relaxed, enjoyable way, it's up to you: practice makes perfect.

I look forward to receiving your comments, criticism, and suggestions for improving this book. Feel free to e-mail me at `kirk@mcelhearn.com`, but make sure you put "Command Line" in the subject of your message so it doesn't get filtered into my spam folder.

Also, for more on using the command line, stop by my blog, Kirkville (`http://www.mcelhearn.com`). I've got a special section on using the command line with Mac OS X, and will regularly add articles about new techniques using the command line with Mac OS X.

Chapter 1

A Guided Tour of the Command Line

When learning something new, the first step is usually the hardest. You need to take the plunge and dive right into a new way of thinking. Working with the command line is like learning a new language—you have to start with simple tasks and take small steps before you can move ahead to the real nitty-gritty.

When you visit a city you have never been to, it can be useful to take a guided tour. Your tour guide can show you the main landmarks and give you basic explanations of what you see. This is what I'm going to do in this chapter. Think of it as a bus tour of a foreign city, where you'll see the sites but you won't get off and wander on your own.

If you have never used the command line, this chapter gives you a brief introduction to entering commands and using Terminal, the Mac OS X program you use to run these commands. This tutorial introduces a few basic commands, and shows you what happens when you run those commands, but I don't give thorough explanations of any of the commands used here. Don't worry; I'll go into detail about all of them in later chapters. The goal of this chapter is to walk you through a few commands and show you that using the command line is not really as difficult as you may have thought. To get the most out of this chapter, sit down in front of your Mac and follow me as I take you on a guided tour of the command line.

NOTE   *If you are familiar with the command line, you can skip this chapter; you probably know everything that's presented here.*

Opening Terminal

Terminal is the program Apple includes in Mac OS X to provide the interface between the commands you type and the operating system. Terminal itself doesn't do much—it merely passes commands and data on to a shell (another program that interprets these commands) and displays the results of these commands.

Start by opening Terminal (see Figure 1.1). This program is located in the `Utilities` folder of your `Applications` folder (or, to use the Unix convention, `/Applications/Utilities`). Double-click the Terminal icon.

The Terminal window displays, showing something like Figure 1.2.
The text in this window tells you several things:

◆ The first line shows the date and time of the last login, followed by the terminal device ("ttyp1") being used.

◆ The second line is the Message of the Day. The default message of the day for Mac OS X (as of version 10.3) is `Welcome to Darwin!`, Darwin being the name of the Mac implementation of BSD Unix.

◆ The third line is the *prompt*. It contains several parts:

  ◆ It first shows the name of the computer being used—in my case, `Walden`. This name comes from the Sharing panel in the System Preferences.

  ◆ The current directory or folder is shown after the colon (:) following the computer name. When you open a new Terminal window, this is by default your home folder, represented by the ~ shortcut.

  ◆ The next part of the prompt is the name of the user, `kirk`, who is logged in. This is the short user name, not the user's full name. (Obviously, your computer name and user are different than mine, which are shown in this example.)

  ◆ The final part of the prompt is the actual prompt character, or `$`. If you're using the `tcsh` shell, you'll see `%` here instead.

FIGURE 1.1
The Terminal icon
in the Utilities folder
of your hard disk

Terminal

FIGURE 1.2
A new Terminal
window

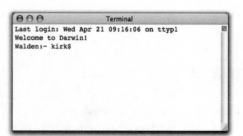

The entire line containing

```
Walden:~ kirk$
```

is known as the *prompt*; it indicates that you can type commands. If Terminal is working on a command or displaying certain processes, you don't see a prompt. In that case, you can always open a new Terminal window to type commands; you can open an unlimited number of Terminal windows, called sessions, at any time.

Typing Your First Command

Now that we've gotten through the basics, you're ready to type your first command. Let's start with echo, a simple command that displays what follows the command name in the Terminal window.

(Note: the commands and text you are to type are shown following the prompt character, $, but without the computer name and user name. You don't type the prompt text; just type what follows the $ character.)

Type the following:

```
$ echo Hello
```

then press Enter or Return.

Terminal displays each character as you type it. The echo command writes arguments to the standard output—in this case, Terminal. After you press Return, it displays the following line:

```
Hello
```

then displays the prompt again, showing that Terminal is ready to go on to its next task, as in Figure 1.3.

Your Mac just said hello to you! Now, you can go even further—after all, you don't know who it was saying hello to. Try this command:

```
$ echo Hello $USER
```

My Mac says:

```
Hello kirk
```

What does yours say? It should say Hello [*your user name*].

FIGURE 1.3
A Terminal window showing the echo Hello command and its results

```
Last login: Wed Apr 21 09:22:57 on ttyp1
Welcome to Darwin!
Walden:~ kirk$ echo Hello
Hello
Walden:~ kirk$
```

That was easy, wasn't it? You've just run your first command with the Mac OS X Terminal. This was certainly a simple command, but you have seen how Terminal works, and you have used basic command syntax.

All commands use a specific syntax; for simple commands, this is often just

```
command argument
```

The command is the order you give to your computer, and the argument is what the order acts on. Arguments are required for some commands; other commands run with no arguments. In the line of text you typed above, the command was echo and the argument was the text you wanted Terminal to display. (Note that when presenting commands in this book, they are shown in monospace font, and arguments follow in the same typeface. This is a standard typographical convention for presenting commands.)

The syntax for the echo command is as follows:

```
echo string...
```

This means that to run the command, you must type echo, then a string of text. This command writes arguments (the text string) to the standard output, whether it be Terminal, as in the above example, or any other output specified, such as a file (see below). You can now try typing the echo command with other text if you want.

Reading Directory Contents

Let's explore some other things you can do with Terminal. In the following series of commands, you will

1. Create a new directory (the Unix word for folder).

2. Examine the contents of the directory.

3. Create a new file.

4. Tell your computer to write some text to that file.

5. Read the file.

6. Delete the file and directory.

The Terminal prompt shows that you are in your home (~) directory. Each user has a home directory that contains their personal files. In the Finder, you can go to this directory by clicking the Home icon (Figure 1.4) in a Finder window sidebar.

FIGURE 1.4
The home folder
icon in a Finder
window sidebar

 kirk

Let's see what's in this directory. If you recall from looking at it in Finder windows, it contains a few folders. Type the following (remember, only type what is *after* the prompt):

```
$ ls
```

(This is the letter l, not the digit 1.) The ls command lists the contents of a directory. Terminal displays the following:

```
Desktop    Library  Music     Public
Documents  Movies   Pictures  Sites
```

This is a list of everything in your home folder. (You may see a different list if you have added files or folders to your home folder.)

Unlike when viewing files and folders in the Finder, this list doesn't tell you which of the above items are files or folders. You can find out by typing the following:

```
$ ls -F
```

Terminal displays this list:

```
Desktop/    Library/  Music/     Public/
Documents/  Movies/   Pictures/  Sites/
```

In the above example, -F is an *option* for the ls command; it is also case-sensitive: -F is not the same as -f. Options tell certain commands to do things in a slightly different way. This option tells Terminal to display a slash (/) immediately after each pathname that is a directory, an asterisk (*) after each executable (application), etc. The slashes here show us that these are directories. If any of the above items were files, there would be nothing after their names.

Creating a New Directory

Now you're going to create a new directory called Test. Type the following:

```
$ mkdir Test
```

The mkdir command, as its name suggests, makes new directories. Let's check to make sure that this directory has been created by repeating the ls -F command:

```
$ ls -F
```

```
Desktop/    Library/  Music/     Public/  Test/
Documents/  Movies/   Pictures/  Sites/
```

There it is: Test/, the directory that you just created.

Now we are going to move into that directory, using the cd command:

```
$ cd Test
```

The cd command changes the current working directory; this is similar to double-clicking a folder in the Finder. After running this command, the prompt changes to show that we are now in the Test directory:

```
Walden:~/Test kirk$
```

This is the part after the colon showing ~/Test. As we have already seen, ~ is a shortcut for your home directory, and the slash means that the following directory is inside the home directory.

Creating a New File

Let's now create a new, empty file inside the Test directory. Type this:

```
$ touch testfile
```

The touch command is typically used to update file access and modification times, but it can also create a new file; the argument, testfile, is the name we're giving to the file.

Let's check to make sure the file was created. Type the following:

```
$ ls -F
```

which should display:

```
testfile
```

Remember that the -F option for the ls command shows a / following a directory; it shows nothing for files. So we now have a new, empty, file called testfile sitting in the Test directory, just waiting for something to do.

Writing Text to a File

Since this file is doing nothing, you might as well write something to it. How about writing Hello [username] in this file? To do so, you can use the echo command that you learned above. Type the following:

```
$ echo Hello $USER > testfile
```

This tells Terminal to echo the text Hello [username] to the file called testfile. Let's check and make sure it worked. Several commands are available to display the contents of your files; one of them is cat. Type this:

```
$ cat testfile
```

Terminal should display:

```
Hello [your user name]
```

But since we only see this in the Terminal window, we don't have the same impression as when we open a window in an application. Let's see how the text looks in this file. Type:

```
$ open .
```

(Make sure you type open, then a space, then a period.)

This tells the Finder to open the current directory (the . is a shortcut for that) in a new window. You should see a new Finder window, entitled Test, with a file, called `testfile`, inside it.

Double-click this file, which should open with TextEdit (a simple text editor that comes with Mac OS X) and display the text `Hello [username]`, as in Figure 1.5.

Quit TextEdit to close the file, then switch back to Terminal by clicking its icon in the Dock.

Deleting Files and Directories

Now that we have finished our brief demonstration, we need to clean up a bit. We don't really need to keep that file and folder, so let's delete them.

WARNING   *Using the command line can be risky. Unlike working in the Finder, some tasks you carry out on the command line are absolute and cannot be undone. The command I am about to present, rm, is very powerful. It removes files permanently and completely. There is no getting them back after running this command, so use it with great care, and always use the -i option, as explained below, so Terminal asks you to confirm deleting each file.*

Your prompt should now look something like this, showing that you are still inside the `Test` directory you created earlier:

```
Walden:~/Test kirk$
```

Type the following:

```
$ rm -i testfile
```

The `rm` command removes files and directories. In the above example, it removes the file called `testfile`. Be careful with this command; it doesn't just put files in the trash, it removes them completely. The -i option tells Terminal to run the `rm` command in interactive mode, asking you to make sure you want to delete the file. Terminal asks:

```
remove testfile?
```

Type **y**, for yes, then press Return or Enter, and the file is removed. If you wanted to leave it there, you could just type anything other than **y** or press Return.

We should check to make sure the file is gone:

```
$ ls
```

FIGURE 1.5
The `Hello`
`[username]`
text as displayed
by TextEdit

After typing 1s, you should just see a prompt. Terminal doesn't tell you that the directory is empty, but it shows what's in it: nothing.

Now, move up into your home folder. Type:

```
$ cd ..
```

This is the same command we used earlier to change directories. Here the command tells Terminal to go up in the directory hierarchy to the next directory (the .. is a shortcut for the parent directory)—in this case, your home directory.

Type 1s again to see what's in this directory:

```
$ ls
```

You should see something like this:

```
Desktop     Library  Music     Public  Test
Documents   Movies   Pictures  Sites
```

The Test directory is still there. It's easy to delete this directory using rm. Type the following:

```
$ rm -d -i Test
```

The -d option tells this command to remove directories.
When Terminal displays:

```
remove Test?
```

Type **y**, then press Return or Enter. (If you didn't remove testfile, as explained above, the rm command cannot delete the directory. It will not delete directories that are not empty.)

Make one final check to see if the directory has been deleted.

```
$ ls
```

```
Desktop     Library  Music     Public
Documents   Movies   Pictures  Sites
```

Summing Up

If you worked through this brief demonstration, you successfully typed commands in Terminal using the Unix command line. You created a directory (folder), created a file, wrote text to it, then deleted the file and the directory. And all that with some very simple commands. While you have not accomplished anything extraordinary, you have seen that using Terminal is not really that complicated. All it requires is a bit of time to learn the different commands and their arguments and options. If you move ahead slowly, learning as you go on, rather than trying to memorize dozens of commands, you'll soon find that you are not only comfortable with the command line, but that you can do things that help you save time and give you much more power than when working with windows and icons.

Chapter 2

Using Terminal

The Terminal application is the gateway to the command line in Mac OS X. This simple program provides an interface with a shell, or command interpreter, which does the real work when you enter commands. In this chapter, you'll learn how to set up Terminal, how to change its display and preferences, how to use keyboard shortcuts to save time, and how to get help.

Terminal (or Terminal.app) is the program Apple provides so you can run commands in Mac OS X. Terminal is one part of a chain that lets you access the Unix underpinnings of Mac OS X. When you enter commands in Terminal, they are funneled through to a shell (the default shell is bash, but you can use others), which interprets these commands and sends them on to the appropriate parts of the BSD subsystem, or the rest of the Mac OS X operating system.

In some cases, commands you run are executed directly by the shell—this is what happens with many commands, such as those used to navigate the file system, control jobs, or manage processes. In other cases, the shell invokes different Unix commands, which are designed to do one or several functions. The shell sends information to these commands, tells them to run, and, if necessary, gets information back from them. The shell can also redirect data from one command to another, or from a command back to the shell, or to files. The shell can even run programs within itself, displaying their data in Terminal.

What Is Terminal?

In the old days of computing, when personal computers weren't even a dream, all computer access was to mainframe computers: large, cumbersome machines in air-conditioned rooms, connected to the outside world by cables that were, in turn, linked to terminals. These devices were initially Teletype machines with rolls of paper; later, in the 1970s, they became simple monitors with keyboards either connected or attached to them. Using a terminal, a user could interact with a computer in another part of the building or, if they had a modem or acoustic coupler (a curious device that looked like an instrument of torture, into which you inserted a phone receiver), anywhere in the world.

These terminal devices were used to enter data, send commands, and receive output from the mainframe computers. When typing on a terminal, each character was echoed through the cables or phone wires to the computer itself, giving users control over sessions initiated from their remote devices. (Users in the computer room worked on terminals as well; at this point in time, this was the only way to work with computers. But it was already an improvement from the days of punch cards.) Since the computers of the time didn't work with audio, video, or graphics, all that was required was simple ASCII text input and output.

Hundreds, even thousands of different types of terminals were created, and each of them worked in a certain way. At first, computer systems were required to have hardcoded drivers; later, they needed a file called `termcap` that contained information about these terminals and which allowed them to correctly interface with the computer.

Apple's Terminal application emulates Digital Equipment Corporation's VT100 terminal, but it combines both the Spartan interface of an old-fashioned terminal emulator with menus and standard interface controls. It offers several ways to customize its environment, with some elements (window size, fonts, colors, etc.) that are accessible from menu items and others that must be set by commands entered in Terminal.

At first glance, Terminal may look like a blast from the past, but as you become familiar with it you will realize that using the command-line interface can let you do certain tasks faster and easier than with the mouse. In addition, you may be impressed to know that, once you have mastered the command line on your Mac, you will have the know-how to pilot most any of the millions of Unix-based computers around the world. You may not need that knowledge right now, but who knows when it will come in handy?

HANDS ON: GETTING QUICK ACCESS TO TERMINAL

If you're planning to use Terminal a lot and you probably wouldn't be reading this book otherwise—it's a good idea to put the Terminal icon in the Dock so you can open it with a click whenever you want. This way you won't have to open folders to get to the application—a single click in the Dock launches it.

There are two ways to do this:

◆ Find the Terminal icon (in the `Utilities` folder, which is in the `Applications` folder) and drag it to the Dock.

◆ Open Terminal by double-clicking its icon, then click and hold its icon in the Dock. Select Keep in Dock. Now, after you quit Terminal, its icon will remain in the Dock, giving you instant access to it.

If you don't want to keep the Terminal's icon in the Dock, you can make an alias of it and place it on your desktop, or in any other frequently used folder. To do this, select the Terminal icon, then select File ➤ Make Alias (or press ⌘-L). Place the alias wherever it will be handy—on the desktop, in your home folder— and double-click it whenever you want to launch Terminal.

The Next Level of Interaction: The Shell

Terminal is merely a wrapper around another program: a shell. Terminal provides a visual interface and little more. When you open Terminal, it calls another program and tells it to open. This program, the shell, runs inside Terminal. When you type commands in Terminal, it is Terminal that sends your input to the shell, and sends the shell's output to the Terminal window. While Terminal is a funnel that sends data in and out, the shell is a command interpreter that takes your commands and changes them to data that the computer can understand. (See Figure 2.1.) When returning information to you, it takes computer data and turns it into characters that you can read.

FIGURE 2.1
How Terminal interacts with other parts of the operating system

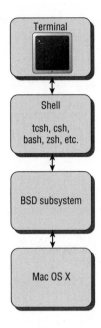

Shells have their own built-in commands for basic operations, and they can invoke other commands stored in various places on your computer. They can also take input or output from different sources (Terminal, files, commands you run) and redirect it to other locations (files, other commands). While a shell's built-in commands are used for many things, much of the work the shell does involves invoking other programs.

There are many shells available for Unix systems. Some of the best known are bash, csh, tcsh, and zsh. Apple has decided to use the bash shell by default; when you open Terminal the first time, this is the shell it uses, though you can change this and use a different shell (see "Customizing Terminal Settings" later in this chapter).

Since a shell is a program, it is invoked like any other Unix command; you can launch a shell by merely typing its name in Terminal and pressing Enter. You can even open a shell within a shell by entering its name as a command.

How the Shell Processes Commands

A shell is an interactive program. When you type text, then press Enter or Return, the shell goes to work, processing that text, looking for the appropriate commands, passing data from one location to another, and returning output, either to the Terminal window or to a file or other program.

In its simplest usage, the shell merely reads the words you type and performs the operations you tell it to do. But it goes much further than that. Depending on the complexity of the command you enter, the shell may perform a number of actions (not necessarily all of these actions, nor in this order):

◆ Break your text into individual "words," which include commands, redirection operators, file and directory names, options, and more.

◆ Analyze these words, one by one, comparing them with programs or data on your computer, to ensure that they are valid references.

◆ Parse your history list to use a previous command, if your command includes a reference to your history list. Command history is discussed in Chapter 6, "Saving Time on the Command Line."

◆ Search your alias list to see if the command you entered is an alias. Aliases are discussed in Chapter 16.

◆ Check the shell's built-in commands to see if the text you type contains one of these commands.

◆ Check the search path to find the commands you entered. If the shell doesn't find all the commands you typed, it will tell you, `Command not found`. For more on setting the search path variable, see Chapter 16.

◆ Perform command, variable, or filename substitution if necessary.

◆ Run the actual commands contained in your text.

◆ Redirect input or output as specified.

◆ Return output from the command to the selected output device (Terminal, a file, etc.)

◆ Display error messages as returned by the command or commands in your text.

◆ Update command history.

As you can see, the shell does a lot of work. This list is not exhaustive, because within simple commands you type after the Terminal prompt, you may have calls to scripts, processes, or programs that set off a complex chain of interactions. In addition, if your command calls part of the Mac OS X operating system, other programs may be called as well, leading to interaction between the shell, the BSD subsystem, and Mac OS X.

Setting Up Terminal

Like any Macintosh application, Terminal has windows, menus, preferences, and shortcuts. You can customize some of the ways Terminal works, but this customization only affects the actual Terminal application, not the shell for which it provides an interface. You can also customize the shell itself, by changing its environment variables, adding aliases to commands, and much more. Shell customization is explored in Chapter 16. Just as with any other application, each user has their own preferences for both Terminal and the shell they use.

WHICH IS YOUR DEFAULT SHELL?

With Mac OS X 10.3, Panther, Apple changed the default shell used by Terminal. In the first iterations of Mac OS X, the tcsh shell was used by default, but with the arrival of Panther, this was changed to bash.

If you update your Mac OS X system from an earlier version to Panther, your user account will retain the tcsh shell. But if you create new accounts, or if you install Panther for the first time, you'll get bash.

You can tell which shell you're using by checking the prompt character that displays in Terminal. The bash shell has a $ prompt, and tcsh uses %.

If you don't work often with Terminal, you'll probably not care one way or another which shell you use; for most operations, they offer similar functions and features. But if you want to change shells, you can do so easily. The chsh (**change sh**ell) command lets you do this. Run the command as follows:

```
$ chsh -s /bin/tcsh username
```

where /bin/tcsh is the path to the shell you want to use. If you're not sure of the full path, run the which command like this:

```
$ which tcsh
/bin/tcsh
```

The result is the full path of the shell you entered as an argument with the which command.

It is important to know which shell you are using if you want to make any configuration changes to the shell. You'll find out all about configuring both bash and tcsh in Chapter 16, "Configuring the Shell."

Customizing Terminal Settings

When you first open Terminal, a new window appears, similar to that shown in Figure 2.2. This window shows some introductory text, then shows a prompt after which you can enter text at the location of the cursor.

Terminal's Window Settings or Terminal Inspector window lets you change many of Terminal's visual elements, from the size of its windows to the type of cursor it uses, and more. To change these settings, select Window Settings from the Terminal menu. (The Terminal Inspector can also be invoked by selecting Show Info from the File menu, or by pressing ⌘-I on the keyboard.) The Terminal Inspector displays Shell options, as shown in Figure 2.3.

FIGURE 2.2

A new Terminal window

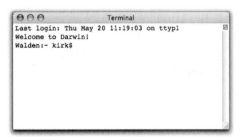

FIGURE 2.3

The Terminal Inspector, showing Shell options

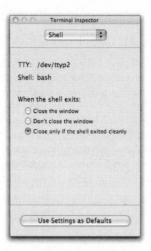

The Terminal Inspector displays a pop-up menu at the top, a middle section for setting options, and a bottom section with a button, Use Settings As Defaults. Select one of the groups of settings from the pop-up menu to make changes. The changes you make apply only to the current window. If you wish to use them as defaults, click the Use Settings As Defaults button.

There are eight groups of settings, each corresponding to the menu items in the pop-up menu at the top of the Terminal Inspector window (see Figure 2.3):

◆ Shell

◆ Process

◆ Emulation

◆ Buffer

◆ Display

◆ Color

◆ Window

◆ Keyboard

The Terminal Inspector is a dynamic window. It changes according to Terminal's frontmost window, and floats above its windows. If you have several windows open and click on different ones, you may see the information in the Terminal Inspector change to reflect differences in the windows.

Shell Settings

If you select Shell from the Terminal Inspector's pop-up menu, you can choose from several shell settings. This window shows the TTY device used by the currently active window, as well as its shell. Figure 2.3 shows these as /dev/ttyp2 and bash, but your window may be different, especially if you have changed the default shell.

Three options are available for actions that occur when the shell exits. The shell will exit when you type exit or logout, and some commands or scripts may tell the shell to exit. You have three choices:

Close the Window	If you choose this option, the Terminal window will close when the shell exits.

Don't Close the Window	If you choose this option, the window won't close and Terminal will display the following:
	
	`% exit`
	`logout`
	`[Process completed]`

Close Only if the Shell Exited Cleanly	This option means that the window only closes when the shell exits normally, following an exit or logout command.

Process Settings

If you select Processes from the Terminal Inspector pop-up menu, the window displays process options, as shown in Figure 2.4.

The Terminal Inspector shows the currently running processes—in this case, login and bash, the current shell. These processes are running in the frontmost window. If you have several windows open and run processes in the background, this can be useful to remember which window is running a specific process.

FIGURE 2.4
Process options
in the Terminal
Inspector

The second part of this window, Prompt before Closing Window, lets you tell Terminal to remind you that processes are active. You have three options:

Always	If you choose this, Terminal will always display a dialog when you close windows.
Never	If you choose this, Terminal will never display a dialog when you close windows.
If There Are Processes Other Than	If you choose this, Terminal will only display a dialog when you close windows with processes other than those in the list. To add a process to the list, click Add and enter the name of the command you wish to add.

The dialog Terminal displays is a sheet that is attached to the window in question. It looks like Figure 2.5.

This dialog reminds you that specific processes are running. In some cases, terminating these processes abruptly may not pose any problems, but some processes need to be shut down in a specific manner.

FIGURE 2.5
A Close Window sheet, alerting you that closing the current window will shut down the processes it is running

Emulation Settings

If you select Emulation from the Terminal Inspector pop-up menu, the window displays input and output options, as shown in Figure 2.6.

FIGURE 2.6
Emulation options in the Terminal Inspector

These options affect input and output, from the way you edit text to the way Terminal responds.

Input Options	Description
Escape Non-ASCII Characters	If you need to enter Unicode characters in Terminal, this option is important. If you use `tcsh` or `bash`, check this option. If you use `zsh`, don't check it. You can then drag files or folders from the Finder or type text with high-bit characters correctly. (`tcsh` and `bash` will show the escaped form of the character; `zsh` will show the actual character.) You may need to uncheck Use Option Key As Meta Key for this to work correctly, and select Unicode (UTF-8) from the Character Set Encoding pop-up menu.
Option Click to Position Cursor	If you set this option, you can move the cursor to any location in the command line by pressing Option and clicking.
Paste Newlines As Carriage Returns	This converts Unix newline characters to returns when you copy text from Terminal and paste it into another Macintosh application.
Strict VT-100 Keypad Behavior	This alters the way keyboard output is passed on to different applications. Only check this if you have problems with key bindings in certain programs such as Emacs.
Reverse Linewrap	This lets you move back up a wrapped line.
Audible Bell	This tells Terminal to use your Mac's default alert sound as an audible alert.
Visual Bell	This flashes Terminal when sending you an alert.

Buffer Settings

Select Buffer from the Terminal Inspector pop-up menu to change buffer options, as shown in Figure 2.7.

Figure 2.7
Buffer options in the
Terminal Inspector

The buffer and scrollback options tell Terminal how much text to keep.

Buffer Size	Description
Unlimited Scrollback	This keeps as many lines in the Terminal buffer as it has displayed. If you use Terminal for a long time and it has a large enough scrollback in its buffer, you may have problems with the application quitting. But in most cases, this is the best choice.
A specific number of lines	If you don't want an unlimited scrollback buffer, enter the number you want here. By default, Terminal uses 3,000 lines.
Disabled	This turns the scrollback buffer off. There's not much reason to do this, unless you have a process running that is constantly generating text (such as a detailed log) and you need to leave it on for a long time. If you do this, Terminal will no longer show a scrollbar at the right side of its windows.

Scrollback	Description
Wrap Lines That Are Too Long	This causes lines that are wider than the Terminal window to wrap to the next line. If you want each long line to go beyond the window's edge, uncheck this.

Scrollback	Description
Rewrap Lines on Window Resize	This tells Terminal to rewrap lines when you change the size of the window. This provides better display. If you uncheck this, you'll have lines that are cut off when you make your windows smaller.
Scroll to Bottom on Input	If you check this option, Terminal will jump to the bottom of the window when you start typing, no matter what you are viewing in the scrollback. This saves you having to scroll back down to the prompt if you are looking at something higher up in the scrollback.

Display Settings

If you select Display from the Terminal Inspector pop-up menu, the window shows display options, as seen in Figure 2.8.

FIGURE 2.8
Display options in the Terminal Inspector

Display options let you choose how the cursor and text are displayed in Terminal.

Cursor Style	Description
Block	This uses a block cursor, which, as shown in the Terminal Inspector, is a gray rectangle.
Underline	This uses an underscore character for the cursor.

Cursor Style	Description
Vertical Bar	This uses a vertical bar for the cursor.
Blink	If you check this, the cursor blinks, making it easier to find in the Terminal window.

TEXT

This is where you choose the font and character size for the Terminal display. The text field shows you the current selection, and if you wish to change this, click Set Font, and the Font window displays, as in Figure 2.9.

Choose the font you want to use, the typeface (regular, bold, etc.), and the size from this dialog. It is best to choose a fixed-width font, such as Courier, which makes it easier to read lists in Terminal, since these lists are always aligned according to a number of characters rather than tabs as in a word processing program. As you make changes in the Font window, they are immediately reflected in the current Terminal window, so you can see exactly what your selected font, size, and other attributes look like. But in the end, you'll probably find that there are very few fonts that are really adapted for reading in Terminal: Courier, Geneva, and Monaco are probably the best choices, but there is no accounting for taste.

You can go further with fonts to get the display that is most comfortable. Remember, since Terminal displays nothing but text, it helps to optimize this display for easy reading. You can adjust the character spacing in both width and height.

When you have decided which font you wish to use, click the Save This Setting As My Default Font button, or close the Font window and click Use Settings As Default in the Terminal Inspector.

FIGURE 2.9
The Font dialog, which lets you choose font, typeface, size, and more

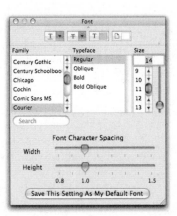

The Display options also contain several settings that you can turn on or off by checking their checkboxes. Table below presents these settings and explains their functions.

Additional Text Settings	Description
Anti-aliasing	If you check this option, Terminal will smooth the edges of your fonts to make the screen display better. Actually, this blurs the edges of the characters; some people like this, others don't. Try it out with your selected font to see if it improves the display. Note that on some slower Macs this might make display take a bit longer. This might not be noticeable unless you have a very long display, or if Terminal is updating something in real time.
Wide Glyphs for Japanese/Chinese/etc.	This uses wide glyphs (characters) for languages with ideograms.
Wide Glyphs Count As 2 Columns	This makes wide glyphs take up two columns in lists. If you are working in Japanese, Chinese, or a similar language, try this to see whether you prefer this type of alignment.
Enable Blinking Text	This allows you to set certain types of text to blink in the Terminal window.
Character Set Encoding	Select from the pop-up menu the character encoding that corresponds to the language(s) you work with. In most cases, it is best to choose Unicode, since this theoretically supports character sets in all other encodings. If you are working in a specific language that requires different encoding (Japanese, Chinese, Russian, etc.), select the appropriate encoding from this pop-up menu. You may need to try several encodings if you work with non-ASCII characters to find the one that displays these characters correctly.
Enable Drag Copy/Paste of Text	If this is checked, you can drag text to and from a Terminal window. You can drag text into other application windows, onto the desktop, or into a Finder window to create a clipping file; or you can drag text from other applications or from clipping files into a Terminal window.

Color Settings

If you select Color from the Terminal Inspector pop-up menu, the window shows color options, as seen in Figure 2.10.

Macs have always been highly customizable, and choices of colors are an expression of individual taste. Terminal gives you free rein as far as colors are concerned. You can choose your own personal colors for the window background, the cursor, normal text, bold text, and selection highlighting. To change any of these colors, click the color box next to one of the item names and select a new color from the color picker that displays. Nothing is stopping you from choosing yellow text and a purple background, and in fact some people find such colors more readable. You are free to experiment as much as you want, and when you have decided which colors you want to use, click Use Settings As Defaults to save them.

Bear in mind that if you select a different color for your cursor, this will have little effect, unless you have selected a block cursor. Choosing a different color for selection highlighting may be useful, since it makes selections stand out from black text more easily.

You can choose a background color or image, but if you do the latter, note the comment in the Terminal Inspector window: you'll find it much slower to resize windows. But if you absolutely must have a background picture, and you don't change your window size often, go for it.

This window also lets you set transparency for the Terminal window. At the default setting, the Terminal window is fully opaque; you can see nothing through it. If you increase the transparency, you will notice that you can see other application windows through Terminal's background. While this is a cool feature of Mac OS X, and some people will want to use it, transparency slows down the display of slower Macs, especially those with less than 16MB of video RAM. I personally find transparency useless for Terminal. However, it does let you keep an eye on what's going on in another window behind it. Say you are using an FTP program to download files and you want to follow the progress while working in Terminal. Instead of switching back and forth, you could set the transparency to a level that allows you to see the FTP program's progress bar. But you'll still find that Terminal text is harder to read this way.

FIGURE 2.10

Color options in the Terminal Inspector

Window Settings

If you select Window from the Terminal Inspector pop-up menu, you can change window options, as seen in Figure 2.11.

DIMENSIONS

While you can resize a window at any time by clicking its lower-right corner and enlarging or reducing it, this part of the Terminal Inspector lets you set the exact size for current or new windows. Window dimensions are very important in Terminal, because some commands only display correctly with a minimum width of 80 columns. This is the case for commands such as `top`, which displays active processes, or `man`, which displays manual pages. The number of rows in the window also affects certain commands. Using `top` as an example again, if you run this in a window with only 10 rows, you'll only see a few processes (though you can resize the window manually, changing the display).

A good choice is to use 80 columns and 35 rows, though if your screen resolution allows it, a higher number of rows is better. You can also choose a specific window size for individual commands or processes, and save them as `.term` files, as explained in the "Using *.term* Files" section later in this chapter.

TITLE

The Terminal Inspector gives you several options for changing the title in your Terminal windows. By default, this is the name of the application: Terminal. You can change the title for all of your Terminal windows by entering a different text in the Title field and saving this as the default. Or you can change the title of a specific window by entering a different title in the Terminal Inspector and then closing it. The custom name will remain on the selected window until you close the window or quit Terminal.

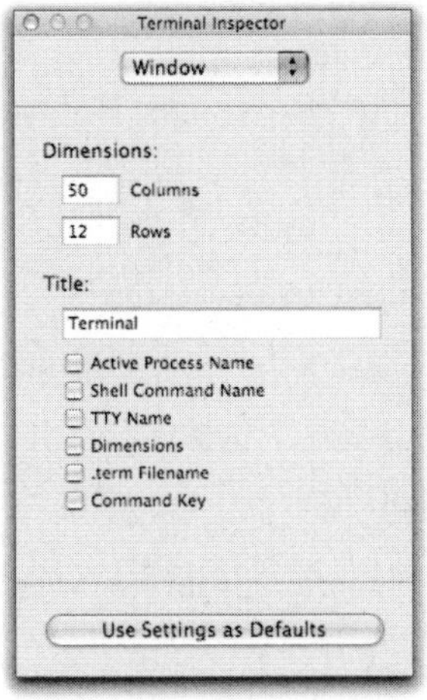

FIGURE 2.11
Window options, which let you adjust window size and Terminal window titles

Other Title Options

The following six options place additional information in the Terminal title bar. You can select any of them alone, any combination of them, or all of them; all of your selections appear in the title bar separated by dashes, provided the title bar is long enough to contain all this information. If not, the title bar text is truncated from the beginning, and an ellipsis prefaces the information that can fit.

Options	Description
Active Process Name	This displays the active process after the title in the Terminal window's title bar.
Shell Command Name	This displays the command name for the active shell (such as `tcsh`).
TTY Name	This displays the name of the TTY device you are logged in on.
Dimensions	This displays the window size, such as 80×35.
.term Filename	This displays the name of a `.term` file, if you have used one to create the window.
Command Key	This displays the command key shortcut for switching to each Terminal window. See "Working with Multiple Windows" below.

Keyboard Settings

If you select Keyboard from the Terminal Inspector pop-up menu, you can change keyboard options, as seen in Figure 2.12.

You can also set specific key mappings, which is where you specify that certain keys (for example the Delete key or the F keys) should perform the action of another key or combination of keys. Select one of the existing key mappings, then click Edit to change it, or click Add to create a new key mapping.

If you check Delete Key Sends Backspace, Terminal sends a backspace character (ASCII BS/8) when you press the Delete key. If this is unchecked, it sends an ASCII DEL/127 character.

If you check Use Option Key As Meta Key, this sets the high-order bit of the character pressed at the same time if you hold down the option key. This may be useful to users of the Emacs text editor.

Terminal Preferences

It may be a bit confusing, but the previous section, which talks about Terminal settings, deals with settings that are accessed by the Window Settings menu item in the Terminal menu. If you select Terminal ➤ Preferences you get a different dialog (see Figure 2.13), which only offers a few choices that affect Terminal and how it acts when it opens, or when it creates new windows.

FIGURE 2.12
Keyboard options, which let you set key mappings and other keyboard options

FIGURE 2.13
Terminal preferences only give you a few choices that affect how Terminal acts when it opens.

Terminal preferences let you choose the following:

When Creating a New Terminal Window You can choose between executing the default login shell, which is specified in NetInfo and read by /usr/bin/login, or a command. If you choose the latter, either you can run a shell, with a simple command such as /bin/tcsh or /bin/bash, or you can have the shell open with a much more complex command, including one that sets specific environment variables.

Declare Terminal Type ($TERM) As You can choose from several terminal types, and this tells Terminal to declare itself as that specific type of terminal. This can affect the way Terminal displays text. In most cases, you'll find that it's probably best to stick with xterm-color, the default choice, but you may need to choose a different terminal type.

Open a Saved .Term File when Terminal Starts If you choose this option, you can have Terminal open a .term file of your choice when starting up. Click Select File and choose the .term file you want to use. For more on .term files, see later in this chapter.

Working with Terminal Windows

Terminal has windows like any other Macintosh application, and most of the same commands and shortcuts apply. This is a bit of a paradox, having a command-line interface so seamlessly integrate with a graphical interface, but this has always been one of the strengths of the Mac OS. There are, however, some differences in the way windows work in Terminal, partly because new windows are not empty in the sense of most other applications, but already run a command (the selected shell) as soon as they open.

Opening New Windows

When you open a new window in Terminal, you begin running a new shell. You do this by selecting File ➤ New Shell, or by pressing ⌘-N. This opens the default shell in a new window, and uses your default window settings for the window size, font, colors, etc.

Terminal windows work just like other Macintosh windows: you can close them by pressing ⌘-W or by clicking the red close button, minimize them (send them to the Dock) by clicking the yellow button, and zoom them by clicking the green button. You can resize them by dragging the lower-right corner of the window, and they have scrollbars like most other windows.

Running Individual Commands

Terminal gives you the possibility of running individual commands without typing them in a Terminal window by selecting File ➤ New Command or pressing ⌘-Shift+N. This opens a small dialog (Figure 2.14) in which you can enter a command.

If you click Run, the command is executed in a new Terminal window and the results displayed. Running the ls command, as shown in Figure 2.14, gives the following output:

```
Desktop       Documents       Library       Movies
Music         Pictures        Public        Sites
[Process completed]
```

When you run a command in this manner, it is the same as running a shell script. However, built-in commands (commands that are built into the shell, and not separate commands that can be called up) won't run in this manner. One example is the **cd** command, which doesn't work from this dialog.

If you check Run Command inside a Shell in the Run Command dialog, the behavior is different. Running the ls command, as in the example above, gives the following results:

```
Last login: Thu May 20 11:54:48 on ttyp1
ls; exit
Welcome to Darwin!
Walden:~ kirk$ ls; exit
Desktop       Movies       Pictures       Sites
Documents     Library      Music          Public
logout
[Process completed]
```

FIGURE 2.14

The Run Command dialog, which displays after selecting the New Command menu item from the File menu

The Run Command dialog sends the command to the shell (including an `exit` command, which it added); the shell opens, displaying its standard welcome message; the `ls` command runs; then the `exit` command causes the shell to log out.

One thing to note is that the shell provides much of the syntax you use in commands. For example, if you were to run a command such as `ls *` or `ls ~` from the Run Command dialog, you wouldn't have much luck, because it is the shell that expands the `*` wildcard or the `~` shortcut to make these commands work.

HANDS ON: OPENING WINDOWS AND RUNNING COMMANDS FROM THE DOCK

If you click and hold the Terminal icon in the Dock, you'll see a number of menu items. In addition to the standard Show in Finder, Hide, and Quit menu items, you'll notice several others. Two of them, New Shell and New Command, open new windows or open the Run Command dialog. These are alternatives to using the File menu or keyboard shortcuts, but you'll probably find using the keyboard to be faster and more practical.

The Dock menu also contains a list of windows (for switching among active windows) and a Connect to Server menu item, which I'll discuss later in this chapter.

Working with Multiple Windows

Like most applications, Terminal lets you work with several windows at a time. But Terminal goes much further, because each window can run a different command, program, or process, allowing you to work in several places from one program. By default, all Terminal windows have the word Terminal in their title bar, but you can change this to help you identify which window is running which process. (See "Window Settings" earlier in this chapter.) If you often use multiple windows, adding the process name to the title bar will make switching from one window to another much easier.

SWITCHING WINDOWS FROM THE WINDOW MENU

There are several ways to switch windows in Terminal. The simplest is to merely click in an inactive window, bringing it to the front. But if you have many windows, you may not see all of them. You can select a window from the Window menu to activate it. But, as you can see from Figure 2.15, unless you have set the title bars to show the current processes, or the command key shortcuts, you won't know which window to select.

Switching windows is much easier if they have clear titles, as in Figure 2.16.

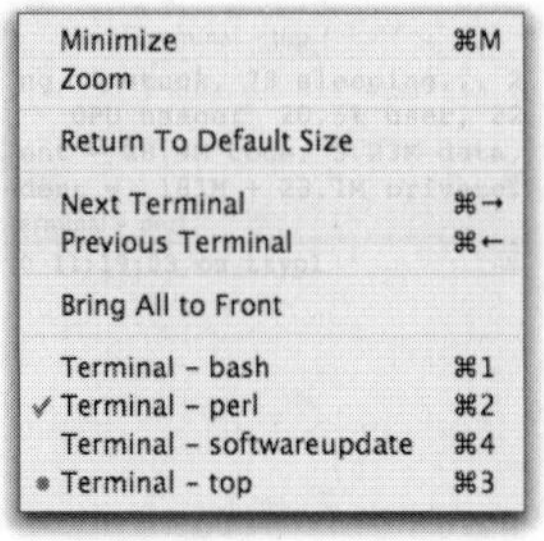

FIGURE 2.15

The Window menu, showing four windows with process names in their titles

FIGURE 2.16

The Window menu, showing four open windows, but all with the same name

Windows with active processes have bullets before their names, and the frontmost window has a check mark before its name. You can see that one window is running bash, which is the shell. This window has no current process running; the prompt is visible, and the shell is waiting for a command to be entered. If you have several windows like this, they are not differentiated in the Window menu.

HANDS ON: CHANGING A WINDOW TITLE ON THE FLY

Terminal window titles can be set from the Window settings window of the Terminal Inspector, but if you need to change the title of a window in a hurry, just press ⌘-Shift+T on your keyboard. This opens the Terminal Inspector to the Window settings window, and selects the window title text. Just type your new title, and press ⌘-W to close the Terminal Inspector.

SWITCHING WINDOWS FROM THE KEYBOARD

As you can see in the Window menu, each window shows a keyboard shortcut—you can switch to any window by pressing this keyboard shortcut. You can also move through all open windows by pressing ⌘-→ or ⌘-←. If you choose to display the command key in the windows' title bars (see "Window Settings" earlier in this chapter), these command keys are displayed both in the title bars of the windows (see Figure 2.17) and in the Window menu.

FIGURE 2.17
A Terminal window title bar, showing the name of the application (Terminal), the current process (top) and the command key shortcut (⌘-3)

Since processes shown in the Terminal title bar may not be indicative, using the command key shortcuts may be more practical. Terminal numbers windows sequentially, so the first window gets the ⌘-1 shortcut, the second ⌘-2, and so on.

HANDS ON: SELECTING WINDOWS WHEN TERMINAL IS HIDDEN

If you launch processes in Terminal and then hide the Terminal application by pressing ⌘-H, you can quickly access any of your Terminal windows from the Dock. Just click the Terminal icon in the Dock and hold the cursor down until the Dock menu displays. This menu shows the names of all open Terminal windows. As long as your Terminal windows have recognizable names, you can select the one you need from the Dock menu.

Of course, you can use the Dock to switch windows even if Terminal is not hidden.

The File Menu

Terminal's File menu offers the standard suite of menu items that you find in just about every graphical application: Open, Close, New (here it is New Shell and New Command), Save, Print, and others. Figure 2.18 shows this menu.

FIGURE 2.18
The Terminal File menu

New Shell	⌘N
New Command...	⇧⌘N
Connect to Server...	⇧⌘K
Library	▶
Open...	⌘O
Close	⌘W
Save	⌘S
Save As...	⇧⌘S
Save Text As...	⌥⌘S
Save Selected Text As...	⌥⇧⌘S
Show Info	⌘I
Set Title...	⇧⌘T
Use Settings As Defaults	
Send Break (Ctrl–c)	⌘.
Send Reset	⌘R
Send Hard Reset	⌥⌘R
Secure Keyboard Entry	
Page Setup...	⇧⌘P
Print...	⌘P

Most of the menu items are self-explanatory, but some call for a bit of explanation.

Connect to Server   This menu item opens a dialog that shows the servers available on your network for certain services.

Using Apple's Rendezvous network discovery technology, this shows you which servers are accessible, and automatically generates the appropriate commands to connect to one of them using the selected service. You can add services by clicking the + button at the left of the window, and you can add servers by clicking the + button at the right. This way you can add servers that Rendezvous does not detect.

Library   If you save .term files (see later in this chapter), the Library menu item lets you access them easily.

Save   As you can see in Figure 2.18, there are several Save menu items. You can save a window as a .term file by selecting Save, save a window under a different name by selecting Save As, save all the text in the current window by selecting Save Text As, and save text you've selected in the window by selecting Save Selected Text As.

Show Info   This displays the Terminal Inspector. See "Customizing Terminal Settings" earlier in this chapter.

Set Title   If you select this, the Terminal Inspector opens to the Window settings, where you can quickly set a title for the current window.

Send Break, Reset, or Hard Reset   If you select one of these menu items, Terminal sends the corresponding metacharacters to the shell.

Secure Keyboard Entry   If you turn this on, other applications on your computer or network cannot detect the keys you type in Terminal.

The Edit Menu

The Terminal Edit menu offers the standard functions, such as cut, copy, and paste, though cut is never enabled since you cannot remove text from Terminal windows. In addition, there is no undo function as there is in most Macintosh applications.

You can copy text from Terminal and paste it in any other application; you can also copy text from other applications and paste it in Terminal, if you need to.

You can use the Copy Style and Paste Style menu items to copy the font and style settings from one window and paste them to another.

The Find submenu offers useful functions for searching for text in the scrollback. If, for example, you are reading a long man page, or a command you run returns a long text, you can search for specific strings easily, and move to the next or previous occurrence of your search string. See Chapter 3, "Getting Help while in Terminal," for more information about finding text in man pages and using Terminal's Find function.

The Scrollback Menu

Terminal can keep an unlimited number of lines of text in its scrollback buffer, or you can select the number of lines you wish to save. (See "Buffer Settings" earlier in this chapter.) This scrollback is practical, because you can return to the output of previous commands without having to save it. Terminal gives you several ways of navigating this scrollback; these functions are available from the Scrollback menu (Figure 2.19).

As you can see from Figure 2.19, the Scrollback menu lets you move up and down in the scrollback buffer. Next to the menu items are keyboard shortcuts, and learning these will save you time working with long text output in Terminal.

To move to the top or bottom of the scrollback, select Scroll to Top or Scroll to Bottom, or press the Home or End keys on your keyboard. If you have checked Scroll to Bottom on Input in the Buffer settings of the Terminal Inspector, you can jump to the bottom of the scrollback just by typing any character. (See "Buffer Settings" earlier in this chapter.)

To move up or down a page (the number of lines visible in Terminal), select Page Up or Page Down, or press the page up or page down keys on your keyboard.

To move up or down one line, select Line Up or Line Down, or press ⌘ and the up or down arrow key on your keyboard. (Note that the up and down arrow keys alone invoke the shell's command history. See Chapter 6 for more on command history.)

If you select Clear Scrollback, or press ⌘-K on your keyboard, the scrollback buffer is cleared, and Terminal again displays nothing but a prompt.

FIGURE 2.19

The Scrollback menu in Terminal

Scroll To Top	⌘\
Scroll To Bottom	⌘\
Page Up	⌘⇞
Page Down	⌘⇟
Line Up	⌘↑
Line Down	⌘↓
Clear Scrollback	⌘K

The Font Menu

The Font menu gives you access to the Fonts dialog (by selecting Show Fonts), which allows you to change the font, size, and style for any window. You can use this even while a process is running to change the font, size, or style of its output.

This menu also lets you change font size incrementally by selecting Bigger or Smaller (or pressing ⌘-+ or ⌘-– on your keyboard). Again, this can be useful when your output is longer than you expected and you wish to change it to make it easier to read.

If you choose Show Colors, the standard color palette displays. You can drag color swatches from this palette to Terminal, applying those colors to different types of text (standard, bold, italic, etc.).

Using .*term* Files

Earlier in this chapter, I examined how to apply custom settings to Terminal windows. While you can use these settings as the default for new windows, you can also save these settings in special files called .term files; they are called this because their names must be followed by the extension .term. But you can do much more than just save window settings in these files—you can also save commands in them, so that these commands run automatically when you open the files.

Saving .*term* Files

To save your Terminal settings as a .term file, select Save from the File menu. Save this file with whatever name you want, but make sure to use the .term extension. While you can save this file anywhere, there is an advantage to saving it in ~/Library/Application Support/Terminal: if you save .term files here, you can easily open them from Terminal's File menu. You will have to create this directory, since it does not exist by default. You can either do it from the Finder or just run the following command:

```
% mkdir ~/Library/Application\ Support/Terminal
```

It is probably much easier to do this from the command line, but note the use of the backslash to escape the space in "Application Support." See Interlude 2, "Names and Paths," for more on typing special characters in Terminal.

Opening .*term* Files

If you save .term files in the location mentioned above, they are available from Terminal's File menu. To open one of these files, select File ➤ Library. A submenu displays, showing a list of all the .term files saved in this directory. To open one of these files, just select it from the submenu.

There are other ways to open .term files, both from Terminal and from the Finder. Since the Finder recognizes the .term extension, you can open a .term file by double-clicking it in the Finder. This opens Terminal, if it is not open, and displays the window according to the settings in the .term file.

You can also open a .term file using the open command, which is Terminal's equivalent of a double-click in the Finder. Run the command like this:

```
% open ~/Desktop/window.term
```

The **open** command is very flexible; for more on this command, see Interlude 5, "The Versatile **open** Command."

Using *.term* Files to Run Commands

A `.term` file is an XML file containing a series of keys and strings, each of which corresponds to one setting. If you open a `.term` file with a text editor, either in Terminal with vi, emacs, or another editor or in the Finder with BBEdit or a similar text editor, you will be able to edit these strings. (If you have installed the Developer Tools, the Property List Editor application makes this even easier, allowing you to edit this type of file in a graphical interface. See Interlude 8, "Using the Developer Tools," for more on using the Property List Editor.)

The key you need to look at is this:

```
<key>ExecutionString</key>
<string></string>
```

You can see that there is nothing between the two string tags. If you want to run a command when launching a `.term` file, enter a command between these two tags.

```
<key>ExecutionString</key>
<string>cd ~/Desktop</string>
```

You can enter several commands sequentially, as long as you separate them by semicolons (;).

```
<key>ExecutionString</key>
<string>cd ~/Desktop; ls -l; cd ~; ls -l</string>
```

Placing the above command in a `.term` file returns the following when the file is opened:

```
% cd ~/Desktop; ls -l; cd ~; ls -l
total 15480
-rw-r--r--   1 kirk  staff  137430 20 May 11:25 Picture 1.pdf
drwxr-xr-x  27 kirk  staff     918  9 May 23:00 Reading
drwxr-xr-x  54 kirk  staff    1836 14 May 17:40 Stuff
-rw-r--r--   1 kirk  staff  580640 19 May 13:24 Walden.txt
drwxr-xr-x   8 kirk  staff     272  9 Feb 09:35 Writing
total 320
drwx------  38 kirk  staff    1292 20 May 13:56 Desktop
drwx------  38 kirk  staff    1292 20 May 11:34 Documents
drwx------  67 kirk  staff    2278 29 Apr 23:01 Library
drwx------   6 kirk  staff     204  5 Feb 20:47 Movies
drwx------  20 kirk  staff     680 21 Mar 21:34 Music
drwx------  10 kirk  staff     340 29 Apr 23:22 Pictures
drwxr-xr-x   8 kirk  staff     272 14 May 17:39 Public
drwxr-xr-x   8 kirk  staff     272 24 Feb 16:15 Sites
```

One thing you notice here is that the different commands are not separated by prompts, so the output runs together.

One of the best reasons to use a command in a `.term` file is to log in automatically to a server. Entering the following allows me to set up an FTP connection when the file opens:

```
<key>ExecutionString</key>
<string>ftp kirk@10.0.1.201</string>
```

Terminal displays this:

```
[Walden:~] kirk% ftp kirk@10.0.1.201
Connected to 10.0.1.201.
220 10.0.1.201 FTP server ready.
331 Password required for kirk.
Password:
```

All I have to do is enter my password and the FTP session begins.

Using a Different Terminal

Apple supplies its own terminal program, Terminal.app, to access the command line in Mac OS X. But there's nothing stopping you from using other terminal programs instead. While Apple's Terminal has many advantages, third-party terminal programs may offer compelling features. Here are two of the most interesting terminal replacement programs.

iTerm

My favorite terminal application is iTerm. This open-source program takes a novel approach to the terminal: it offers tabbed windows, similar to those used on some web browsers, so you can have multiple terminal sessions open with just one window. If you use lots of terminal sessions, it keeps your desktop from getting messy. It has many other interesting features, but this one is a strong selling point for me.

For more information on iTerm, go to `http://iterm.sourceforge.net`.

GLTerm

This program solves one of the weaknesses of Apple's Terminal, which is its relatively slow display. It takes a different tack on the terminal: it uses OpenGL 3D rendering to display text, making output appear almost instantly on any OpenGL-compatible Mac. However, it doesn't allow you to choose from more than a handful of built-in fonts, so your display options are limited. But it sure is fast.

For more on GLTerm, go to `http://www.pollet.net/GLterm`.

Summing Up

When you work in Terminal, you combine two programs: the Terminal application and the shell. Like any graphical application, Terminal offers you a full range of customization features, such as window size, fonts, colors, and more. Setting up Terminal to fit your working style helps you be more productive and lets you adapt the application to your needs.

Interlude 1: Command Syntax

When working on the command line, you are bound by certain rules: you must enter the different parts of a command in a specific order. Commands you enter on the command line are a kind of language, and the appropriate word order is essential for them to work correctly. Some commands function very simply, with just a single word necessary to run them. Others offer additional options, allowing you to change the way they run. And some commands cannot run without arguments such as filenames or other specific data.

Command syntax varies greatly from one command to another. For the most basic commands, syntax is easy to understand, but it can get complex when you start working with complex commands, adding redirection operators or pipes, or gluing several commands together to make complex commands.

Unix commands can contain several parts:

Command The command is, in some cases, the only item that is required. Many commands can run in a basic form with no options or arguments. Commands are always case-sensitive. In most instances they are all lowercase, but there are some notable exceptions, such as the `MvMac` and `CpMac` commands, which are part of the Mac OS X Developer Tools. (See Interlude 8, "Using the Developer Tools," for more on the Developer Tools.)

Options Options, also known as flags or switches, change the way a command works, or tell the command to return additional information. In most cases they are written as letters or words following a dash (-) or double dash (--). Single dashes are used with letter options (such as `-i`) and double dashes are used with word options (such as `--version`); there are exceptions to this, such as the `find` command, which uses single dashes before *primaries*, which are words used to tell the command to search for specific criteria. Letter options can usually be combined.

Arguments Arguments usually come at the end of the command and are often filenames or directory names, indicating the data on which the command operates.

Redirection Symbols or Pipes You can string commands together with pipes, or redirect input or output using specific characters.

Each command has its own syntax, which is presented in this form:

```
command -options arguments
```

Each command's man page (see Chapter 3, "Getting Help while in Terminal," for more on using man pages) tells you the syntax required under the "SYNOPSIS" heading.

Commands That Function Alone

Some commands are so simple that they have no options and require no arguments. One such command is `whoami`. If you look at the man page for this command (see Chapter 4 for more on viewing man pages), you see that there is nothing you need to enter, other than the command itself, when running it:

```
NAME
     whoami - display effective user id

SYNOPSIS
     whoami
```

The fact that the SYNOPSIS shows nothing following the command tells you that there is effectively no syntax other than the command itself. This is not surprising, because when you run the whoami command you can see that it doesn't do very much:

```
$ whoami
kirk
```

As the man page says, it displays "effective user id"—that is, the current user's name. This type of command is relatively rare, however; most commands offer at least one or more options, or require arguments.

Commands That Require Arguments

The next level of complexity is found in the type of command that requires an argument following it, and nothing else. Here is a simple example: the syntax of the locate command from its man page:

```
locate pattern
```

You can find out more about the locate command in Chapter 9, "Editing Text," but here you can see that this command runs with nothing more than a pattern following it. However, this pattern is not optional; if it were, the command's syntax would be presented like this in the man page:

```
locate [pattern]
```

The brackets indicate an optional part of a command.

A command such as locate cannot do anything on its own, and can only locate what you tell it to look for. This pattern, or search string, is the word or expression that you want it to find.

Some commands allow for multiple arguments. One example is the whatis command, whose syntax is as follows:

```
whatis keyword ...
```

This means that you can run the whatis command with one or more arguments; the first keyword is required, and additional keywords are optional.

Commands That Include Options

As I pointed out above, commands always include the command name and may include options or arguments. Some commands, such as those mentioned in the previous section, run with just the command name and one or more arguments. Other commands offer options that alter the way the command runs, or that change the output the command returns. Options are, as their name indicates, optional; most commands that use options never *require* that an option be used.

One such command is the `jobs` command, which is built into the `bash` shell. This command has the following syntax:

```
jobs [-l]
```

In its basic form, without the -l option, this command returns a list of currently active jobs. If the -l option is added, it also lists process IDs.

There are only a handful of commands like this that offer options but do not use arguments.

Commands That Include Options and Arguments

The majority of commands available include both options and arguments, and their level of complexity can vary greatly, as the examples below show:

```
cat [-benstuv] [-] [file ...]

man [-adfhkotw] [-m machine] [-p string] [-M path] [-P pager]
        [-S list][section] name ...

touch [-acfhm] [-r file] [-t [[CC]YY]MMDDhhmm[.SS]] file ...

find [-H | -L | -P] [-EXdsx] [-f pathname] [pathname ...] expression
```

Most commands are not as complex as `man` and `find`, but many commands have a large number of options.

WORKING WITH OPTIONS

The options available for commands change the way they run, or change the information they return. Options must be separated from commands by at least one blank space, and you can usually combine several options to combine their effects. A good example of this is the `ls` command, which lists the contents of a directory, and which is presented in depth in Chapter 5, "Navigating the File System." Its syntax is as follows:

```
ls [-ACFLRSTWacdfgiklnoqrstux1] [file ...]
```

The `ls` command has 25 options, and allows for one or more arguments to be added to it. When running a command with several options, you have two choices: you can either indicate each option with a dash preceding it:

```
ls -a -l -F
```

or you can combine the options after a single dash:

```
ls -alF
```

Both of these `ls` commands return the same information. Note that the following is incorrect, and returns an error:

```
ls-alF
```

because there is no space between the command and dash. However, the following command will work, because Unix commands can have any number of spaces separating the command and options:

```
ls        -alF
```

The `ls` command allows you to add options in any order, but some commands require that options be in a certain order, or have certain options that may cancel out other options. The man page for `ls` mentions some options that override each other:

```
The -1, -C, -l, and -x options all override each other;
the last one specified determines the format used.
```

Options, like commands, are read from left to right. Whenever options conflict, the rightmost (or last) option takes precedence.

Some commands offer options that *must* be followed by arguments; this is the case with the find command, and, with this command, these options, which are specified by whole words, are called primaries. Some primaries must be followed by arguments before the next primary; other primaries, such as `-empty`, are entered alone. Look at the following example:

```
$ find ~ -mtime 1 -name "*.plist" -user kirk -size -10
```

In the above example, the primaries are `-mtime`, `-name`, `-user`, and `-size`. Each of these primaries must be followed by a string in the appropriate form: `-mtime` would not work if it were followed by "one" instead of "1"; `-user` will only work with a user name, or the `find` command will return nothing. Also, in this type of command, each primary and its respective string must have spaces before the primary, between the primary and the string, and after the primary (if another primary follows).

WORKING WITH ARGUMENTS

Arguments used with commands, except those following primaries as in the example above, are usually files or directories but may also be device names. When arguments represent input files or directories, commands can often accept several arguments. Take the `ls` command, which allows you to list the contents of a directory or, if you specify one or several filenames, only the information for those files:

```
$ ls -l cashb10.txt rhout10.txt
-rw-r--r--    1 kirk     staff      170512 Feb 20 11:30 cashb10.txt
-rw-r--r--    1 kirk     staff      319080 Feb 20 11:31 rhout10.txt
```

Adding two filenames as arguments returns information about both of these files.

Some commands, however, only accept one argument for input. A good example of this is the cd command, which changes the current working directory:

```
$ cd Documents Pictures
cd: Too many arguments.
```

Attempting to run this command with two arguments returns an error message.

When commands can accept several arguments, these arguments may be individual file or directory names, or expressions using wildcards that the shell interprets as one or several files or directories. For more on using wildcards in commands, see Interlude 6, "Wildcards and Globbing."

Command syntax is simple for the most commonly used commands, though for some of them—such as find—it can be quite complex. The best way to find out a command's syntax is by checking its man page. But command syntax is not an absolute science. As one user pointed out to me, "The path to being a *real* Unix user includes the acceptance that the question of how to define command syntax has no answer.

```
<command> <some stuff> ...
```

is about as good as it gets."

HANDS ON: GROUPING COMMANDS

The above section on command syntax focuses on the structure within a given command: the command itself, its options, and its arguments. When you have written a command correctly, you press Enter or Return and the shell runs the command. After the command is run and any output is returned, the shell displays a prompt showing you that the command has completed. You can then enter another command.

If you want to run several commands sequentially, you don't have to wait for the prompt to appear. You can string several commands together on one line and separate them with semicolons (;). This tells the shell to execute each command, one after another, until it reaches the end of the line. Only when one command is completed does another begin; this shortcut is just like waiting for the prompt and typing a new command. Here is an example:

```
$ ls -l ; cd .. ; pwd ; ls -l > file2.txt
```

This simple command does four things: it lists the contents of the current working directory (ls -l), moves up to the parent directory (cd ..), prints the name of the current working directory (pwd), then saves the contents of the directory to a text file (ls -l > file2.txt).

You can combine any kind of command in this way, and this is especially useful if you know that one command is going to take a long time and want to launch a string of commands without waiting for it to finish.

Chapter 3

Getting Help while in Terminal

The huge number of commands available in any Unix system is matched only by the vast amount of documentation that these systems contain. By default, several dozen megabytes of documentation are installed on your Mac, giving you almost instant access to a wealth of information about the many command-line tools on your system. While I cover as much of the basics as possible in this book, the man pages cover everything about each command available.

But before looking at using the man pages, or manual pages, the heart of the Unix documentation, there are a couple of other very useful commands for finding out about what's hidden in the Unix underpinnings of Mac OS X.

Finding Out What a Command Does with *whatis*

One of the commands you can use to find out what a command does is `whatis`. Its name is self-explanatory—it tells you what a command is—but an example is worth a thousand words:

```
$ whatis ls
ls(1)                    - list directory contents
```

As this example shows, `whatis` gives a one-line summary of what a command does, taken from the first line of the command's man page.

Sometimes `whatis` returns several lines of text, and you have to look for the command you want.

```
$ whatis whatis
apropos(1), whatis(1)    - search the whatis database
getNAME(8)               - get NAME sections from manual source for
                           whatis/apropos data base
makewhatis(8)            - create a whatis.db database
```

As you can see here, the word `whatis` is included in three command descriptions: two of them are commands that contain that word, and one has a description that contains it. For other commands, `whatis` may return dozens of lines, because the keyword you include as an argument is in many command descriptions.

The previous example shows that there is another command, `apropos`, that also searches the `whatis` database. The advantage to using `apropos` is that you can use regular expressions when searching the `whatis` database; `whatis` only searches for whole words. For more on using these regular expressions, type `man grep` in Terminal.

ON THE COMMAND LINE

Overview of the *whatis* and *apropos* Commands

COMMAND SYNTAX

```
whatis [keyword]
apropos [keyword]
```

FINDER EQUIVALENT

None.

OVERVIEW OF OPTIONS FOR *WHATIS* AND *APROPOS*

whatis   The whatis command searches a database file containing short descriptions of system commands for keywords and returns the result. It only displays complete word matches.

apropos The apropos command searches a database file containing short descriptions of system commands for keywords and returns the result. This command can search for regular expressions.

GETTING MORE INFORMATION

To display the manual page and learn more about whatis and apropos, type man whatis or man apropos in Terminal. The two commands share a man page.

HANDS ON: BUILDING THE *WHATIS* DATABASE

When you first install Mac OS X, it doesn't have a whatis database—without this file, you cannot use the whatis or apropos commands. This database is automatically built the first time one of Mac OS X's weekly maintenance scripts runs. Unfortunately, this script only runs in the wee hours on Sunday morning, so if your Mac is not running 24/7, it won't get built.

You can build this database manually, though, and you should not only do it now, so you can use whatis and apropos, but you should also do it regularly. (For more on these maintenance scripts, see Chapter 15.)

Only a user with administrator access can run this command, so you need to precede it with sudo. (For more on sudo, see Interlude 7, "Using sudo.") Run the command as follows:

```
$ sudo periodic weekly
```

Terminal will ask you to type your administrator's password. Do this, then press Enter. It may take a few minutes for this command to complete, and the periodic weekly command generates the whatis database (among other tasks it performs). You can check by running the whatis command for any command you know is on your Mac.

You can also save this database to a text file, if you want to browse through it and see what commands are available. To do this, you again need administrator access using sudo. Run the following:

```
$ apropos . > ~/Desktop/whatis.txt
```

This saves the contents of the whatis database in a text file on your desktop. If you open this file, you'll see that many of the lines are not commands that you can call in Terminal, but are programming tools and functions.

Using man Pages

The online help system included in the BSD subsystem of Mac OS X is made up of several thousand manual pages, or man pages. These text files are stored in /usr/share/man, together with the whatis database (see the sidebar "Building the whatis Database"). This directory contains a series of numbered subdirectories named man1 through man9. Theoretically, these nine directories break the man files up into a coherent organization (see Table 3.1), though in practice this is not always the case. In addition, not every command has a man page in Mac OS X; some of Apple's own commands lack man pages.

While in most cases you won't need to know which man directory contains a given command's documentation, this may be important if you are a programmer and need information on using functions and libraries. If you type man chmod, for example, the man command will display the man page for chmod(1). The number in parentheses indicates which man directory contains the command. But since the chmod *function* is in man2, you need to run the man command differently to get the man page for chmod(2):

```
$ man 2 chmod
```

This tells the command to only look in directory man2.

TABLE 3.1: CONTENTS OF THE NINE MAN DIRECTORIES

DIRECTORY	CONTENTS
man1	User commands: these are the most common commands for navigating the file system, managing files and directories, etc. This contains such commands as pwd, whatis, cd, etc.
man2	System calls: information on APIs and other information for programmers. It also contains such system calls as setuid and symlink.
man3	Subroutines or library functions: mostly of interest to programmers.
man4	Devices: more information for programmers regarding using and programming device drivers.
man5	File formats: information on system configuration files.
man6	Games: information on games installed by the Unix subsystem. Mac OS X contains no command-line games; this directory is empty.
man7	Miscellaneous: whatever doesn't fit in one of the other categories.
man8	System administration: commands used to manage the system. This is where you find such commands as fsck and reboot.
man9	Kernel interfaces: information for programmers on interfacing with the kernel.

You can use the whatis command, presented earlier, to find out which commands and man pages exist. This command returns all of the commands, functions, libraries, etc. that are referenced in the man directories, showing the directory number in parentheses.

```
$ whatis chmod
chmod(1)                   - change file modes
chmod(2), fchmod(2)        - change mode of file
```

In this example, there are two references to chmod: the first is the command, the second the function, as shown by the man directory numbers.

Reading man Pages

To read the man page for a given command, just run the man command followed by the name of the command you want to learn about. If you run this command:

```
$ man apropos
```

the corresponding man page displays in Terminal:

```
APROPOS(1)        System General Commands Manual        APROPOS(1)

NAME
      apropos, whatis - search the whatis database

SYNOPSIS
      apropos keyword ...
      whatis keyword ...

DESCRIPTION
      apropos searches a set of database files containing short
      descriptions of system commands for keywords and displays
      the result on the standard output.  whatis displays only
      complete word matches.

      keyword really is a regular expression, please read
      grep(1) manual page for more information about its format.

DIAGNOSTICS
      The apropos utility exits 0 on success, and 1 if no
      keyword matched.

SEE ALSO
      grep(1), makewhatis(1), man(1)


BSD                       January 15, 1991                      BSD
```

Each man page includes a series of sections, though not all of these sections are present in every man page:

Command Name	In this case, it is apropos(1), showing that this is the apropos command and it is located in the man1 directory.
Name	Here, it is apropos, whatis - search the whatis database. This is also the short description that the whatis command displays.
Synopsis	This shows how you run the command. In most cases, this is command [option(s)] [argument(s)], though some commands have no options and others have no arguments. In the present case, it is merely command keyword.

Description	This is the meat of the man page, a description (which may be more or less easy to understand, depending on the command) of how the command works, what the various options do, and how to use arguments. The example I have chosen is a very simple command; many commands have several pages of description.
Options/ Arguments	Some commands have a separate section for options or arguments. (This section is not present in the example.)
Environment Variables	This discusses which environment variables, if any, affect the operation of the command. (This section is not present in the example.)
History	This tells when the command first appeared, and in which version of Unix. (This section is not present in the example.)
Files	This tells which files are used, read, or created. (This section is not present in the example.)
Examples	These are examples of configurations or sample commands. (This section is not present in the example.)
Diagnostics	This tells what the command returns if successful or if errors occur.
Compatibility	This discusses questions of compatibility with Posix standards. (This section is not present in the example.)
See Also	This tells you some other commands that may be related, or that may help you understand the current command.
Standards	Like the Compatibility section, this discusses compatibility with any standards. (This section is not present in the example.)
Bugs	This lists known bugs, if any. (This section is not present in the example.)
Author(s)	This gives the name(s) of the author(s) of the program. (This section is not present in the example.)
Notes	This gives additional notes, as required. (This section is not present in the example.)
Date	This final line shows the last update to the man page, as well as the operating system.

Moving through man Pages

When using the man command, the shell displays the man pages via the less command; less is a pager, a command designed to present text one page at a time. When you type man [command name] and press Enter, the man command automatically pipes its output through less to the shell.

The first page (as much as will fit in your window) is displayed immediately after you call the man command. If this is not the only page in the file, you will see a colon (:) at the bottom of the Terminal window indicating that there is more text to come. To move to the next page, just press the spacebar. You can keep doing this until you reach the end of the man page.

To move back up in the man page, use the Terminal window's scrollbar. You can scroll down one line by pressing Enter or Return, and scroll up one line by pressing K on your keyboard. (There are other key bindings, or keyboard shortcuts, that you can use with less: see Chapter 9, "Viewing Files," for more on this command, or type man less in Terminal, or type h when using less to view its help screen.)

You can jump up one page (or screen) by pressing Control+B, and you can jump down one page by pressing Control+F.

When you reach the end of the man page, Terminal displays (END) at the bottom of the window; this text is highlighted in black. To continue, and exit the less program, press the spacebar a final time: this causes a prompt to be displayed.

If you find yourself in a long man page and want to stop displaying it (say you typed man cd, and the builtin man page is showing), just press the Q key on your keyboard. This exits less and displays a prompt.

Finding Text in man Pages

The less pager, used to display man pages, lets you find text in these documents so you don't have to read through them entirely. Just like a find function in any word processor, the find function in less allows you to search for a specific string either forward or backward in the text.

To search for text in a man page, use the following search form:

```
/[search string]
```

ON THE COMMAND LINE

Overview of the *man* Command

COMMAND SYNTAX

```
man [option(s)] [-P [pager]] [section] command name
```

(This syntax is simplified; man offers many more options.)

FINDER EQUIVALENT

Similar to the Finder's online help function, which uses Apple's Help Viewer, but only provides help for command-line tools.

OVERVIEW OF OPTIONS FOR *MAN*

`man command name`	This displays the man page for the command specified.
`-P [pager]`	This option tells man to use the specified pager.
`[section]`	This tells the man command to only look in a specific man directory. See Table 3.1 for the contents of these directories.

GETTING MORE INFORMATION

To display the manual page and learn more about man, you can naturally type man man in Terminal. I have only shown the most common options here, but there are many others.

When you type the slash (/), the colon at the bottom of the window changes to show the slash. Enter your search string immediately following the slash, then press Enter or Return. The less command finds the next occurrence of your search string, highlights it, and scrolls the text of the man page to display it.

To find the next occurrence of the same search string, just press N on your keyboard.

If you want to search backward in the man page, use the following search form:

```
?[search string]
```

Just as when you search forward, you can find the next occurrence by pressing N on the keyboard. For a full list of key bindings and options available under less, type the following in Terminal:

```
$ less --help
```

This displays the less command's online help, which is a summary of the many shortcuts and options available. Note that many of these shortcuts offer several key bindings. For example, the key bindings available to move forward or backward are as follows:

```
e  ^E  j  ^N  CR  *  Forward  one  line
```

```
y  ^Y  k  ^K  ^P  *  Backward one line
```

Choose the one you prefer, or the one that is easiest to remember. For more on `less` navigation shortcuts, see Chapter 9.

HANDS ON: SAVING MAN PAGES AS TEXT FILES

The Unix documentation system, with online help available for almost every command just a few keystrokes away, is a boon for novices and experts alike. But negotiating some of the longest man pages can be a headache. For these pages, especially if you need to look at them often, the best idea is to save them as text files. The bash man page, for example, takes up dozens of screens; the `find` and `grep` man pages are long and include many options. Saving them as text files lets you read through them with any text editor and use more efficient text searching.

You cannot simply save a man page from its source file—man pages contain special formatting characters for bold text, underlined text, etc., which the man program converts when displaying in Terminal. To save a man page as a text file, run the following command (this example shows how to save the bash man page as a text file):

```
$ man bash | col -b > bash.txt
```

You can name the result file whatever you want, and set a location to save it. If you want to save it to the desktop, you would run the command as follows:

```
$ man bash | col -b > ~/Desktop/bash.txt
```

Note that these text files will not be formatted perfectly. There are extra spaces interspersed throughout the file, but this does not pose any problem of readability.

If you have installed the X11 package with Panther, you'll have a command called `rman`, which lets you reformat man pages in many formats including HTML. You can run the following command to save a man page as a neatly-formatted HTML page, complete with hyperlinks to the different sections of the file:

```
$ man bash | /usr/X11R6/bin/rman -f HTML > ~/Destkop/bash.html
```

Note that the above command uses the full path of the `rman` command. By default, when you install X11, its `bin` directory is not added to your PATH variable. To add this directory to your PATH variable so you don't need to enter the full path of the command, see Chapter 16, "Configuring the Shell."

OTHER TOOLS FOR VIEWING MAN PAGES

While it's easy to view man pages in Terminal, it is useful to use a separate program for displaying them to keep your Terminal windows free for entering commands. Sure, you can open as many Terminal windows as you want, but you need to find the ones containing man pages.

There are a few programs that you can use to view man pages, some of which offer useful features that Terminal doesn't have.

Continued on next page

OTHER TOOLS FOR VIEWING MAN PAGES *(continued)*

Xcode (or ProjectBuilder, if you're running Jaguar), part of Apple's Developer Tools, provides a man page display function. If you have installed the Developer Tools, this program is found in /Developer/ Applications. Select Help ➤ Open man Page and enter the name of the man page you want to read. You can search for text in man pages, and ProjectBuilder displays clickable links that take you to other parts of the page or to other pages.

ManOpen, a freeware available for Mac OS X, Mac OS X Server, and OpenStep, offers a simple display of man pages. You select File ➤ Open Title, then enter the name of the page to display. You can choose which section to look in, if you know where the page is, and you can choose from recent items in the File menu as well. The program's find function lets you search for text strings in the man pages; clickable links to other pages, when they occur, open new windows with these pages. This program is available from http:// www.clindberg.org/projects

Summing Up

Terminal gives you instant access to thousands of pages of documentation on the command-line tools included in Mac OS X. Learning to use this documentation efficiently can save you time when trying to understand how a command works or how to implement its options. These man pages are easy to use and easy to search, providing you with a wealth of documentation just a few keystrokes away.

Interlude 2: Names and Paths

When working with the command line, there are certain rules of the road that you must follow. Unlike when you work in the Finder, the command line gives no quarter; if you make a typing error or indicate a filename or path incorrectly, you'll see the soon-to-become-familiar `Command not found` or `No such file or directory` error message. In order to avoid these messages and make sure your commands work correctly, you need to know the correct way to name files and directories and how to work with filepaths.

File and Directory Names

Mac users have long been able to name their files and folders with just about any characters they want. But with Mac OS X and its Unix base, there are some limits to how you name your files and folders. While you can still use *almost* any character, it is much easier to avoid certain characters if you are going to work on the command line often. New users need to be aware of the constraints imposed by the two layers of the operating system. Both layers allow you to enter filenames up to 255 characters long, and the Unix layer is very forgiving: there is only one forbidden character, the slash (/). You are not allowed to use this character for filenames because it is the directory separator.

However, the graphical layer of Mac OS X *does* allow you to enter slashes in filenames. If you do this, you'll find it very difficult to work with these files in Terminal. If you name a file with slashes in the Finder, Terminal does not see the slashes and instead shows you the filename with colons. This is because the Finder actually changes the name, or at least changes what you see in Finder windows. A file named Plans/Projects in the Finder displays like this in Terminal:

```
Plans:Projects
```

Historically, Mac OS has long used colons as directory separators; in fact, if you try to name a file Plans:Projects, the Finder will display an alert saying that this name cannot be used. If you name a file Plans:Projects in Terminal, nothing will stop you—but the Finder will show you the file as Plans/Projects. Because of this confusion, it's best to avoid using either slashes or colons in filenames.

Since Mac filenames were never limited to the 8.3 DOS file format (eight characters followed by a three-character extension), Mac users have long used spaces in their filenames and were free to use more descriptive filenames, such as "Third Quarter Report" or "Picture of my dog on the beach." You can use spaces in Unix filenames, but this leads to greater difficulty when entering names for these files in Terminal.

Unix has a number of characters that have special meanings (see the sidebar "Using Special Characters in Unix" below); these characters are used as wildcards or control characters. To enter one of these characters on the command line, you must *escape* it with a backslash (\), or enclose the entire filename in quotes.

Using the ls (list directory contents) command as an example, here are two ways to enter a filename that contains spaces:

```
$ ls -l 'Final Report'
-rw-r--r--    1 kirk     staff        0 Feb 23 15:13 Final Report

$ ls -l Final\ Report
-rw-r--r--    1 kirk     staff        0 Feb 23 15:13 Final Report
```

In the first example, the filename is surrounded by single quotes; this tells the shell to treat the contents of the quotes literally, to ignore any special meaning that the characters in quotes have. The second example uses a backslash to escape the space in the filename. Both versions work the same, but both require that you do more than just enter the filename as you see it.

If you avoid using these special characters in filenames, you'll save time in Terminal when typing their names, and also when trying to find files.

HANDS ON: USING SPECIAL CHARACTERS IN UNIX

Unix shells give special meanings to certain characters, using them as wildcards or other control characters. Unix file systems give special meaning only to the / character. While you can use these characters in filenames, as long as you escape them or enclose the filenames in quotes (see above), it is probably best to avoid them.

Here is a list of these special characters:

```
( ) [ ] { } < > / | \ * ? ! ' ` " $ # ; & ^ space newline tab
```

The newline and tab characters are very difficult to use in filenames; in fact, you cannot use them when naming files in the Finder.

One special character that should only be used in certain positions is the tilde (~) character. If you use this character, which is a shortcut for the current user's home directory, at the beginning of a file or directory name, the shell will substitute the home directory for the tilde. You can, however, use it in other locations. This is fortunate, because you may have files whose names contain this character. This is what Mac OS used in the past to indicate truncated filenames when copying files with long names from Windows:

```
questi~1.doc
```

If you have such files on your Mac, and want to work with them from the command line, you don't need to escape the tilde.

Another character to be careful with is the dash (-). While this won't cause problems with most commands, some might interpret a filename beginning with a dash as an option. If you don't use this character at the beginning of file or directory names you should be safe.

HANDS ON: WORKING WITH SPECIAL CHARACTERS IN ANOTHER WAY

As I pointed out above, when entering filenames containing special characters, you generally need to escape these characters using a slash, or type the filenames in quotes. Escaping all the special characters can be annoying if there are a lot of them.

If you work with languages other than English, you may also have problems using accented characters in Terminal.

But there is a simple way to get around this: use the ? wildcard to replace any special characters in filenames. This is safe as long as you don't have more than one file that can match the name containing the wildcards.

Here is an example. For the file named "Picture of my dog on the beach," you could type its name as:

```
Picture?of?my?dog?on?the?beach
```

The same is true of files with names such as these:

```
Persée
Final (draft) report
Whose book?
```

which you can type like this:

```
Pers?e
Final??draft??report
Whose?book?
```

The ? wildcard matches any character, including itself.

If you are sure there are no other files in your directory containing the same characters at the beginning of the file you want to access, you can also use the * wildcard. Here are examples for the three files above:

```
Per*
Final*
Whose*
```

See below for more on using the ? and * wildcards.

The standard convention for naming files in Unix is to separate words with the underscore (_) character, which results in filenames such as these:

```
Third_Quarter_Report
Picture_of_my_dog_on_the_beach
```

They have the advantage of showing a clear separation between words, yet remaining unbroken by spaces.

If, in spite of all this, you still have to work with filenames that contain spaces or other special characters, there are still ways to make this easier. One way is to use filename completion (see Chapter 6, "Saving Time on the Command Line") to have the shell complete the names for you. The other way

HANDS ON: MAKING HIDDEN FILES

As I pointed out above, any file whose name begins with a dot is hidden, and is invisible to the Finder. So, if you ever want to hide a file or directory, just change its name via Terminal to have a dot in front of it. You can use the following command:

```
$ mv filename .filename
```

The mv command, used in this way, merely renames the file. (For more on the mv command, see Chapter 5, "Working with Files and Directories.")

To make the file visible again, invert the command:

```
$ mv .filename filename
```

You can also make directories invisible in the same way.

is to drag files, folders, or applications from the Finder directly into Terminal to have the shell enter their names for you (see Chapter 2, "Using Terminal").

The only other filename constraint when in the Finder is that you cannot use a dot (.) at the beginning of a filename. If you attempt to name a file with a leading dot, you'll see an alert telling you, "These names are reserved for use by the system." This is because files whose names begin with dots are "invisible"—well, sort of. They are invisible to the Finder, and invisible to Terminal if you don't use specific options for commands to display them. However, you can create files and directories whose names begin with . from Terminal.

If you run the ls command to display the contents of a directory without using the -a option, you won't see any files with . at the beginnings of their names. But create a file via the command line with a name beginning with a dot, and run the ls -a command to see all these invisible files and directories:

```
$ ls -a
.   ..   .file
```

As you can see, the above directory contains nothing but "invisible" files and directories: the . and .. directories (see Chapter 4, "Navigating the File System") and a file created manually with a dot at the beginning of its name.

Absolute and Relative Paths

Whenever you enter commands in Terminal that act on files or directories, you must specify the paths of the target items. There are two ways to specify paths: you can use either absolute or relative paths. The way you specify a path depends on the type of command you are running and where you are in the file system. If you are running a command on files in the current working directory, it is easiest to use relative filepaths. If, however, you are running a command on a file in a distant location, use its absolute path: there is less chance for error.

The difference between absolute and relative paths is simple, and a telephone number analogy makes this clear. If I am in a phone booth in Manhattan and I want to call my friend Jay, I can dial his number, which is 555-6789. This is a relative phone number, which looks for a subscriber with that phone number in the current area code (in this case, 212). But if I'm in San Francisco, I need to dial Jay's number preceded by its area code: 212-555-6789. This is the absolute number. No matter where I am, I can call Jay using the full number with the area code, while dialing the relative number only connects me with whoever has that number in the area code I'm calling from.

Working on the command line, you are always in a given directory (see Chapter 4). Relative paths begin from that point, the current working directory, which you can find by entering the `pwd` command in Terminal; they never begin with a /. Absolute paths, however, always start from the root level of your file system, which is represented by /, and always begin with that character. And absolute paths are always the same no matter where you are in the file system.

ABSOLUTE PATHS

As I mentioned above, absolute paths always begin with /, the root level of the file system, and always contain the entire path of the file or directory being specified. Say I have a file called `Walden.txt` in my home directory. If I want to read that file with the `less` command, using an absolute path, I must run the command like this:

```
$ less /Users/kirk/Walden.txt
```

You might be tempted to consider this as an absolute path:

```
$ less ~/Walden.txt
```

In a way, this is absolute, but only for user kirk. If I add a command that refers to a file using the ~ shortcut to my home directory in a script, for example, and give the script to another user, it may not work; they need to have the same file at the same location in *their* home directory. You can consider paths starting with ~ as absolute if you are the only user on your computer, but they are not absolute for every user.

Absolute paths are precise, yet to use them you must know the exact path to the file or directory you want to refer to. This is usually easy to find out, but can be long to type. In some cases you will have to navigate through the file system to find the exact location of a given file. But remember that Terminal and the Finder can work hand in hand: if you need to enter the full path of a file or directory, just drag it from the Finder onto the Terminal window, and Terminal automatically enters its absolute path. For more on using Terminal and the Finder together, see Chapter 2.

RELATIVE PATHS

Since relative paths begin at the current working directory, you can often run commands by entering nothing more than the name of a file, if you are in its directory. If I have a file called `Walden.txt` in my home directory, and I have moved into that directory, I can read that file by running the following command:

```
$ less Walden.txt
```

Since the path does not begin with a slash, the shell looks no further than the current working directory. But if the file `Walden.txt` is in the `Documents` directory, inside my home directory, and I am in the home directory, running the same command does not work:

```
$ less Walden.txt
less: Walden.txt: No such file or directory
```

In that case, I would need to run the command as follows:

```
$ less Documents/Walden.txt
```

This tells the shell to look inside the `Documents` directory for a file named `Walden.txt` and read the file. Every directory contains two directory shortcuts: `.` (dot) and `..` (dot dot). (See Chapter 4 for an explanation of these shortcuts.) You can use these shortcuts in relative filepaths to indicate the current working directory (`.`) or the parent directory of the current working directory (`..`). In the same directory as for the above examples, you can reference the `Walden.txt` file as follows:

```
./Walden.txt
```

and the `less` command shown above becomes:

```
$ less ./Walden.txt
```

Using `..` to refer to the parent directory can save time when you know that a file is in this directory. In the above examples, `Walden.txt` is in the `~/Documents` directory. If I know there is a file called `thoreau.txt` in my home directory (`~`), I can view this file by running the following command while remaining in the `~/Documents` directory:

```
$ less ../thoreau.txt
```

I can refer to files by using the `..` shortcut several times; all of the following commands refer to the same file:

```
$ less ../Documents/Walden.txt
$ less ../../kirk/Documents/Walden.txt
$ less ../../../Users/kirk/Documents/ Walden.txt
```

It is very unlikely that you would want to refer to files in this manner when working from the command line; it is so much easier to either move into the file's directory and use a relative path or simply use an absolute path. In fact, the last command in the above example is merely an absolute path preceded by three `..` shortcuts. However, this type of path may be useful if you write shell scripts and you know exactly what the hierarchical relationship is among certain files.

Chapter 4

Navigating the File System

The first thing you need to learn about traveling in any new land is how to get from one place to another. In the land of the command line, you need to learn how to use Terminal to get around your Macintosh's file system. As you have already discovered (especially when you couldn't find where you saved a file), your files are organized in a complex hierarchy of directories (the Unix word for folders). When moving around in the Finder, you open folders—which display other folders and files—and you drag, copy, and paste files and folders among the windows that the Finder displays. In the Unix world, you navigate directories using commands, displaying lists of files and directories, moving and copying files and directories by typing commands.

In most cases, you're probably better off using the Finder for your everyday activities. But navigating the file system with Terminal has several advantages:

◆ It's fast. You can jump from one directory to another in a split second, as long as you know its path. There is no need to open window after window to get where you want. You can also get information about the contents of a directory without actually moving to that directory.

◆ It gives you more information about your files and directories, and more easily. While you can access most of the same information from the Finder—such as file permissions—Terminal shows you this information more quickly. For example, if you want to know the permissions for an entire folder of files, you can use the Finder's Get Info window to find it out. But you need to do this individually for each file. With Terminal, you can display a list showing all this information almost instantly.

◆ You can access hidden or invisible files and directories. While in most cases you're better off leaving these files and directories alone, you may sometimes want or need to access them. If you need to see which hidden or invisible files and directories are on your computer, or if you need to work with them, Terminal is the quickest way to go. (There are some third-party programs that can show you invisible files and directories in the Finder, but using Terminal is quicker and easier.)

◆ Some system commands or functions can only be accessed from Terminal. This includes commands for maintaining the system as well as for configuring certain parts of it.

◆ Finally, Terminal can be the only way to delete recalcitrant files. Sometimes the Finder won't let you delete certain files from the Trash; Terminal will. Be careful, though; this kind of operation is irreversible.

As you can see, there is a place for both the Finder's graphical interface and Terminal's command-line interface. It's up to you to choose which is best suited for each task you need to accomplish.

In this chapter, I'll show you how to find out where you are in the file system, how to list the contents of your directories in a variety of ways, and how to move from one directory to another. I'll look at the commands you use for these tasks, which are among the most common and most important things you'll do on the command line.

About the Mac OS X File System

Mac OS X, like all other operating systems, uses a *file system* to organize files, folders, and applications. The basic principle behind this system is that of hierarchy: at the top of the hierarchy is a single point (called the *root* of the file system, indicated by / under Unix systems), and below that point, a tree structure spreads out from directory to subdirectory, with an almost unlimited number of branches possible.

In the Finder, you can easily see how this tree structure is organized by looking at a window in column view, as seen in Figure 4.1.

The computer in this example has several volumes (partitions of a single hard disk, though they could also be individual disks), each of which contains a number of folders. My home folder, called kirk, is selected, and you can see that it is a subfolder of the Users folder, as well as a parent for eight other folders. Each of these subfolders can contain other files and folders, and so on. Each folder is considered to be a node in the tree structure, and each new subfolder another branch.

Under previous versions of Mac OS, such as Mac OS 9, which you may be familiar with, the folder in the above figure would have a path of Panther:Users:kirk. Under Mac OS X, at least in Terminal, this path is /Users/kirk/. (Curiously, the Finder still uses this colon-separated filepath when displaying the path in the Get Info window.) As you can see, the difference is not only in the characters used to separate the names of the folders or directories, but also in the beginning of the path itself.

When looking at this structure in the Finder, as in Figure 4.1, the user is led to believe that the partitions shown in the left-hand column of the above window are at the top of the tree. Mac OS X uses an abstraction to present these volumes in a manner that is familiar to Mac users. (To complicate things, the Finder window sidebar also displays an iDisk, if you have a .Mac account, and a Network icon, which allows you to access network volumes quickly.)

FIGURE 4.1
Looking at a user folder in the Finder, in column view

In reality, the boot volume (in the above example, the partition named Panther) is mounted at the root mount point (/) and the other partitions are at a lower level, in a directory called /Volumes. The root level also contains a group of standard Unix directories that the Finder hides from view.

To see the same structure in Terminal, you need to think in a different manner. The following sequence of commands moves among the directories, listing their contents, ending with the contents of my home directory (my username is kirk), which is shown in the right-hand column of Figure 4.1. (I have added some line breaks to make this easier to visualize.)

```
1:
$ cd /
$ ls
AppleShare PDS          Network                 etc
Applications            Network Trash Folder    mach
Desktop DB              System                  mach.sym
Desktop DF              Users                   mach_kernel
Desktop Folder          Volumes                 private
Developer               automount               sbin
File Transfer Folder??  bin                     tmp
Icon?                   cores                   usr
Library                 dev                     var


2:
$ cd Users
$ ls
Shared          henrydthoreau   kirk          perceval
emerson         jsbach          mariefrance   samuelpepys


3:
$ cd kirk
$ ls
Desktop     Library   Music      Public
Documents   Movies    Pictures   Sites
```

In the first command of this example, I moved to the root level of the file system, or /. I then listed its contents; this directory includes the Users directory. (I'll explain all the commands I used in the above example later in this chapter.) In the second command, I moved into the Users directory; listing its contents shows eight directories. Then, in the third command, I moved into my home directory, and lists its contents. These directories are the same as the folders in Figure 4.1. (But as you can see, the root level of the file system, or /, contains some folders that you *don't* see in the Finder. Don't worry about this right now; this is another example of the way Mac OS X hides things from you in the Finder to make the system easier to use.)

Finding Your Way Around

In the rest of this chapter I'll show you how to move around in your computer's file system using Terminal. You'll learn how to list the contents of a directory, how to change directories, and how to find the current path to where you are in Terminal.

WHAT ARE ALL THOSE DIRECTORIES?

When you look at the root level of your file system, you may be perplexed by the many directories with short, cryptic names: dev, var, bin, etc and others. These directories are all part of the standard Unix file system. If you're curious and want to know what they contain, type this command in Terminal:

```
$ man hier
```

The hier man page gives "A sketch of the filesystem hierarchy," listing each directory and subdirectory in the standard Unix file system and explaining what they contain. This list does not discuss directories specific to Mac OS X, such as Applications, Library, and System.

One thing you need to bear in mind is that when you open Terminal you are at a specific location in the file system. Unless you have made changes to the way Terminal acts when it opens, you will always begin in your home directory, the one with your username. No matter what you do in Terminal, you are always someplace. Terminal is like a window looking at a map of your file system, and you are always at a given point on that map. (You can work in multiple Terminal windows. In that case, each window is at a given point on the map. They may be at the same point or at different points.)

Finding Where You Are with *pwd*

Just like when you are traveling and you look at a map to find where you are, you may sometimes need to know where you are in Terminal. The pwd (print working directory) command does just that; it is like a You Are Here! balloon pointing to your current location. It tells Terminal to print the current working directory. (When we say a Unix command *prints*, it does not always mean that it is sending something to a printer; it often means that it is displaying something in Terminal. This convention dates back to the days when all command output was actually printed.)

The pwd command is one of many Unix commands that does just one thing, and does it well. When you enter this command and press Enter or Return, Terminal shows the full path to the current working directory on the following line:

```
Walden:~ kirk$ pwd
/Users/kirk
```

I have left the complete prompt visible in this example to show you the difference between the directory information visible in the prompt (the ~) and what pwd displays. The only difference, as you can see in the above example, is that my user's home directory is replaced by the ~ shortcut. In this example:

```
Walden:~/Documents kirk$ pwd
/Users/kirk/Documents
```

you can see that I am in the Documents folder, within my home directory. The ~ shortcut is again used to replace /Users/kirk.

But look at the next example. When I'm outside my home directory, there is no difference between what is shown in the prompt and what pwd returns.

```
Walden:/Library/Preferences kirk$ pwd
/Library/Preferences
```

If you use the `tcsh` shell, the prompt may not always display the complete path to the current directory. Look at the following prompt:

```
Walden:2/3/4 kirk$
```

The prompt here shows that I am in directory 2/3/4. But when I type `pwd`, it tells me more:

```
$ pwd
/Users/kirk/Documents/1/2/3/4
```

In this example, I am in a folder that is several levels down in the hierarchy of my Mac's file system. The `tcsh` prompt limits the length of its display to three levels of hierarchy, no matter how long the names of the directories. (The `bash` prompt displays the entire path, no matter how long, by default.) In the case of long directory names, the prompt may cover several lines, as in this example:

```
Walden:A very long folder name/A much longer folder name/
A really, really long folder name, much longer than the
first two kirk$
```

So, if you have many nested folders and use `tcsh`, `pwd` will give you more information than the prompt—it tells you both where you are (the current working directory) and how to get there (the full path to that directory). In most cases, the information given in the prompt is sufficient; you won't need to use `pwd` unless you need to find out a long directory path.

ON THE COMMAND LINE
Overview of the *pwd* Command

COMMAND SYNTAX

```
pwd [option]
```

FINDER EQUIVALENT

None (the Finder displays the name of the current folder in the title bar of every window, but not its path; if you have a Path button in the Finder window toolbar, this will show you the logical path).

OVERVIEW OF OPTIONS FOR *PWD*

pwd	The pwd command prints (displays) the current working directory. By default, this is the physical path to the directory.
-L	This option displays the logical path to the current working directory. This is only different if you have entered a directory through a symbolic link.

GETTING MORE INFORMATION

To display the manual page and learn more about pwd, type man pwd in Terminal.

Using *pwd* to Resolve Symbolic Links

Symbolic links are the Unix equivalent of Finder aliases—sort of. (There are some important differences between the two. See Chapter 5, "Working with Files and Directories," for a discussion of aliases and symbolic links.) The pwd command has an option that lets you preserve symbolic links. When you have moved into a directory through a symbolic link, pwd shows you the path you followed: the physical path. But if you run pwd -L, Terminal returns the logical path, or the actual route to the original directory that you entered through a symbolic link. Look at the following:

```
Walden:~/Current kirk$ pwd
/Volumes/Files/Current
Walden:~/Current kirk$ pwd -L
/Users/kirk/Current
```

I entered the Current directory through a symbolic link that I created in my home directory. In both cases, the prompt shows that I am in ~/Current. In the first example, running pwd alone shows the actual physical path to the directory I am in. In the second example, Terminal remembers how I got there, and displays the logical path to the same directory. If I had moved to the Current directory without using a symbolic link, there would be no difference between the two.

Listing Directory Contents with *ls*

The ls (list directory contents) command is one of the most useful commands for navigating the file system, and is probably the command you will use the most. You are certainly used to seeing the contents of folders when opening new windows in the Finder; when you move to a new directory in Terminal, you see nothing. Terminal only displays the contents of a directory after you tell it to with the ls command.

When you are in your home directory, and run the ls command, you should see something like this:

```
$ ls
Desktop     Library   Music      Public
Documents   Movies    Pictures   Sites
```

The ls command returns a simple list of the current working directory's contents, but nothing in this list tells you anything about what these items are. There may be directories, files, or applications, but the basic ls command does not give you any clues about which are which. This is one case when the Finder is far more efficient—its visual clues tell you immediately if a given item is a file, folder, or application.

Compare the above list to Figure 4.2, which shows what you see in a Finder window when looking in your home folder:

It's clear that these are all folders, and their names and icons help you know at a glance what's inside them. (Of course, these icons are specific to the contents of your home folder; other folder icons are plain, unless you have added your own custom icons.)

In addition, if you get info for an item in the Finder, you get more details on what it is and what it contains.

Figure 4.3 shows the results of the File ➤ Get Info command performed on my Documents folder. It tells the kind of item, its size, its file path, and its creation and modification dates. By clicking the triangles at the bottom of the Info window, you can also find out more about the item, including its ownership and permissions.

FIGURE 4.2

The contents of my home folder, seen in a Finder window

FIGURE 4.3

Examining the Documents folder with the Get Info command

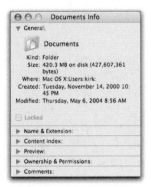

The ls command gives you a plethora of options for displaying the contents of a directory and for the type of information it returns. As you will see, you can find out much more about any file, folder, or application on your computer by using the command line than you can from the Finder.

VIEWING EVERYTHING IN A DIRECTORY

The basic ls command displays the contents of a directory in a simple manner. But what this command doesn't tell you is that there are other items in the directory. In fact, every Mac OS X directory contains hidden items, either files or folders. To view the entire contents of a directory, use the ls command with the -a option.

```
$ ls -a
.                       .gimp-2.0           .xnap
..                      .gimp-2.0-etc       Desktop
.CFUserTextEncoding     .history            Documents
.DS_Store               .inputrc            Furthur
.Network Trash Folder   .java               Library
.Trash                  .links              Movies
```

```
.Xauthority          .lpoptions          Music
.bash_history        .mysql_history      Pictures
.bash_profile        .ssh                Public
.fonts.cache-1       .tcshrc             Sites
.furthur             .thumbnails
.giFT                .viminfo
```

Your home directory will probably contain different files, but many of them are the same as in the example. As you can see, many of these files have names beginning with . (dot). All files and directories beginning with . are invisible files, but the ls -a command displays all files, including these invisibles. While you won't need to access most of these files (you probably shouldn't touch some of them), you can see them and know they are there. Later in this chapter, when examining the cd command, we will see what . and .. do. Some of the files or directories are self-explanatory: .Trash is a trash directory; .CFUserTextEncoding stores information about the type of text encoding used; and .bash_history is a record of commands you have entered in Terminal (if you are running the default bash shell).

But ls -a still doesn't tell you if these items are files, directories, or applications. You can use the -F option, in addition to -a, to get additional information about the contents of your directory. (When running commands with multiple options, you can string them together following the dash; you can also type each option with its own dash. So, for the following example, you could type ls -aF or ls -a -F. For more on command syntax, see Interlude 1, "Command Syntax.")

```
$ ls -aF
./                      .gimp-2.0/          .xnap/
../                     .gimp-2.0-etc/      Desktop/
.CFUserTextEncoding     .history            Documents/
.DS_Store               .inputrc            Furthur/
.Network Trash Folder/  .java/              Library/
.Trash/                 .links/             Movies/
.Xauthority             .lpoptions          Music/
.bash_history           .mysql_history      Pictures/
.bash_profile           .ssh/               Public/
.fonts.cache-1          .tcshrc             Sites/
.furthur/               .thumbnails/
.giFT/                  .viminfo
```

The display here is slightly different: directories are now shown with slashes (/) after their names, and you have a much better idea of what your home directory contains. In addition, items with an asterisk (*) following their names are executables.

VIEWING THE CONTENTS OF A SPECIFIC DIRECTORY

The ls command displays the contents of the current working directory (the one Terminal is in) if you do not add the name of a directory to the command as an argument. You can list the contents of any directory on your computer, as long as you know its path. To do this, you must specify the full path of the directory. For example, if you want to list the contents of the /Library/Fonts directory, you must enter the following:

```
$ ls /Library/Fonts
AmericanTypewriter.dfont      Hoefler Text.dfont
Apple Chancery.dfont          Lucida Blackletter
Apple Symbols.ttf             Lucida Bright
Arial                         Lucida Calligraphy
Arial Black                   Lucida Fax
Arial Narrow                  Lucida Handwriting
Arial Rounded Bold            Lucida Sans
Baskerville.dfont             Lucida Sans Typewriter
[etc.]
```

When you run this command, you have to use the complete path of the directory /Library/Fonts/, because you are specifying an absolute filepath. (For more on absolute and relative paths, see Interlude 2, "Names and Paths.")

You can also use ls to display the contents of directories using relative filepaths. When in my home directory, I can display the contents of the Pictures directory without moving into that directory, by simply entering the following:

```
Walden:~ kirk$ ls Pictures/
iPhoto Library
```

As you can see from the prompt, I am still in my home directory (~). If you don't specify an entire filepath, beginning with /, the shell considers that you want to run the ls command starting in the current working directory. If, however, no directory corresponds to the name you add to the ls command, the shell returns an error message, saying that there is no such directory.

Viewing Long Information

So far, we have only seen the ls command present the names of files and directories. Another option to this command, -l (that's the letter l in lowercase), returns much more complete information about the contents of a directory, going much further than what you can find out from the Finder's Get Info command.

If I run ls -l in my home directory, Terminal returns the following information:

```
$ ls -l
total 320
drwx------   17 kirk    staff    578  8 May 12:11 Desktop
drwx------   36 kirk    staff   1224  6 May 08:56 Documents
drwx------   67 kirk    staff   2278 29 Apr 23:01 Library
drwx------    6 kirk    staff    204  5 Feb 20:47 Movies
drwx------   20 kirk    staff    680 21 Mar 21:34 Music
drwx------   10 kirk    staff    340 29 Apr 23:22 Pictures
drwxr-xr-x    8 kirk    staff    272  6 May 10:59 Public
drwxr-xr-x    8 kirk    staff    272 24 Feb 16:15 Sites
```

When using the -l option, the following information is displayed:

◆ The first line shows the number of 512-byte blocks used by files in the directory.

◆ The first part of each line shows the file or directory's permissions. For more on permissions, see Chapter 12, "Working with Users, Groups, and Permissions."

◆ The next part is the number of file system links the file or directory uses. When files have additional hard links, this count reflects the total number of directory references. Files with no additional hard links show a count of 1, files with one hard link show 2, etc.

◆ Then comes the username. In the example, I am in my home directory, so all the files belong to me.

◆ Next is the group the file belongs to. In this case, the files belong to staff, which I am a member of.

◆ The next number is the size of files in bytes. This number is useful for files; the directory number is less useful.

◆ The date and time shown correspond to the last time the file or directory was modified. If the file has not been modified in the last year, the date and year are shown.

◆ Finally, the name of the file or directory is shown.

Let's look at another example, to see some of the other information this command can display. If I run the same command, ls -l, at the root level of my file system, I get the following:

```
$ ls -l
total 13025
-rwxr-xr-x    1 kirk   unknown    208896   3 Feb   2002  AppleShare PDS
drwxrwxr-x  130 root   admin        4420   8 May  10:45  Applications
-rw-r--r--    1 root   admin      372224   8 May  11:49  Desktop DB
-rw-r--r--    1 root   admin     1661106   6 May  16:01  Desktop DF
drwxr-xr-x    3 kirk   unknown       102  29 Jul   2003  Desktop Folder
drwxrwxr-x   12 root   admin         408  20 Feb  12:09  Developer
-rw-r--r--    1 kirk   admin           0  29 Jul   2003  Icon?
drwxrwxr-x   47 root   admin        1598  10 Mar  18:46  Library
drwxr-xr-x    1 root   wheel         512   8 May  14:53  Network
drwx---rwx    3 root   nobody        102  29 Jul   2003  Network Trash Folder
drwxr-xr-x    5 root   wheel         170  23 Apr  08:12  System
drwxrwxr-t   12 root   admin         408  28 Jan  11:36  Users
drwxrwxrwt    7 root   admin         238   8 May  11:33  Volumes
drwxr-xr-x    4 root   admin         136  29 Oct   2003  automount
drwxr-xr-x   35 root   wheel        1190  16 Mar  12:56  bin
drwxrwxr-t    3 root   admin         102  12 Sep   2003  cores
dr-xr-xr-x    2 root   wheel         512   7 May  10:22  dev
lrwxr-xr-x    1 kirk   staff          11  25 Feb  19:46  etc -> private/etc
lrwxr-xr-x    1 root   admin           9   7 May  10:22  mach -> /mach.sym
```

```
-r--r--r--    1 root  admin    568124   7 May 10:22 mach.sym
-rw-r--r--    1 root  wheel   3832636   5 Mar 23:23 mach_kernel
drwxr-xr-x    5 root  wheel       170   7 May 10:22 private
drwxr-xr-x   61 root  wheel      2074   4 May 12:36 sbin
lrwxr-xr-x    1 kirk  staff        11  25 Feb 19:46 tmp -> private/tmp
drwxr-xr-x   11 root  wheel       374  13 Sep  2003 usr
lrwxr-xr-x    1 kirk  staff        11  25 Feb 19:56 var -> private/var
```

HANDS ON: ANOTHER WAY TO VIEW THE CONTENTS OF A DIRECTORY

The ls command is the standard command for viewing the contents of a directory. But another command can also show you what is in a directory, and give you different and perhaps more useful information about its contents. The file command, which attempts to determine the type of file or files specified in the command, is a practical tool. Here's what the file command returns when I run it followed by the * wildcard in my Documents directory:

```
$ file *
AppleWorks User Data:   directory
Data.dmg:               data
Inspiration Data:       directory
Other:                  directory
Windows Shared Folder:  directory
Work:                   empty
cashb10.txt:            English text
iChats:                 directory
main.html:              HTML document text
pepys.txt:              English text
rhout10.txt:            English text
```

As you can see, this displays the names of the files and directories, and also tells which files are empty. (The file named Work is a Finder alias, but since the file command uses a database of common Unix file types, many Macintosh files appear as empty.)

This command does not show hidden files, though—files whose names begin with . (dot). You can run the command as follows to display only hidden files and directories:

```
$ file .*
.:        directory
..:       directory
.DS_Store: data
```

To display both hidden and visible files at the same time, you can run the command as follows:

```
$ file .* *
```

This returns all the information the first two examples display. For more on the file command, see Chapter 8, "Viewing Files."

Several of these items display information that is not seen in my home directory:

◆ There are items belonging to an additional user, root. (For more on the root user, see Chapter 12.)

◆ There are more groups than in my home directory—you can see wheel, unknown, and admin, in addition to staff. (For more on groups, see Chapter 12.)

◆ Some items contain -> in their names. These are *symbolic links*, similar to Mac OS aliases. For example, var -> private/var is a symbolic link pointing from var to private/var. (For more on symbolic links, see Chapter 5.")

While you don't need to see this information all the time, the ls -l command tells you just about everything you could ever want to know about your files.

More Options for *ls*

When you only have a few items in a directory, the basic options just discussed are the most useful. But the ls command has many other options, some of which can help you better view the items contained in a directory. Just as you can in the Finder, you can sort the items by size, in alphabetical order, or by the last time they were accessed; you can even display a list containing the contents of any subdirectories. Here are a few useful options to use with ls.

SORTING ALPHABETICALLY

By default, ls returns an alphabetical list of the items in a directory. But if you use the -r option, this sort is inverted, and the items are shown in the opposite order. Running ls -r in my home directory returns the following:

```
$ ls -r
Sites       Pictures    Movies      Documents
Public      Music       Library     Desktop
```

When running ls with a short display, the order is top-to-bottom, left-to-right. If I run the same command with a long display, the following displays:

```
$ ls -lr
total 320
drwxr-xr-x   8 kirk  staff   272 24 Feb 16:15 Sites
drwxr-xr-x   8 kirk  staff   272  6 May 10:59 Public
drwx------  10 kirk  staff   340 29 Apr 23:22 Pictures
drwx------  20 kirk  staff   680 21 Mar 21:34 Music
drwx------   6 kirk  staff   204  5 Feb 20:47 Movies
drwx------  67 kirk  staff  2278 29 Apr 23:01 Library
drwx------  36 kirk  staff  1224  6 May 08:56 Documents
drwx------  17 kirk  staff   578  8 May 12:11 Desktop
```

The reverse alphabetical order is more obvious here.

DISPLAYING FILE SIZE

While the `ls -l` command shows the size of files, there are some cases where this figure is incorrect. Using the `-s` option adds a column at the left of the list, showing the number of 512-byte blocks each file takes up on disk. Look at the following example:

```
$ ls -ls
328 -rw-r--r--  1 kirk  staff  30819 Nov 14 18:06 Perceval.jpg
 64 -rw-r--r--  1 kirk  staff  30819 Nov 14 18:07 PercevalCopy.jpg
```

These two files seem to have the same size (30,819 bytes) but the first file takes up much more space on disk: the number of 512-byte blocks for each file shows this difference (328 for the first file, but only 64 for the second). This is because the first file, a picture, has an additional resource that Terminal does not see. This thumbnail takes up much more space than the actual file, and the Finder clearly shows the difference in size. But Terminal does not, unless you use the `-s` option.

SORTING BY SIZE

In some cases, you may want to display the contents of a directory in size order. The `-S` option does that, showing the largest item first.

```
$ ls -S
Library    Pictures  Public  Sites
Documents  Desktop   Music   Movies
```

But this doesn't give you much useful information. Combining `-S` with `-l`, however, does. Here are the first few entries from a directory inside my `iPhoto Library` directory:

```
$ ls -lS
total 19464
-rw-r--r--     1 kirk  staff  73463 Oct  2 17:53 P1010013.jpg
-rw-r--r--     1 kirk  staff  69554 Oct  2 17:54 P1010017.jpg
-rw-r--r--     1 kirk  staff  68790 Oct  2 17:54 P1010014.jpg
-rw-r--r--     1 kirk  staff  66221 Oct  2 17:54 P1010015.jpg
-rw-r--r--     1 kirk  staff  64024 Oct  2 17:53 P1010038.jpg
[etc.]
```

As we saw above, the `-r` option lets you reverse the sort order. So, in this same directory, I can run `ls -lSr` to have the files sorted from smallest to largest.

```
$ ls -lSr
total 19464
-rw-r--r--     1 kirk  staff  24890 Oct  2 17:53 P1010036.jpg
-rw-r--r--     1 kirk  staff  31733 Oct  2 17:54 P1010071.jpg
-rw-r--r--     1 kirk  staff  32076 Oct  2 17:53 P1010057.jpg
-rw-r--r--     1 kirk  staff  33301 Oct  2 17:53 P1010059.jpg
-rw-r--r--     1 kirk  staff  33676 Oct  2 17:54 P1010091.jpg
[etc.]
```

This is especially useful if you have a long list of files and want to find which are the smallest.

SORTING BY TIME MODIFIED

The -t option sorts the results by the time modified; the most recently modified item is displayed first.

```
$ ls -t
Desktop  Documents  Public  Sites
Library  Pictures   Music   Movies
```

Combining this with the -l option gives you long information, sorted by time modified:

```
$ ls -lt
total 320
drwx------  17 kirk  staff   578  8 May 12:11 Desktop
drwxr-xr-x   8 kirk  staff   272  6 May 10:59 Public
drwx------  36 kirk  staff  1224  6 May 08:56 Documents
drwx------  10 kirk  staff   340 29 Apr 23:22 Pictures
drwx------  67 kirk  staff  2278 29 Apr 23:01 Library
drwx------  20 kirk  staff   680 21 Mar 21:34 Music
drwxr-xr-x   8 kirk  staff   272 24 Feb 16:15 Sites
drwx------   6 kirk  staff   204  5 Feb 20:47 Movies
```

You can tell at a glance which are the most recently modified directories.

DISPLAYING PRECISE TIME INFORMATION

The above examples showing the long information merely show abbreviated times—they show the month, day, and time (in hours and minutes). If you need more detailed time information, you can use the -T option. (Note that this option only works if you are using the -l option; if you run ls alone, with short results, adding -T won't change anything.)

```
$ ls -lT
total 320
drwx------  17 kirk  staff   578  8 May 12:11:13 2004 Desktop
drwx------  36 kirk  staff  1224  6 May 08:56:43 2004 Documents
drwx------  67 kirk  staff  2278 29 Apr 23:01:38 2004 Library
drwx------   6 kirk  staff   204  5 Feb 20:47:26 2004 Movies
drwx------  20 kirk  staff   680 21 Mar 21:34:52 2004 Music
drwx------  10 kirk  staff   340 29 Apr 23:22:02 2004 Pictures
drwxr-xr-x   8 kirk  staff   272  6 May 10:59:52 2004 Public
drwxr-xr-x   8 kirk  staff   272 24 Feb 16:15:13 2004 Sites
```

As you can see, this command only adds the seconds to the time, and adds the year. This additional information is not useful in many cases, but you can compare two files and see, to the second, which is the more recent.

SHOWING USER AND GROUP ID NUMBERS

If you add the -n option to the ls command, when displaying information in long format, Terminal displays the users and groups as numbers. The following example shows my home directory after running ls -ln:

```
$ ls -ln
total 320
drwx------   17 501  20    578  8 May 12:11 Desktop
drwx------   36 501  20   1224  6 May 08:56 Documents
drwx------   67 501  20   2278 29 Apr 23:01 Library
drwx------    6 501  20    204  5 Feb 20:47 Movies
drwx------   20 501  20    680 21 Mar 21:34 Music
drwx------   10 501  20    340 29 Apr 23:22 Pictures
drwxr-xr-x    8 501  20    272  6 May 10:59 Public
drwxr-xr-x    8 501  20    272 24 Feb 16:15 Sites
```

You can see that all these files are owned by user 501, who is a member of group 20. This option can be useful when you have files owned by many users; it can be easier to see who owns them by their numbers than by their names, in some cases.

Running the same command on your / directory shows several group numbers:

```
$ ls -ln
total 13025
-rwxr-xr-x     1 501  99    208896  3 Feb  2002 AppleShare PDS
drwxrwxr-x   130 0    80      4420  8 May 10:45 Applications
-rw-r--r--     1 0    80    372224  8 May 11:49 Desktop DB
-rw-r--r--     1 0    80   1661106  6 May 16:01 Desktop DF
drwxr-xr-x     3 501  99       102 29 Jul  2003 Desktop Folder
drwxrwxr-x    12 0    80       408 20 Feb 12:09 Developer
-rw-r--r--     1 501  80         0 29 Jul  2003 Icon?
drwxrwxr-x    47 0    80      1598 10 Mar 18:46 Library
drwxr-xr-x     1 0    0        512  8 May 15:08 Network
drwxr-xr-x     5 0    0        170 23 Apr 08:12 System
drwxrwxr-t    12 0    80       408 28 Jan 11:36 Users
drwxrwxrwt     6 0    80       204  8 May 15:07 Volumes
drwxr-xr-x     4 0    80       136 29 Oct  2003 automount
drwxr-xr-x    35 0    0       1190 16 Mar 12:56 bin
drwxrwxr-t     3 0    80       102 12 Sep  2003 cores
dr-xr-xr-x     2 0    0        512  7 May 10:22 dev
lrwxr-xr-x     1 501  20        11 25 Feb 19:46 etc -> private/etc
lrwxr-xr-x     1 0    80         9  7 May 10:22 mach -> /mach.sym
-r--r--r--     1 0    80    568124  7 May 10:22 mach.sym
-rw-r--r--     1 0    0    3832636  5 Mar 23:23 mach_kernel
drwxr-xr-x     5 0    0        170  7 May 10:22 private
drwxr-xr-x    61 0    0       2074  4 May 12:36 sbin
lrwxr-xr-x     1 501  20        11 25 Feb 19:46 tmp -> private/tmp
drwxr-xr-x    11 0    0        374 13 Sep  2003 usr
lrwxr-xr-x     1 501  20        11 25 Feb 19:56 var -> private/var
```

As you saw earlier, there are many files that belong to groups other than group 20, such as `admin` (group 80) and `wheel` (group 0)

DISPLAYING INFORMATION FOR A SINGLE FILE

We have looked at how the `ls` command displays information about the contents of a directory; it can also display the same information about just one file. You may want to find out the permissions for a single file, but not want to display the entire contents of a directory. To do this, just run the `ls` command as above, using whatever options you need, adding the name of the file after the command and options. Here's an example:

```
$ ls -l P1010096.jpg
-rw-r--r--  1 kirk  staff  53269 Oct  2 17:53 P1010096.jpg
```

DISPLAYING INFORMATION FOR SEVERAL FILES

The `ls` command allows you to enter several arguments: as in the above section, where you saw how to display information for a single file, you can specify the names of as many files as you want and the command will display information for only those files.

```
$ ls -l P1010090.jpg p1010093.jpg p1010096.jpg
-rw-r--r--  1 kirk  staff  41365 Oct  2 17:54 P1010090.jpg
-rw-r--r--  1 kirk  staff  40014 Oct  2 17:54 P1010093.jpg
-rw-r--r--  1 kirk  staff  53269 Oct  2 17:53 P1010096.jpg
```

You can also use the `*` wildcard character to display information about files whose names fit certain criteria. In the example below, I want to see information for all files whose names begin with P101009:

```
$ ls -l P101009*
-rw-r--r--  1 kirk  staff  41365 Oct  2 17:54 P1010090.jpg
-rw-r--r--  1 kirk  staff  33676 Oct  2 17:54 P1010091.jpg
-rw-r--r--  1 kirk  staff  40014 Oct  2 17:54 P1010093.jpg
-rw-r--r--  1 kirk  staff  42302 Oct  2 17:53 P1010094.jpg
-rw-r--r--  1 kirk  staff  53269 Oct  2 17:53 P1010096.jpg
```

(For more on using wildcards in commands, see Interlude 6, "Wildcards and Globbing.")

If you use multiple directory names as arguments for `ls`, the command returns the contents of each directory, formatted in a way that is easy to read:

```
$ ls Music Sites Public
Music:
Dead Songs.rtf  iTunes

Public:
Drop Box  Network Trash Folder  TheVolumeSettingsFolder

Sites:
```

HANDS ON: DISPLAYING *LS* OUTPUT IN COLOR

By default, Terminal displays its output in whatever color text you set in its preferences (see Chapter 2, "Using Terminal" for more on Terminal preferences). You can set the ls command to display different types of items in different colors—this works best when you use black text on a white background, but you can adjust the colors to fit your Terminal settings.

If you haven't changed your terminal type in the Terminal preferences, the default is xterm-color, which allows you to run the ls command like this to get color output:

```
$ ls -G
```

If you use another terminal type, such as vt100 or xterm, you can do the same thing by adding the three following lines to your .bash_profile file:

```
CLICOLOR=1
LSCOLORS=ExFxCxDxBxegedabagacad
export CLICOLOR LSCOLORS
```

(See Chapter 16, "Configuring the Shell," for more on setting variables and adding items to your .bash_ profile file.)

If you use tcsh, you'll need to add the following two lines to your .tcshrc file:

```
setenv CLICOLOR 1
setenv LSCOLORS ExFxCxDxBxegedabagacad
```

Now, when you run ls, you'll get color display, with different items showing as different colors. See the ls command's man page for more on setting and changing these colors.

You will notice that Sites is listed even though it is empty; since it was one of the arguments used in the command, it is shown.

Going one step further with multiple directories, you can use the asterisk wildcard to get a neat list of all the contents in each of your home directory's subdirectories by running this command when in your home directory:

```
$ ls *
```

This returns a long list of files and directories.

And if you want to list *everything* from the current working directory down to the furthest of its subdirectories, run this command:

```
$ ls -R
```

This recursively lists all the subdirectories contained by the current working directory, or by another directory if specified as an argument. Each file in each directory is listed, as are the contents of each subdirectory.

But we won't examine what this command returns to Terminal—it can be very long. Try this, if you want, and see all the files you have in your home folder.

Overview of the *ls* Command

COMMAND SYNTAX

```
ls [option(s)] [directory(s)/file(s)]
```

FINDER EQUIVALENT

Standard Finder window display, with some additional information.

OVERVIEW OF OPTIONS FOR *LS*

ls   The ls command displays all visible items contained in a directory. If the directory is empty, nothing is returned.

-a   This option tells the shell to display invisible items as well; invisible items have names that begin with . (dot).

-F   This option displays a slash (/) after each pathname that is a directory, an asterisk (*) after each executable, an at sign (@) after each symbolic link, a percent sign (%) after each whiteout (which is a special directory entry that hides the original filename—this is unique to BSD Unix), an equal sign (=) after each socket, and a vertical bar (|) after each FIFO.

-l   This option (lowercase l) displays information in long format.

-n   When used with -l, this option shows users and groups as their ID numbers rather than their names.

-r   This option reverses the sort order. If used alone, it reverses the alphabetical order; if used with other sort options (-t, -S), it reverses their order (time, size).

-R   This option recursively lists the contents of all subdirectories. Every file and directory contained in the directory listed is shown. The output can be very long.

-s   This option adds a column to the left of the list, when used with the -l option, showing the number of 512-byte blocks each file takes up on disk.

-S   This option returns information sorted by size.

-t   This option returns information sorted by time modified.

-T   This option returns precise time information (seconds and year).

GETTING MORE INFORMATION

To display the manual page and learn more about ls and the many options available, type man ls in the Terminal. The ls man page is long, since this command has more than two dozen options.

HANDS ON: SAVING THE CONTENTS OF A DIRECTORY TO A TEXT FILE

When you run the ls command, you see a list of items in a directory. If you need to save a list of files, you can use the ls command, with a few additional arguments, to save this list to a text file. Run the following simple command to do this:

```
$ ls > files.txt
```

You can give the file any name you want. (The > symbol is the *output redirection operator*. For more on redirection, see Interlude 3, "Redirecting Input and Output.")

When you run ls again in the same directory, you will see that files.txt has been created.

```
$ ls
Desktop    Library  Music     Public  files.txt
Documents  Movies   Pictures  Sites
```

Open this file, and you will see a list of files in the directory. This procedure is especially useful for long lists of files. You can use any of the additional options with ls to fine-tune this list to meet your needs.

Changing Directories with *cd*

When navigating your computer's file system under the Finder in Icon view, you have two choices: you can have the Finder either open a new window when you open a folder or open the folder and remain in the same window. When working in this second way, you always have just one window open; you can go backward and forward in your file system hierarchy, but always within the same window.

Moving around in Terminal works in this second way: no matter where you move to, you are always *in* one window. As we saw above, the Terminal prompt tells you which directory you are in, and the pwd command tells you where you are in the file system hierarchy.

The **cd** (change **d**irectory) command moves you from one directory to another. In Unix lingo, it changes the working directory; this is the directory in which you are located, and the one in which you can act on files without specifying a filepath.

Let's start by looking at the following:

```
Walden:~ kirk$ ls
Desktop    Library  Music     Public
Documents  Movies   Pictures  Sites
```

This shows the contents of my home directory after executing the ls command. (Yours will be similar, though you may have more items in it.)

To move to the Library directory, enter the following:

```
$ cd Library
```

The prompt changes to reflect the current working directory:

```
Walden:~/Library kirk$
```

Then, to see what it contains, type ls and press Enter.

```
$ ls
Address Book Plug-Ins    FontCollections      PreferencePanes
Application Support      Fonts                Preferences
Assistants               Icons                Printers
Audio                    Indexes              Recent Servers
Caches                   Internet Plug-Ins    Safari
Calendars                Keyboard Layouts     Snapz Pro X
ColorPickers             Keychains            Sounds
Cookies                  Logs                 StickiesDatabase
Documentation            Mail                 iMovie
Favorites                Mirrors              iTunes
```

You can move into one of these directories with cd:

```
$ cd Calendars
```

and look at its contents using ls:

```
$ ls
French Holidays.ics    US Holidays.ics
Home.ics               Work.ics
```

By this time, you may have forgotten where you are in your file system. Run the pwd command to find out exactly where you are:

```
$ pwd
/Users/kirk/Library/Calendars
```

You can now use the cd command to move back up in the hierarchy, running cd with the complete filepath of the folder you want to move to. Say you want to go back to the Users directory; just run the following:

```
$ cd /Users
Walden:/Users kirk$
```

The prompt shows that you are in the Users directory.

And if you want to go back to the Library directory, where you were before, you could type the following:

```
$ cd /Users/kirk/Library/
Walden:~/Library kirk$
```

If you attempt to move into a directory that does not exist, or if you misspell the name of a directory, the following message is returned:

```
$ cd Proust
Proust: No such file or directory.
```

The shell doesn't search for the directory you specify; if the directory is not where it's supposed to be, the shell just tells you that and nothing else.

Using the Finder to Save Time in Terminal

While you may think that the Finder and Terminal are mutually exclusive, they can work together to save you time. Sometimes you may need to type a lot to get into a deeply nested directory, but it's a cinch to navigate there in the Finder. If you want to move into a directory using cd, type cd [space] in Terminal. Then switch to the Finder, look for the folder you want to move to, and drag that folder into the Terminal window, as shown in Figure 4.4.

The Terminal adds the path of the item you dragged to the command you just typed.

```
Walden:~ kirk$ cd /Users/kirk/Documents
```

Press Return, and the Terminal moves to that directory.

You can do the same thing to act on a file. Just type the beginning of the command you want to use (don't forget to type a space before dragging the file), then locate the file in the Finder and drag it to the Terminal window.

Navigation Shortcuts

The cd command offers several ways for you to quickly move to certain locations, or to move back and forth between directories. Instead of typing the path of the directory you want to move to, use these shortcuts to save time.

THERE'S NO PLACE LIKE HOME

The cd command, in its basic usage, lets you move to any directory by specifying either its *relative* file-path (the path starting from the current working directory) or its *absolute* filepath (the entire filepath, beginning with the root (/) of your file system).

FIGURE 4.4
Drag a folder from a Finder window to the Terminal—the Terminal displays the folder's complete path.

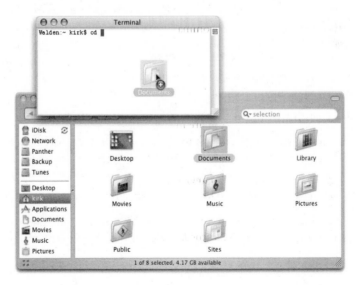

But cd, which is a command built into the bash shell (and into most other shells), also offers many shortcuts to let you navigate quickly and easily through the file system.

The most useful shortcut is to type cd and press Enter.

```
$ cd
Walden:~ kirk$
```

As you can see from the prompt, this takes you to your home directory. (Remember, the tilde character (~) is a shortcut for the current user's home directory.) This gives you a very quick way to get back home, even faster than clicking your heels three times. The logic in a Unix system is that most users will only be working in their home directory or one of its subdirectories. If you type the following:

```
$ cd ~
Walden:~ kirk$
```

you will also be taken immediately to your home directory. There is no reason to type the tilde character to get there, as we saw above, but the tilde is a shortcut that lets you move easily to sub-directories within your home directory. If you want to move to your Documents directory, you can type the following:

```
$ cd ~/Documents
Walden:~/Documents kirk$
```

This saves you typing the full filepath of the Documents directory:

```
/Users/your_user_name/Documents
```

This not only saves time, but also keeps you from having to retype the command if you make a typo.

Note that the ~ shortcut works with any command you use in Terminal and is not limited to just the cd command.

MOVING TO A USER'S HOME DIRECTORY

While the tilde character (~) is a shortcut that can take you to your home directory, you can also use it with cd to move to any other user's home directory, as in:

```
$ cd ~samuelpepys
```

Just enter the user's short name after the tilde (with no space between them).

You can combine this with any subdirectory, or any filepath within a user's home directory as well:

```
$ cd ~samuelpepys/Documents
/Users/samuelpepys/Documents: Permission denied.
```

But as you can see above, you'll need to have the permission to move into this directory; you need to be a superuser or root to do this. (For more on the superuser and root, see Chapter 12.)

MOVING BACK AND FORTH

The cd command has a few other interesting shortcuts to make it much easier for you to move up and down in the file system, as well as back and forth. The first is the use of a dash (-) following the cd command. Look at the following as I move through a few folders in my file system:

```
Walden:~ kirk$ cd Documents
Walden:~/Documents kirk$ cd -
Walden:~ kirk$ cd -
Walden:~/Documents kirk$ -
```

the first line shows that I am in my home directory (the prompt shows ~). I type cd Documents to move into my Documents directory; the prompt then shows that I moved there.

I then type cd - to move back to the previous directory; again the prompt shows that I am back in my home directory. Typing cd - again takes me back to my Documents directory. In a way, it toggles between two directories.

In the previous example, I am merely moving from one directory to a subdirectory. But as you can see below, this option works with directories at any location in the file system.

```
Walden:/Applications/Utilities kirk$ cd
Walden:~ kirk$ cd -
Walden:/Applications/Utilities kirk$ cd -
Walden:~ kirk$
```

I first begin in the Applications/Utilities directory. If I move there in the Finder, this would be the Utilities folder inside my Applications folder. I then type cd to move to my home directory, then cd - to go back to the Utilities directory. Typing cd - again takes me back to my home directory.

The advantage of using this option is that you can toggle between two directories; the disadvantage is that you can only move back and forth between two directories. There are other commands that let you move through a *stack* of directories that you have already visited. (See below for information about these commands, pushd and popd.)

MOVING UP AND DOWN

Every directory in your file system contains at least two entries. When you create a new, empty directory, these two "files" are automatically added to them. They are . (dot) and .. (dot dot).

Look at the following:

```
$ mkdir New_Directory
$ cd New_Directory
$ ls -a
.  ..
```

In the first line above, I created a new directory, and in the second line, I moved into that directory. I then ran the ls -a command, which displays the contents of that directory; the -a option shows invisible files. You can see that the only files in this new directory are . (dot) and .. (dot dot).

HANDS ON: MOVING QUICKLY TO YOUR FAVORITE DIRECTORIES

You are probably familiar with the way the Finder works with favorites—you can add a folder to the favorites and move to it more quickly by selecting it from the Favorites menu in any Open or Save dialog.

Well, Terminal lets you do something similar, though it's a bit more work to add these favorites. The bash and tcsh shells use a variable, called CDPATH (for bash) or cdpath (for tcsh), that contains a list of directories that the shell checks automatically each time you run the cd command. When this variable is set and you run cd from a directory, the shell will check this list as well as the current directory's subdirectories.

You set this variable like other shell variables, by adding it to your ~/.bash_profile or ~/.tcshrc file. (For more on using these files, see Chapter 16.) You must set the variable as follows:

For the bash shell:

```
CDPATH=:directory1:directory2: ...
```

Each directory name must be separated by a colon, and there is no colon at the end. Here's an example:

```
CDPATH=:~:~/Documents:~/Pictures:/Volumes
```

For the tcsh shell, use the following:

```
set cdpath = (directory1 directory2 ...)
```

The directory names are separated by spaces. Here's an example:

```
set cdpath = (~ ~/Documents ~/Pictures /Volumes)
```

In the above examples, running cd causes the shell to check the following directories to see if the directory you entered as an argument is inside them:

~	Your home directory
~/Documents	The Documents directory in your home directory
~/Pictures	The Pictures directory in your home directory
/Volumes	Any mounted volumes

The first entry, ~, means that any directory in your home directory will be found if used as argument for the cd command. You can type the following to go directly to your Documents directory:

```
$ cd Music
```

The next two arguments tell the shell to look in both your Documents and Pictures directories. Any directories you place in these two locations will also be examined.

The final argument is an extra time saver. Every volume mounted on your computer is found in /Volumes/. If you add this argument to the CDPATH or cdpath variable, you can easily move to any volume on your computer, any mounted network volume, or any removable medium mounted on your computer.

These two files are very useful. The first one, ., represents the current working directory. This can save you time in certain commands involving files within that directory. The second one, .., is a shortcut to the parent directory, or the next directory up in the file system. No matter where I am, I can always type the following:

```
Walden:~/Documents/New_Directory kirk$ cd ..
Walden:~/Documents kirk$
```

As you can see from the prompts in this example, typing cd .. takes me up to the parent directory of New_Directory, or Documents.

Any time you move into a subdirectory using the cd command, you can back up by using cd .. But you can also move up the file system from the current directory until you reach the top. Look at the following:

```
Walden:~/Documents kirk$ cd ..
Walden:~ kirk$ cd ..
Walden:/Users kirk$ cd ..
Walden:/ kirk$
```

As you can see in the prompts, I was in my Documents folder, then moved up three times to reach the root level of the file system, or /.

You can now combine the cd .. command with cd - to move up and down in the file system—but remember, the cd - command only moves back one step. There is no simple equivalent (in the cd command) to move down the file system to where you started.

```
Walden:/Users kirk$ cd ..
Walden:/ kirk$ cd -
Walden:/Users kirk$
```

In the first line, I moved up from /Users to /; in the second line, I moved back to the previous working directory, /Users.

The . and .. shortcuts have many other uses on the command line, such as specifying the parent directory of a directory in a script or other command.

OPENING A DIRECTORY IN THE FINDER

Sure, Terminal lets you move around quickly and easily, but sometimes you yearn to see icons again. Wherever you are in Terminal, no matter what directory you are in, you can run the following command at any time to open the current working directory in the Finder:

```
$ open .
```

You will recall that . (dot) represents the current working directory. The open command lets you open many kinds of items just as if you're double-clicking them. This command even lets you open directories that are normally hidden from view by the Finder. (For more on the open command, see Interlude 5, "The Versatile *open* Command.")

MOVING TO OTHER VOLUMES

While many people only have one hard drive on their computer, others may have multiple drives (both internal and external), partitions (your internal hard drive, or any external hard drive, can be split into several volumes), or network volumes (hard disks on other computers, connected via a network and mounted on a different Mac).

If you look at a Finder window (Figure 4.5), of your computer (the iMac icon), you will see that any network volumes show up in the same location as any other disks or partitions you have on your computer.

In Figure 4.5, my iMac has two partitions, and another volume, Backup, is mounted from another computer on the network, as is my iDisk.

But in Terminal, network volumes don't show up in the same place. We already saw that Mac OS X moves things around, showing you the startup volume (in the above example, Panther) in the same location as other volumes, whereas it is actually mounted elsewhere in the file system. Or, more accurately, the startup volume is mounted at the root (/) level of the file system, and the other partitions are mounted elsewhere.

ON THE COMMAND LINE

Overview of the *cd* Command

COMMAND SYNTAX

    cd [directory]

FINDER EQUIVALENT

None (this is similar to navigating folders in Finder windows).

OVERVIEW OF OPTIONS FOR CD

cd [directory]	This moves you into the directory whose name is specified. If no directory with the name specified exists, the following error message is returned: No such file or directory.
cd	Running the cd command alone takes you to your Home directory.
cd ~	This also takes you to your Home directory.
cd ..	This takes you to the next level up in the file system.
cd -	This takes you back to the previous working directory. Repeating this command toggles between two directories.

GETTING MORE INFORMATION

There is no man page for cd; information about this command is included in the bash shell man page. If you run man cd, the bash man page opens; you have to scroll through it to find the short section on cd.

FIGURE 4.5
A Finder view of the volumes mounted on an iMac

The same goes for network volumes. In the file system, all other volumes show up in /Volumes. If I move to that directory and look at its contents, I see the following:

```
Walden:/Volumes kirk$ ls
Backup  Panther  Tunes  iDisk
```

You can see that this is the same as Figure 4.5, with the exception of the Network icon. But your startup volume (Panther, in my case), is not really mounted in /Volumes—it is mounted at the root level of the file system, even though it shows up in /Volumes. Running ls -l shows you that the startup volume is a symbolic link:

```
$ ls -l /Volumes/
total 12
drwx------  26 kirk     admin      840  8 May 15:26 Backup
lrwxr-xr-x   1 root     admin        1 29 Apr 18:02 Panther -> /
drwxr-xrwx  99 kirk     unknown   3366 15 Apr 09:34 Tunes
dr-x------  18 kirk     unknown    612  8 May 11:31 iDisk
```

When you want to examine files on other volumes—whether hard disks, partitions, or network volumes, including your iDisk, if you have one—you must remember that their location in the file system always begins with /Volumes.

Jumping Around the File System with *pushd* and *popd*

While the cd command is practical and useful, it has limits: moving back and forth between distant directories is not very simple. Say you are working on a project whose files are in the Documents directory of your home directory, but you need to switch often to another directory, such as one in /Library. The pushd and popd commands let you store a *stack*, or list of directories, and switch between them much more easily than with cd.

You can use pushd instead of cd; it not only stores the directory in a stack but moves to it as well. Think of a stack as a pile of file cards. Each time you move to a directory with pushd, a new card, with the name of the directory, is added to the stack. Look at the following:

```
1:
Walden:~ kirk$ pushd Documents
~/Documents ~
```

```
2:
Walden:~/Documents kirk$ pushd ..
~ ~/Documents ~
```

```
3:
Walden:~ kirk$ pushd Library
~/Library ~ ~/Documents ~
```

```
4:
Walden:~/Library kirk$ pushd Preferences
~/Library/Preferences ~/Library ~ ~/Documents ~
```

You can see that I started in my home directory (~) and moved to my Documents directory using pushd (1). Section 2 shows, in the prompt, that I am in ~/Documents, and Terminal then printed a line showing three directories: my home directory, followed by ~/Documents, followed by my home directory again. This is the stack that has been stored by pushd.

I then moved to the ~/Library directory (3), then to the ~/Library/Preferences directory (4). Each time, pushd prints a line showing the list of directories in the stack.

Now, pushd on its own is not very useful; adding these directories to a stack is only interesting if there is a way to get them back out. This is where popd comes in.

Remember, pushd works like cd, but stores the directories in a stack. The popd command also works like cd, but takes its directory from the top of the stack.

If I continue from the above example, entering popd several times, look at what happens:

```
Walden:~/Library/Preferences kirk$ popd
~/Library ~ ~/Documents ~
```

```
Walden:~/Library kirk$ popd
~ ~/Documents ~
```

```
Walden:~ kirk$ popd
~/Documents ~
```

```
Walden:~/Documents kirk$ popd
~
```

```
Walden:~ kirk$
```

(Again, I have added line breaks and left the prompt text visible for clarity.) Each time popd is run, the topmost directory in the stack is called, and Terminal moves into that directory, then prints a line with the remaining directories in the stack.

Silencing *pushd* and *popd*

One disadvantage to using pushd and popd is the fact that they litter the Terminal window with lines showing the directory stack. If you use the tcsh shell, you can turn this off by setting the pushdsilent shell variable. To do this, run the following command:

```
$ set pushdsilent
```

The pushd and popd commands will no longer return a line showing the directory stack. However, if you want to see this line, run the pushd or popd command with the -1 option.

If you have set the pushdsilent variable and want to know what directories are in the stack, you can always run the dirs command, which returns the same line you turned off above.

```
$ dirs
~/Library/Preferences /Library / ~
```

Finally, if you want pushd and popd to again display the directory stack, run the following:

```
$ unset pushdsilent
```

When setting the pushdsilent variable in this manner, the shell will only remember this change during the current session. If you quit Terminal or quit your shell session, the next time you start a session this variable will be reset to the default, which is for pushd and popd to return the directory stack. For more on setting shell variables, and making them stick, see Chapter 16.

HANDS ON: JUMPING FROM DIRECTORY TO DIRECTORY—ANOTHER WAY

While pushd and popd are useful commands, there is another way to move quickly from one directory to another distant directory. The default shell, bash, and the tcsh shell have a built-in command history. If you type a command, you can later press the up arrow on your keyboard to backtrack through this history. When you find the command you want to run again, just press Enter or Return.

If you use cd with absolute paths, this command history will allow you to move into directories without retyping long names.

Say you want to move back and forth between the following directories:

```
/Volumes/Backup/Files/Docs/Web\ pages
/Library/Desktop\ Pictures/Abstract
```

If you move to these directories using their full paths, as above, rather than moving into one directory, then using cd to move into a subdirectory, and so on, the commands you run are recorded in the command history. To move back to one of these directories, press the up arrow until you find the right cd command, then press Enter or Return. (For more on using command history, see Chapter 6, "Saving Time on the Command Line.")

Overview of the *pushd*, *popd*, and *dirs* Commands

COMMAND SYNTAX

```
pushd [option(s)] [directory]
popd
dirs
```

FINDER EQUIVALENT

In a way, this is similar to the Finder's Recent Items, accessible from the Apple menu. The Forward and Back buttons in a Finder window toolbar can also move you through your navigation history.

OVERVIEW OF OPTIONS FOR *PUSHD*, *POPD*, AND *DIRS*

pushd [directory]	This command adds the current directory to the directory stack, then moves you into the directory whose name is specified. If no directory with the name specified exists, the following error message is returned: No such file or directory.
pushd	The pushd command run alone takes you to your home directory and adds that directory to the directory stack.
pushd ~	This command takes you to your home directory and adds that directory to the directory stack.
pushd ..	This command takes you to the next level up in the file system and adds that directory to the directory stack.
pushd -	This command takes you back to the previous working directory, and adds that directory to the directory stack. Repeating this command toggles between two directories.
-l	This option tells pushd to display the directory stack if the pushdsilent variable has been set. (Used only with the tcsh shell.)
popd	This command takes you to the directory at the top of the directory stack.
dirs	This command displays the directory stack.
set pushdsilent	This command tells the shell to not print a line with the directory stack after running pushd or popd. (Used only with the tcsh shell.)
unset pushdsilent	This command resets the pushdsilent shell variable to its default, which is to print a line with the directory stack after running pushd or popd. (Used only with the tcsh shell.)

GETTING MORE INFORMATION

There are no man pages for pushd, popd, or dirs; information about these commands is included in the builtin man page. If you run man pushd, popd, or dirs, the builtin manual page opens (or the tcsh man page, if you use tcsh).

Summing Up

This chapter presented some of the most useful and commonly used commands: those needed to navigate the file system. Commands such as `ls` and `cd` are the basics for finding your way around, `pwd` for finding where you are, and `pushd` and `popd` for helping you move around more quickly. You will find that these commands are the foundation of your work in Terminal, and becoming familiar with them will help you feel comfortable on the command line.

Interlude 3: Redirecting Input and Output

One of the basic principles of Unix is that the operating system includes many small tools, each of which usually does just one thing. The corollary is that these tools must have some way of working together so complex tasks can be carried out. It's no good to be able to find files with certain text in them if you cannot then move, copy, concatenate, or otherwise process these files. Input and output redirection is the glue that lets you combine these tools in just about any way you want. You can tell a command to send its output to a file; you can tell a command to get its input from a file; or you can pipe the output of one command into the input of another.

Every Unix system uses three channels for input, output, and error messages:

◆ stdin: standard input, or whatever gives data to a command. This can be Terminal, or it can be a file or other command.

◆ stdout: standard output, or what a command returns. This can be sent to Terminal, to a file, or to another command.

◆ stderr: standard error, or error messages returned by a command. This can be sent to Terminal, to a file, or to another command.

If you only use Unix commands individually, you will never need to know how to glue them together using input and output redirection and pipes. But if you want to harness the full power of these commands, understanding what you can redirect and how is essential.

Note that the following examples discuss redirecting input and output using both the bash and tcsh shells. I'll specify whenever input or output redirection differs between these two shells, but if you use another shell, redirection may function differently. See the appropriate documentation for your shell.

Redirecting Output

The most basic operation involving redirection is that of sending the output of a command, or stdout, to a file. This is extremely common, and can be very useful when you run a command, such as a find or grep command, that returns a great deal of data. If you run such a command normally, the output is sent to Terminal. But if you use the > character after your command, you can redirect the output to a file.

Here is a simple command, ls -l, that displays long information on the contents of a directory. The command is run in my home directory and returns the following:

```
$ ls -l
total 1456
drwx------  14 kirk  staff   476 22 Jun 10:06 Desktop
drwx------  35 kirk  staff  1190 20 Jun 14:52 Documents
drwx------  69 kirk  staff  2346 21 Jun 17:58 Library
```

```
drwx------     6 kirk  staff     204  5 Feb 20:47 Movies
drwx------    12 kirk  staff     408  3 Jun 09:30 Music
drwx------    10 kirk  staff     340 29 Apr 23:22 Pictures
drwxr-xr-x     8 kirk  staff     272 27 May 15:02 Public
drwxr-xr-x     8 kirk  staff     272 24 Feb 16:15 Sites
```

This is not much information, since my home directory only contains eight subdirectories. But if the contents were very long, or if I needed a list of its contents in a file, I could run the following command:

```
$ ls -l > file.txt
```

where `file.txt` is the name of the file I want the output written to. You can see here that after running the above command, the file called `file.txt` is now seen in my home directory:

```
$ ls -l
total 1464
drwx------    14 kirk  staff     476 22 Jun 10:06 Desktop
drwx------    35 kirk  staff    1190 20 Jun 14:52 Documents
drwx------    69 kirk  staff    2346 21 Jun 17:58 Library
drwx------     6 kirk  staff     204  5 Feb 20:47 Movies
drwx------    12 kirk  staff     408  3 Jun 09:30 Music
drwx------    10 kirk  staff     340 29 Apr 23:22 Pictures
drwxr-xr-x     8 kirk  staff     272 27 May 15:02 Public
drwxr-xr-x     8 kirk  staff     272 24 Feb 16:15 Sites
-rw-r--r--     1 kirk  staff     628 22 Jun 12:25 file.txt
```

If I open that file in a text editor, I can see that it contains the exact same text as Terminal displayed when running the `ls -l` command.

When redirecting output to a file, the shell creates the file if it does not exist. But beware: if the file does exist, the shell just overwrites its contents without warning. If you want to append the output of a command to a file, run the command like this:

```
$ ls -l >> file.txt
```

If the file following >> does not exist, it is created. Opening the file in a text editor, I can see that it now contains two lists of files in my home directory. Try this and see what happens.

Deciding whether to overwrite a file's contents or not depends on what you are planning to use the file for. If it contains log data, you probably want to save the history and not overwrite the file, but if it is a list of files in a directory, it may be more logical to overwrite it so the file contains only the latest data.

Redirecting Input

Sometimes you want to redirect input, or send data into a command from a source other than the standard input or Terminal. In this case, you can use the < character. The simplest example of redirecting input is using `mail`, which is a command-line e-mail program:

```
$ mail me@mydomain.com < file.txt
```

HANDS ON: PROTECTING FILES WITH THE *NOCLOBBER* VARIABLE

The bash and tcsh shells both have a variable called noclobber, which, when set, protects existing files from being overwritten when redirecting output to a file. If this variable is not set, the > redirection character tells a command to overwrite a file, if one with the name used in the command exists, and to create one if none exists.

If the noclobber variable is set, however, the shell returns an error message if the file output is redirected to exists; if the file does not exist, the shell creates it.

Using the >> characters to append output to a file appends normally if the file exists and the noclobber variable is set, but if the file does not exist, the shell returns an error message.

You can override the noclobber variable by adding a | after the redirection characters, with bash, or by adding ! after the redirection characters with tcsh:

```
$ ls >| file.txt
$ ls >>| file.txt


% ls >! file.txt
% ls >>! file.txt
```

In the first example in each set above, the file is overwritten if it exists. In the second example, it is created if it does not exist.

For more on setting shell variables, see Chapter 16, "Configuring the Shell."

This sends file.txt to me@mydomain.com using the mail command. But few people use command-line e-mail any more. Actually, input redirection is not very common, since most commands take their input from filenames that are entered as arguments. The following two commands do the same thing:

```
$ sort < pepys.txt
$ sort pepys.txt
```

because the sort command gets its input from the filename that follows it.

As you can see from the above example, which is just a hint of what redirection can do, you can use output from different commands that has been redirected, or saved in files, and make it function as the input for other commands.

Redirecting Input and Output

You rarely need to redirect both input and output, since commands that can use input from files almost always get that input from arguments, as we saw above with the sort command. So, running this command:

```
$ sort < pepys.txt > pepys_sort.txt
```

is the same as running this command:

```
$ sort pepys.txt > pepys_sort.txt
```

One way input and output redirection are used together is in a command such as this:

```
$ tr '\r' '\n' < pepys.txt > pepys_unix.txt
```

In the above command, the file I have called `pepys.txt` was created on a Macintosh and uses Mac line breaks. Unix commands, however, only understand Unix line breaks. To be able to work with this file from the command line, I must translate these line breaks using the `tr` command. This command gets its input from `pepys.txt`, translates Mac line breaks (`\r`) into Unix line breaks (`\n`), and saves the output as `pepys_unix.txt`. For more on `tr`, see Chapter 9, "Editing Text."

Redirecting Error Messages

When commands generate error messages, they write these messages to standard error. In some shells, you can redirect standard error, or `stderr`, to a file. In `bash`, this is easy to do. The `find` command, when not run using `sudo` or as root, generates a number of "Permission denied" errors when it tries to move into directories that the user does not have privileges for.

To redirect only error messages with `bash`, use the following:

```
$ find / -name pepys 2> errors.txt
```

This runs the `find` command and sends any errors to a file called `errors.txt`. You can append error messages to an existing file like this:

```
$ find / -name pepys 2>> errors.txt
```

If you simply want to ignore errors, you can send them to /dev/null, the Unix bit-bucket (/dev/null is a "device" that contains nothing, and swallows anything that is sent to it):

```
$ find / -name pepys 2> /dev/null
```

This displays the results of the `find` command and tosses all the error messages into the ether.

The `tcsh` shell can do this as well, but only with a bit of tweaking. Here's a `find` command where the results are displayed in Terminal and the error messages are sent to a file:

```
% (find / -name pepys > /dev/tty) >& errors.txt
```

The above command sends those errors into a text file and only displays the results of the search.

Here is another way to work with the same command, this time sending the error messages to /dev/null:

```
% (find / -name pepys > /dev/tty) >& /dev/null
```

Running this command makes the `find` part of the command run in a subshell; the results of the search are sent to Terminal while the error messages, sent to /dev/null, just disappear.

You can also redirect output to a file using the same type of command while sending error messages to /dev/null:

```
% (find / -name pepys > file.txt) >& /dev/null
```

This lets you save only the results of the find command in a file. Naturally, you can also save the results to one file and error messages to another:

```
% (find / -name pepys > file.txt) >& errors.txt
```

Or you can save results to one file and append error messages to another file:

```
% (find / -name pepys > file.txt) >>& errors.txt
```

Using redirection of results and error messages, as in the above example, you have a full range of options for dealing with the results of any command.

Using Pipes

We saw above how to redirect input and output separately, getting input from a file or redirecting output to a file. Another way to redirect input and output is called a *pipe*; this represented by the | character. A pipe redirects the output of one command into the input of another. You can pipe any two commands together, as long as the command following the pipe can work with the type of data returned by the first command. Here are a few examples:

```
$ ls | wc -l
```

The above command first gets a list of the contents of the current working directory, then pipes the results into the wc (word count) command; this command's -l option returns the number of lines in the input. The result is the number of items in the directory.

```
$ locate string | wc -l
```

The above command searches the locate database for string, then sends the results to the wc command. The result is the number of occurrences of string in the locate database.

```
$ ps -aux | grep kirk
```

The above command uses the ps (process status) command to find running processes, then looks through them to find which ones contain kirk.

Pipes are useful in find and grep commands to refine results. Here is one example:

```
$ grep -wr ball ~/Documents/* | grep -w pitcher
```

The above command uses grep to look for the word "ball" in any file in my Documents directory. After finding occurrences of this word, it pipes the data to grep, which searches, this time, for the word "pitcher". The final result is any line containing *both* "ball" and "pitcher".

You can combine a pipe and output redirection. Using the above command, if you wanted to save the results to a file, you could run the following:

```
$ grep -wr ball ~/Documents/* | grep -w pitcher > results.txt
```

You are not limited to using just one pipe in a command. You can pipe together several commands, each time sending the output of one command into another. Here is an example with two pipes:

```
$ grep -wr ball ~/Documents/* | grep -w pitcher | sort | less
```

The above command does the same search as the previous example, then passes this on to sort, which sorts the lines in alphabetical order, then passes that on to less, so you can view the results one screen at a time.

HANDS ON: REDIRECTING INPUT AND OUTPUT WITH *PBCOPY* AND *PBPASTE*

In addition to the standard ways of redirecting input and output, Mac OS X offers two unique tools that send output to the clipboard (pbcopy) or redirect input from the clipboard (pbpaste). Actually, calling these redirection tools is perhaps not correct, but functionally they can work as such.

These two commands provide a link between the Finder's clipboard and Terminal. You can use them in one-line commands or in shell scripts to manage data and move it in either direction. For example, as I write these words in Microsoft Word, I can copy this sentence and insert it into Terminal using pbpaste:

```
$ pbpaste
For example, as I write these words in Microsoft Word,
I can copy this sentence and insert it into Terminal
using pbpaste:
```

Admittedly I could do the same thing by simply pasting the text into Terminal with ⌘-V, but the pbpaste command lets you use data in the clipboard within a command without having to worry about escaping characters, or without worrying about how long it is.

In the same manner, pbcopy lets you send output to the clipboard, after which you can paste it into any application. For example, say you want to be able to convert characters in text you have copied to the clipboard. If you want to turn all the text into uppercase characters, you can copy the text in any application, then run this command:

```
$ pbpaste | tr 'a-z' 'A-Z' | pbcopy
```

This pipes the data from the clipboard into the tr command, which, here, changes lowercase characters to uppercase characters and pipes it into pbcopy, which puts it back into the clipboard.

These two commands are inherited from NeXTStep, which used a pasteboard, hence their names. You can find out more about them by typing man pbpaste and man pbcopy in Terminal.

You'll notice that pbpaste can paste text in PostScript and RTF formats as well as ASCII text.

HANDS ON: PIPING OUTPUT AND ERROR MESSAGES

Pipes only pass standard output into the following command; any error messages are displayed in Terminal. To pipe both standard output and standard error, use this form (the first example is for bash, the second for tcsh):

```
$ find / -name "pepys*" 2>&1 | grep 'pepys'
% find / -name "pepys*" |& grep 'pepys'
```

The 2>&1 _ or |& operator tells the shell to redirect output and error messages to the following command, and grep then filters them, removing error messages and displaying only the results of the find command. Since in this case the command returns many Permission denied messages (for directories that I don't have permissions to search), this command limits the number of results to those containing my search string.

You can also send standard output and standard error to a file, if you use tcsh:

```
% find / -name "pepys*" >& file.txt
```

This allows you to save both your output and errors to examine later.

Redirecting Output to Two Places with *tee*

Another tool that can be useful when redirecting output with pipes is the **tee** command. This command gets its name from a T-shaped pipe, which sends water in two directions. It allows you to send output to a file while piping the same output into another command. Here is one example of how you can use **tee**:

```
$ ls ~/Library/Preferences | sort -r | tee prefs.txt | grep apple | less
```

Looking at this command from left to right, here is what it does:

1. First, it uses ls to get a list of the files in ~/Library/Preferences.

2. It pipes this into sort, which sorts the list in reverse alphabetical order (the -r option tells sort to sort in reverse order).

3. Next, it pipes this through tee; tee is always used with a pipe preceding it. The tee command saves its input (the results of the sort command) in a file called prefs.txt, then pipes it on to the next command.

4. The grep command obtains its input from the previous pipe. This input is the sorted list of preferences. If the | tee section of the command were not there, the rest of the command would not change; grep would have the same input.

5. The grep command then searches for lines containing "apple".

6. The results of the grep command, lines containing "apple", are piped into less so they can be viewed in Terminal, one screen at a time.

As you can see from the above example, tee creates a file but does not stop the "flow" of the command, sending its data on, without altering it in any way, to the next pipe. Some basic knowledge of plumbing certainly helps in understanding this kind of command.

The tee command offers an -a (append) option, which works like a >> redirection operator. If you use this option, output is appended to a file. If not, and the file exists already, tee overwrites the file.

Overview of the *tee* Command

COMMAND SYNTAX

```
tee [option(s)] [file ...]
```

FINDER EQUIVALENT

None.

OVERVIEW OF OPTIONS FOR *TEE*

tee   The tee command copies standard input to standard output, making a copy in zero or more files.

-a   This option tells the tee command to append its output to the specified file, rather than overwriting the file if it already exists.

GETTING MORE INFORMATION

To display the man page and learn more about tee, type man tee in Terminal.

Chapter 5

Working with Files and Directories

One of the strongest features of the Mac OS X Finder, and of other graphical user interface operating systems, is its ability to make file management actions so intuitive that they seem effortless. When you drag a file from one window to another, for example, the Finder is merely putting a graphical face on a basic action, that of issuing a command to move a file from one location to another. Figure 5.1 is an example of what you see in the Finder.

But what you would type to carry out this same operation from the command line is this:

```
$ mv ~/My\ Folder/My\ File.txt ~/My\ Other\ Folder
```

FIGURE 5.1

Moving a file in the Finder

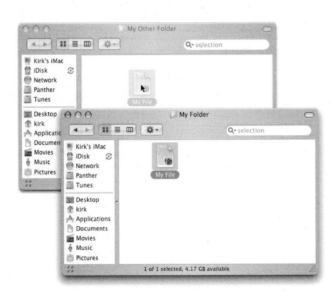

You have to admit, there's something to be said for dragging and dropping files in Finder windows! But the command line offers many advantages over using the Finder for moving, copying, or deleting files and folders. Here are just a few:

◆   You can copy or move files from one directory to a distant directory, without having to open any windows.

◆   You can easily copy or move multiple files using wildcards. You can even select which files to copy according to certain attributes, such as parts of filenames or extensions.

◆   You can copy or move files that are hidden by the Finder.

◆   You can make files invisible with one simple command.

◆   You can rename files and directories in a jiffy. You can even move and rename a file or directory with just one command.

◆   You can delete files or directories quickly (but irreversibly—see the section "Removing Files with *rm*" below for a warning on deleting files).

◆   You can delete files that the Finder refuses to delete. Occasionally, a recalcitrant file that you have placed in the Trash just won't go away. Using the command line, you can eliminate it for good.

As you get more familiar with working via the command line, you will discover more advantages to using Terminal.

A CAVEAT ON MOVING AND COPYING FILES

Mac OS has historically used a unique way of saving files. Many files are in two parts, called the *data fork* and the *resource fork*. Back in the days of Mac OS 9 and earlier, the data fork contained data (the contents of a file, or code for applications) and the resource fork contained settings, icons, and other information. Most files used this two-part system; if you have ever copied files to a PC disk and looked on a Windows computer, you have seen additional folders copied together with your files.

When copying or moving files containing a resource fork, this can be a problem: some files still contain information in their resource fork, especially those files used by Mac OS 9 or Classic applications.

If you are using files with Mac OS 9 or Classic, the cp and mv commands may strip any resources the files contain. (The mv command is usually safe, and only strips resource forks when moving a file to another volume; this is, in essence, copying the file, since it creates a new copy of the file on the other volume and then deletes the original.) Some applications need these resource forks, and stripping them may cause files you've moved or copied with these commands to be unusable. But Apple created some additional commands, called CpMac and MvMac (the capitalization is important here), to resolve these issues. CpMac and MvMac are installed with the Developer Tools. (For more on using the Developer Tools, see Interlude 8, "Using the Developer Tools.") These command-line tools allow you to retain resource forks when copying and moving files and applications, ensuring that everything you copy or move with them remains usable.

Copying Files with *cp*

The `cp` (**copy**) command does exactly what its name suggests: it copies files from one location to another. At its simplest implementation, `cp` copies a file (specified by its filename, with either a relative or absolute path) to a directory (also specified by its name, with either a relative or absolute path). The basic form is as follows:

```
cp source destination
```

With this in mind, let's look at a few examples of copying files.

```
$ cp ~/Documents/MyFile.rtf ~/Public
```

In the above example, I copied a file from the `Documents` directory in my home directory to the `Public` directory, a location where any user can access files. As you can see in the command, the first part, `cp`, is the command, the second, `~/Documents/MyFile.rtf`, is the source, and the third, `~/Public`, is the destination. Both the source and destination in this example use absolute filepaths; I could be anywhere in the file system when running this command.

However, if I were already in the `Documents` directory, I wouldn't need to use an absolute filepath for the source. Since it's perfectly legal to mix absolute and relative filepaths in a command, I could merely type the following:

```
$ cp MyFile.rtf ~/Public
```

Let's say I'm in my `Documents` directory and want to copy a file there from my `Public` directory. I could use the following command, using the `.` and `..` shortcuts:

```
$ cp ../Public/MyFile.rtf .
```

The source, `../Public/MyFile.rtf`, tells the shell to look at the `Public` directory, which is a sub-folder of the next directory up in the hierarchy (`..`, or my home directory), and to copy the file called `MyFile.rtf`. The destination, `.`, is the shortcut for the current directory.

When copying files in this simple form, the source is a filename and the destination a directory. (The destination can also be a filename; see below for more ways to use `cp`.) But the source can also be multiple filenames. When executing this command, the shell checks the contents of the directory you refer to, making sure that the file or files exist. If there are several files listed and they all exist, then the shell goes ahead and copies them all to the destination. You can run a command like this:

```
$ cp MyFile1.rtf MyFile2.rtf MyFile3.rtf ~/Public
```

and copy the three files after the `cp` command to the destination directory.

Using Wildcards to Copy Files

For an even shorter version of this command, you can use a wildcard and save your typing fingers:

```
$ cp MyFile* ~/Public
```

WARNING: COPYING FILES REPLACES EXISTING FILES

By default, the cp command replaces any like-named files in the destination—unlike the Finder, which gives you an alert, asking if you really want to replace them. The same goes for the mv command (see the section "Moving Files and Directories with *mv*" below). This is one of the dangers of using the command line. New actions call for new habits, and the safest way to work with these two commands is to use the -i (interactive) option, which tells the shell to ask you if any files with the same name are present. When using this option, type y for yes (to replace files) and n for no.

Here's an example:

```
$ cp -i MyFile1.rtf New_Directory/
overwrite New_Directory/MyFile1.rtf? y
$
```

I typed y when Terminal asked me if I wanted to overwrite the file. If I typed n, or pressed Return, at the overwrite question, the command would stop.

The * wildcard tells the shell to look for all files whose names begin with MyFile and copy them to ~/Public. Of course, if you have 10 files like that, all 10 will be copied. If you only want the first three copied, you need to enter each name individually, or you could use the following command:

```
$ cp MyFile[1-3].rtf ~/Public
```

If you want to copy all .rtf files from the source directory, you can use the following:

```
$ cp *.rtf ~/Public
```

This will copy all files ending with .rtf to the Public folder. You can use the asterisk wildcard at any location in a filename. Table 5.1 demonstrates some ways it can be used.

For a more thorough presentation of wildcards, see Interlude 6, "Wildcards and Globbing."

TABLE 5.1: EXAMPLES OF USING THE ASTERISK AS A WILDCARD

WILDCARD USAGE	WHAT THE SHELL MATCHES
MyFile*.rtf	This string tells the shell to look for any file beginning with MyFile and ending with .rtf. It will copy, for example, MyFile1.rtf, as well as MyFileBackup.rtf.
My*.rtf	This string tells the shell to look for any file beginning with My and ending with .rtf. It will also copy MyReport.rtf or MyBicycle.rtf.
*File.rtf	This string tells the shell to look for any file ending with File.rtf. It will copy OldFile.rtf, NewFile.rtf, etc.
My*le[1-3].rtf	This string tells the shell to look for any file beginning with My, followed by any characters, then by le1, le2, or le3, then .rtf. It will copy MyVeryOldFile1.rtf, but not MyFileBackup1.rtf.

HANDS ON: COPYING ALL THE FILES IN A DIRECTORY

As seen in Table 5.1, wildcards save you from typing lots of filenames. You can go the ultimate distance with the * wildcard and use it to copy all the files from a directory to another directory. To copy all the files from the current working directory (the directory Terminal is currently in), run the following:

```
$ cp * [destination]
```

For example, to copy all the files in your Pictures directory to your home directory, you can run this while in the Pictures directory:

```
$ cp * ~
```

If you are not in the directory you want to copy from, you merely need to specify that directory in the source, like this:

```
$ cp ~/Pictures/* ~
```

Not only does this save you a lot of keystrokes, but you'll find that it can be even quicker than using the Finder.

Copying a File and Changing Its Name

In the above examples, the sources used were files and the destinations directories. But the destination can also be a filename. This is useful if you want to copy a file and change its name at the same time. For example, to copy MyFile.rtf to your Public folder, renaming it MyFile1.rtf, run the following command:

```
$ cp MyFile.rtf ~/Public/MyFile1.rtf
```

Unless you want to change the name, you won't need to specify a filename in the destination; a directory will do.

You can do the same thing to make a copy of a file, with a different name, in the same folder. Just run the command like this:

```
$ cp MyFile.rtf MyFile1.rtf
```

The system will make a copy of the file, with the new name.

PRESERVING FILE INFORMATION WHILE COPYING

When you copy a file with cp, some of the information about the file may be lost or changed. This notably includes the file's modification date and time. The cp command normally updates this information when copying, but if you run this command with the -p (preserve) option, this will be preserved. This is very useful when you are concerned about knowing which of your files is the newest or most recently modified.

In the following example, I had a file called testfile, which I copied normally as testfile1, then again using cp -p as testfile2. You can see that in the first case the modification time was changed and in the second it was preserved.

```
-rw-r--r--    1 kirk      staff           0 Jan 13 09:49 testfile
-rw-r--r--    1 kirk      staff           0 Jan 13 10:19 testfile1
-rw-r--r--    1 kirk      staff           0 Jan 13 09:49 testfile2
```

This option preserves more than just the modification time. According to the cp man page, it "causes cp to preserve in the copy as many of the modification time, access time, file flags, file mode, user ID, and group ID as allowed by permissions." Not all this information is preserved in all cases. For more on using this option, see the cp man page.

Copying Directories with *cp*

You can use cp to copy directories as well as files, but it works a bit differently. For cp to work with directories, it needs the -R (recursive) option. This tells the command to copy not only the directory specified, but all subdirectories it contains as well as any other contents. To copy a directory, you need to run the following:

```
$ cp -R [source] [destination]
```

All the other options and ways of copying, shown above for files, work the same with directories. Note, however, that while you rename the directory while copying—giving the new directory a different name than the original—you cannot change the name of its subdirectories or other contents.

ON THE COMMAND LINE

Overview of the *cp* Command

COMMAND SYNTAX

```
cp [option(s)] source destination
```

FINDER EQUIVALENT

Copy and Paste.

OVERVIEW OF OPTIONS FOR *CP*

cp   This command copies the source argument to the destination. You can use multiple sources or wildcards. You can specify a directory as the destination, or specify a path containing a file name, if you wish to change the name of the file being copied.

-p   This option causes cp to preserve in the copy as many of the modification time, access time, file flags, file mode, user ID, and group ID as allowed by permissions.

-R   If the source is a directory, with this option tells cp to copy the directory and all its subdirectories.

-i   This is the interactive option. The shell will ask you to confirm before copying a file that would overwrite an existing file. If you type y, the copy will continue. If you type n, it will stop.

GETTING MORE INFORMATION

To display the man page and learn more about cp, and the options available, type man cp in Terminal. Several options are available that can be useful in certain situations.

THE INCREDIBLE SHRINKING FILES

The `cp` command does not copy the resource forks of files. For most files, this doesn't make a difference, but some programs still put information in resources. One example is graphics programs that may put thumbnail images in the resources of picture files.

You can use `cp` to remove these resources, making the files much smaller, so you can send them more easily by e-mail or just save space. (If you have a lot of pictures, you can save several megabytes by removing these thumbnails.)

To do this, just copy a file, giving it a new name.

```
$ cp Perceval.jpg PercevalCopy.jpg
```

In the above example, I copied a picture of my son Perceval, renaming it, in the same directory. If you look in the Finder, you can see the difference, as shown here:

The original file displays a thumbnail and the copy just shows a standard JPEG icon.

Curiously, when examining the file info in Terminal, there seems to be no difference:

```
$ ls -l
-rw-r--r--  1 kirk  staff  30819 Nov 14 18:06 Perceval.jpg
-rw-r--r--  1 kirk  staff  30819 Nov 14 18:07 PercevalCopy.jpg
```

But as you can see here, the Finder shows that the difference is significant:

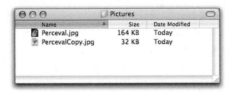

This is because Terminal does not see the resource fork of the files, and calculates the size only by looking at their data. However, running `ls -ls` shows the difference (the `-ls` option adds a column at the beginning of the line with the number of 512-byte blocks each file takes up):

```
$ ls -ls
```

Continued on next page

THE INCREDIBLE SHRINKING FILES *(continued)*

```
328 -rw-r--r--  1 kirk  staff  30819 Nov 14 18:06 Perceval.jpg
 64 -rw-r--r--  1 kirk  staff  30819 Nov 14 18:07 PercevalCopy.jpg
```

Removing this thumbnail reduces the size of the file fivefold. If you are sending a number of pictures by e-mail, this can save a lot of time. However, if you want to strip resource forks from many files at once, you can use the cp command to copy the files to another folder. Run the command like this:

```
$ cp *.jpg /folder
```

sending the copies to another folder. In this manner using the * wildcard to match all filenames with a jpg extension the resource forks of all the files are removed.

Moving Files and Directories with *mv*

The mv (**move**) command moves files or directories from one location to another. When these locations are on the same volume, mv works the same as when you drag files from one Finder window to another. If you run the mv command across volumes, the files or directories are removed from their original location, whereas the Finder merely copies them. The mv command acts like a cut-and-paste operation, cutting the file or directory from its original location, and pasting it in its new location. This command works almost exactly like the cp command, the main exception being that you never have to use the -R option to move directories. To run this command, do the same things as described in the previous section, substituting mv for cp.

```
$ mv MyFile.rtf ~/Public/MyFile.rtf
```

In this example, the file called MyFile.rtf is moved to my Public folder. The operating system first writes the file then, after checking to make sure the copied file was written correctly, deletes the original.

HANDS ON: RENAMING FILES IN A JIFFY

As we saw earlier, the mv command lets you choose a new name for a file at the destination. But you can also quickly rename a file with this command. All you need to do is move a file to the same directory it's in while changing its name. Run the following:

```
$ mv OldFileName NewFileName
```

The mv command takes OldFileName and replaces it with NewFileName in the same directory (since no different path is specified in the destination). But it gets even better: this command does not differentiate between files and directories, and you can use mv to rename a directory, retaining all its contents, no matter how many subdirectories or files it contains.

```
$ mv Photos Photos-copy
```

But be warned: as with many Unix commands, there is little room for error. You are safest copying files and directories if you want to change their names. When doing this, you are left with both the original and the copy, whereas mv leaves you with only the copy.

I must warn you that by default, the mv command (like cp discussed earlier) replaces any like-named files in the destination, unlike the Finder, which gives you an alert asking if you really want to replace them. You can run the mv command with the -i (interactive) option, as with many commands, to protect against this. If you run the command in the following manner, you will get an alert if a file exists with the same name:

```
$ mv -i MyFile.rtf ~/Public
overwrite /Users/kirk/Public/MyFile.rtf? y
```

Type y to overwrite the file, or type n or Return to stop the move operation and keep the file in the destination.

ON THE COMMAND LINE

Overview of the *mv* Command

COMMAND SYNTAX

```
mv [option(s)] source destination
```

FINDER EQUIVALENT

Cut and Paste; changing filenames by clicking and editing them.

OVERVIEW OF OPTIONS FOR MV

mv   This command moves the source argument to the destination. You can use multiple sources or wildcards. You can specify a directory as the destination, or specify a path containing a filename, if you wish to change the name of the file being moved.

-i   This is the interactive option. The shell will ask you to confirm before moving a file that would overwrite an existing file. If you type y, the move operation will continue. If you type n, or press Return, it will stop.

GETTING MORE INFORMATION

To display the man page and learn more about mv, and the options available, type man mv in Terminal.

Creating Directories with *mkdir*

We have seen above how to move and copy files from one directory to another, but you will also need to create directories to put these files in. The mkdir (**make dir**ectory) command is very easy to use. Here's an example:

```
$ mkdir Test
```

This command creates a new directory, called Test, in the current directory. Since the filename does not begin with a /, the shell knows that you are specifying a relative path. If you want to create the same directory in, say, your `Documents` directory, you could run the above command after using `cd` to move to that directory, or run the following from anywhere:

```
$ mkdir ~/Documents/Test
```

The `mkdir` command can also make several directories at a time. If you want to create three directories, called `Test1`, `Test2`, and `Test3`, you can run the following:

```
$ mkdir Test1 Test2 Test3
```

This command will create the three directories in the current working directory. To do the same using absolute paths, the command looks like this:

```
$ mkdir ~/Documents/Test1 ~/Documents/Test2 ~/Documents/Test3
```

If you want to create directories in hierarchy, `mkdir` can help as well. The only condition is that you set up your command in hierarchical order, creating the parent directory before the subdirectory, and before the sub-subdirectory, etc. If you want to create a series of directories and subdirectories like this:

```
Test1/Test2/Test3
```

you need to run the command as follows:

```
$ mkdir -p Test1/Test2/Test3
```

ON THE COMMAND LINE

Overview of the *mkdir* Command

COMMAND SYNTAX

```
mkdir directory ...
```

FINDER EQUIVALENT

New Folder.

OVERVIEW OF OPTIONS FOR *MKDIR*

`mkdir`   This command creates a new directory. You can specify either a relative or an absolute path for the directories you create.

`-p`   This option tells `mkdir` to create all intermediate directories when you specify a hierarchy of directories.

GETTING MORE INFORMATION

To display the man page and learn more about `mkdir`, and the options available, type `man mkdir` in Terminal. There are several options involving permissions for the directories created, which may be useful in some cases.

The -p (path) option tells the command to create each intermediate directory as required. The command first creates the Test1 directory, then the Test2 subdirectory, and finally, further down in the hierarchy, Test3.

Removing Directories with *rmdir*

The rmdir (**r**e**m**ove **dir**ectories) command is self-explanatory: it lets you remove directories, deleting them forever. Like the rm command (covered in the next section), which works on files, rmdir is very powerful: once you remove a directory in this manner, there is no getting it back. (See the section "A Safer Way to Remove Files" below for a way to safeguard this command.)

However, rmdir only works with empty directories. You may find it easier to use rm for both files and directories in all cases—after all, it's much easier to use just one command instead of two, and if you apply the safeguard shown below, you need only set it for one command: rm.

To delete an empty directory, run the following:

```
$ rmdir Files
```

If you try to remove a directory that contains files or other directories, Terminal will display the following:

```
$ rmdir Files
rmdir: Files: Directory not empty
```

ON THE COMMAND LINE

Overview of the *rmdir* Command

COMMAND SYNTAX

```
rmdir [option] [directory1] [directory2] ...
```

FINDER EQUIVALENT

Move (Folder) to Trash (though rmdir deletes the directory immediately).

OVERVIEW OF OPTIONS FOR *RMDIR*

rmdir   This command removes directories. You can specify a single directory or several directories as arguments.

-p   This option tells rmdir to remove all intermediate directories when you specify a hierarchy of directories. All the directories in the hierarchy must be empty.

GETTING MORE INFORMATION

To display the man page and learn more about rmdir and the options available, type man rmdir in Terminal. There is one option that can be useful in certain situations.

You can remove several empty directories in one command. Just separate their names with single spaces, specifying either just their names (for relative paths, within the current working directory) or their paths (for absolute paths). Here's an example:

```
$ rmdir Files ~/Documents/OldDocuments ../Video
```

You can also use `rmdir` to remove a hierarchy of directories, as long as all the directories are empty. Use the `-p` option as follows:

```
$ rmdir -p Directory1/Directory2/Directory3
```

One disadvantage to using the `rmdir` command is that, unlike the `rm` command, it has no `-i` (interactive) option, which asks you to confirm the deletion, and no `-v` (verbose) option ; these deficiencies limit its value.

Removing Files with *rm*

The `rm` (remove) command is one of the most powerful and dangerous commands you can use in Terminal. Be forewarned: when you remove a file with `rm`, it is deleted *forever*. While some file recovery programs may be able to find files deleted in this manner, it is safest to assume that what is eliminated with `rm` is gone for good.

While many Unix commands are safe to run, even if you have little experience, `rm` is like a loaded gun. For this reason, you should use this command with the utmost care. However, there is a simple way to apply a safeguard to this command (and others); see the next section for a safety measure that will take the worry away.

Running the `rm` command is relatively simple. Look at the contents of this directory:

```
$ ls
File1 File2 File3
```

To remove one of these files, run the following:

```
$ rm File1
```

You can check to make sure it worked:

```
$ ls
File2 File3
```

You can see that the file you removed is indeed gone; it no longer shows up in the list.

A Safer Way to Remove Files

The first way of removing files, as shown above, is really for those people who are totally confident with the command line. It's working without a net, though; as I said above, `rm` is very powerful, but there is a safeguard you can use to protect yourself. The `rm` command has an option, `-i` (for interactive), which tells Terminal to ask you to confirm that you really want to delete each file.

To use this option, run the command as follows:

```
$ rm -i File2
```

Terminal will ask you to confirm.

```
remove File2?
```

Type y for yes or n for no.

```
remove File2? y
```

If you type **y**, the file will be deleted. If you type **n**, or press Return, the file will not be touched. In both cases, Terminal will display a new prompt; it gives no other information, and you need to run the ls command again to see what's in the directory.

A good thing to do is set rm -i as an alias for rm, so you can type rm and use the interactive option without needing to remember it or typing those extra characters. See Chapter 16, "Configuring the Shell," for an explanation of how to do this.

AN EVEN SAFER WAY TO REMOVE FILES

There is one good thing about deleting files in Mac OS X (and in previous versions of Mac OS): file deletion is always a two-step procedure. You first move files to the Trash, then you delete them (unless you are deleting files on a remote volume; they are deleted immediately when you move them to the trash).

With the command line, this is much more radical. You remove files, and they are gone.

But there's a safeguard you can use, combining the best of both worlds. Instead of removing files with the rm command, you can use the mv command to move them to the Trash. This lets you work with a safety net to make sure you haven't goofed and deleted the wrong file.

To do this, use the following command:

```
$ mv filename ~/.Trash
```

If you look in the Trash, you'll see the file you moved. You can later empty the Trash when you are sure you want to delete the file.

There is one thing to note, however. Unlike when you drag or send files to the Trash in the Finder, the above command replaces any like-named file that is in the Trash. So make sure that you don't want to get back other files that are already in the Trash and that may have the same name.

You can also create your own command alias to do this more easily. See Chapter 16 for instructions on creating this alias.

Getting More Feedback with *rm*

The rm command has another option, -v (verbose), which shows the names of files as it removes them. If you use this option, Terminal will show the following:

```
$ rm -v File3
File3
$
```

I have added the prompt after the file removal to illustrate how this is displayed in Terminal. All this option does is show the name of the file, but it can serve to confirm exactly which file has been removed. Of course, if you made a typo and removed the wrong file, it's too late now!

Removing Directories with *rm*

While there is a special command for removing empty directories (`rmdir`; see above), the `rm` command also lets you do this through the `-d` option. I cannot repeat often enough how dangerous this command is. Don't forget to check the "A Safer Way to Remove Files" section above to see the best safeguard to protect against accidental deletions.

To remove a directory, use the following:

```
$ rm -d Directory1
```

You can use the `-i` and `-v` options, as mentioned above, for additional security:

```
$ rm -div Directory1
```

HANDS ON: SHREDDING FILES WITH *RM*

There are many programs on the market that shred files: what they do is not only delete files but overwrite the disk space they used to make sure that file recovery programs cannot get them back. This is a useful security measure for many people, and it's no surprise that there is a Unix command that can do this without the need for additional software.

The trick is to use the `-P` option with `rm`. This overwrites files first with the byte pattern 0xff, then 0x00, and then 0xff again; this triple protection may seem overkill, but if you are really concerned about shredding your files it's reassuring to know that you're covering all bases.

The command is run as follows:

```
$ rm -P fileName (fileName2 ...)
```

Naturally, you can also use the `-i` option, presented above, to confirm removal of the file(s), or the `-v` option to show the names of the files being removed.

Note that the `rm` command's three-pass deletion is good, but not the best way of shredding your files. The Finder offers a U.S. Department of Defense–approved system of deletion offering seven passes, which is guaranteed to prevent recovery. Some companies or government agencies may need to use this system, and in such cases, the `rm` command's secure deletion is insufficient.

The `rm` command can also remove directories recursively, using the `-r` (recursive) option, deleting a directory and all its subdirectories, as well as any files they contain. This is like dragging a folder that contains subfolders and files to the Trash in the Finder, except you can't drag it back out of the Trash if you want to keep it.

Let's look at how this works, and how you can use the `-i` option for minimal protection.

First, create a few nested directories:

```
$ mkdir Directory1 Directory1/Directory2 Directory1/Directory2/Directory3
```

Overview of the *rm* Command

COMMAND SYNTAX

```
rm [option(s)] file1/directory1 file2/directory2 ...
```

FINDER EQUIVALENT

Move to Trash (though rm deletes the files or directories immediately).

OVERVIEW OF OPTIONS FOR RM

rm	This command removes (deletes) the file(s) and/or directory(ies) specified in its arguments. This deletion is quick and painless. It is also permanent: when removing files or directories, there is no way to get them back.
-i	This is the interactive option. The shell will ask you to confirm before removing a file that would overwrite an existing file. If you type y, the deletion will continue. If you type n, it will stop.
-v	This is the verbose option. It tells the shell to display the name(s) of files or directories removed after running the command.
-d	This option removes directories.
-P	This option shreds files by overwriting them. This overwrites files first with the byte pattern 0xff, then 0x00, and then 0xff again.
-r (or -R)	This is the recursive option. It removes directories and files recursively, starting from the directory specified, it removes every subdirectory and file within that directory.

GETTING MORE INFORMATION

To display the man page and learn more about rm and the options available, type man rm in Terminal. Several additional options can be useful in certain situations.

Then, to remove all three of these directories, run the following:

```
$ rm -ir Directory1
remove Directory1? y
remove Directory1/Directory2? y
remove Directory1/Directory2/Directory3? y
```

Obviously, if you don't use the -i option, the command will just remove all the directories without any feedback.

But what if you decide that you don't want to remove one of the directories? You can type n at any point to keep it. Watch what happens then:

```
$ rm -ir Directory1
remove Directory1? y
```

```
remove Directory1/Directory2? y
remove Directory1/Directory2/Directory3? n
rm: Directory1/Directory2: Directory not empty
rm: Directory1: Directory not empty
```

If at any point in the hierarchy you don't want to delete a file or directory, the system cannot let you keep an item without its parent directory. In the above example, the decision to not remove Directory3 means that Directory2 (its parent directory) could not be deleted; Directory1 (the parent of Directory2) could also not be deleted, so none of these three directories will be removed. However, if they contain files, and you answer y to the rm command's confirmation requests for these files, they will be removed.

Aliases and Links

When the Finder sees an alias or a symbolic link, it treats them both the same—they will be displayed the same, and double-clicking on either one will take you to its source (if a folder) or will open the file or application. Prior to Mac OS X 10.2, aliases maintained references to files or folders through their unique identity first and their filepath second. Beginning with Mac OS X 10.2, the filepath was given priority. This means that from 10.2 on, you can delete the original file or folder and create a new one with the same name and the alias will still work. The advantage to aliases is that the Finder can keep track of the original if it is moved.

CAN'T EMPTY THE TRASH?

While in the Finder, you'll occasionally find that you cannot fully empty the Trash. There may be one or more files that you cannot empty because of their permissions, or because they are locked. The rm command lets you empty the Trash easily.

The first thing you need to know is that there are several Trashes. Each user has their own Trash directory (~/.Trash) and each volume has one (/.Trashes). So, if you have several volumes, you'll have one Trash directory to empty for your user account and one per volume. Run these commands to empty all the Trash:

```
$ sudo rm -rfi ~/.Trash/*
$ sudo rm -rfi /.Trashes/*
$ sudo rm -rfi /Volumes/<volumename>/.Trashes/*
```

The first command empties your user Trash, the second the startup volume's Trash, and the final one empties the trash for any other volume (enter the name of the volume where the command shows <volumename>).

Since these commands use the -i (interactive) option, Terminal will ask you to confirm deletion of each file. If you're sure you want to delete all these files, you can leave this option out.

The second and third commands empty the Trash for *all users*. So only use them if you really need to do this. If you just want to empty the Trash for your user account, run these commands:

```
$ sudo rm -rf /.Trashes/`id -u`/*
$ sudo rm -rf /Volumes/*/.Trashes/`id -u`/*
```

The above commands get your user ID number and delete the contents of the appropriate Trash subdirectories.

Symbolic links work strictly according to filepaths. If you move the original, the symbolic link is broken. But only symbolic links work in Terminal—you cannot do anything with aliases from the command line.

Creating Symbolic Links with *ln*

The ln (link) command creates links from Terminal. As mentioned above, these symbolic links function like Finder aliases (though if the original is moved, the link breaks). Its syntax is very similar to that of the cp or mv commands: you type the command followed by a source and target path.

```
$ ln -s /Volumes/Files/Current ~/Current
```

In the above example, I created a link for the Current directory, located in the Files partition, and placed it in my home directory. Inspecting this directory shows the following:

```
$ ls -F
Current@  Documents/  Movies/  Pictures/  Sites/
Desktop/  Library/    Music/   Public/
```

Remember, ls -F shows the directory contents in short form, but adds a slash after a directory and an @ after a symbolic link.

You can also run ls -l to get more information:

```
$ ls -l
total 0
lrwxr-xr-x    1 kirk    staff      33 Nov 21 09:42 Current -> /Volumes/Files/Current
drwxr-xr-x    7 kirk    staff     238 Nov 20 22:24 Desktop
drwxrwxrwx   17 kirk    staff     578 Nov 20 22:23 Documents
drwxr-xr-x   43 kirk    staff    1462 Nov 20 21:17 Library
drwxr-xr-x    2 kirk    staff      68 Jan 10  2002 Movies
drwxr-xr-x    5 kirk    staff     170 Sep 24 01:02 Music
drwxr-xr-x   10 kirk    staff     340 Jun 25 19:26 Pictures
drwxr-xr-x    7 kirk    staff     238 Nov 20 22:12 Public
drwxr-xr-x    4 kirk    staff     136 May 28 16:56 Sites
```

As you can see, Current points (->) to /Volumes/Files/Current and the entry type flag is l, showing that it is a link.

Now that you have a symbolic link in this directory, you can use cd to move into it:

```
Walden:~ kirk$ cd Current/
Walden:~/Current kirk$
```

The prompt treats the symbolic link like a directory—it does not show the actual path. But if you run the pwd command, you will see where you really are:

```
$ pwd
/Volumes/Files/Current
```

whereas running `pwd -L` shows the logical path to the directory, or how you got there:

```
$ pwd -L
/Users/kirk/Current
```

(For more on `pwd`, see Chapter 4, "Navigating the File System.")

ABSOLUTE VERSUS RELATIVE PATHS FOR SYMBOLIC LINKS

Unlike Finder aliases, symbolic links are not updated when you move their targets in your file system. If you create an alias to a file using the Finder and move the file somewhere else on the same volume, the Finder will still know where it is and be able to open it. (The Finder won't follow aliases copied to other volumes, because when moving a file to another volume you copy it. It only follows the original file the alias points to.) If you copy the alias somewhere else (even to another volume), it will still find the original file.

With symbolic links created in Terminal, the situation is a bit different. If you create a symbolic link then move the original, the link breaks. But if you create a new file with the same name as the original, in the original location, the symbolic link will work again.

If you move the symbolic link, there are two possibilities for what will occur: if you specified a relative filepath as the source, the link may break. But if you used an absolute filepath when creating the link, it will still work. In this example:

```
$ ln -s Current ~/Current
```

I created a link with an absolute filepath. I told the shell to make a link to `/Volumes/Files/Current` and place it in `~/Current`. If I were in my home directory and ran the following command:

```
$ ln -s /Volumes/Files/Current ~/Current
```

it would have the same effect, at least at first. I would have a link in my home directory that points to `/Volumes/Files/Current`. But since this link has a relative filepath, it would break if I decided to move it anywhere else.

ALIASES AND THE COMMAND LINE

Most Mac users are familiar with aliases—they allow you to create virtual pointers to files or folders that can be placed anywhere on your computer. When you double-click an alias to an application, the application opens; when you double-click a file alias, that file opens; and when you double-click a folder alias, a window opens displaying the contents of that folder.

Aliases are very practical on the Mac for organizing frequently used files, folders, and applications in different locations. You can put aliases to all your common applications in one folder, and, instead of opening lots of windows to get to the applications, can open them easily with just a double-click. You can also use file and folder aliases to group pointers to common files and folders, again saving time.

Continued on next page

ALIASES AND THE COMMAND LINE *(continued)*

Unix systems don't grok Mac OS aliases. (But note that an *alias* under Unix has a totally different meaning. See Chapter 16 for information on shell aliases.) Unix systems have an equivalent to Mac OS aliases called *symbolic links*. These are pointers to files, directories, or applications that work from the command line almost the same as aliases work in the Finder.

If you try to use cd to move into a directory alias, you will see the following:

```
$ cd Current
Current: Not a directory.
```

When running ls to look at the contents of a directory, there is nothing to indicate that Current is an alias:

```
$ ls
Current      Library      Pictures
Desktop      Movies       Public
Documents    Music        Sites
```

But if you run ls -l you can see the difference:

```
$ ls -l
total 320
-rw-r--r--   1 kirk  staff      0 21 Nov 10:06 Current
drwx------  17 kirk  staff    578  8 May 16:29 Desktop
drwx------  36 kirk  staff   1224  6 May 08:56 Documents
drwx------  67 kirk  staff   2278 29 Apr 23:01 Library
drwx------   6 kirk  staff    204  5 Feb 20:47 Movies
drwx------  20 kirk  staff    680 21 Mar 21:34 Music
drwx------  10 kirk  staff    340 29 Apr 23:22 Pictures
drwxr-xr-x   8 kirk  staff    272  6 May 10:59 Public
drwxr-xr-x   8 kirk  staff    272 24 Feb 16:15 Sites
```

Terminal sees Current, the alias to another folder, as a kind of file. Note the flags at the left of this line:

```
-rw-r--r--   1 kirk  staff      0 21 Nov 10:06 Current
```

The first flag, the entry type flag, shows whether the item is a directory (the d flag), a symbolic link (the l flag), or one of several other types of special items. Since this flag is blank, Terminal sees it as just another file.

ALIASES, SYMBOLIC LINKS, AND HARD LINKS

Symbolic links are very similar to Finder aliases though they react differently when moved, depending on whether you used absolute or relative filepaths when creating them.

Unix systems offer another kind of link, called *hard links*. A hard link is more than an alias, and different from a symbolic link, because it links directly to the original file's location in the file system. When you delete a hard link, the target remains in its original location. When you delete the target of a hard link, the hard link remains, with the content of the file.

An example may help you clarify this. Imagine a puppet held by several strings to its frame (the wooden piece that the puppeteer holds). If hard links were strings, you could cut one, two, even three of these strings (depending on how many there are) and, as long as there is still one string holding on to the puppet, it remains attached to the frame. Cut the last string and the puppet falls.

Filenames in the file system are actually hard links. Each bit of data that makes up a file is referenced by a filename. When you move a file, you aren't moving its data, just its name within the file system tree. When you delete a file, you delete the reference to that data, not the data itself.

For all intents and purposes, a hard link is the exact same thing as its target file; unlike symbolic links or aliases, deleting the target does not actually delete the file. It is more like giving a file several names. As long as there is at least one hard link to a file, the file system maintains the file and only deletes the file when there are no more hard links to it. In addition, you can move a hard link or its target and the link will still work, and if you move a hard link to another volume, it becomes a file—no longer linked to the original target, it is exactly the same as the original file and can be edited accordingly.

If you are used to working with aliases, you may find the concept of hard links a bit confusing. The fact that you can delete the original file, yet not actually delete it, may lead to confusion. The other problem with hard links is that they cannot refer to directories and cannot be used to refer to files on other volumes, whether on the same computer or a different computer on a network. In most cases, symbolic links will be sufficient.

As you can see in Table 5.2, aliases, symbolic links, and hard links have different properties and different usages. The one to use depends on how you need to work with it.

When looking at links in Terminal, you can tell which type they are by using the `ls -l` command. Here are three files: a normal file, a hard link, and a symbolic link.

```
-rw-r--r--   2 kirk    staff    0 Jan 13 10:51 testfile
-rw-r--r--   2 kirk    staff    0 Jan 13 10:51 hardlink
lrwxr-xr-x   1 kirk    staff    8 Jan 13 10:51 symlink -> testfile
```

The first file is a normal file, but you can tell by looking in the second column that a hard link to this file exists. If the file had no hard links, the directory link count in this column would be 1; since it is 2, you know there is a hard link, though you don't know where.

The second file, a hard link to the first file, shows the same information except for its name. The only way you know it was created as a hard link is because of its name.

The third file is a symbolic link, and this shows in two ways. First, the file mode section at the beginning of the line starts with the letter l, indicating this is a symbolic link. Second, the filename shows both the name of the link and the file it points to, with the -> symbol between them. Also, the size of this file is equal to the length of the file it links to; since `testfile` is 8 letters, `symlink` has a size of 8 bytes.

TABLE 5.2: PROPERTIES AND USAGE OF ALIASES, SYMBOLIC LINKS, AND HARD LINKS		
FINDER ALIASES	**SYMBOLIC LINKS**	**HARD LINKS**
Aliases can link to files, directories, or applications.	Symbolic links can link to files or directories. They can link to command-line applications as well, and when created to Finder applications, appear and work like Finder aliases.	Hard links can only link to files. (The only exceptions are the `.` and `..` hard links, which are created with each new directory, but only the `mkdir` command can create these links.)
The Finder resolves aliases when files are dragged onto them.	The Finder resolves symbolic links when files are dragged onto them.	You cannot create hard links to directories or applications, so there is no reason to drag items onto them.
The Finder resolves aliases when you double-click them.	The Finder resolves symbolic links when you double-click them.	The Finder resolves hard links to files when you double-click them.
Aliases can refer to items across volumes.	Symbolic links can refer to items across volumes.	Hard links cannot refer to items across volumes.
Aliases can be moved and still work. The targets of aliases can also be moved and still work.	Symbolic links can be moved and still work (if absolute filepaths are used). If you use a relative filepath, the link breaks when moved. (However, a relative link using `../` at the beginning of its path will still work if it is moved to another directory that is one level below its target.)	Hard links can be moved on the same volume and still work, whether you use an absolute or relative filepath when creating them. If moved to another volume, they become copies of the original files.
Aliases give visual indications in the Finder (the alias icon has an arrow), and the Get Info window shows their paths. They also maintain any custom or application icons the item has.	Symbolic links give visual indications in the Finder (the symbolic link icon has an arrow), and the Get Info window shows their paths. They also maintain any custom or application icons the item has.	Hard links are blank file icons, showing nothing about what they are. They do not take on specific custom or application icons.
Aliases give no indication of what they are in Terminal.	Symbolic links show clearly in Terminal; a link name is shown like this: *link_name -> original_file*.	Hard links give no indication of what they are in Terminal, but they are equivalent to their targets.
You cannot follow aliases in Terminal.	You can open (if links to files) or follow (if links to directories) symbolic links from Terminal.	You can open hard links (or, more correctly, the files they point to) from Terminal.

HANDS ON: USING LINKS TO WORK WITH THE DEVELOPER TOOLS

If you have installed the Developer Tools provided with Mac OS X, you probably want to access some of their special commands, such as MvMac and CpMac. (For more on the Developer Tools, see Interlude 8.) Since these commands are located in /Developer/Tools, you cannot invoke them without specifying their entire path, unless you add this path to your shell's PATH variable. (See Chapter 16 for more on the PATH variable.)

Another way to do this is to create symbolic links to the commands you use often and put them into /usr/local/bin, where the shell looks automatically. This saves you from changing your PATH variable, but it also ensures that the commands remain where they belong. Though you could physically move these commands, they would be in the wrong place when you install the next Developer Tools upgrade.

To create these links, run the following commands:

```
$ sudo ln -s /Developer/Tools/CpMac /usr/local/bin/cpmac
$ sudo ln -s /Developer/Tools/MvMac /usr/local/bin/mvmac
```

If you run the commands as above, you'll do something else that will make using these Developer Tools commands a bit easier: by naming the links in lowercase letters, you won't need to remember that the original commands actually contain a combination of both uppercase and lowercase. (These names are case-sensitive.)

Once you have created these links, you can use these commands by simply typing their names instead of their full paths. If you use bash, run the hash -r command; if you use tcsh, run the rehash command so the system finds the new links in /usr/local/bin and you can use them.

ON THE COMMAND LINE

Overview of the *ln* Command

COMMAND SYNTAX

```
ln [option(s)] source [target]
```

FINDER EQUIVALENT

Make Alias.

OVERVIEW OF OPTIONS FOR LN

ln   This command creates a link between a source (original) file or directory and a target file or directory. If you don't use the -s option, this is a hard link.

-s   This option creates a symbolic link.

GETTING MORE INFORMATION

To display the man page and learn more about ln, and the options available, type man ln in Terminal.

Copying Directories with *ditto*

As we saw earlier, the cp command copies both files and directories but has one important disadvantage: it does not copy resources and certain other file information that is required by the Finder. Because of this, Apple has provided a special command-line tool with its Developer Tools: CpMac copies files so all Finder information is maintained. Together with MvMac, which is an enhanced version of the mv command, these two tools offer "safe" copying of files and applications. (For more on using these tools, see Interlude 8.)

There is another program included in the basic OS X installation for copying directories and their contents: ditto. This command is most useful for two things:

◆ Copying Mac OS X resources and metadata. The ditto command correctly copies Mac OS X applications, which are stored as a kind of folder, and also copies other metadata that the Finder uses.

◆ Backing up data. The ditto command can back up your data safely, keeping all attributes the Finder needs, and can also make a bootable clone of your startup volume.

This command works in two ways. In the first form, you can copy a directory to another location, specifying the source directory and the name of the new target directory. You can run the command like this:

```
$ ditto directory1 directory2
```

The command creates the new directory and copies the source directory to the destination, which can have either the same name as the source (if in a different parent directory) or a different name.

To use ditto to copy Mac OS X resources and metadata (this includes Mac OS aliases and custom icons), you must use the -rsrcFork option. If the destination is on a file system that does not support resource forks, ditto will store this data in AppleDouble files.

```
$ ditto -rsrcFork directory1 directory2
```

If you specify the name of the destination directory and it does not exist, ditto creates it. In the following command, this works more like the cp command:

```
$ ditto -rsrcFork ~/Documents ~/Desktop/DocumentsBackup
```

As you can see, I copied my Documents directory to the desktop. Since I specified the name of the destination (DocumentsBackup), ditto created this directory, then copied the contents of my Documents directory into it.

But ditto becomes very interesting when copying into an existing directory. In this case, the ditto command copies the *contents* of the source directory into the destination directory. This is very different from how cp works. As the ditto man page says, "If the destination directory does not exist it will be created before the first source is copied. If the destination directory already exists then the source directories are merged with the previous contents of the destination."

When copying a directory with cp, the source directory and its contents are copied to the destination directory. If you have a directory called `dailyFiles` that contains seven files (Monday, Tuesday, etc.) and you run the following command:

```
$ cp -R dailyFiles Backup
```

you end up with the following structure:

```
$ ls Backup
dailyFiles
```

The `dailyFiles` directory was copied to the Backup directory.

But when doing this:

```
$ ditto dailyFiles Backup
```

the result is as follows:

```
$ ls Backup
Friday  Monday  Saturday  Sunday  Thursday  Tuesday  Wednesday
```

As you can see, `ditto` did not copy the `dailyFiles` directory to Backup, but only its contents.

This difference is both subtle and tricky. On the one hand, it allows you to copy or back up the contents of a directory or volume to another directory or volume, maintaining the exact same structure as the original, without replacing the parent directory. If you back up your entire Users directory to a Backup volume, for example, you will not see a Users directory after the backup, but rather a group of directories with the names of each user. The structure is that which was *inside* the source directory.

But this is also tricky. You are probably used to copying a directory and finding that directory inside the destination. So you need to make sure that if you want to back up all your user folders, you run `ditto` with the Users directory, not each individual user directory, as the source.

Finally, `ditto` overwrites all existing files, symbolic links, and directories in the destination, but ensures that all these items have the same mode, owner, and group as the source items. Files cannot overwrite directories or vice versa, so if you have a directory with the name of a file, it will not be copied.

Copying Applications with *ditto*

As I mentioned earlier, only `ditto` and CpMac can copy applications correctly under Mac OS X. If you haven't installed the Developer Tools, `ditto` is the only way you can do this.

When copying items with `ditto`, remember that `ditto` copies the contents of a directory. You may also recall that Mac OS X applications are actually directories masquerading as single items. So, with this in mind, you can probably imagine what will happen if you try to copy an application with `ditto`.

```
$ sudo ditto -rsrcFork /Applications/Calculator.app ~
```

(Notice the use of `sudo` before this command—in many cases, you will get a `"Permission denied"` result from Terminal if you run `ditto` on an application without `sudo`. For more on using `sudo`, see Interlude 7, "Using *sudo*.")

In the above example, I tried to copy the Calculator application to my home directory. But when I look in my home directory, I see the following:

```
$ ls ~
Contents   Desktop  Library  Music  Public
Documents  Movies   Pictures Sites
```

There's nothing called Calculator, but there is something called `Contents`. If you recall from the section on the `cp` command, copying an application has surprising consequences (at least copying native Mac OS X applications, which are, in fact, directories containing other files and directories). The `cp` command strips the resources and metadata that the application needs to appear as an application, leaving behind nothing but a directory called `Contents`. But `ditto`, with the `-rsrcFork` option, is supposed to keep this data, right?

Well, it does, but you need to run `ditto` differently. Instead of specifying a source (the application) and a destination (the directory to which you want to copy the application), you need to run `ditto` like this:

```
$ ditto -rsrcFork /Applications/Calculator.app ~/Calculator.app
```

When done in this manner, `ditto` copies the application as is, and it works fine.

One final note: I have used the `-rsrcFork` option here, but if you run the above command without it, it will work just fine. Most of Apple's own applications (such as Calculator) have no resource forks, but other applications may have them. It is safer to use this option, though if you copy an application without it you'll probably find out right away whether it works or not.

Backing Up Your Files with *ditto*

As we saw above, `ditto` is the safest way to copy Mac OS X files and applications. If you want to regularly back up your files, you can use `ditto` to do this.

Start by choosing a location for your backups. The best way is to have a separate partition or hard disk for backups. But if you haven't partitioned your hard drive, you could also use an external medium such as a Zip drive.

To use a removable medium such as a Zip drive, insert your Zip cartridge and run the following commands:

```
$ cd /Volumes
$ ls
```

The first command moves you to the `Volumes` directory, which contains the names of all mounted volumes. The second lists these volumes. Use the exact name of the Zip cartridge or other medium, as shown here. When I insert a 250MB Zip cartridge in my drive, it shows up as ZIP 250.

If you have a partition dedicated to backups, you can copy everything to this location. If not, create a directory on this partition with the same name as your user name. (I'll show the following commands with my user name, kirk; replace this with your user name.)

```
$ cd /Volumes/'Zip 250'
$ mkdir kirk
```

WHY USE *DITTO*?

The ditto command is the command-line equivalent of a Finder drag-and-drop copy. So why use ditto instead of copying in the Finder? The main reason to use this command is so you can add it to scripts, or have it run automatically using cron. (For more on cron, see Interlude 9, "Automating Commands.") Otherwise, unless you cannot access the Finder (because of problems on a computer, or because you have logged in remotely) there is little reason to use it. Drag-and-drop copies are generally faster and easier than command-line copies.

However, there is one thing you can do with ditto that you cannot do from the Finder: you can use it to create a bootable backup of your startup volume, and one reason you would want to do this is to copy invisible files. For a complete explanation on cloning your startup volume, see Interlude 4, "Cloning your Mac OS X Startup Volume."

If you are backing up your home directory, first make sure there is enough room on the destination; if there isn't, you will have to back up something that will fit—your Documents directory, for example. Run the following command, changing *partitionName* to the name of your partition or external backup medium:

```
$ ditto -rsrcFork /Users/kirk /Volumes/partitionName/kirk
```

If I run this command to my backup partition (called **Backup**), it would be as follows:

```
$ ditto -rsrcFork /Users/kirk /Volumes/Backup/kirk
```

If I run this command to my Zip cartridge, it would be as follows (note the use of quotes, because of the space in the name of the Zip cartridge):

```
$ ditto -rsrcFork /Users/kirk /Volumes/'Zip 250'/kirk
```

Backup may take a few minutes, depending on how many files you have in your directories. The copy will be finished when Terminal displays a prompt.

When running this command, you may see some messages like this:

```
/Users/kirk/Library/Preferences/com.apple.loginwindow.plist:
Permission denied
```

This means that there is an issue with permissions that you don't have. These files are not copied, but the rest of your files and directories are copied. (To copy *every* file, you can run the command using the sudo command. For more on sudo, see Interlude 7.)

ON THE COMMAND LINE

Overview of the *ditto* Command

COMMAND SYNTAX

```
ditto [option(s)] [source] [destination]
```

FINDER EQUIVALENT

Copy.

OVERVIEW OF OPTIONS FOR *DITTO*

ditto   This command copies the source argument to the destination. If the destination directory does not exist, it will be created before the copy is made. If it does exist, the contents of the source are merged in the destination directory.

-rsrcFork   This is the resource fork option. It tells ditto to copy Mac OS resource forks and metadata.

GETTING MORE INFORMATION

To display the man page and learn more about ditto, and the options available, type man ditto in Terminal. This command has several options that can be useful in certain situations.

HANDS ON: BACKING UP FILES ACROSS A NETWORK

The ditto command is a great tool for backing up files locally, but if you want to back up files and synchronize directories across a network, the rsync command is what you need. This command can set up a secure connection and copy files and directories to another computer, maintaining an exact copy of the source directory on both sides—it can delete any files in the destination that are not in the source.

For more on the rsync command, see Chapter 13, "Using the Network."

Summing Up

This chapter has shown you the essential commands for copying, moving, and deleting files and directories, as well as creating directories. These commands—cp, mv, rm, mkdir, rmdir, and ditto— do similar things as drag-and-drop copying in the Finder but, as some of the examples show, offer more power and flexibility. While the Finder remains easier to use for most operations, these commands give you a powerful alternative and in some cases provide tools that the Finder cannot offer.

Interlude 4: Cloning Your Mac OS X Startup Volume

While backing up your personal files is essential to make sure you don't lose any data in case of a crash or hardware problem, backing up your startup volume is purely optional, yet can be useful as insurance. If you do this from time to time, such as before making any new system upgrades, you can always revert to a working system if you encounter any problems. It can take a long time to reinstall the system and all its upgrades if you do have problems; a clone of your startup volume lets you get up and running in a short time.

Under previous versions of Mac OS, you could merely copy your System Folder to another volume to make a backup and recopy it to your startup volume in case of problems. You could even boot off this backup easily, as long as your backup System Folder was *blessed*, or set to be bootable (usually, it was sufficient to open the System Folder for this to occur).

Under Mac OS X, you cannot just copy your startup volume to another disk. Well, you can, but you won't be able to boot from this backup. There are many files that don't get copied if you do a drag-and-drop copy, and many of the Unix permissions and links are either changed or damaged during copy. To make a useful copy of your Mac OS X startup volume, you must *clone* it, making an exact copy not only of all the files, but also of the permissions and settings.

While you can use third-party tools to clone your Mac OS X startup volume (using a program such as Mike Bombich's shareware Carbon Copy Cloner, `http://www.bombich.com/software/ccc.html`, or Intego Personal Backup X, `http://www.intego.com`), you can also accomplish this task using the command line.

Note: this procedure covers Mac OS X 10.3 (Panther) and 10.2 (Jaguar) and does not work with older versions of Mac OS X.

Considerations for Cloning a Mac OS X Startup Volume

Several issues must be considered when cloning a Mac OS X startup volume. The following is adapted from Mike Bombich's "Guide to Backing Up Mac OS X," found at `http://www.bombich.com/mactips/image.html`.

File Permissions Must Be Preserved Many files belong to the root user, so you cannot simply copy these files from the Finder. There are other issues with permissions, such as the `setuid` bit, a feature of a file that, when executed, gives the file or application the same privileges as the owner of the file; if the owner of the file is root, then root privileges are granted during the execution of this file. Copying via the Finder sets the owner of the new files to the user who copied them and assigns a default set of permissions. Many applications and system files will not work properly with the default Finder settings.

The Invisible Unix System Files Must Be Copied Some of the essential directories for Mac OS X are invisible: these are `/private`, `/bin`, `/usr`, and `/sbin`. These directories hold critical files that allow the computer to boot and operate. There are also other invisible files at the root level of the file system that the Finder cannot copy.

Unix-Style Links Must Be Preserved   Symbolic links and hard links are different from Mac aliases, and the Finder does not copy them correctly. Because there are some critical symbolic links on a Mac OS X volume, the integrity of these files must be preserved when you clone the volume.

Special Directories   Some directories are populated by the system. For example, the `Volumes` directory is populated with directories corresponding to the names of volumes you have on your system. These directories are called mountpoints and are created on the fly by Apple's `autodiskmount` utility. Because these directories do not contain data on your startup volume, they do not need to be copied during a clone operation. The `Volumes` directory is just a placeholder (and Mac OS X recreates the `Volumes` directory on startup). The `/dev` directory is also a placeholder, for system devices such as disk drives, output devices, and communications devices. The list of devices in this directory is created each time the computer is started up and when new hardware is added, so it is unnecessary to copy the items in this directory. Because this is a Unix system directory, however, you will not have a bootable volume unless this directory is recreated on the cloned disk. Creating an empty directory is sufficient. Likewise, it is important to back up `mach_kernel` (the most important file in the system), but `mach` and `mach.sym` are destroyed and recreated each boot by the `/etc/rc` boot script. Finally, the `Network` folder at the root level does not need to be backed up because it is populated by the system on startup.

Resource Forks Must Be Preserved   While Apple is trying to move away from resource forks, many applications and documents still use them. Because of this, any backup or cloning utility must preserve the resource forks. If you try to clone a Mac OS X disk without preserving resource forks, many of your personal documents will be damaged.

Preparing to Clone a Mac OS X Startup Volume

Do the following before cloning your Mac OS X startup volume:

◆ Make sure the Ignore Ownership on This Volume setting is not checked for your target volume. To check this setting, click on the target volume's icon in the Finder, select File ➤ Get Info, then click the disclosure triangle next to Ownership and Permissions. Make sure the box at the bottom is *not* checked, otherwise permissions and ownership settings will not be preserved, no matter how you copy files.

◆ Run Disk Utility on the target and source volumes before cloning. This is not required, but is a good idea to avoid disk- or directory-related problems during cloning. If you are cloning to an external FireWire device, it's a good idea to reformat (not simply erase) the drive with Disk Utility prior to cloning.

Cloning a Mac OS X Startup Volume with *ditto*

The `ditto` command preserves permissions when run as root and preserves resource forks when run with the `-rsrcFork` option. (For more on `ditto`, see Chapter 5, "Working with Files and Directories.") This command is easy to use to clone a Mac OS X startup volume, and you can clone a disk with just a few steps. Here's what you need to do to clone your startup volume. (Note: use the following procedure at your own risk. Make sure, before erasing your original volume, that you are able to boot from the clone and that no files are missing.)

In the following procedure, the volume used for the clone is called /Volumes/Backup. Change this to reflect the name of the actual volume you are using. Also, you must have an administrator password to run these commands. Terminal will ask you to enter that password after you type the first command.

Note that some of these commands may take a while to run, and the commands don't give you any feedback in Terminal. You may have a couple hundred megabytes of files in your /Applications folder, for example, and this takes a long time to copy.

1. Use ditto to copy each of the visible directories from your startup volume to your backup volume. You need to repeat this step for each of these files or directories at the root level of your drive:

```
$ sudo ditto -rsrcFork /Applications /Volumes/Backup/Applications
$ sudo ditto -rsrcFork /Developer /Volumes/Backup/Developer
$ sudo ditto -rsrcFork /Library /Volumes/Backup/Library
$ sudo ditto -rsrcFork /System /Volumes/Backup/System
$ sudo ditto -rsrcFork /Users /Volumes/Backup/Users
$ sudo ditto -rsrcFork /System\ Folder /Volumes/Backup/System\ Folder
```

If you have not installed the Mac OS X Developer Tools, you won't have a Developer directory; if you haven't installed Mac OS 9 on the same volume as Mac OS X, you won't have a System Folder.

If you have installed Mac OS 9, you'll also want to copy the Mac OS 9 Applications folder (the following command should all be on one line):

```
% sudo ditto -rsrcFork '/Applications (Mac OS 9)'
     '/Volumes/Backup/Applications (Mac OS 9)'
```

You don't need to back up any of these files or directories at the root level of your file system:

```
dev
Volumes
Network
etc
tmp
var
automount
.vol
mach
mach.sym
.DS_Store
Cleanup At Startup
```

```
TheVolumeSettingsFolder
File Transfer Folder
Trash
.Trashes
TheFindByContentFolder
```

However, if you find any other files or directories there, you should copy them. Use the same syntax as above to copy these additional items.

2. Use `ditto` to copy your system files:

```
$ sudo ditto -rsrcFork /cores /Volumes/Backup/cores
$ sudo ditto -rsrcFork /private /Volumes/Backup/private
$ sudo ditto -rsrcFork /usr /Volumes/Backup/usr
$ sudo ditto -rsrcFork /bin /Volumes/Backup/bin
$ sudo ditto -rsrcFork /sbin /Volumes/Backup/sbin
$ sudo ditto -rsrcFork /mach_kernel /Volumes/Backup/mach_kernel
$ sudo ditto -rsrcFork /.hidden /Volumes/Backup/.hidden
```

3. Recreate symbolic links and empty directories:

```
$ cd /Volumes/Backup
$ ln -s private/etc etc
$ ln -s private/var var
$ ln -s private/tmp tmp
$ mkdir dev Volumes Network
```

4. Bless the system (Mac OS X) and System Folder (Mac OS 9), if copied, on the target:

```
$ sudo bless -folder /Volumes/Backup/System/Library/CoreServices
$ sudo bless -folder9 /Volumes/Backup/System\ Folder -bootBlocks
```

The last step is required if you want to be able to boot from your clone. Another way to accomplish this is to select it as the startup disk in the Startup Disk pane of the System Preferences.

You should now have a bootable clone of your Mac OS X startup volume. To check that it works, select this volume as the startup disk in the Startup Disk pane of the System Preferences and restart. If all went correctly, you'll be able to start up from this volume.

If you ever need to copy this clone back to your startup volume, repeat the procedure using the volume containing the clone as the source and the desired startup volume as the destination.

Chapter 6

Saving Time on the Command Line

One of the main reasons Mac users may shy away from using the command line is the time it takes to type in commands. Since we are all so familiar with the ease of pointing and clicking in our WIMP (window, icon, mouse, pointer) interfaces, typing arcane commands may seem like moving back to the Stone Age of computing. But as you have seen in the other chapters of this book, the command line and Terminal can give you quicker access to many functions, and provide a way to access hidden features of Mac OS X.

But time is certainly an issue. For users who don't type fast, it seems like a burden to open Terminal and start typing commands and long filepaths. It may seem daunting to have to type a filepath like this:

```
/Library/Preferences/ByHost/com.apple.SoftwareUpdate.003065c6ec5e.plist
```

Not only is it long, but it is arcane. Look at those numbers and letters at the end of the filename, just before the .plist extension. Those characters don't inspire you to type in Terminal, and it's easy to make mistakes when typing such long filenames.

In this chapter, I'll show you how to save lots of time when working in Terminal. I'll show you how you can get around typing long filenames and filepaths, how to recycle commands you've already run, and how to use keyboard shortcuts to save even more time. I'll look at both the default bash shell, and the tcsh shell, for those users who prefer using the latter.

WHICH SHELL?

In this chapter, I discuss a number of techniques and variables that are different for the bash shell and the tcsh shell. I point out, each time, which command or variable to use for each shell, but to make sure you know which shell you're using, just check the prompts shown in the commands. The tcsh shell uses the % prompt and the bash shell uses the $ prompt.

Using Filename Completion

Fortunately, you *don't* need to type out those long, complex filepaths and filenames. The `bash` and `tcsh` shells provide a nifty feature called *filename completion*. This allows you to type only the first few letters of a filename you need—Terminal fills in the rest for you.

Let's start with a simple example. If I look at my `Users` directory (the one that contains the home directories of all the users on my computer), I see the following:

```
$ ls
Shared         jsbach  mariefrance  samuelpepys
henrydthoreau  kirk    perceval
```

The first directory, `Shared`, is exactly what it looks like: a directory that is shared by all users—any user can place files or directories in it. The other directories are the home directories for the users on my Mac.

If I want to move to one of these home directories—say, the one belonging to Henry D. Thoreau—I could type the following:

```
$ cd henrydthoreau
```

But using filename completion, I can save keystrokes and get there in a jiffy:

```
$ cd henry [TAB]
$ cd henrydthoreau/
```

The above notation, which I'll use for the rest of this chapter, means that after typing **henry** I pressed the Tab key. (I do not type a space before the Tab key; I only show a space to make these examples more readable.) When I do this, Terminal (or, more correctly, the shell) expands the text I typed to display the next line. So, each time [TAB] is in an example, the following line is displayed automatically; you don't have to type it. You can see in the above example that the shell not only entered the name of the directory but also added a slash after it. This is another time-saving feature: the shell always adds slashes after directory names and spaces after filenames. The assumption is that you may need to continue typing your command with a subdirectory, or you may have another argument to add after the filename.

Using filename completion, I just type **henry**, press Tab, then, after the shell expands the filename, press Enter or Return and the command is run.

The shell is always aware of what is in the current working directory. When you start typing a command that requires a file or directory name as an argument, the shell looks through the directory and reacts immediately when you press Tab—you don't need to wait, even if there are lots of files or directories. Since these completions only work from the beginnings of file and directory names (you type the first few characters, not characters in the middle or at the end), it's a very rapid process of elimination.

But the fewer items you have in the directory, the less you have to type. In the above example, I typed "henry" before pressing Tab. I could just as well have typed the following:

```
$ cd h [TAB]
$ cd henrydthoreau/
```

Since there is only one directory beginning with "h," I don't need to give the shell any more information for it to figure out what I want. But if there were two or more directories whose names begin with "h," I would have to type more. Look at what is in my home directory:

```
$ ls
Desktop    Library  Music     Public
Documents  Movies   Pictures  Sites
```

You can see that there are two directories whose names begin with "D" and two that begin with "P." To move into one of those directories, I have to type more than the first letter. For example, to move to the Pictures directory, I have to type the first two letters:

```
$ cd Pi [TAB]
$ cd Pictures/
```

The shell just needs enough information to differentiate which item is being asked for. Once it has that bare minimum, it can do the rest.

Filename completion can save you the trouble of typing backslashes (\), which you need to use when entering spaces in filenames. (For more on using spaces in filenames, see Interlude 2, "Names and Paths.") When in the Pictures directory, within my home directory, I can save time moving into my iPhoto Library directory by typing the following:

```
$ cd iP [TAB]
$ cd iPhoto\ Library/
```

The shell correctly expands the name of this directory, adding the backslash before the space as required.

Capitals Count

You may have noticed that capital letters do not always count when using Terminal. If you're in your home directory and you want to move into your Documents directory, either of the following will take you there:

```
$ cd Documents
$ cd documents
```

In addition, if you type the lowercase word, the prompt will show it as the name of the current working directory (though it *incorrectly* shows it as having a lowercase name):

```
Walden:~/documents kirk$
```

When using filename completion, however, capitals do count (it is case-sensitive). If you type the following from the same location, Terminal will beep, indicating that it can't find any match for what you have typed:

```
$ cd doc[TAB]
```

Bear in mind, therefore, that to use filename completion, the characters you type must match the case of the files or directories you are searching for. (You can turn off case-sensitivity; see the sidebar below, "Turning Off Filename Completion Case-Sensitivity," and, for a more permanent change, see Chapter 16, "Configuring the Shell.")

Going Further with Filename Completion

Once you get the hang of filename completion, you'll be able to move around a lot more quickly. Say I want to execute the following command and move to my Mail directory:

```
$ cd /Users/kirk/Library/Mail
```

I could, of course, type out the entire path, but I could also type much less:

```
$ cd /U [TAB]k [TAB]L [TAB]M [TAB]
```

That's a bit difficult to read, so let's see how the shell expands the directory names one bit at a time:

```
$ cd /U [TAB]
$ cd /Users/

$ cd /Users/k [TAB]
$ cd /Users/kirk/

$ cd /Users/kirk/L [TAB]
$ cd /Users/kirk/Library/

$ cd /Users/kirk/Library/M [TAB]
$ cd /Users/kirk/Library/Mail/
```

Each step corresponds to one tab, which is one completion.

Using Multiple Completions for Files

The above examples showed a pretty simple situation, where the names of the items in the directory are different enough that you only need to type two letters before pressing Tab to have the shell complete the filenames. But even if you have lots of files, with very similar names, filename completion can help.

Say you want to copy a picture from your iPhoto Library directory. If you look in this directory, you will see it is divided into many subdirectories—one for each month—which have another level of subdirectory for each day of the month that you imported pictures. Since most digital cameras save files with an incremental number in the filename, all the files are similar. Here's what one of my iPhoto directories contains:

```
$ ls
Data            P1010022.jpg    P1010061.jpg    P1010086.jpg
P1010009.jpg    P1010023.jpg    P1010062.jpg    P1010088.jpg
P1010010.jpg    P1010024.jpg    P1010063.jpg    P1010089.jpg
P1010012.jpg    P1010033.jpg    P1010064.jpg    P1010090.jpg
P1010013.jpg    P1010034.jpg    P1010066.jpg    P1010091.jpg
[etc.]
```

To copy a file from this directory, I can use filename completion, but since the names are very similar, it works a bit differently. Say I want to copy P1010086.jpg. I can start by typing the following:

```
$ cp P [TAB]
$ cp P10100
```

Since all the files begin with P10100, the shell begins completing the filename as much as it can until there are differences. After displaying P10100 it beeps.

Next, I type 86 (after what is already displayed) and press Tab:

```
$ cp P1010086 [TAB]
$ cp P1010086.jpg
```

and the shell completes the filename.

HANDS ON: TURNING OFF FILENAME COMPLETION CASE-SENSITIVITY

Remember earlier when I said that capitals count? Well, what this heading means is that you can set the shell so you don't need to worry about typing capital letters to have file and directory names completed.

To do this for bash, you must add the following line to the ~/.inputrc file (which you can create, if you don't already have one):

```
set completion-ignore-case On
```

This turns on a variable for the Readline library, which bash uses for some of its functions. The change will take effect the next time you launch a shell.

For tcsh, you can type the following command, or add it to your ~/.tcshrc file:

```
% set complete = enhance
```

and press Enter or Return.

Now, if you type this when in your home directory:

```
$ cd do [TAB]
```

the shell will expand it like this:

```
$ cd Documents/
```

This not only searches for completions in both uppercase and lowercase, but also displays the correct case after the completion.

You can turn case-sensitivity on again for bash by simply removing the line you added to ~/.inputrc, or by running this command to turn it off temporarily:

```
$ bind 'set completion-ignore-case off'
```

Or for tcsh, run this command:

```
% unset complete
```

and press Enter or Return.

However, if you think this option is useful all the time, you can add either of these lines to your .inputrc file or your .tcshrc file. For more on using these files, see Chapter 16.

Refreshing Your Completion Memory

When entering file or directory names, you may not remember which items are actually in the directory you are working in. You can, of course, run the ls command to get a list, but you have to drop out of your current command and start retyping it again. Fortunately, there is another time-saving shortcut to display the items available for completion.

Say you want to move into a directory in your Library directory, but you're not sure exactly what its name is. You begin by typing cd, then the beginning of the path (/Users/kirk/Library/) but you want to know what your choices are. Just press Tab twice (with bash) and Terminal displays a list of possible completions, then again displays the prompt and whatever you had typed before.

```
$ cd /Users/kirk/Library/ [Tab Tab]
.DS_Store                        Internet Search Sites
.nisus                           Keyboards
.rdb.stkdc-itrwcdadvxth.cdit.lcf Keychains
.rdb.stkdc-itrwcdadvxth.pvtci.lcf LauncherItems
Acrobat User Data                Logs
Address Book Plug-Ins            Mail
Addresses                        Mirrors
Application Support              Open With Items
Assistants                       Plug-ins
Audio                            PreferencePanes
[etc.]
$ cd /Users/kirk/Library/
```

Note that with bash, the second Tab press only lists completions if the results of the first Tab press were ambiguous and did not expand anything, completely or partially. If there is only one possibility, the first Tab press completes this possibility; if this occurs, the second press won't give a list, since there is nothing to list. If a partial completion occurs, the first Tab performs this partial completion, the second Tab fails, and pressing Tab a third time gives a full list.

If you use tcsh, the technique is slightly different. Press Control+D to view a similar display.

```
% cd /Users/kirk/Library/ [Ctrl+d]
Acrobat User Data/               Keychains/
Address Book Plug-Ins/           LauncherItems/
Addresses/                       Logs/
Application Support/             Mail/
Assistants/                      Mirrors/
Audio/                           Open With Items/
Books/                           Plug-ins/
Bundles/                         PreferencePanes/
Caches/                          Preferences/
[etc.]
% cd /Users/kirk/Library/
```

When displaying the completion list, the `tcsh` shell uses `ls -F`, which appends slashes to directory names, and other characters to certain types of files. (For an explanation of `ls -F`, see Chapter 4, "Navigating the File System.") You can see that after displaying this list, the shell redisplays what you had typed before, so you can continue where you left off.

The `bash` shell, however, gives a different display. It uses `ls -a`, showing invisible files, but not indicating directories with slashes. (But if you don't want this display of hidden files, you can add `set match-hidden-files Off` to your `~/.inputrc` file.)

It doesn't matter how many possible completions there are; the shell displays them all. Look at the following:

```
$ cd /Users/kirk/Library/P [Tab Tab] or [Ctrl+d]
PreferencePanes/ Preferences/     Printers/
Walden:~/Library kirk$ cd /Users/kirk/Library/P
```

After I've narrowed down my choice by adding P to the path, then pressed Tab Tab or Control+D, Terminal displays all the possible completions that begin with P.

HANDS ON: SETTING COMPLETION AUTOLIST WITH *TCSH*

As you saw above, `bash` and `tcsh` both offer filename completion, but do it in a different manner. With `bash`, you press Tab Tab, and with `tcsh`, you press Control+D. If you set the `autolist` variable in `tcsh`, you can simplify this operation: you'll only need to press Tab. Granted, this is not a major difference, but you may find it easier to press Tab than Control+D.

To set this variable, type the following:

```
% set autolist
```

In the example below, I was in my `Library` directory and wanted to go to a directory whose name starts with S. I typed the following:

```
% cd S [TAB]
Screen Savers/ Services/     Sounds/
Scripts/       Snapz Pro X/  Spelling/
$ cd S
```

After I pressed Tab, the shell displayed a list of possibilities then redisplayed what I had typed.

You can do the same thing when you need to by pressing Control+D, but if you think it's good to have Terminal display this list all the time, you can add the `set autolist` command to a `.tcshrc` file. If you want to have this display all the time in `bash`, add `set show-all-if-ambiguous` to your `.inputrc` file. For more on using these files, see Chapter 16.

FILENAME COMPLETION VARIABLES

Filename completion is not a command, but a function of the shell. There are many variables that change the way filename completion works. The following list presents just a few of these.

FILENAME COMPLETION VARIABLES

`Complete`	(tcsh) When set to enhance, this tells the completion function to ignore the case of what you type. Capitals and lowercase letters are treated as equal, and the shell can complete file and directory names no matter which you type.
`completion-ignore-case`	(bash) When set to on, this tells the completion function to ignore the case of what you type. Capitals and lowercase letters are treated as equal, and the shell can complete file and directory names no matter which you type.
`show-all-if-ambiguous`	(bash) If you set this variable, the shell automatically lists all possible completions whenever it is unable to expand the characters you have typed. After Tab is pressed, the shell displays this list, then redisplays the previously typed command.
`Autolist`	(tcsh) If you set this variable, the shell automatically lists all possible completions whenever it is unable to expand the characters you have typed. After Tab is pressed, the shell displays this list, then redisplays the previously typed command.

GETTING MORE INFORMATION

To learn more about variables that affect filename completion, type **man bash** or **tcsh** to read the man pages for these shells. Since both of these are very long, it is easiest to open them in a word processor and search for "completion" to find these variables. See Chapter 16 to learn how to save these man pages to files that you can use with any word processor.

Using Command Completion

Just like filename completion, the bash and tcsh shells offer a command completion function. This allows you to type the first few letters of a command, press Tab, and have the shell expand the command for you. Let's say you want to run the command-line version of Apple's Software Update tool, but you're not sure how it's written (it might have capital letters, or be separated with an underscore). Type the following:

```
$ soft [TAB]
```

which the shell expands to:

```
$ softwareupdate
```

A completion list is also available, as for filename completion, by pressing Tab (`tcsh`) or Tab Tab (`bash`) after you have begun typing a command name.

```
% set [Tab]
set        setenv     setkey     setregion settc      setty
% set

$ set [Tab Tab]
set        setenv     setkey     setregion settc      setty
$ set
```

After displaying the list of possible completions, the shell redisplays what you had already typed.

You can also use this, if you're curious, to browse through the available commands. If you want to know which commands exist that begin with the letter m, type either of the following:

```
$ m [Tab Tab]
% m [Tab]
```

and the shell will provide you with the following list:

m4	mesg	mount_afp
mDNS	metaflac	mount_cd9660
mDNSResponder	mib2c	mount_cddafs
mac	mig	mount_devfs
mach_init	mk-amd-map	mount_fdesc
machine	mkafmmap	mount_ftp
mail	mkbom	mount_hfs
mailq	mkdep	mount_msdos
mailstat	mkdir	mount_nfs
make	mkextunpack	mount_ntfs
makedbm	mkfifo	mount_smbfs
makeinfo	mkfile	mount_synthfs
malloc_history	mklocale	mount_udf
man	mknod	mount_volfs
manpath	mkslapdconf	mount_webdav
md	mktemp	mountd
md5	mmroff	msgs
md5sum	more	mtree
merge	mount	mv

The shell only looks at the directories set in the path variable when attempting to complete commands. If you have installed the Developer Tools and want the shell to use the `/Developer/Tools/` path as well, you need to add this to your path variable. For more on setting your path variable, see Chapter 16.

Using Command History

Do you remember that long filepath I showed you at the beginning of the chapter? It went like this:

```
/Library/Preferences/ByHost/com.apple.SoftwareUpdate.003065c6ec5e.plist
```

Imagine that you type this filepath, then move around to a few other directories and run a few commands, then realize you need it again. You don't really want to have to retype it, even though, as we saw above, you can use filename completion to make it a bit easier.

Well, there's another way to save time when working in Terminal: it's called command history. The shell keeps a record of the commands you run, and you can access this history with a few simple keystrokes to run commands again, or edit them, so you don't have to retype them.

In the following example, I move around in a few directories and list files and directories. (I have added line breaks to make the commands easier to read.)

```
$ ls
Desktop    Library  Music     Public
Documents  Movies   Pictures  Sites

$ cd ..
```

```
$ ls
Shared         jsbach   mariefrance  samuelpepys
henrydthoreau  kirk     perceval

$ cd kirk
$ ls
Desktop    Library  Music     Public
Documents  Movies   Pictures  Sites

$ cd Pictures
$ ls
35.jpg       hobbiton.jpg    shire.jpg
ford.jpg     iPhoto Library  thoreau.gif
gandalf.jpg  pepys.jpg       white background.jpg
```

I issued the following commands, in this order:

```
$ ls
$ cd ..
$ ls
$ cd kirk
$ ls
$ cd Pictures
$ ls
```

The command history is saved in last-in-first-out order, which means that the first command in the history list is the last command issued. If I want to run the `ls` command again, all I have to do is press the Up arrow key and the shell displays the last run command at the prompt.

```
$ ls
```

Press Enter and the command will run.

If you want to run this command again:

```
$ cd kirk
```

you can access it in the history by pressing the Up arrow key four times (since it is the fourth command back in the list). As you press the arrow key, the shell cycles through your last commands, displaying each one at the prompt. If you go too far, you can then press the Down arrow key to move forward through the history list until you find the command you want to use. If you decide that you don't want to use a command in the history list, just press the Delete key to erase what the history added after the prompt and enter a different command.

Another way to run the last command in the history is to enter the following:

```
$ !!
```

While this does the same thing as pressing the Up arrow key, it allows you greater flexibility. You can use this in conjunction with other operators, or to run the previous command while appending something to the beginning of the command.

There are many shortcuts for using command history, but one of the most useful is the !$ shortcut. This takes the last argument from the previous command and substitutes it in the current command. Here's an example of how this works:

```
$ mkdir Documents/Archives
$ mv pepys.txt !$
mv pepys.txt Documents/Archives
$ ls -l !$
ls -l Documents/Archives/
total 6640
-rw-r--r--   1 kirk     staff     6796982 Feb 14 22:04 pepys.txt
```

In the first line, I create an Archives directory in my Documents directory. Then I move a file (pepys.txt) into this directory, but the !$ shortcut lets me call up the directory name from the previous command. The next line shows the substitution made, and the shell executes the mv command.

Finally, I want to check to make sure the file is there, so I use the ls -l command with the same shortcut to view the contents of that directory. Again, the shell makes the substitution, then displays the contents of the directory.

Modifying Commands from the History

Using the command history, you can rerun previous commands, but you can also modify commands and run them with different arguments. One of the simplest ways to do this is using the !! command to run the previous command, appending new information to it. Let's say you want to list the contents of a directory, like this:

```
$ ls /Users/kirk/Library/Preferences/ByHost
```

and then, after reading the list, decide you want to save this list to a file. You can run the following:

```
$ !! > list.txt
```

This is the same as running this command:

```
$ ls /Users/kirk/Library/Preferences/ByHost > list.txt
```

but it saves you a few keystrokes. There are many possibilities for modifying commands in this manner, using substitution modifiers.

Editing Commands from the History

As we saw above, you can move up and down the command history by pressing the Up and Down arrow keys. The advantage is that each command is displayed in Terminal, at the prompt. You can then edit the command, or add arguments to it, as you wish. This saves time when you need to run a command that is very similar, yet not exactly the same.

Say you want to copy a file; you type the following command:

```
$ cp /Users/kirk/Pictures/P101068.jpg /Users/shared
```

and Terminal returns this:

```
cp: /Users/kirk/Pictures/P101068.jpg: No such file or directory
```

But you're sure the file exists. When you go to the directory and check, you see that there is indeed a file with a similar name, but you had left out a zero and it should be P1010068.jpg. Using the command history, you can press the Up arrow and have the same command displayed after the prompt. Use the left arrow to move the cursor to the location where you need to add the zero, type **0**, then press Enter (you don't need to move the cursor back to the end of the line). The command now works fine.

You can use command editing to change commands and run them on different files, for example. If you have several files in your Pictures directory, as above, you can use the Up arrow to redisplay the previous command, change the filename, and run the new command each time.

```
$ cp /Users/kirk/Pictures/P101068.jpg /Users/shared
$ [up arrow; move cursor; change name]
```

Move the cursor with the left arrow, change the filename by pressing the Delete key and entering a new name, then press Enter. Continue this for each file:

```
$ cp /Users/kirk/Pictures/P101053.jpg /Users/shared
$ [up arrow; move cursor; change name]
$ cp /Users/kirk/Pictures/P101047.jpg /Users/shared
$ [up arrow; move cursor; change name]
$ cp /Users/kirk/Pictures/P101026.jpg /Users/shared
```

In this example, the change is just in the last two characters before the .jpg extension, but you could change the entire filename as well.

You can also use command editing to change a command's arguments. Using the above example again, I copied some pictures into my /Users/shared directory. But I could run the command to copy one of the files to a different location without retyping the entire line:

```
$ cp /Users/kirk/Pictures/P101068.jpg /Users/shared
$ [up arrow]
```

Here, you don't need to move the cursor, but can just use the Delete key to erase shared and replace it with your user directory followed by Desktop:

```
$ cp /Users/kirk/Pictures/P101068.jpg /Users/kirk/Desktop
```

In the first line I copied a picture to the /Users/shared directory, and in the second I changed the destination of the file to the desktop.

Command editing is also a way of changing the options issued in a command. Say you list the files in a directory, then decide you want to use the -1 option to display a long list. No need to retype this command either:

```
$ ls /etc/periodic
daily   monthly  weekly
$ [up arrow; move cursor; type option]
```

After pressing the Up arrow, move the cursor to the left and add -1:

```
$ ls -1 /etc/periodic
total 0
drwxr-xr-x    4 root     wheel         136 Jul 14 13:33 daily
drwxr-xr-x    3 root     wheel         102 Jul 14 13:33 monthly
drwxr-xr-x    3 root     wheel         102 Jul 14 13:33 weekly
```

The shell now displays the directory contents in long list form.

OOPS! FORGOT *SUDO*?

There are many commands you cannot run without root user privileges; there are many areas on your computer you cannot access without these privileges as well. If you have administrator rights to your computer, you can use the sudo command to prompt you for a password to run these commands or access these files or directories (see Interlude 7, "Using sudo," for more on sudo).

But it can be annoying to type a long command only to have Terminal dourly reply "Permission denied":

```
$ periodic daily weekly monthly
/usr/sbin/periodic: /var/log/daily.out: Permission denied
/usr/sbin/periodic: /var/log/weekly.out: Permission denied
/usr/sbin/periodic: /var/log/monthly.out: Permission denied
```

If you forgot to prefix the command with sudo, you can use a shortcut to run it again:

```
$ sudo !!
```

This is the command history operator that tells the shell to run the previous command. By adding sudo before it, you tell the shell to run the previous command as sudo. Terminal displays the following:

```
$ sudo !!
sudo periodic daily weekly monthly
Password:
```

Enter your password at the prompt, then press Enter, and the command will run as sudo without you needing to retype the command.

Displaying the Command History

You can check to see what commands are in your history at any time by running the following command:

```
$ history
```

Terminal displays a list of the commands in the history list; it looks something like this:

```
$ history
    1  10:13    ls
    2  10:13    cd ..
    3  10:13    ls
    4  10:13    cd kirk
    5  10:13    ls
    6  10:13    cd Pictures
    7  10:13    ls
    8  10:13    ls -1
    9  10:24    history
[etc.]
```

You can see that it shows the number of the command (from the first to the last), the time you ran the command, and the command you entered. It includes the `history` command you just ran, and includes all commands, whether or not they were successful. This means that erroneous or misspelled commands are contained in the history.

The `history` command displays the entire history list by default; this list is limited to a certain number of commands, according to your shell settings. When this list gets very long, you're better off not displaying the entire list. There are several ways of displaying just a part of your history list. In most cases, you want to see the most recent commands. One way to do this is to run the history command with an argument telling how many commands you want to display.

```
$ history 5
  329  10:47    locate walden
  330  10:49    history
  331  10:49    ls
  332  10:49    cd ..
  333  10:49    ls -a
```

This tells the shell to display the last five commands in the history list. You can enter any number as an argument for the `history` command; if your history list is shorter than the number you specify, the shell will display the entire list:

```
$ history 10
    1  11:12    cd /
    2  11:12    ls -a
    3  11:12    cd ~
    4  11:12    ls -al
    5  11:12    history 10
```

Running a Specific Command from the History

As we saw above, you can move up or down your history list by pressing the arrow keys. This is the easiest way to rerun a command that you recently executed. But if your command is farther back in the list, there are other ways to tell the shell which command to run.

If you have displayed your history list, and part of it is like this:

```
328  10:44    history
329  10:47    locate walden
330  10:49    history
331  10:49    ls
332  10:49    cd ..
333  10:49    ls -a
334  10:49    history
335  10:50    cd /
336  10:50    ls -a
337  10:50    ls -l
```

you will know the number of the command you want to run. Say you want to re-execute command number 329, `locate walden`. Just enter the following:

```
$ !329
```

The exclamation point (!) is a shortcut for a command in the history list; if you enter a number with it (with no space between them), it runs the command with that absolute number in the history.

Another way to specify a previous command is using a relative number, or the *n*th command back from the end of the list. If you want to run the fifth command back, enter this:

```
$ !-5
```

You can also tell the shell to run the last command beginning with a specific string of characters. Again using the history list above, you could run the `locate walden` command by typing the following (again, with no space after the exclamation point):

```
$ !loc
```

You can enter as few characters as you want after the exclamation point, but the shell will stop at the first occurrence of a string that matches these characters. In the example above, I could have entered `lo` since there were no other commands that begin with those letters. But if I had merely entered `l`, it would have run command 337, the `ls -l` command, because this would have been the first match.

Command History with *bash*

So far, the command history information I've given is the same for both `bash` and `tcsh`. This section will look at some history commands and techniques that are specific to `bash`. In fact, the way `bash` lets you work with your command history is a compelling reason for using `bash`. It offers much more flexibility, and lets you work a lot faster, providing valuable shortcuts to recent commands.

One of the most useful history functions in `bash` is the ability to run the last command beginning with a specific string. Say you ran the following command a few hours ago:

```
$ pico /Volumes/Backup/Texts/Transcendentalist/Walden.txt
```

If you want to run it again you could scroll through your history list, only to find it was 207 commands ago, find its number, then call it up using the history shortcuts mentioned earlier. Or you can use the `bash` way.

If you add the following two lines to your `.bash_profile` file, you'll set up a powerful history search shortcut:

```
bind '"\M-[A": history-search-backward'
bind '"\M-[B": history-search-forward'
```

After you've done this, exit your shell and open a new Terminal window. To find the previous commands you ran that began with a specific string, you can use these shortcuts with the arrow keys: type `pico`, then press the Up arrow. This brings to the prompt the last command you ran that began with `pico`.

If you have run many commands beginning with `pico`, just press the Up arrow again to see other commands you've run. Or you can type more before pressing the Up arrow. For the above command, you could type `pico /Vol` and then press the Up arrow, if you know that you haven't run any other commands with `pico` and files beginning with that path.

You can also use this technique to move back to another directory (if you specified the full path) by typing `cd` and pressing the Up arrow. You can use this with any command you have run, as long as you type a few letters it began with.

QUICKLY SEARCHING YOUR COMMAND HISTORY

There is another way to find commands you've run recently that are stored in your history file. With `bash`, press Control+R to bring up a reverse search prompt. When you do so, the following displays:

```
(reverse-i-search)`':
```

Type a few characters—the beginning of the command you're looking for—and the shell automatically fills in the rest. If the command shown is the one you want, press Enter to run it.

If not, you can press Control+R to run through other commands that begin with the same string. This is the same as pressing the Up arrow in the previous technique.

THE *FC* COMMAND

One command that is specific to `bash` is the `fc` command. This built-in command (it's part of the shell, not a separate command) lets you edit and interact with your history in many ways.

First, the `fc -l` command lists the last 16 entries in your history file. This is the same as running `history 16`, so it's not really special:

```
$ fc -l
500     exit
501     bash
```

```
502     history 10
503     ls
504     ls
505     ls  | wc
506     history
507     ls
508     man bash
509     history -10
510     history 10
511     man fc
512     fc
513     man fc
514     fc
515     man fc
516     fc -1
```

But the fc command becomes more valuable when you begin to use it to edit a previous command. Say you've typed a long command like this:

```
$ tr -d '\015' < Walden.txt | awk 'BEGIN { RS = ""; OFS= " "}
   { $1 = $1; printf "%s\r", $0}' > Walden2.txt
```

The above command (which is run all on one line) seems to invite typing errors. And suppose you did make a mistake in the command, in either a filename or one of the argument references or a quote.

There are several ways to edit this command, including simply pressing the Up arrow to bring it back to the prompt and making changes, as I explained earlier in this chapter. But the fc command lets you edit commands in your favorite text editor, which, for complex commands, can be much easier than doing so on the command line.

When you run the fc command with no arguments, it opens the previous command in your text editor. You can then make any changes, save them, and exit the text editor. The bash shell then runs the command as you edited it.

You can run the fc command with arguments, such as a number (fc loads the command with that number in your history list) or a string (fc loads the last command you ran beginning with that string).

HANDS ON: SETTING THE *FCEDIT* VARIABLE

The fc command uses the text editor you have set with your EDITOR variable or, if you want to use a different one for fc, the editor set with the FCEDIT variable. Enter the following in your .bash_profile file if you want to use pico, for example:

```
FCEDIT=/usr/bin/pico
```

If you've already set your EDITOR variable and want to use the same text editor, then you don't need to set the FCEDIT variable, but this allows you to use a simpler text editor for the fc command than for other text processing.

Setting the Command History Variable

The command history records an almost unlimited number of commands. Depending on how you use Terminal, you may want the history to record a large number of commands or just a few. There are several variables that let you choose how large your history file is, and whether the file saves duplicates.

SETTING HISTORY VARIABLES IN *BASH*

The `bash` shell records your history by default; unlike `tcsh`, where you have to set a variable to record history, this is automatic. This history file, by default, contains the last 500 commands you have run.

But you may not want to store 500 commands: you may only want to save the last few dozen commands, or you may want to store thousands. You can change this value by setting the `HISTSIZE` variable. To do this, add the following line to your `.bash_profile` file:

```
export HISTSIZE=n
```

where *n* is the number of commands you want to save.

You can also choose to have the history file ignore duplicate commands, or at least sequential duplicates. To do this, add the following line to your `.bash_profile` file:

```
export HISTCONTROL=ignoredups
```

You'll have fewer commands in your history because any time you run the same command twice or more it will only appear once in your history file. This makes it easier to go back and find old commands and run them again.

SETTING HISTORY VARIABLES IN *TCSH*

To save your command history with `tcsh`, you first need to turn on the `savehist` variable. If you do this, the shell saves a `.history` file in your home directory, adding each new command you execute to this file. If you log out and later begin a new shell session, the shell reads this file and uses the command history it contains in its current history list.

To set this variable, add the following to your `~/.tschrc` file:

```
set savehist
```

In this form, the shell saves the entire history list. You can also tell the shell to only save the last *n* history events:

```
set savehist = n
```

where *n* is any number.

If you often work in multiple shell sessions or Terminal windows, you might want to merge your command history into a single file. This doesn't affect the way the history displays in each individual window as you work, but when you log out the history lists of all the windows are merged, in time order, into your `.history` file. To do this, set the `savehist` variable as follows:

```
set savehist = (n merge)
```

where *n* is the number of history events you want to save. No matter how many windows you have open, your history list will be merged into a single list after logout. In the example below, running `history` in a window where I have run five commands shows this:

```
% history
     1  11:55   cd
     2  11:55   ls -a
     3  11:55   cd ..
     4  11:55   ls
     5  11:56   history
```

But another window I just opened merely shows this:

```
% history
     1  11:56   cd /
     2  11:56   ls -al
     3  11:56   history
```

If I log out of both windows now, then run the history command again, the shell returns the following:

```
% history
     1  11:55   cd
     2  11:55   ls -a
     3  11:55   cd ..
     4  11:55   ls
     5  11:56   history
     6  11:56   cd /
     7  11:56   ls -al
     8  11:56   history
     9  11:56   logout
    10  11:56   logout
    11  11:56   history
```

You can see that the lists have been merged, in time order (including two `logout` commands), and I can now access any of the commands that were run in either window.

For more on setting shell variables, see Chapter 16.

Clearing the Command History

Most of the time it is useful to record the last few hundred commands you have run. But occasionally you may find a shorter command history list to be more practical. As we saw above, you can display just part of your history list by running the `history` command followed by a number; this displays the last *n* commands you have run.

But if you want a shorter history list while still keeping your command history, you can clear the list Terminal displays without actually erasing the history list itself. To do this, run the following:

```
$ history -c
```

As you've seen above, you can set your history to store the number of commands you want. But be careful if you set it to a small value. If you use 10 commands, for example, then run the history command to see what has been recorded, you'll see something like this:

```
$ history
     7   10:43    ls
     8   10:43    more .tcshrc
     9   10:43    history
    10   10:43    ls
    11   10:43    ls -al
    12   10:43    cd kirk
    13   10:43    history
    14   10:44    who
    15   10:44    locate tcsh
    16   10:44    ls
```

You can see that it shows 10 commands, but numbers them starting at 7 and ending at 16. The last 10 commands are shown, but each command is still recorded with its incremental number. You need to remember this if you want to rerun a command using its number. If you are used to running commands from your history in this manner:

```
$ !5
```

which means the fifth command in the history, the shell will return the following if there is no command number 5 in the history:

```
5: Event not found.
```

So you need to bear in mind that once your command history exceeds the value set for the history variable the command count no longer begins at one, and you have to display your history to know the actual number of a given command.

Your history list will be erased, but only for the current session (if you are running **bash**, or if you use **tcsh** and have set the **savehist** variable). If you run the history command again, you'll see something like this:

```
$ history
    17   13:42    history
```

This shows that the latest command is number 17; the list is not reset to zero, but the previous entries have been erased from the history. If you open a new session in another window, or log out of Terminal and log back in again, this history list is saved, and running the history command will show the entire list, including what the history -c command cleared.

If you don't set the **savehist** variable, your history is not saved across sessions.

Overview of the *history* Command

COMMAND SYNTAX

```
history -[option(s)] [number of events]
```

FINDER EQUIVALENT

None.

OVERVIEW OF OPTIONS FOR *HISTORY*

history	This displays all the commands recorded in the command history.
history [*n*]	This displays the last *n* commands in the command history.
![*n*]	This runs the command number *n* in the command history.
!-[*n*]	This runs the *n*th previous command in the command history.
!$	This substitutes the last argument of the previous command in the current command.
history -c	Clears the command history buffer.

GETTING MORE INFORMATION

To display the man page and learn more about history, type man history in Terminal. This opens the bash builtin man page for bash, or the tcsh man page, since history is a command built into the shell. The section on history is long and thorough, and explains many additional ways to call previous commands.

Keyboard Shortcuts in Terminal

Like most graphical user interface programs, Terminal—or the shell, actually—offers a wide range of keyboard shortcuts to make things quicker and easier. The Unix world calls these *key bindings*. In addition to using the Up and Down arrow keys to move through the history and using the Left and Right arrow keys to move through commands for editing, there are dozens of other shortcuts available, some of which are essential, others merely useful.

While I won't present them all—you can get a list in Terminal by typing bind -P with bash or bindkey with tcsh—I will discuss some of the most useful and practical shortcuts. (In sticking with the Macintosh tradition, I'll call these *shortcuts*, rather than key bindings.)

Arrow Key Shortcuts

The arrow keys serve two purposes: the Up and Down arrow keys are used to move up and down the command history; the other arrow keys are used to navigate within commands when editing. Shortcuts using the Control key are also available for the same actions. (See Table 6.1.)

HANDS ON: CLEARING THE TERMINAL BUFFER

Terminal retains a number of lines of its display, called a buffer. You set this buffer size in the Window Settings dialog of the Terminal application. (See Chapter 2, "Using Terminal," for more on Terminal settings.)

It is generally practical to set this buffer to Unlimited, but there are times when you will find it gets in your way. If you want to clear this buffer, just press Command+K on your keyboard. Terminal empties its buffer and puts a new prompt at the top of the window. This does not delete the history, so you can still access previous commands; it just gives you a nice empty window.

Other Editing Shortcuts

Both bash and tcsh offer emacs and vi key-binding modes. These allow you to use the standard key bindings for those two common text editors. By default, emacs mode is used, and the following shortcuts, which are the same as those used by emacs, let you edit text on the command line. They all use the Control key, and some of them accomplish the same actions as the arrow key shortcuts. (See Table 6.2.)

The bash and tcsh man pages give you lots of information on using these two modes, as well as long lists of default key bindings.

GETTING MORE INFORMATION

For more on the bash shell, see *Learning the bash Shell*, 2nd ed. by Cameron Newham and Bill Rosenblatt (O'Reilly, 1998). For more on the tcsh shell, see *Using csh & tcsh* by Paul Dubois (O'Reilly, 1995). For an excellent overview of the five main Unix shells—C, Bourne, Korn, bash, and tcsh—see *Unix Shells by Example*, 4th ed. by Ellie Quigley (Prentice Hall, 2005).

TABLE 6.1: COMMAND HISTORY KEYBOARD SHORTCUTS

KEYS	ACTIONS
Down	Moves down the command history
Up	Moves up the command history
Left	Moves to the left when editing commands
Right	Moves to the right when editing commands
Shift+Home	Moves to the beginning of the line
Shift+End	Moves to the end of the line

TABLE 6.2: COMMAND EDITING SHORTCUTS FOR *TCSH* AND *BASH*

KEYS	ACTIONS
Ctrl+N	Moves down the command history.
Ctrl+P	Moves up the command history.
Ctrl+B	Moves one character to the left.
Ctrl+F	Moves one character to the right.
Delete	Deletes one character to the left.
Ctrl+D	Deletes one character to the right.
Ctrl+A	Moves to the beginning of the line.
Ctrl+E	Moves to the end of the line.
Ctrl+W	Deletes an entire word to the left of the cursor in bash. Deletes the entire line, from the cursor to the beginning of the line, in tcsh.
Esc, then Ctrl+H	Deletes an entire word to the left of the cursor in tcsh.
Ctrl+U	Deletes the entire line in bash.
Ctrl+K	Deletes from the cursor to the end of the line.

HANDS ON: CORRECTING TYPOS ON THE FLY

When you type commands, you sometimes make typos. It's only natural to misspell names of files, especially when they are complex. When these names are embedded in long commands, it's a hassle to go back and edit the commands, even though the tcsh shell allows this.

There's a quick way to correct typos and run the corrected command with just a few keystrokes.

Say I want to copy a file called testfile, and misspell its name in my command:

```
$ cp testfille ~/Desktop/testfile
cp: testfille: No such file or directory
```

Terminal soberly points out my mistake. But I can easily correct my typo and run the command by doing the following:

```
$ ^testfille^testfile
```

Type a caret, then the incorrect spelling, then a second caret followed by the correct spelling, then press Return. The shell runs the command again, substituting the second term for the first term, displaying the corrected command.

```
$ cp testfile ~/Desktop/testfile
```

You can also use this technique to run the same command on several different files or directories. Just substitute the new filename for the old one each time.

Summing Up

One thing that keeps many people from using the command line is the amount of time it takes to type commands. But, as we have seen in this chapter, there are many ways to save time when working in Terminal: filename completion, command completion, command history, and command editing can speed up your work on the command line. These simple yet powerful functions are essential to using Terminal efficiently.

Interlude 5: The Versatile *open* Command

The open command is one of the handful of commands that are specific to Mac OS X and aren't found in other Unix-based operating systems. Inherited from the NeXTStep operating system, the open command is extremely versatile and crosses the breach between the graphical Finder interface and the text-only interface of the command line. Experienced Unix users may find this command a bit strange, even useless; more traditional Macintosh users, familiar with the graphical metaphors of the Finder interface, will find the open command to be the ideal tool for integrating the graphical with the command line. With this command, you can open files, folders, directories, applications, and more. It is the command-line equivalent of double-clicking an icon in the Finder.

Opening Directories with *open*

The first thing you can do with the open command is open directories in the Finder. This can be useful when you are working on the command line and want to switch over to the Finder to move, copy, or delete files manually. You can open a directory by using the open command followed by the directory's name, as follows:

```
$ open ~/Documents
```

This opens my Documents folder in the Finder.

You can also open more than one directory by using several directories as arguments for the open command:

```
$ open ~/Documents /bin /Users/kirk/Library
```

One advantage to using the open command is that it can open directories that the Finder normally hides. Many of the directories at the root (/) level of your file system are hidden—directories such as /bin, /usr, /tmp, and others. The open command can allow you to view these directories and their contents in the Finder. But be careful what you do when viewing these directories; you are not really meant to play around with their files. (Note that you *can* access these directories from the Finder; select Go ➤ Go to Folder and enter the name of the directory you want to open in the sheet that displays, then click Go.)

You can open the current working directory, the one you are *in* in Terminal, by using this command:

```
$ open .
```

The . (dot) shortcut represents the current working directory. (See Chapter 5, "Working with Files and Directories," for more on the . shortcut.)

You can also open the parent directory of the current working directory with the following command:

```
$ open ..
```

The .. (dot dot) shortcut represents the directory immediately above the current working directory in your file system. (See Chapter 5 for more on the .. shortcut.)

Opening Applications with *open*

The **open** command can open applications, and does so very easily. You just need to use the -a (application) option and enter the application's name as argument for the command:

```
$ open -a TextEdit
```

After you press Return, it may take a second or two before TextEdit opens and comes to the front. You can open any application in this manner, as long as it is in the "right" place: for OS X applications, this is the /Applications folder or the /Applications/Utilities folder, and for Classic applications this is the /Applications (Mac OS 9) folder. But in most cases, you *must* enter the exact name of the application as shown in the Finder. In the following example, the **open** command cannot launch Acrobat Reader:

```
$ open -a "Acrobat Reader"
2004-05-08 12:18:40.196 open[16931]
Couldn't launch application:  Acrobat Reader
```

This problem arises because the program's actual name is Acrobat Reader 6.0.

If you have Mac OS 9 installed on your computer and want to open an application that exists in both OS 9 and OS X versions, you may need to run the command like this:

```
$ open -a iTunes.app
```

If you don't add the .app extension, you may find the OS 9 application opening in the Classic environment.

When opening an application whose name contains a space, you must put the name in quotes. If you don't, the following is returned to Terminal:

```
$ open -a Activity Monitor
2004-05-08 10:46:22.468 open[7433] No such file: /Users/kirk/Monitor
```

In the above example, the **open** command did not find the Activity Monitor application. The correct way to run this command is as follows:

```
$ open -a "Activity Monitor"
```

You can also use a backslash to escape the space:

```
$ open -a Activity\ Monitor
```

Note that you can also open Classic applications using the **open** command. If the Classic environment is not running, it will launch and the application you open from the command line will launch after Classic has booted.

You can also launch the Classic environment from the command line. Hidden in your Mac is an application called Classic Startup that does nothing more than launch Classic. You can use the following:

```
$ open -a "Classic Startup"
```

This only boots the Classic Environment, but later when you want to open a Classic application it will open much faster. If you want to boot the Classic Environment and open an application, just use the **open** command to launch the application, as explained above.

HANDS ON: USING THE *OPEN* COMMAND AS AN APPLICATION LAUNCHER

As we saw above, you can open any application from the command line using the open command no matter where it is on your Mac. Just type:

```
$ open -a [application]
```

to open any application that is in its expected location. If you use Terminal regularly, and often have a Terminal window open, it can be quicker to open applications this way than to move through Finder windows to eventually double-click an application's icon.

You can even use shell aliases to make the job quicker. Say you want to open a program such as Safari from the command line. You could create an alias like this:

```
alias safari='open -a Safari'
```

and add it to your ~/.bash_profile file. Then, to open Safari from the command line, just type this:

```
$ safari
```

You can also create aliases using the open command to open several applications at once. Here's an example that opens Mail, Safari, and iCal with one command:

```
alias myapps='open -a Mail ; open -a Safari ; open -a iCal'
```

Add that line to your ~/. bash_profile file then type the myapps alias on the command line to see all three programs open immediately.

For more on using shell aliases, see Chapter 16.

Opening Files with *open*

You can use the open command to open files from the command line, using the following syntax:

```
open [filename]
```

This opens files as if you double-click them in the Finder, with the application that created them or the application that is registered to open them.

You can open several files at once like this:

```
$ open file1.txt file2.txt file3.txt
```

If the default application allows you to open more than one file, they will all open. If not, usually only the last file in the list will open.

You can also use shell wildcards to open multiple files. To open all PDF files in a directory, use the open command like this:

```
$ open *.pdf
```

And you can open files created by different applications. Remember, the open command works exactly like double-clicking files in the Finder: if you select multiple files and double-click them, they each open with the application that created them.

```
$ open Walden.txt Walden.doc Walden.pdf
```

If you try to open a file and the Finder cannot find an application to open it, Terminal returns a long error message (I've added line breaks in the example below):

```
$ open songs.puz
2004-05-08 09:40:30.846 open[21528] LSOpenFromURLSpec() returned
-10814 for application (null) path /Users/kirk/Documents/songs.puz.
2004-05-08 09:40:30.848 open[21528] Couldn't open file: /Users/kirk/Documents/
songs.puz
```

When you try opening the same file in the Finder, an alert displays telling you "There is no default application specified to open the document," and asking you to choose an application.

If you use the open command to open text files, they open by default with TextEdit.

```
$ open ~/.bash_profile
```

You can open your .bash_profile file with TextEdit in this manner, and edit it using a graphical interface. (For more on editing this file, see Chapter 16.) If you want to open files with a different application, see below.

Opening Files with a Specific Application

There are times when you want to open a file with an application other than the default application, or with a different application than the one used to create the file.

You can force any file to open with TextEdit by using the -e option with the open command.

```
$ open -e walden.txt
```

Even if the Finder shows that this file has a different icon and would open it with a different application when double-clicking it, this forces it to open with TextEdit. This is the same as dragging the file's icon onto the TextEdit icon in the Finder.

HANDS ON: UNZIPPING ZIP ARCHIVES QUICKLY FROM THE COMMAND LINE

Since Panther includes a built-in zip archive function, you can compress files from the Finder, creating zip archives. To open these zip archives in the Finder, you merely need to double-click them and they expand automatically.

Well, you can probably see that, since the open command works like a text version of a double-click, you can use this command to expand any zip archives you have. Just type the following:

```
$ open archive.zip
```

replacing *archive* with the name of your zip archive. If you have many zip archives in one directory, just run this command to expand them all:

```
$ open *.zip
```

Bingo! Fast unzipping with a single command!

You can also open any file with a specific application by specifying that application in the command, using the following syntax:

```
open -a [application] [filename]
```

For example, to open a PDF file with Preview (if you have set Acrobat Reader as the default application), use the following:

```
$ open -a Preview Walden.pdf
```

You don't need to specify the full path for the application; the **open** command interacts with the Finder, which keeps track of where your applications are. However, if you have both Classic and OS X versions of applications you must enter the full path, specifying the *exact* name of the application as it appears in the Finder. The following does not work, because while Across Lite is the name of the application, it is not the exact name shown in the Finder:

```
$ open -a "Across Lite"
2004-05-08 10:18:09.911 open[26080]
Couldn't launch application:  Across Lite
```

Running the command as follows does work however:

```
$ open -a "Across Lite OS X v1.2"
```

If you plan to use the **open** command as an application launcher, you could create shell aliases to open some of your applications without having to type their entire names. See Chapter 16 for more on shell aliases.

Opening URLs with *open*

The **open** command can also open URLs in the appropriate application as defined by your system preferences. To open URLs you must enter the full URL, which includes the beginning with the protocol information. For example, `www.apple.com` won't work, but `http://www.apple.com` will.

```
$ open www.apple.com
2004-05-08 13:50:31.919 open[21847]
No such file: /Users/kirk/www.apple.com
```

Without the protocol information the command looks for a file, and in the example above finds no file with that name. Typing the following opens the URL in your default browser:

```
$ open http://www.apple.com
```

You can open any type of URL, including, for example, FTP URLs. Here's an example:

```
$ open ftp://ftp.apple.com
```

This opens Apple's FTP site as a network volume in the Finder.
You can open an iDisk in the Finder using this command:

```
$ open afp://idisk.mac.com
```

The Finder displays a connection dialog where you must enter your username and password, then mounts your iDisk on the desktop.

You can also tell your e-mail program to create a new message with a specified e-mail address using the command as follows:

```
$ open mailto:name@domain.com
```

While many of these usages are no quicker than typing URLs directly into web browsers or other programs, they can be useful to integrate into shell scripts. (For more on shell scripting, see Interlude 9, "Automating Commands.")

ON THE COMMAND LINE

Overview of the *open* Command

COMMAND SYNTAX

```
open [-a application] [file ...]
open [-e] [file ...]
```

FINDER EQUIVALENT

Open (double-clicking directories, applications, or files, dragging files onto application icons).

OVERVIEW OF OPTIONS FOR *OPEN*

open The open command opens files, directories, applications, or URLs.

-a This option, followed by the name of an application and file, tells the open command to open the specified file with the specified application.

-e This option tells the open command to open the file with TextEdit.

GETTING MORE INFORMATION

To display the man page and learn more about open, type man open in Terminal.

Chapter 7

Finding Files, Directories, and Everything Else

Computers are full of files, directories, and applications. That's what they're for: collecting files, working with them, sorting them, and processing them. Gone are the days of compact operating systems that took up just a few dozen megabytes (and further gone are the days of single floppy-disk operating systems). Today's computers use intricate operating systems that require hundreds of megabytes of disk space and thousands of files.

While you probably store your files in a limited number of places—if you follow Apple's lead, you'll have most of your files in your home folder—you may still want or need to find other files that are scattered all over your hard disk or disks, as well as on network volumes.

In this chapter, you'll learn how to find any kind of file on your Mac, and learn about three different tools that find files in different ways. You'll also learn how to find text within your files, and how to use regular expressions that match specific types of search strings.

Finding Files in Mac OS X

A basic Mac OS X installation takes up well over a gigabyte of hard disk space, and contains several tens of thousands of files. If you add the Developer Tools and a few applications, this can bring you to over 50,000 files and more than 2 gigabytes, and that's before you start saving your own files. You can easily understand why Apple provides a powerful find function in the Mac OS X Finder.

To efficiently work with a computer, you need to organize your files. Figure 7.1 shows the eight folders included in your Mac OS X home directory, which gives you a good way to organize personal files.

These eight folders help you organize your files in a logical manner, storing your personal files in the Documents folder, your movies, music, and pictures in their respective folders, and providing a Public folder to share files and a Sites folder for website files if needed. The Library folder is a catchall for system files and preferences, and the Desktop is, well, the desktop, where you can toss things like recently used files and aliases. In addition to these folders, Mac OS X suggests that you store your applications in the Applications folder, located higher up in the file system, which is accessible to all users of your computer.

The Finder's built-in find function offers a powerful tool for searching for files. In its simplest form, as in Figure 7.2, you can search for files by name.

But you can also add a variety of criteria to fine-tune your search, as in Figure 7.3.

This is sufficient for searching for most files, directories, or applications on your computer, at least for "normal" items that the Finder can work with.

FIGURE 7.2

The Finder's Find dialog

But once you start working with the command line you will find that there are plenty of other files—tens of thousands, actually—that you may want to access to find information, change system settings, or configure applications. The Finder's find function is excellent for searching for your word processing documents, pictures, MP3 files, and movie trailers, but it's not as good at finding many of the files you want to use from Terminal.

Here's an example: I wanted to find a file called `locate.database`, which I know is hidden in some corner of my Mac. I searched in the Finder for files whose names contain the text "locate". As you can see in Figure 7.4, the Finder found some files, but not the one I was looking for.

But when I added invisible files to my search criteria, it did find what I was looking for. Look at Figure 7.5.

FIGURE 7.3
The Find dialog showing all possible search criteria

FIGURE 7.4
The results of a Finder search for files whose names contain "locate"

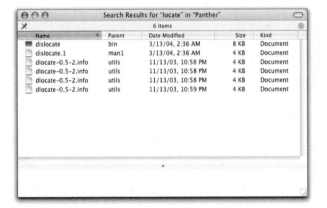

When you look for files in the Finder you need to specify whether to look for invisible files, but when searching for files from Terminal all files are checked, regardless of their visibility to the Finder. This is a good thing, because, as you will see, many of the files you need to work with from the command line are invisible to the Finder.

FIGURE 7.5

The results of a Finder search for invisible files whose names contain "locate"

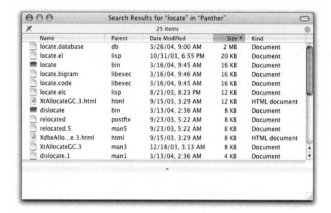

WHAT THE FINDER HIDES FROM YOU

I said earlier that the Finder hides some directories. The following shows the contents of your startup volume in the Finder:

There are only five folders shown in the startup volume (four, if you haven't yet installed the Developer Tools). But when you look in Terminal, you see many more:

```
$ ls -F
AppleShare PDS*      Network/         mach@
Applications/        System/          mach.sym
Desktop DB           Users/           mach_kernel
Desktop DF           Volumes/         private/
Desktop Folder/      automount/       sbin/
Developer/           bin/             tmp@
```

Continued on next page

```
File Transfer Folder??/ cores/              usr/
Icon?                  dev/                 var@
Library/               etc@
```

While this list shows you more than what the Finder does, it only shows the files and directories that are not invisible. Running ls -aF shows all the items at /:

```
$ ls -aF
./                     Desktop DB           cores/
../                    Desktop DF           dev/
.DRM_Data*             Desktop Folder/      etc@
.DS_Store              Developer/           mach@
.TechToolProItems/     File Transfer Folder??/ mach.sym
.Trashes/              Icon?                mach_kernel
.audacity_temp/        Library/             private/
.hidden                Network/             sbin/
.hotfiles.btree        System/              tmp@
.vdb                   Users/               usr/
.vol/                  Volumes/             var@
AppleShare PDS*        automount/
Applications/          bin/
```

We have seen that a file or directory whose name begins with a dot (.) is normally invisible to Terminal as well (running ls with the -a option displays these items). But how does the Finder know not to show you the rest of them?

Do you see the file called .hidden? Run the following command to see what it contains:

```
$ cat .hidden
```

Terminal displays its contents:

```
automount
bin
cores
Desktop DB
Desktop DF
Desktop Folder
dev
etc
lost+found
mach
mach_kernel
mach.sym
opt
private
sbin
tmp
Trash
```

Continued on next page

WHAT THE FINDER HIDES FROM YOU *(continued)*

```
usr
var
VM Storage
Volumes
```

This list corresponds to the items that the Finder does not display. The .hidden file is nothing more than a list that the Finder parses to know what not to show. The .hidden file only works for the current system, telling the Finder to hide files and directories at the root of the file system.

Finding Files with *locate*

The command line offers several tools for finding files, the simplest of which is locate. As its name suggests, this program locates files, directories, and anything else on your computer. It is lean and mean, and works in a jiffy. Here's a simple example of how it works:

```
$ locate locate
/private/etc/postfix/relocated
/private/tmp/locate.list.5421
/private/var/db/locate.database
/usr/bin/locate
/usr/libexec/locate.bigram
/usr/libexec/locate.code
/usr/libexec/locate.updatedb
/usr/share/doc/postfix/examples/sample-relocated.cf
/usr/share/emacs/21.2/lisp/locate.el
/usr/share/emacs/21.2/lisp/locate.elc
/usr/share/man/man1/locate.1
/usr/share/man/man5/relocated.5
/usr/share/man/man8/locate.updatedb.8
/usr/X11R6/lib/X11/doc/html/XdbeAllocateBackBufferName.3.html
/usr/X11R6/lib/X11/doc/html/XdbeDeallocateBackBufferName.3.html
/usr/X11R6/lib/X11/doc/html/XtAllocateGC.3.html
```

You can see that these are the same items the Finder found after searching for "locate" among invisible files. The files themselves are not invisible, but their directories (/private and /usr) are, so the Finder, in normal search mode, didn't look there.

The locate command does not offer any options, and its usage is among the simplest of all command-line programs. Its syntax is:

```
locate pattern
```

where pattern is any text string: this string can be either whole words or other strings and may contain wildcards such as * or ?, but any wildcards must be escaped with a backslash (\), or surrounded by quotes (' '').

The locate command performs a quick-and-dirty search on the filepaths in its database, returning a list of files and directories containing the search pattern in their paths. This can be very useful to

HOW MANY HITS?

In the previous example, I mentioned that `locate` returned 24,949 occurrences of "kirk" in my file system. Since this is my username, this is no surprise. But you may be wondering how I know that number. The `locate` command does not give you that information.

It's a simple trick, actually. Since you can pipe data from one command to another, I used the `wc` (word count) command, with the `-l` option (to count lines; each filename is on one line), to give me that figure. The command I ran is as follows:

```
$ locate kirk | wc -l
```

The `locate` command sent its results to `wc`, and all I saw in Terminal was the number of lines. For more on using the `wc` command, see Chapter 9, "Editing Text." For more on pipes and redirection, see Interlude 3, "Redirecting Input and Output."

find files stashed away in the nether depths of the file system, but in other cases may provide you with more than you can handle.

If I search for my name, kirk, `locate` returns a list of thousands of files. These files don't all have my name in them, but my name does appear in the path for every file in my home directory. Here are a few lines of this list:

```
/Users/kirk/Public
/Users/kirk/Public/.DS_Store
/Users/kirk/Public/Drop Box
/Users/kirk/Public/Drop Box/.DS_Store
/Users/kirk/Public/Icon?
/Users/kirk/Public/Network Trash Folder
/Users/kirk/Public/TheVolumeSettingsFolder
/Users/kirk/Sites
/Users/kirk/Sites/.DS_Store
[etc.]
```

You can see that this is not much help in finding a file whose name contains kirk, since there are so many of them. Actually, when I ran the `locate` command searching for kirk, it returned 24,949 occurrences—far too many to look at in Terminal.

One thing to remember is that the pattern you use with the `locate` command is case-sensitive. Running the following:

```
$ locate Kirk
```

with my name capitalized returned only 899 files.

The `locate` command is more effective at finding unique filenames. For example, if I want to look for files containing `bash` (the name of the default shell that Terminal uses), I get the following list:

```
$ locate bash
/bin/bash
/Library/Documentation/Commands/bash
/private/etc/bashrc
```

```
/Users/henrydthoreau/.bash_history
/Users/kirk/.bash_history
/Users/kirk/.bash_profile
/usr/bin/bashbug
/usr/share/emacs/21.2/etc/emacs.bash
/usr/share/info/bash.info
/usr/share/man/man1/bash.1
/usr/share/man/man1/bashbug.1
/usr/share/zoneinfo/Africa/Lubumbashi
/usr/share/zsh/4.1.1/functions/bashcompinit
/usr/share/zsh/4.1.1/functions/_bash_completions
```

This shows the location of the bash command, as well as some of the essential files for configuring the bash shell. (These files are examined in Chapter 16, "Configuring the Shell.")

ON THE COMMAND LINE
Overview of the *locate* Command

COMMAND SYNTAX

```
locate [pattern]
```

FINDER EQUIVALENT

Similar to the Finder's find command, yet much more limited in scope.

OVERVIEW OF OPTIONS FOR *LOCATE*

The locate command has no options.

GETTING MORE INFORMATION

To display the manual page and learn more about locate, type man locate in Terminal. This is one of the shortest man pages, since the command has no options.

HANDS ON: CREATING THE *LOCATE* DATABASE

Using the locate command is very simple, as we saw in the preceding example. However, you may be surprised when you try it for the first time and get no results from your search, no matter what you look for. This is because locate searches for files in a database, which is found here:

```
/private/var/db/locate.database
```

When you install Mac OS X, this database is installed, but the file is empty. In some cases, this file is updated regularly, but if your computer is not running in the wee hours of Sunday morning this won't occur. (For more on these periodic system tasks, see Chapter 15, "System Maintenance from the Command Line.")

Continued on next page

HANDS ON: CREATING THE *LOCATE* DATABASE *(continued)*

You can run the following command to create or update your locate database:

```
$ sudo /usr/libexec/locate.updatedb
```

(You need to use the sudo command, and enter an administrator password, to run this script. For more on sudo, see Interlude 7, "Using sudo.") This command may take a few minutes to run; Terminal displays a prompt when it has completed.

It is useful to run this command occasionally, if you don't run the periodic system tasks. Since locate only searches its database, which is a list of all the filepaths for all the files on your computer, it can only find files that existed on your computer the last time the update was performed. Each search only reflects the state of your computer at the time of the last update. If you need to look for files or directories and want to use locate, remember to update the database first.

HANDS ON: FINDING COMMANDS WITH *WHATIS*, *WHEREIS*, AND *WHICH*

While these three commands are limited in their actions, they can be useful for finding information about other commands. The first command, whatis, searches a database of commands installed on your computer, and returns a line for each command found describing the command. For example, if you want to find a command that works with a calendar, you can run the following:

```
$ whatis calendar
cal(1)                   - displays a calendar
calendar(1)              - reminder service
```

This command returns one line for each command that contains the keyword you enter as an argument. For more on whatis, see the section "Finding Out What a Command Does with whatis" in Chapter 3, "Getting Help while in Terminal."

The whereis command is different: it tells you the location of a given command. Similar to locate, or find, this command returns the full path of the command whose name you enter as argument:

```
$ whereis locate
/usr/bin/locate
```

As the program's man page specifies, the whereis utility checks the standard binary directories for the specified programs, printing out the paths of any it finds.

The which command tells you something else about a command but gives you different information. It looks through the directories defined in your shell's PATH variable, as well as any aliases you have defined in your ~/.bash_profile file, to find the location of the command given as an argument. This is useful when you want to find out exactly which version of a command is being used. Here's an example:

```
$ which ls
/bin/ls
```

This tells you that when you use the ls command, it is /bin/ls that is run. This command will also tell you if a specific command is a shell builtin.

Continued on next page

HANDS ON: FINDING COMMANDS WITH *WHATIS*, *WHEREIS*, AND *WHICH* (continued)

If you have aliases in your ~/. bash_profile file, the which command won't help you, at least if you're using bash. If you use tcsh, the which command will tell you what your aliases represent:

```
% which rm
rm:       aliased to rm -i
```

In the previous example, the rm command is set to run an alias, rm -i, so each time the rm command is run, the interactive option is used. The equivalent command for bash is type; it shows whether the argument you run after the command is an alias:

```
$ type rm
rm is aliased to 'rm -I'
```

While the which command works in bash for commands other than aliases, the type command will also tell you where other commands are to be found:

```
$ type which
which is hashed (/usr/bin/which)
```

For more on using shell aliases, see Chapter 16, "Configuring the Shell."

Finding Anything with *find*

The find command is everything you would want a find tool to be: it is a Swiss-army knife for finding just about everything on your computer. You can use it to find files by name, by size, by modification date, by user, by type, or almost anything else you can think of. While its options may seem endless, it is surprisingly easy to start using. Its basic operation is relatively simple, and its options can be seen as add-ons that extend its capabilities.

Finding Files by Name

At its simplest, the find command uses the following syntax:

```
find path [option(s)] expression ...
```

This means that you type the find command, then a filepath where the search begins, then any options that allow you to refine your search, and finally the string you are searching for. Here's a simple example:

```
$ find ~ -name "Pictures"
/Users/kirk/Library/LauncherItems/_Folders/Pictures
/Users/kirk/Pictures
```

In this example, the find command starts searching in my home directory (~), and looks for files or directories whose names are Pictures. It searches for the exact name; partial names are not returned. (The example does not return files or directories called My Pictures, School Pictures, or any other variant.)

The `path` argument for this command can be any directory. The `find` command "walks a file hierarchy" starting at that path. If you specify, as in the example, your home directory (~), it will search that directory and all of its subdirectories. If you want to search your entire file system, use a slash (/) as the path. (Remember that this path (/) also includes the /Volumes directory, which is where any other volumes are mounted. This can include internal partitions, external devices and disks, and network volumes. If you use / as the search path, your search may take a long time. However, if you use the `-x` option with the `find` command, only the current volume will be searched.)

You can also specify any directory as the path for `find` to start with, or specify the current directory by using the dot (.) shortcut.

The `find` command only searches in directories you have permission to read. If you try to run the same command in another user's directory, you'll be turned away coolly:

```
$ find /Users/samuelpepys -name "Pictures"
/Users/samuelpepys: /Users/samuelpepys/.Trash: Permission denied
/Users/samuelpepys: /Users/samuelpepys/Desktop: Permission denied
/Users/samuelpepys: /Users/samuelpepys/Documents: Permission denied
/Users/samuelpepys: /Users/samuelpepys/Library: Permission denied
/Users/samuelpepys: /Users/samuelpepys/Movies: Permission denied
/Users/samuelpepys: /Users/samuelpepys/Music: Permission denied
/Users/samuelpepys/Pictures
/Users/samuelpepys: /Users/samuelpepys/Pictures: Permission denied
/Users/samuelpepys: /Users/samuelpepys/Public/Drop Box: Permission denied
```

As you can see, each of the first six directories returned a `Permission denied` message. Then the `Pictures` directory was shown as a result of the search, but the `Permission denied` message appeared again as the command attempted to look inside it. The `find` command then looked into the `Public` directory (which you can access) but couldn't go any further. If you have administrator rights on your Mac, you can run the command using `sudo`:

```
$ sudo find /Users/samuelpepys -name "Pictures"
/Users/samuelpepys/Pictures
```

The `find` command returns the only occurrence of `"Pictures"`, which is the `Pictures` directory, and shows no `Permission denied` messages.

The `-name` option is case-sensitive. This means that searching for "`pictures`" and "`Pictures`" is different. While there are times you want to use case-sensitivity, in most cases you probably don't. To avoid having to run the command once for each case (or even more often, if you suspect that filenames may have capitals in several locations), use the `-iname` option instead of `-name`. It works the same but doesn't care about case.

Using Wildcards to Find Files

The power and flexibility of the `find` command increase exponentially when you learn to use wildcards in your commands. Instead of looking for an exact name (after all, you can't remember exactly what you called that file), you can use standard wildcards to look for partial filenames. (Note that you must surround search strings containing wildcards with quotes so the shell does not expand them.)

If, for example, you want to find all the PDF files in your home directory (assuming their names end in .pdf; file extensions can be useful), run the following:

```
$ find ~ -name "*.pdf"
/Users/kirk/Music/Misc Music stuff/staff_paper_double.pdf
/Users/kirk/Music/Misc Music stuff/staff_paper_single.pdf
/Users/kirk/Sites/Web pages/perceval1.pdf
/Users/kirk/Sites/Web pages/perceval2.pdf
/Users/kirk/Sites/Web pages/perceval3.pdf
/Users/kirk/Sites/Web pages/perceval4.pdf
[etc.]
```

HANDS ON: GETTING RID OF *PERMISSION DENIED* MESSAGES

If you try to run the find command in directories you don't have read permission for, you will see a string of Permission denied messages, one for each directory the command attempts to enter. This can be annoying, especially if you run a find command starting at the root level of the file system (/), because you need to sift through the results to find the hits that interest you.

There are three ways to get rid of these messages. The first is to preface your find command with sudo, to give yourself permission to access every directory on your computer. But this only works if you are indeed authorized to use the sudo command.

There is another way to avoid these messages. If you're using bash, run a find command like this (you can't do this with tcsh):

```
$ find /Users -name "pepys*" 2> /dev/null | grep 'pepys'
```

This sends error messages to /dev/null, a special "bit-bucket" directory where you can send anything you don't want to see or keep, using the 2> error redirection argument; it then pipes the results through grep, which, in this case, returns all lines containing the string between single quotes. With this command, Terminal only displays the lines containing matches, saving you from sifting through a long list of Permission denied messages. (For more on grep, see later in this chapter.)

See Interlude 3, "Redirecting Input and Output," for more on the 2> error redirection argument.

As you can see, the command found several PDF files in my home directory. This list shows just a few of them.

You can use the asterisk (*) wildcard either before or after your search string; you can even use it in both locations to find any file or directory containing the search string at any point in its name. Here's an example looking for any file or directory containing "bash" in its name:

```
$ sudo find / -name "*bash*"
/bin/bash
/Library/Documentation/Commands/bash
/private/etc/bashrc
/private/var/root/.bash_history
/Users/henrydthoreau/.bash_history
```

```
/Users/kirk/.bash_history
/Users/kirk/.bash_profile
[etc.]
```

The command returns the bash command (/bin/bash), but also my .bash_profile file, as well as several others. There are many other ways you can use wildcards with the find command. For more on using wildcards, see Interlude 6, "Wildcards and Globbing."

Finding Files by Type

When running a find command, you may only be interested in finding a certain type of item: files, directories, symbolic links, etc. The -type option lets you limit your search to a given type of file. If, for example, you want to find directories whose names include "cache", run the following:

```
$ find ~ -type d -iname "*cache*"
/Users/kirk/.java/deployment/cache
/Users/kirk/Documents/AppleWorks User Data/Starting Points/Cache
/Users/kirk/Library/Application Support/AddressBook/Images/CachedMacDotComPhotos
/Users/kirk/Library/Caches
/Users/kirk/Library/Caches/iPhoto Cache
/Users/kirk/Library/Preferences/Software Update/Software Update Cache
```

In this example, I used asterisks to find any occurrence of cache as part of a string, and the -iname option to run the search as case-insensitive. As you can see, it returned a list of directories containing the word cache. Since this word is in a large number of filenames, running it without the -type d option results in a much larger number of results (379 to be exact), which must be read through if you only want to find the directories.

Table 7.1 shows the different file types you can look for with this option.

TABLE 7.1: FILE TYPES SEARCHABLE WITH THE *-TYPE* OPTION

TYPE FLAG	FILE TYPE
b	block special
c	character special
d	directory
f	regular file
l	symbolic link
p	FIFO
s	socket

Note that, unlike other options added to commands, you cannot combine these file type arguments.

You can use this option to find all the files of a certain type. For example, to find all the symbolic links within your home directory, run this command:

```
$ find ~ -type l
```

You don't need to specify a name when running the `find` command with this option; you can search for all occurrences of any type of item in this manner.

Finding Files by Date

Sometimes you want to find files modified on or after a certain date, such as when you want to find recent files on your computer. The `-mtime` (modification time) option lets you do this, but it is not the most efficient way to do so. Let's say you want to find all files in your home directory that were modified two days ago. This command will return such a list:

```
$ find ~ -mtime 2
```

With the `-mtime` option, the number following the command represents a 24-hour period ending now (the time you run the command). So, in this example, the command looks for files modified between 48 hours ago and 24 hours ago (the second 24-hour period). This is not extremely intuitive, because it does not look for actual days, but rather 24-hour periods. If you run it at 10 a.m. on Wednesday, it doesn't tell you what was updated on Monday, but returns a list of files modified between 10 a.m. Monday and 10 a.m Tuesday.

Another way to find files by date is to compare them to the modification date of a reference file. You can do this with the `-newer` option. First, find a file with a modification date that you want to use as a reference. Then run the `find` command like this:

```
$ find ~ -newer filename
```

where *filename* is the name of your reference file or directory. The command returns a list of everything in your search path that is more recent.

The problem with this option is finding a file or directory that was modified at the date and time that you want as a reference. Rather than search through your files for one with the right date and time, there is a way to create a file with the modification date and time you want. The **touch** command, which is used to update the modification date and time of a file, creates a file if one doesn't exist, and you can use it to make a new file with the exact modification date and time you want.

Run the **touch** command with the `-t` option, and follow it with the date and time you want in the following format: mmddhhmm, where mm is the month in two digits, dd is the day in two digits, hh is the hour in two digits and mm is the minutes in two digits. To create a file with a modification date and time of February 10, at 12:00, run the following command:

```
$ touch -t 02101200 ref_file
```

If you run the `ls -l` command, you can check that this file indeed shows this date and time:

```
$ ls -l
-rw-r--r--    1 kirk      staff           0 Feb 10 12:00 ref_file
```

You can then run your `find` command with this file as your reference file. It will find any files modified after its date and time:

```
$ find ~ -newer ref_file
```

If you often need to find files using the `-newer` option, you could name your reference files with their date and time (such as calling the file I just made 02101200), and save them in a special directory.

A BETTER WAY TO FIND NEWER FILES

In the previous section I told you how to find files with the -newer argument added to the find command. While this is an effective way to find files newer than a certain date and time, it's not the best way. The find command offers another way to do this, which, while a bit more complex, is more efficient in the long run.

The -newerXY <file> argument lets you look for files accessed, changed, or modified after a certain date. (The difference between changed and modified is as follows: changed means that the file's inode was altered; this occurs when you move, link, or unlink a file, or when you change its ownership or permissions. Modified means that a file was updated, that you modified data in a file.) The X parameter of this argument is a, c, or m, specifying whether you want find to search for accessed, changed, or modified dates and times. The Y parameter is a, c, m, or t. The first three options are the same as for the X parameter, and the t option specifies a CVS date specification. These dates can be ISO 8601 dates (such as 2004-06-04 06:00), RFC 822 dates (June 4, 2004 06:00 AM), or even relative dates (such as "1 month ago", "4 hours ago", or "yesterday."

You can therefore check, for example, to find any files modified since last Saturday like this:

```
$ 'find ~ -newermt "last Saturday"'
```

Or you could run the following command to find all files last modified before January 1, 2002:

```
'find ~ -not -newermt "2002-01-01"'
```

Once you get the hang of this argument, it's a mighty powerful way to search for files according to their access, changed, or modification date or time.

Finding Files by Size

Another way to look for files is by their size. You may want to find files that are larger than a certain size, smaller than a given size, or exactly a specific size. You can use the -size primary and enter the file size in bytes, followed by the letter c (without a space between the two). So, to find files that are exactly 500 kilobytes, run the following:

```
$ find ~ -size 50000000c
```

Chances are that you won't find any such file, unless you know the exact size of the file you are looking for. An easier way is to look for files that are bigger than 50 megabytes; this command does the trick:

```
$ find ~ -size +50000000c
/Users/kirk/Library/Mirrors/000a95bc0684/kirkmc.dmg
/Users/kirk/Movies/Cat Story.mov
/Users/kirk/Movies/Perceval.mov
```

Naturally, you can use a minus sign before the number of blocks to look for a file that is smaller than the given size, and you can also use two -size arguments to find files that are between two sizes. Here's an example:

```
$ find ~ -size -500000c -size +100000c
```

This command finds all files between 100 kilobytes and 500 kilobytes.

You can also use the -size primary without c to specify the number of multiples of 512 kilobytes. For example:

```
$ find ~ -size +10000
```

searches for files greater than 5 megabytes in size.

Finding Files That Belong to a Specific User or Group

Another of the many options available with the find command is -user, which allows you to find files that belong to a specific user. However, in most cases you won't get very far with this command unless you prefix it with sudo to give you permission to read other users' files. If you look for your own files you won't need to, as long as you search only in your home directory, but to find any other user's files you will need either sudo or a root account. You can run the command as follows:

```
$ sudo find /Users -user samuelpepys
```

This finds all files belonging to samuelpepys in the /Users directory. You can also enter a user's ID number instead of their name as argument after the -user option.

You can do the same with groups, using the -group option and entering either the name or ID number of the group you want to use.

Finding Files That Belong to No User or Group

If you add and remove users often, you may find that there are files on your computer that belong to deleted users. Running the find command with the -nouser option lets you find all these orphaned files and clean up your computer. As when looking for files belonging to specific users or groups, you need to prefix this command with sudo to have access to all the locations where these files may be. Running this command will show a few files that were not deleted when user accounts were removed:

```
$ sudo find / -nouser
/Library/Caches/com.apple.dock.iconcache.alice
/Library/Caches/com.apple.IntlDataCache.502
/Library/Caches/com.apple.IntlDataCache.sbdl.502
/Library/Caches/Desktop Pictures/alice.4270140
```

To find files belonging to no groups, use the -nogroup option instead of -nouser.

Gluing Together Several Options

We have seen how to use a number of options with the find command, and, as you have probably guessed, these options can be glued together to make very complex searches. You can use as many options as you want in a find command, and, as long as you respect the basic syntax of this command (find path [option(s)] expression ...), you are free to stick them together as you want. Here's one example:

```
$ find ~ -mtime 1 -name "*.plist" -user kirk -size -10
```

This command searches in my home directory (~) for files modified in the past 24 hours (`-mtime 1`) whose names end with .plist (`-name "*.plist"`) belonging to me (`-user kirk`) that are less than 5KB in size (`-size -10`).

The complexity of `find` statements is limited only by your imagination and the precision you need to use when searching for files.

Displaying File Information for *find* Results

In its basic form, the `find` command returns only the names of files or directories it finds, with their full filepaths. This is often insufficient, since you may want to know more about these files and not want to have to run the `ls -l` command on each one individually. If you use the `-ls` option in a `find` command, the command returns a long line of information for each file found.

This option returns the following for each file: its inode number, size in 512-byte blocks, file permissions, number of hard links, owner, group, size in bytes, last modification time, and pathname. If the file is a block or character special file, the major and minor numbers will be displayed instead of the size in bytes. If the file is a symbolic link, the pathname of the linked-to file will be displayed preceded by ->. The display is the same as if you run `ls -dgils`. It looks like this (I have inserted a line break before the file's pathname, since this line is too long to fit on the page):

```
235189   60 -rw-------   1 kirk    staff    25570 Feb 11 21:24
/Users/kirk/Library/Preferences/com.apple.iTunes.plist
```

This is a lot of information, but it has the advantage of telling you just about everything you could ever want to know about your files.

There is another way to get the `find` command to return a line of information, and you can adjust the information returned by using whatever options you want for the `ls` command. Here's an example:

```
$ find ~ -name "*pdf*" -exec ls -l "{}" \;
-rwxrwxrwx  1 kirk  staff    500 20 Jan  2001 intro
-rwxrwxrwx  1 kirk  staff   4872 20 Jan  2001 perceval1
-rwxrwxrwx  1 kirk  staff  10219 20 Jan  2001 perceval1.pdf
```

```
-rwxrwxrwx  1 kirk   staff   36863 20 Jan  2001 perceval2
-rwxrwxrwx  1 kirk   staff   40163 20 Jan  2001 perceval2.pdf
-rwxrwxrwx  1 kirk   staff   13504 20 Jan  2001 perceval3
-rwxrwxrwx  1 kirk   staff   19547 20 Jan  2001 perceval3.pdf
-rwxrwxrwx  1 kirk   staff   32229 25 Aug  2001 perceval4
-rwxrwxrwx  1 kirk   staff   34447 25 Aug  2001 perceval4.pdf
[etc.]
```

This example looks in my home directory for files whose names contain "pdf" and displays the results using `ls -l`, which is more concise than the `-ls` option for find. The `-exec` option lets you execute any command on the results of the `find` command (and for this reason, must be located at the end of the `find` statement, after any other `find` options). I won't go any further with this option, but you can obviously run just about any command on `find` results using `-exec`. You could delete files, move them, copy them, change their permissions, and more. Here's just one example to show you what this option can do:

```
$ find ~ -name "*pdf*" -exec cp "{}" ~/Desktop \;
```

This command finds files whose names contain "pdf" and copies them to the desktop. The `find` part of the command looks in my home directory (`~`) for files whose names contain "pdf" (`-name "*pdf*"`) and then runs (`-exec`) the copy command (`cp`) on the files found ("`{}`" represents the file-name returned, and must be in quotes; each filename is processed one at a time), places the copies on the desktop (`~/Desktop`) and exits (`\;`).

HANDS ON: USING OPERATORS WITH

In addition to the many options available with the `find` command, you can use logical operators, such as and, or, and not. We have already seen how to find files that do not meet your search criteria; this uses the `!` character, escaped with a backslash (`\`) in front of it, such as the following:

```
$ find ~ \! -name test
```

The `-and` and `-or` operators (or `-a` and `-o`) allow you to create `find` commands that combine different criteria and evaluate the results according to their combinations. The following example shows how you can use the `-and` (or `-a`) operator:

```
$ find ~ -iname "Kirk"
/Users/kirk
/Users/kirk/Library/Keychains/kirk

$ find ~ -iname "Kirk" -a -type d
/Users/kirk
```

The first `find` command looks for any item with "Kirk" in its name, and is case-insensitive. It returns two results: the first is a directory, the second a file.

Continued on next page

HANDS ON: USING OPERATORS WITH *(continued)*

The second command looks for any item with "Kirk" in its name, case-insensitive, which is also a directory (-type d). In this simple example, the -a operator is not actually necessary; the find command evaluates each option as they are presented in the command. Running this command would offer the same results:

```
$ find ~ -iname "Kirk" -type d
```

But the -and operator can be useful when creating more complex find commands, or when using find in shell scripts, to evaluate criteria which find cannot check on its own.

The -or (or -o) operator is more interesting. It lets you search for items that meet one or another criteria. Here is a simple example:

```
$ find ~ -name hello -o -name goodbye
```

This searches for any items whose names are either hello or goodbye. You can use the -and and -or operators with any combination of criteria, allowing you to cover a wider range of searches.

ON THE COMMAND LINE

Overview of the *find* Command

COMMAND SYNTAX

```
find path [option(s)] expression ...
```

FINDER EQUIVALENT

Find.

OVERVIEW OF OPTIONS FOR *FIND*

find	Searches a file hierarchy for files and directories containing the search string.
-x	This option restricts the search to the current volume, and does not search through volumes found at /Volumes/.
-name	This option tells the find command to search for files whose names are specified following the option. It is case-sensitive.
-iname	This option is the same as -name but is case-insensitive.
-type	This option tells the find command to search for files whose types are specified following the option. See Table 7.1 for a list of types.
-mtime	This option tells the find command to search for files whose modification times are specified following the option.

Continued on next page

ON THE COMMAND LINE

Overview of the *find* Command *(continued)*

-newer	This option tells the find command to search for files that are newer than a reference file, whose path is specified following the option.
-newerXY	This option tells the find command to search for files that have been accessed, changed, or modified since a certain time.
-size	This option tells the find command to search for files whose sizes, in 512-byte blocks, are specified following the option. Using a value followed by c tells the find command to look for the size in bytes.
-user	This option tells the find command to search for files belonging to the user whose name or ID number is specified following the option.
-group	This option tells the find command to search for files belonging to the group whose name or ID number is specified following the option.
-nouser	This option tells the find command to search for files belonging to no user.
-nogroup	This option tells the find command to search for files belonging to no group.
-exec	This option runs a command on the results of the find command. The -exec option must be placed after all other options used with this command.

OPERATORS FOR USE WITH *FIND*

Operator	Usage
-and -a	The -and operator (or -a) lets you find items that meet a first criterion *and* a second criterion (or more).
-or -o	The -or operator (or -o) lets you find items that meet a first criterion *or* a second criterion (or more).
\!	The ! operator lets you find items that *do not* meet specific criteria.

GETTING MORE INFORMATION

To display the manual page and learn more about find and the many options available, type man find in Terminal. This man page is long, since find has a great deal of options.

Finding File Contents with *grep*

The grep (globally search for the regular expression and print) command is an extremely powerful command that searches for strings within files of all kinds. It can return results to Terminal, displaying either the lines containing the search string, the files containing it, or other results, or it can be used together with other commands. The grep command is often used to process output from other commands, or to process text and input it into different commands.

Unlike the find command, grep lets you find what is inside files. On a basic level, this is useful when you don't remember the name of a file but remember something that's in it. This is similar to the content criteria of the Finder's find function. On a higher level, grep returns the string you search for and the complete line of text that contains it. You can therefore see where the string appears and act accordingly. Say you have a list of names and phone numbers; with grep, you can find anyone's phone number quickly. Finally, at a much higher level, grep lets you act on text, taking the results of one command and passing it on to another.

It is important to note that, while grep under Mac OS X works the same as it does on most other versions of Unix, many Mac files are formatted differently than under Unix, which changes the way you should use this command.

Finding Files with *grep*

The first use of grep is to find a file by its contents. Say you can't recall which file you saved something in, but you are sure it's somewhere within your Documents folder. If you remember part of its contents—ideally something unique enough that won't be in many files—you can use grep to find it. The grep command's syntax is simple:

```
grep [options] [search string] [file...]
```

A simple search in one directory looks like this:

```
$ grep baseball ~/Documents/*
```

The asterisk indicates that grep should look in every file in the directory. The command returns this:

```
grep: /Users/kirk/Documents/Servers: Is a directory
/Users/kirk/Documents/cashb10.txt:for playing baseball,
like the big clubs they have in
/Users/kirk/Documents/cashb10.txt:place as captain of the
baseball club.  He says that
/Users/kirk/Documents/cashb10.txt:baseball club.''
[etc.]
```

As you can see, there are three occurrences of the search string "baseball", each in the same file. So only one file contains that string. The grep command also tells me that there are directories; since I didn't use a recursive option, it didn't go into those directories looking for any other files.

To tell grep to look inside all subdirectories, use the -r (recursive) option.

```
$ grep -r baseball ~/Documents/*
```

The grep command is case-sensitive by default. To run it case-insensitive, use the -i option.

```
$ grep -i baseball ~/Documents/*
```

This command finds additional lines, such as the following:

```
/Users/kirk/Documents/rhout10.txt:Worcester Baseball Club, as the newspapers
```

In some cases, you only want to know that a given file contains your search string; you don't need to see it displayed. The grep command offers an option, -c (count), which returns the number of occurrences of the search string in each file, and nothing more.

```
$ grep -c baseball ~/Documents/*
/Users/kirk/Documents/Writing:0
/Users/kirk/Documents/cashb10.txt:3
grep: /Users/kirk/Documents/iChats: Is a directory
/Users/kirk/Documents/iChats:0
/Users/kirk/Documents/main.html:0
/Users/kirk/Documents/music reviews:0
/Users/kirk/Documents/rhout10.txt:95
[etc.]
```

But this gives you a lot of files that show the number 0. You can use another option, -l (list) to only display the names of files containing your search string. In the following example, it is combined with the -r option:

```
$ grep -lr baseball ~/Documents/*
/Users/kirk/Documents/cashb10.txt
/Users/kirk/Documents/rhout10.txt
```

This command only returns the names of the files found, with their full paths if you specify an absolute path in your grep command, or with relative paths if you specify a relative path. The example given shows how to get grep to return full paths. You could get it to return relative paths by moving to the Documents directory, then using just * as the path in the grep command. Either way, if you need to open the files, you know where to find them.

Another option, -h (no-list), only displays the lines of text, and does not return the filenames (again combined with the -r option):

```
$ grep -hr baseball ~/Documents/*
for playing baseball, like the big clubs they have in
place as captain of the baseball club.  He says that
baseball club.''
league baseball.  It was Delaney's pride, as it was
[etc.]
```

To look for the search string as a whole word, you can use the -w (word) option. This only matches search strings that are not part of a longer word.

```
$ grep -wr ball ~/Documents/*
/Users/kirk/Documents/rhout10.txt:When the gong rang at the ball grounds there
/Users/kirk/Documents/rhout10.txt:Of course what Red did off the ball grounds
/Users/kirk/Documents/rhout10.txt:cover off the ball.
[etc.]
```

In this example, searching for "ball" does not return "baseball".

THE SPECIAL CASE OF MACINTOSH FILES

The grep command was designed to work on Unix files, which use standard formatting and, above all, Unix line breaks. Macintosh files are different. Mac text files use different line breaks, and files created by most applications are not formatted in a way that grep can work with them.

The basic grep command can still find text in these files, though it doesn't return the same information, such as the line of text containing the search string. For these binary files, it will, however, indicate which files contain the string.

In the following example, I have a folder of classical music CD reviews I have written with Microsoft Word. I want to find which files mention Tobias Hume, an English composer who lived in the 16th and 17th centuries. While some of the files contain Hume in their names, others don't, since they are reviews of discs containing music by other composers as well. So I can use this command to find which files contain the word Hume:

```
$ grep Hume *
Binary file Pill.doc matches
Binary file dowland_v_hume.doc matches
Binary file hume.doc matches
Binary file hume_poeticall_savall.doc matches
Binary file ostinato.doc matches
Binary file queens_goodnight.doc matches
Binary file two_ground.doc matches
```

The grep command returns a list of files containing my search string. The asterisk (*) tells grep to search all the files in the directory, and each match is shown on one line. Since these are not normal text files, it prefaces the results with "Binary file" and follows it with "matches".

But there are other problems with text files, at least with those created by Macintosh applications. Different platforms use different characters for line breaks, and the grep command does not recognize Macintosh line breaks. It uses line breaks to display the results of its search—one result per line—but if these lines are too long, it returns useless data.

There are several ways to get around this problem. The first is to use a program that saves text files with Unix line breaks. Many text editors, such as Apple's TextEdit and BBEdit, can do this. The second is to add extra commands to your grep command to replace Macintosh line breaks by Unix line breaks. To do this, run the grep command like this:

```
$ tr '\r' '\n' < file | grep string
```

The tr (translate characters) command works like a find and replace command, and changes Macintosh line breaks (\r) for Unix line breaks (\n) from the file specified after the < sign. The results of this command are then piped into grep, which searches for the specified string. This does not change the file at all, but merely reads its data, changes it, and runs grep. With this technique, you can use grep to search for text in any Macintosh text file without needing to convert it. This is especially practical if you have a large number of files to search, which would take a long time to convert.

Searching for Two Strings with *grep*

In the preceding sidebar ("The Special Case of Macintosh Files"), you saw how you can pipe data into a grep command. Since you can pipe data from any command into grep, you can also pipe the results of one grep command into another. This allows you to search for two (or more) strings in the same text.

Earlier in this chapter, we saw this example:

```
$ grep -wr ball ~/Documents/*
```

which looks for the string "ball" in all the files in a directory. But suppose you want to look for any lines that contain both "ball" and "pitcher"? You can run the following command:

```
$ grep -wr ball ~/Documents/* | grep -w pitcher
```

The first part of the command, before the pipe (|), is the same as our previous example. The pipe passes the results of this command on to the second part, which looks for the string "pitcher". This second part has no filename, since it is getting its input from the pipe, rather than from a file. Also, it doesn't need the -r (recursive) option, since it is not searching within a directory. This command returns:

```
/Users/kirk/Documents/rhout10.txt:handed pitcher whose most
effective ball for them
/Users/kirk/Documents/rhout10.txt:pitcher let the ball go,
Ash was digging for
/Users/kirk/Documents/rhout10.txt:pitcher.  There was only
one kind of a ball that
/Users/kirk/Documents/rhout10.txt:ball.  See, the pitcher's
got it now.  Boys, it's all
/Users/kirk/Documents/rhout10.txt:Doran hit to the pitcher.
The ball caromed
/Users/kirk/Documents/rhout10.txt:As Wayne received the ball
in the pitcher's box,
```

All of these lines contain both search strings. You can combine as many grep statements as you want, in order to narrow down your search—this is like doing a search with an Internet search engine, entering several key words, and telling the search engine to only return those pages that contain all the words.

Saving *grep* Results to a File

There may be times when you want to go fishing for certain text in a bunch of files and save the results to another file. Just as when you piped the results of a grep search to another grep command, you can redirect its output to a file.

Starting from the example used in the previous section, you merely add a redirection symbol to the command followed by the name of the file you want to save the data to:

```
$ grep -wr ball ~/Documents/* > file.txt
```

You need to make sure the file does not exist, unless you want to overwrite it—the command writes the results to the file but doesn't ask you to confirm if it already exists. Saving results to a file can have several advantages: you have a clear record of your search that you may want to use elsewhere; it can be easier to read if it is long; and it can be quicker, since Terminal does not have to display each line.

If you already have a file and want to append the results of your `grep` search to the end of that file, use the following format:

```
$ grep -wr ball ~/Documents/* >> file.txt
```

The double angle bracket (>>) tells the shell to append the data to the file.

For more on redirection, see Interlude 3.

HANDS ON: SEARCHING FOR TEXT IN COMPRESSED ARCHIVES

If you use the `gzip` or `compress` commands to create compressed archives, and want to search for text inside these compressed files, you can use the `zgrep` command to pass `grep` searches on to files in `.gz` archives. This can save you from having to decompress and recompress archives if you store files in this format.

A similar tool, `bzgrep`, is available for passing `grep` searches on to `.bz2` archives, created with `bzip2`.

Searching for Character Patterns with *grep*

While the `grep` command is useful for finding which file contains a certain text string, or locating a word within a file, its real power comes from its ability to find just about anything. Macintosh users may be familiar with `grep` in several programs which use similar search capabilities: BBEdit offers a `grep` feature in its find box, and Nisus Writer has long offered PowerFind, which is an implementation of `grep`-like searching. Those familiar with these functions know just how powerful this type of searching can be. For example, you could search for any words that begin with a "c" and end with "g"; you could search for phone numbers with the pattern "nnn-nnnn"; or you could find any strings that contain letter-digit-letter-digit. The power of `grep` is almost unlimited, and works because of its wide range of wildcard characters.

One important thing to remember about using regular expressions in `grep` statements is that the wildcards that represent any character match not only letters and numbers but also spaces and punctuation. For this reason, it is best to use the `-w` (whole word) option whenever you are searching for a string that is to be a whole word, though this works best when you aren't using wildcards in your search string—that is, when your search string is a complete word.

Below is an overview of regular expressions, as well as many examples of using them with `grep` commands. Mastering this type of `grep` search involves learning a series of wildcards and what they represent. Table 7.2 shows some of these wildcards. (Note: the wildcards used for `grep` regular expressions are also used in other programs such as `sed` and `awk`, but differ from those used in basic shell commands such as `cp` and `mv`. For more on these wildcards, see Interlude 6.)

The `grep` command comes in two flavors: `grep` and `egrep` (extended `grep`). The `egrep` command allows you to use some extra operators when creating regular expressions, but it might be easier to just run `grep` followed by the `-E` option (which does the same thing) instead of having to remember to type a different command if you want to use those operators. The wildcards for extended regular expression are specified in Table 7.3.

TABLE 7.2: REGULAR EXPRESSION WILDCARDS FOR USE WITH THE *GREP* COMMAND

WILDCARD	MATCHES
. (dot)	Matches any single character, except a new-line.
*	Matches the preceding character zero or more times.
[abc] [135] [lmnop]	Matches any single character in the list enclosed in the brackets.
[a-z], [A-Z], [0-9], etc.	Matches any character in the range specified in brackets.
[^a-z], [^A-Z], [^0-9], etc.	Matches any character *not* in the range specified in brackets.
^	Matches the beginning of a line, with the following character(s).
$	Matches the end of a line, with the preceding character(s).
\<	Matches the beginning of a word, with the following character(s).
\>	Matches the end of a word, with the preceding character(s).

TABLE 7.3: EXTENDED REGULAR EXPRESSION WILDCARDS

WILDCARD	MATCHES
?	Matches the preceding character zero or one times.
+	Matches the preceding character one or more times.
|	Matches either the expression before the pipe or the expression after the pipe.
{x}	Matches the character or regular expression preceding this pattern x times.
{x,}	Matches the character or regular expression preceding this pattern x or more times.
{x,y}	Matches the character or regular expression preceding this pattern from x to y times.
()	Used to group expressions.

EXAMPLES OF REGULAR EXPRESSION MATCHES

The examples in Table 7.4 show how the regular expressions presented in Table 7.2 can be applied in grep command statements. Expressions that require egrep or the -E option are noted with (egrep). While some of these patterns may work without quotes, many of them will not. It is therefore assumed that all these patterns take quotes around them.

HANDS ON: USING CHARACTER CLASSES WITH *GREP*

In addition to the many wildcards, you can search for text with grep by specifying *character classes*, which are also sometimes called *bracket expressions*. These are special predined sets of characters, whose names are generally self-explanatory:

```
[:alnum:]     <alphanumeric characters>
[:alpha:]     <alphabetic characters>
[:blank:]     <blank characters>
[:cntrl:]     <control characters>
[:digit:]     <numeric characters>
[:graph:]     <graphic characters>
[:lower:]     <lower-case alphabetic characters>
[:print:]     <printable characters>
[:punct:]     <punctuation characters>
[:space:]     <space characters>
[:upper:]     <upper-case characters>
[:xdigit:]    <hexadecimal characters>
```

Make sure you specify class names as [:classname:]. You'll find some examples of using character classes in Table 7.4.

If you want to use any of the wildcard characters for their real value, you must escape them by preceding them with a backslash (\). In Table 7.4 below, the "Match as is" column shows what specific strings match when run with grep in the standard way, with no special options. In the "Match with -w option" column, the table shows what the search patterns match when run with the -w (whole word) option.

TABLE 7.4: EXAMPLES OF REGULAR EXPRESSIONS USED WITH THE *GREP* COMMAND

PATTERN	MATCH AS IS	MATCH WITH -W OPTION
grail	Finds the string **grail**, but also **grail**s, **grail**'s, etc.	Finds the string **grail**.
[Gg]rail	Finds **Grail** or **grail**, but also **grail**s, **Grail**'s, etc.	Finds **Grail** or **grail**.
g...l	Finds **grail**, but also **grail**s, being **well**, **gentle**man, cosmo**gonal**, etc.	Finds **grail**, but also any other whole word beginning with **g** and ending with **l**, such as **girl**, **grill**, etc.
gr[aeiou]il	Finds **grail**, or any other string containing **gr**[any vowel]**il**, such as **grail**s.	Finds **grail**, or any other string containing **gr**[any vowel]**il**.
gr[^eiou]il	Finds **grail**, but no words with any other vowel in the same position, but also **grail**s.	Finds **grail**, but no words with any other vowel in the same position.

Continued on next page

TABLE 7.4: EXAMPLES OF REGULAR EXPRESSIONS USED WITH THE *GREP* COMMAND *(continued)*

PATTERN	MATCH AS IS	MATCH WITH -W OPTION
`[a-z]rail` `[:lower:]rail`	Finds **grail**, or any word containing **-rail**, and preceded by one lowercase letter, such as **trail**, **frail**, **trail**er, **frail**ness, etc.	Finds **grail**, or any word ending with **-rail**, and beginning with one lowercase letter, such as **trail**, **frail**, etc.
`^[A-Z].*\.$`	Find any line that begins with a capital letter and ends with a period.	Find any line that begins with a capital letter and ends with a period.
`[a-g]rail`	Finds **grail**, or any string containing **-rail,** preceded by a–g, such as **frail**, **frail**ness, etc.	Finds **grail**, or any word ending with **-rail** and beginning with a–g, such as **frail**, etc.
`[^a-f]rail`	Finds **grail**, or any word containing **-rail** and not preceded by a–f, such as **trail**, _**rail**road, etc.	Finds **grail**, or any word ending with **-rail** and not beginning with a–f, such as **trail**, etc.
`[a-z][a-z][a-z][a-z][a-z]`	Finds any five-letter string, with all letters in lowercase.	Finds any five-letter word, with all letters in lowercase.

`[A-Z][a-z][a-z][a-z][a-z]`
`[[:upper:]][[:lower:]]`
`[[:lower:]][[:lower:]]`
`[[:lower:]]`
	Finds any five-letter string containing a capital letter followed by four lowercase letters, such as abc**Defgh**ijk, **Bronx**, etc.	Finds any five-letter word beginning with a capital letter, such as **Bronx**.

`[A-Za-z][a-z][a-z][a-z]`
`[a-z]`
`[[:alpha:]][[:lower]]`
`[[:lower:]][[:lower:]]`
`[[:lower:]]`
	Finds any five-letter string containing either a lowercase or uppercase letter followed by four lowercase letters.	Finds any five-letter word, with or without initial capitalization.

`^grail`	Finds **grail** at the beginning of any line, but also **grail**s, etc.	Finds **grail** at the beginning of any line.
`grail$`	Finds **grail** at the end of any line, but also any string ending with **grail** at the end of a line.	Finds **grail** at the end of any line.
`^grail$`	Finds **grail** alone on any line.	Finds **grail** alone on any line.
`\<gra`	Finds any word beginning with **gra**.	Finds the string **gra** on its own.
`ail>\`	Finds any word ending with **ail**.	Finds the string **ail** on its own.

Continued on next page

TABLE 7.4: EXAMPLES OF REGULAR EXPRESSIONS USED WITH THE *GREP* COMMAND *(continued)*

PATTERN	MATCH AS IS	MATCH WITH -W OPTION
grail|trail	Finds either **grail** or **trail** anywhere in a line, but also foo**trail**, or any other word containing **grail** or **trail** (egrep).	Finds either the word **grail** or **trail**. (egrep).
grail|trail|frail	Finds any string containing **grail, trail** or **frail**, including **grail**s, **trail**s, etc. (egrep)	Finds **grail, trail** or **frail**. (egrep)
happ(y|ier|iest)	Finds any string containing **happy, happier,** or **happiest**, including un**happy**, un**happier**, etc. (egrep).	Finds **happy, happier** or **happiest** (egrep).
[0-9][0-9][0-9]-[0-9][0-9][0-9][0-9]	Finds any string containing three digits followed by a dash followed by four digits, such as **555-1234,** 12**345-1234**5, etc.	Finds any number in the form **555-1234**.
[0-9]{3}-[0-9]{4}	Finds any string containing three digits followed by a dash followed by four digits, such as **555-1234,** 12**345-1234**5, etc. (egrep).	Finds any number in the form **555-1234** (egrep).
[0-9]{9}	Finds any string containing [nine digits (egrep).	Finds any string containing exactly nine digits (egrep).
[abc][123][a-z][0-9] [abc][123][[:alpha:]][[:digit:]	Finds any string containing a letter followed by a digit followed by a letter followed by a digit, such as **a1b1, c3p0**, Doppler.jar-7f7c**c2b8**.idx, etc.	Finds any word of the type **a1b1, c3p0**, etc.
^.....$	Finds any line containing exactly five characters.	Finds any line containing exactly five characters.
^\.....$	Finds any line containing a dot followed by exactly four characters.	Finds any line containing a dot followed by exactly four characters.
[a-z][a-z][a-z]\.[a-z][a-z][a-z]	Finds any string containing three lowercase letters, a dot (.), and another three lowercase letters, such as Wal**den.txt**, Cred**its.mpe**g, etc.	Finds any word made up of exactly three lowercase letters, a dot (.), and another three lowercase letters.

Continued on next page

TABLE 7.4: EXAMPLES OF REGULAR EXPRESSIONS USED WITH THE *GREP* COMMAND *(continued)*

PATTERN	MATCH AS IS	MATCH WITH -W OPTION
[a-z]+\.[a-z][a-z][a-z]	Finds any string containing one or more lowercase letters, a dot (.), and another three lowercase letters, such as a filename in the form filename.txt, filename.doc, Background **image.tiff**, etc. (egrep).	Finds any word consisting of one or more lowercase letters, a dot (.), and another three lowercase letters, such as a filename in the form filename.txt, filename.doc, etc. (egrep).
[a-z]+\.txt	Finds any string containing one or more lowercase letters, a dot (.), and txt, such as a filename in the form filename.txt, Who's on **First.txtn**, etc. (egrep).	Finds any word containing one or more lowercase letters, a dot (.), and txt, such as a filename in the form filename.txt (egrep).
[a-z][a-z][a-z][a-z] [a-z][a-z]*	Finds any string containing five or more lowercase letters.	Finds any word containing five or more lowercase letters.
[a-z]{10}	Finds any string containing ten or more letters (egrep).	Finds any word containing exactly ten letters (egrep).

As the examples in Table 7.4 show, you can find literally anything with grep and regular expressions. While this may seem complex at first, trial and error will help you refine your understanding of these wildcards.

HANDS ON: USING *FGREP* TO FIND EXACTLY WHAT YOU TYPE

You saw earlier in this chapter how the grep command can find just about anything, but you've also seen that it can be complex to set up the correct regular expression for certain strings of characters. In addition to using wildcards, you need to escape these wildcards when you want to use them for their exact value.

Enter the fgrep, or fixed grep, command.

The fgrep command is useful when you want to find something that's really hard to find, and when you want to be able to type it exactly as it is, without scratching your head to figure out which characters need to be escaped.

Using fgrep, you can search for the most complex and weird strings easily. Say you want to find 4/16/1904-*Bloomsday[1:2]* in a file. As you can see, it contains some characters that are annoying at best when using grep: the * and the / characters, among others. Using fgrep, you can search by simply running this:

```
$ fgrep '4/16/1904-*Bloomsday[1:2]*' file.txt
```

No need to worry about escaping the characters correctly, since fgrep only looks for what it sees: and exactly what it sees.

ON THE COMMAND LINE

Overview of the *grep* Command

COMMAND SYNTAX

```
grep [options] search string file...
```

FINDER EQUIVALENT

Find by content, on steroids.

OVERVIEW OF OPTIONS FOR *GREP*

`grep`	Searches a file hierarchy for files and directories containing the search string.
`-r`	This option, the recursive option, tells the `grep` command to look at all subdirectories within the target directory.
`-i`	This option tells the `grep` command to look for the search string as case-insensitive.
`-c`	This option tells the `grep` command to only return a count of the number of occurrences of the search string in each file examined.
`-l`	This option tells the `grep` command to only return a list of files containing the search string.
`-h`	This option tells the `grep` command to only return lines of text containing the search string.
`-w`	This option tells the `grep` command to only look for the search string as a whole word, rather than within words.
`-E`	This option tells the `grep` command to use extended regular expressions (this is the same as using `egrep`).

GETTING MORE INFORMATION

To display the manual page and learn more about `grep` and the many options available, type `man grep` in Terminal. The best book available on the subject is *Mastering Regular Expressions*, 2nd ed., by Jeffrey Friedl (O'Reilly, 2002).

Summing Up

The commands in this chapter, `locate`, `find`, and `grep`, are powerful tools for finding files and text. A thorough understanding of these commands not only helps you find anything on your Mac, but also opens the door to more complex commands, where you act on the results of these commands with other tools. The `grep` command is commonly used in shell scripts to filter input and output, or to find specific files or text strings to process for other purposes, and is the most powerful tool available for finding text. Combined with wildcards, you can find just about anything with `grep`.

Interlude 6: Wildcards and Globbing

When working on the command line, you can use wildcards in many different contexts to help you find files or expressions. There are several types of wildcards or metacharacters used on the command line; unfortunately, the same wildcard can have different meanings when working with different tools. Commands such as grep, sed, and awk use wildcards in certain ways, and, in these commands, the patterns created using wildcards and metacharacters are called *regular expressions*. This section deals with the type of wildcards used in the shell for filename matching, in combination with such commands as ls, find, cp, mv, rm, or other basic commands.

You may be wondering what *globbing* means. This strange word comes from the name of an old Unix program called glob, which expanded wildcards in early versions of the Unix shell. Globbing means expanding wildcards or metacharacters in filenames, and in certain shell options.

There are only a handful of wildcards that you can use to match filenames, but they are very powerful. Unlike regular expressions (see Chapter 7, "Finding Files, Directories and Everything Else"), these wildcards only allow you to match characters within a given string, rather than matching the location of a search pattern in a line or at other locations.

The * Wildcard

Wildcards help you locate files whose names match specific strings, or perform operations on a number of files with similar names. The simplest example is displaying information about selected files, limiting the display to files with specific strings in their names. If you have a directory that contains a large number of files and only want information about the ones whose names end with .txt, you can run the following command:

```
$ ls -l *.txt
-rw-r--r--    1 kirk     staff      170512 Feb 20 11:30 cashb.txt
-rw-r--r--    1 kirk     staff     6796982 Feb 14 22:04 pepys.txt
-rw-r--r--    1 kirk     staff      319080 Feb 20 11:31 rhout.txt
```

As you can see, this command returns only files with the .txt extension. (For more on the ls command, see Chapter 4, "Navigating the File System.") The * (asterisk) wildcard matches zero or more occurrences of any character, except for . (dot) at the *beginning* of a file or directory name and / (slash), since these two characters have important meanings for the system. (The . at the beginning of a filename indicates that the file is hidden; the slash is the directory separator in file paths.) The * is the most commonly used wildcard, since it is the most flexible. Since it can match any number of characters, you don't need to specify how many characters you are looking for.

The * wildcard alone matches every item in the directory specified by the command. This can be useful when copying or removing files, for example, to not have to enter every filename. Here is one example:

```
$ cp * ~/backup/
```

The above command copies the contents of the current working directory into ~/backup, which must exist before the command is run. (Note that the cp command, in this form, only copies files and not directories or their contents. See Chapter 5, "Working with Files and Directories", for more on the cp command.) Using the * like this is a big time-saver, since you don't need to type any filenames at all.

The ? Wildcard

Another common wildcard is the ? (question mark) character. This matches any character (except a leading . and /), but exactly once for each time it is used. To get information on the file pepys.txt, using the ls -l command as in the above example, you would need to run one of the following commands:

```
$ ls -l ?epys.txt
$ ls -l ??pys.txt
$ ls -l ???ys.txt
$ ls -l ????s.txt
$ ls -l ?????.txt
$ ls -l ??????txt
$ ls -l pepys????
```

Any of the above commands returns the following:

```
-rw-r--r--   1 kirk    staff   6796982 Feb 14 22:04 pepys.txt
```

The ? wildcard is also useful for replacing characters such as accented characters or others that are difficult to type.

The [ ] Wildcard

While the [] characters are not really wildcards themselves, what they contain acts like wildcards, in a way. The [] characters let you match any of the characters contained within the brackets. Here is an example of how to use this wildcard:

```
$ ls -l [mnop]epys.txt
-rw-r--r--   1 kirk    staff   6796982 Feb 14 22:04 pepys.txt
```

This matches any file that begins with m, n, o, or p and ends with epys.txt. You can use these brackets at any location in a filename. Here is another example:

```
$ ls -l pepy[clmstv].txt
-rw-r--r--   1 kirk    staff   6796982 Feb 14 22:04 pepys.txt
```

Combining this with the * wildcard, you can list, for example, all commands beginning with the letter a that are in the /usr/bin directory:

```
$ ls /usr/bin/[a]*
/usr/bin/a2p          /usr/bin/at_cho_prn
/usr/bin/aclocal      /usr/bin/atlookup
```

```
/usr/bin/aclocal-1.6    /usr/bin/atos
/usr/bin/addftinfo      /usr/bin/atprint
/usr/bin/addr           /usr/bin/atq
/usr/bin/aexml          /usr/bin/atrm
/usr/bin/afmtodit       /usr/bin/atstatus
[etc.]
```

Note the construction of this command: an absolute path is used, followed by the specified directory (/usr/bin) and the string that the ls command must look for ([a]*).

You can also use the [] wildcard to look for items that *do not* contain specific characters. To do this, use an ! (exclamation point) at the beginning of the list of characters:

```
$ ls /usr/bin/[!a]*
/usr/bin/CFInfoPlistConverter    /usr/bin/malloc_history
/usr/bin/b2m                     /usr/bin/man
/usr/bin/banner                  /usr/bin/manpath
/usr/bin/basename                /usr/bin/md
/usr/bin/bashbug                 /usr/bin/merge
[etc.]
```

NOTE   *The* bash *shell uses the* ! *character to negate a bracketed list of characters. Other shells may use different characters, such as the* ^ *character, which the* tcsh *shell uses for the same purpose.*

You can specify a range of characters when using the [] wildcard. To find only those commands beginning with a letter from a to e, use the following form:

```
$ ls /usr/bin/[a-e]*
/usr/bin/a2p            /usr/bin/checknr
/usr/bin/aclocal        /usr/bin/chflags
/usr/bin/aclocal-1.6    /usr/bin/chfn
/usr/bin/addftinfo      /usr/bin/chgrp
/usr/bin/addr           /usr/bin/chpass
[etc.]
```

You can also use ranges of numbers, such as [1-5], in this string.

It is important to remember that all such strings are case sensitive. While the above command, using [a-e], returned dozens of results, the following returns only one:

```
$ ls /usr/bin/[A-E]*
/usr/bin/CFInfoPlistConverter
```

Since almost all Unix commands are in lowercase letters, this is no surprise. Apple, however, has named its proprietary commands using capitals to set them apart.

The {} Characters

Similar in effect to the [] wildcard examined above, the {} characters let you specify a number of possibilities, any of which are acceptable. They work something like an either/or wildcard. (The {} characters tell the shell to perform a textual transformation before any globbing occurs. But the way they work allows you to use them something like a wildcard.)

To use these brackets, you separate your arguments with commas, as in this example:

```
$ ls -l {pepys,james,thoreau}.txt
```

The above command, `ls -l {pepys,james,thoreau}.txt`, is equivalent to the command `ls -l pepys.txt james.txt thoreau.txt`; it will list information for any file named `pepys.txt`, `james.txt`, or `thoreau.txt`.

```
$ ls -l {pepys,james,thoreau}.txt
ls: james.txt: No such file or directory
-rw-r--r--    1 kirk    staff   6796982 Feb 14 22:04 pepys.txt
-rw-r--r--    1 kirk    staff    580764 Feb 28 15:33 thoreau.txt
```

Since there was no file called `james.txt`, the `ls` command returned a not found message, but went on to display information for the files it found.

These `{}` characters can also be combined with wildcards to expand a single argument into a series of similar wildcard patterns:

```
$ cp image/*.{jpg,jpeg,gif,tiff} ~/Desktop
```

would be the same as running this command:

```
$ cp image/*.jpg image/*.jpeg image/*.gif image/*.tiff ~/Desktop
```

These brackets are a time-saving shortcut that allow you to limit the number of matches to a specified range of strings.

Testing Wildcards

While you only use a few wildcards for matching filenames, these wildcards are very powerful, and, with a little bit of practice, allow you to match just about any filenames you want. One word of advice, however: when using these wildcards with certain commands (such as `rm`, the remove command), you should test them first. The `rm` command is irreversible, and if you make a mistake in your use of wildcards, the consequences could be serious.

The best way to test wildcards is using the `echo` command. Running the following command in my Documents directory checks which filenames end with "txt", and returns the following:

```
$ echo *.txt
cashb.txt pepys.txt pepys_diary.txt thoreau.txt roget.txt
```

This reassures me that if I want to do something to these files—copy them, move them, or delete them—only these files will be acted on. I use the `*.txt` argument in a command.

It is best to be safe whenever you are running a command that erases, moves, or otherwise acts on a lot of files. You can *never* undo a command you run on the command line, though in some cases you can reverse its operations.

Escaping Wildcards

The wildcard characters we have looked at so far (* ? [] {}) have special meanings when used in filenames on the command line. Yet there may be times when these or other metacharacters are part of a filename, and you need to enter them for their real value, not for their wildcard value. When talking about filenames earlier in this interlude, I mentioned a number of characters that should be avoided when naming files:

```
( ) [ ] { } < > / | \ * ? ! ' ` " $ # ; & ^ space newline tab
```

These characters all have special meanings when used in commands, and in order to use them for their actual values they must be *escaped*. This means that other special characters must be used to turn off the special meanings of these characters.

The basic escape character is the \ (backslash). This character turns off the special meaning of the character that immediately follows it. For example, to view a file named my file.txt (note the space in the filename; the space is a special character), you must do the following:

```
$ less my\ file.txt
```

Sometimes a filename contains several special characters; in this case, you need to use the backslash for each one:

```
$ less Abbott\ \&\ Costello.txt
```

In the above example, three characters (two spaces and the & character) must be escaped.

The more special characters a filename contains, the more complicated it can be to escape them. If there are just one or two special characters, this is easy, but files with complex names, such as the following, present a real challenge:

```
My long and **exciting** vacation
Quarterly Report (US/UK;EU;ASIA)
The "Olde" Pub!
```

Each of the above filenames contains several special characters, and making sure you get the backslashes in the right place is not simple. There are two ways of dealing with filenames like this. The first is to use filename completion. The bash shell has a powerful function that enters filenames for you after you type the first couple of letters and press Tab. See Chapter 6, "Saving Time on the Command Line," for a detailed explanation of using filename completion.

The other way of working with these filenames is to use quotes. The first two filenames above can be entered on the command line as follows:

```
'My long and **exciting** vacation'
'Quarterly Report (US/UK;EU;ASIA)'
```

But the third name contains a special character that is truly special: the !. Even in quotes, this character retains its special meaning (in tcsh, but not in bash), and, if you use tcsh, you must use the backslash character, as follows:

```
'The "Olde" Pub\!'
```

In the above examples, I have used single quotes. I could have used double quotes as well, but there are differences between the two. If single quotes are used, only the ! character retains its special meaning in tcsh, but if double quotes (") are used, the !, $, and ` characters retain their special meanings and must be escaped with a \.

USING THE FINDER TO HELP YOU ENTER FILENAMES

Entering the names of files with special characters can be quite a challenge, though filename completion can help. There is another way to enter complex filenames in Terminal: you can get help from the Finder.

If you drag a file or folder from the Finder onto the Terminal window, Terminal enters its filename at the current location in the command. If a file or folder name contains special characters, these are immediately translated into the appropriate form.

Begin by typing the first part of your command, and when you get to the point where you need to enter the file or directory name, type a space (to separate the file or directory name from the command, options, or arguments), and drag the item from the Finder onto Terminal.

Dragging a file with this name:

```
The *Long* and Winding(!!!) File Name with many $trange Characters...
```

makes Terminal immediately convert it to this:

```
The\ \*Long\*\ and\ Winding\(\!\!\!\)\ File\ Name\ with\ many\ \$trange\
Characters...
```

So if you have strange filenames, save yourself time with the help of the Finder.

Wildcard Summary

Table Int. 6.1 is a summary of the filename wildcards presented above.

TABLE INT. 6.1: FILENAME WILDCARDS

WILDCARD	FUNCTION
*	Matches any zero or more characters (except . (dot) or / (slash).
?	Matches any character (except . or /).
[]	Matches any of the characters [abc] or ranges [0-9] inside the brackets.
{}	Expands the contents of the strings within the curly brackets. These strings must be separated by commas, such as: {1,2,3}.
[!]	Matches all but the characters [!abc] or ranges [!0-9] inside the brackets. (For the tcsh shell, the equivalent is the ^.)

Remember that these wildcards are not used in exactly the same way for regular expressions, such as those used with grep, sed, and other commands. For more on regular expressions, see Chapter 7.

Chapter 8

Viewing Files

When you work in the Mac OS X Aqua environment, you have a variety of options as to which programs you can use to view files. For many files you must use the program that created them, but for plain text files you can use Apple's TextEdit or any other text editor or word processor. Yet not all of these programs can let you view files used by the Unix part of Mac OS X.

Working with Terminal, you often need to look inside files to see what they contain. You may want to read log files, man pages, text files, or configuration files. Mac OS X's Unix subsystem contains a full suite of tools for viewing files, including programs that let you see entire files screen by screen or just the beginning or end of a file.

In this chapter, you'll learn about the different tools available for viewing the contents of files. (I'll tell you about programs to edit files in Chapter 9, "Editing Text.") It helps to be familiar with all these tools, since each one is designed to display files in a specific way, and they can save you a lot of time when you only need to read some information in a file.

Finding Out What Kind of Files You Have with *file*

When using the Finder, you depend on icons to tell you which program files were made with, or file extensions to tell you which type of files they are. When working with the command line you'll discover that most files don't need extensions, and they certainly don't have icons. Viewing the contents of a directory may not tell you much about specific files; you'll see their names, dates of creation and modification, permissions, and other information that has nothing to do with the files' contents, but you won't be able to tell what's inside them.

The `file` command looks at the contents of a file and attempts to return the type of file it is. While this does not work for all files, it works for several thousand different file types, ranging from simple text files to graphics files, audio files, video files, and many others. A complete list of file types is found in /etc/magic, which is some 4,500 lines long and lists many file types you have never heard of.

To run the `file` command on a file, use the following syntax:

```
file filename
```

Here is an example:

```
$ file /usr/share/man/man1/file.1
/usr/share/man/man1/file.1: troff or preprocessor input text
```

The file I examined above is the `file` command's man page. Here are some other examples:

```
Ssh.bin:          data
backup.txt:       Bourne shell script text
bison.simple:     C program text
cron:             Mach-O executable ppc
page.html:        HTML document text
pepys_diary.txt:  English text
report.pdf:       PDF document, version 1.4
whatis.db:        English text
```

You can see that in some cases `file` returns very precise information, such as for `cron` or `report.pdf`. It also knows that the text in certain files is English, spots HTML tags, and shows that one is a C program.

You can get this information on all the items in a directory by using the * wildcard as the command's argument. Running the `file` command in my home directory shows the following:

```
$ file *
Desktop:    directory
Documents:  directory
Library:    directory
Movies:     directory
Music:      directory
Pictures:   directory
Public:     directory
Sites:      directory
testfile:   empty
```

It tells me that some items are directories, and that one, `testfile`, is an empty file.

The `file` command is not very good at spotting what's in binary files, though. The three files below have extensions that tell you what types of files they are, but the `/etc/magic` file does not contain information about them:

```
file_sharing.doc: data
invoice.xls:      data
report.cwk:       data
```

While the `/etc/magic` file does have entries for Word and Excel files, they are for older versions, and the command cannot recognize current versions of these files. If you're willing to try compiling the source code for the program, a much more recent version of `file` is available at `ftp://ftp.astron.com/pub/file`.

ON THE COMMAND LINE
Overview of the *file* Command

COMMAND SYNTAX

```
file [option(s)] filename ...
```

FINDER EQUIVALENT

Similar information is available from the Finder's Get Info window.

OVERVIEW OF *FILE*

file   The `file` command attempts to determine the file types for the file(s) included as argument(s).

GETTING MORE INFORMATION

To display the manual page and learn more about `file`, type `man  file` in Terminal. This command has several options.

Viewing Files with *cat*

The `cat` (concatenate) command is one of the easiest to remember because of its name. But it doesn't meow; it is designed to concatenate (join) and display files, though it is often used to view short files. To view a file with `cat`, run the command as follows:

```
$ cat .bashrc
FCEDIT=/usr/bin/pico
export HISTCONTROL=ignoredups
```

The `cat` command displays the entire contents of the file whose name is included as an argument. For files that are no longer than one screen in Terminal, this is an easy way to view their contents. But for longer files, `cat` is not very useful. Running the `cat` command on a longer file causes the contents of the file to zip by in Terminal, much too fast to read. If the file is only a few screens long, you can move up and down in Terminal with the scroll bar. But anything longer is not meant for viewing with `cat`. Pagers such as `less` and `more` are much more appropriate (see later in this chapter).

The main usage for `cat`, as I mentioned above, is to concatenate files. You can use `cat` like this to join two or more files and display the results in Terminal:

```
$ cat file1 file2 file3 ...
```

If you want to save the concatenated file, you can use output redirection as follows:

```
$ cat file1 file2 file3 > newfile
```

And if you want to append the concatenated files to another file, you can run the command like this:

```
$ cat file1 file2 file3 >> oldfile
```

ON THE COMMAND LINE
Overview of the *cat* Command

COMMAND SYNTAX

```
cat [option(s)] file1 file2 ...
```

FINDER EQUIVALENT

None.

OVERVIEW OF OPTIONS FOR CAT

cat   The cat command concatenates and prints files.

-n   This option tells the cat command to number the lines in its output.

-b   This option is the same as -n but does not number blank lines.

GETTING MORE INFORMATION

To display the manual page and learn more about cat, type man cat in Terminal.

When using output redirection, make sure that, in the first case, no file already exists with the same name. For more on output redirection, see Interlude 3, "Redirecting Input and Output."

The cat command offers several options that may be useful when using this command to view long files (more than one screen) in Terminal. The -n (number) option displays the text with numbers at the beginning of each line:

```
$ cat -n Walden.txt
     1  WALDEN
     2  Or Life In The Woods
     3  by Henry David Thoreau
     4
     5  ECONOMY
     6
     7  When I wrote the following pages, or rather the bulk
     8  of them, I lived alone, in the woods, a mile from
     9  any neighbor, in a house which I had built myself,
    10  on the shore of Walden Pond, in Concord, Massachusetts,
[etc.]
```

And using the -b option does the same thing, but does not number blank lines:

```
$ cat -b Walden.txt
     1  WALDEN
     2  Or Life In The Woods
     3  by Henry David Thoreau

     4  ECONOMY
```

```
5  When I wrote the following pages, or rather the bulk
6  of them, I lived alone, in the woods, a mile from
7  any neighbor, in a house which I had built myself,
8  on the shore of Walden Pond, in Concord, Massachusetts,
[etc.]
```

The `cat` command is useful to learn because of its multiple applications: from viewing short files to combining several files and numbering lines, it's one of the most commonly used Unix commands.

Viewing the Beginning of a File with *head*

Sometimes you only want to see the first few lines of a file to find out what it contains. The `head` command lets you do this. By default this command displays the first 10 lines of a file:

```
$ head Walden.txt
WALDEN
Or Life In The Woods
by Henry David Thoreau

ECONOMY

When I wrote the following pages, or rather the bulk
of them, I lived alone, in the woods, a mile from
any neighbor, in a house which I had built myself,
on the shore of Walden Pond, in Concord, Massachusetts,
```

You can use the -n option to tell `head` to display the exact number of lines that you want:

```
$ head -n 6 Walden.txt
WALDEN
Or Life In The Woods
by Henry David Thoreau

ECONOMY
```

Blank lines count as lines when using `head`.

You can run the `head` command with more than one file as argument. In this case, the command returns the first 10 or *n* lines of each file with a header specifying the filename:

```
$ head -n 6 Walden.txt CivDis.txt
==> Walden.txt <==
WALDEN
Or Life In The Woods
by Henry David Thoreau

ECONOMY


==> CivDis.txt <==
```

```
Civil Disobedience

[1] I heartily accept the motto, That government is
best which governs least; and I should like to see
it acted up to more rapidly and systematically.
Carried out, it finally amounts to this, which also
```

If you need to see the beginnings of all the files in a directory, you can run the **head** command as follows:

```
$ head *
```

This returns a list of filenames followed by the first 10 lines of each file.

The **head** command does not distinguish between files and directories, and in the example below, run in my home directory, it returns the following:

```
$ head *
==> Desktop <==

==> Documents <==

==> Library <==

==> Movies <==

==> Music <==

==> Pictures <==

==> Public <==

==> Sites <==
```

It attempts to read the beginning of each of these directories—to a Unix system, directories are just another type of file—but finds nothing and returns only their names.

HANDS ON: SAVING PART OF A FILE TO ANOTHER FILE

As we saw above, you can run the head command with the -n option to specify the number of lines it displays. If you want to see the first 50 lines of a file, you can run the following:

```
$ head -n 50 file.txt
```

If you want to save these 50 lines in a file, you can do so by redirecting the output of the head command as follows:

```
$ head -n 50 file.txt > 50lines.txt
```

You can also do this with the tail command (see below) to save the last *n* lines in a file.

COMMAND SYNTAX

```
head [-n count] [file ...]
```

FINDER EQUIVALENT

None, though the Finder's preview function in column view displays the first few lines of text files.

OVERVIEW OF OPTIONS FOR *HEAD*

head   The head command displays the first 10 lines of a file.

-n [count]   This option tells the head command to only display the number of lines following the
              -n option.

GETTING MORE INFORMATION

To display the manual page and learn more about head, type man head in Terminal.

Viewing the End of a File with *tail*

The tail command is similar to the head command, except that it displays the last few lines of a file. This command is commonly used to view the most recent entries in a log file. Run tail as follows on a log file to see the last ten lines of your system.log file:

```
$ tail /private/var/log/system.log
```

The tail command includes an option, -f, that keeps a file open and appends new lines to its display in Terminal as they are added to the file. If you want to observe a log and always see the latest entries as they are added, run the command like this:

```
$ tail -f /private/var/log/httpd/access_log
```

You can keep a Terminal window open in the background and check it occasionally to see what activity has occurred. To stop tail from displaying entries to this log, press Control+C on the keyboard.

Like head, tail lets you choose the number of lines to display using the -n option. To see the last line of the system.log file, run this command:

```
$ tail -n 1 /private/var/log/system.log
Apr 23 10:21:35 Walden WindowServer[188]: CGXDisableUpdate:
Updates disabled by connection 0xd103 for over 1.000000 seconds
```

You can use any number following the -n option.

Overview of the *tail* Command

COMMAND SYNTAX

```
tail [option(s)] [file ...]
```

FINDER EQUIVALENT

None.

OVERVIEW OF OPTIONS FOR *TAIL*

`tail`	The `tail` command displays the last 10 lines of a file.
`-f`	This option tells the `tail` command to display the last lines of a file, and to display any additional lines as they are written to the file.
`-n [count]`	This option tells the `tail` command to only display the number of lines following the `-n` option.

GETTING MORE INFORMATION

To display the manual page and learn more about `tail`, type `man tail` in Terminal.

Viewing Files with *less*

Unix systems come with several *pagers*, or programs that allow you to view the contents of long files one screen at a time. The first pager you will become familiar with is `less`, because this is the default pager for man pages under Mac OS X. The `less` command—defined on its man page as "opposite of `more`," since `less` is an enhanced version of `more`—allows you to move through text screen by screen, and also to move backwards in the text, something `more` does not allow you to do. (Note that on Mac OS X, `more` *is* `less`. That's not just some advertising slogan; the original `more` program is replaced by `less`, so even if you run `more`, `less` will open.) In practice, moving backward is not a problem in Apple's Terminal, since you can always scroll back up in its display, unless your Terminal buffer is set very short.

The first and simplest way to see `less` in action is to view a man page. Try typing `man less` in Terminal to see this page. See the section "Moving through man Pages" in Chapter 3, "Getting Help while in Terminal," for more on using `less`. You can also search for text within the `less` command's display. For more on how to find text in `less`, see "Finding Text in man Pages" in Chapter 3.

To use `less` on other files, simply run the `less` command followed by a filename:

```
$ less Walden.txt
WALDEN
Or Life In The Woods
by Henry David Thoreau
```

ECONOMY

```
When I wrote the following pages, or rather the bulk
of them, I lived alone, in the woods, a mile from
any neighbor, in a house which I had built myself,
on the shore of Walden Pond, in Concord, Massachusetts,
[etc.]
```

Press the spacebar to move to the next screen, and press Q to quit the display.

Earlier in this chapter, we saw how the `tail` command can be used to display a growing file, one that is continually added to, such as a log file. The `less` command can do this as well, using the `-F` option. Run the command like this:

```
$ less -F /private/var/log/httpd/access_log
```

and new lines are added to the end of the display as they are written to the file.

You can enter several filenames as arguments for `less`; this displays the first file, then, when it has ended, displays the next file, and so on.

```
$ less Walden.txt CivDis.txt
```

The `less` command displays the first screen of text, and, instead of displaying a : as prompt at the bottom of the screen, displays this:

```
Walden.txt (file 1 of 2)
```

This prompt will continue to tell you which file you are viewing. This is very practical for viewing a group of files in a directory. You can run the command like this to view the contents of all the files in a directory:

```
$ less *
```

The first file displays in Terminal. When you get to the end of the file, the prompt shows this:

```
Archives (file 1 of 12) (END) - Next: CivDis.txt
```

When You Need to Edit Files You Are Viewing

The tools used for viewing files are practical for this purpose because they are designed to be simple and fast, and in most cases are easier to use for viewing files than text editors, such as vi, Pico, or Emacs.

But at times, you may be viewing a file and then decide that you want to edit it. If you view a file with `less` or `more`, you can switch to vi quickly by just pressing the V key. This opens the file in vi, allowing you to edit it immediately at the current location. When you are finished editing the file, you can quit vi (by pressing :Q and Return) and return to `less`, continuing to view it as you started. (The `less` and `more` commands use the VISUAL and EDITOR variables to know which editor to open. If you set either of these variables to another editor, it will open that editor instead. By default, if nothing is specified, `less` and `more` open vi.)

For more about setting your EDITOR environment variable, see Chapter 9.

HANDS ON: VIEWING MACINTOSH TEXT FILES WITH *LESS*

Macintosh text files use Mac line breaks, and Unix programs do not interpret these line breaks as breaks. Displaying a Macintosh text file in Terminal is not very practical, since the lines do not break, and include control characters. Here is what a Mac file looks like when viewed with less:

```
WALDEN Or Life In The Woods ^Mby Henry David Thoreau ^M^MECO
NOMY^M^MWhen I wrote the following pages, or rather the bulk
 of them, I lived alone,^Min the woods, a mile from any neig
hbor, in a house which I had built myself,^Mon the shore of
Walden Pond, in Concord, Massachusetts, and earned my living
```

While this is readable, it is not very comfortable. In addition, any file where the line breaks should break lines, sending the following text to a new line, will not display correctly. To view a Mac text file in Terminal, you need to combine an additional command with less:

```
$ tr '\r' '\n' < file | less
```

This translates the Mac line breaks (\r) to Unix line breaks (\n) before passing the data through a pipe to less.

For more on the tr command, see Chapter 9. For more on input and output redirection, see Interlude 3.

ON THE COMMAND LINE

Overview of the *less* Command

COMMAND SYNTAX

```
less [option(s)] [file ...]
```

FINDER EQUIVALENT

None.

OVERVIEW OF *LESS*

less   The less command displays the contents of a file or standard output one screen at a time.

-F   This option tells the less command to display a file, and to display any additional lines as they are written to the file.

GETTING MORE INFORMATION

To display the manual page and learn more about less, type man less in Terminal. This command has dozens of options, and has a full range of commands for navigating and searching for text strings.

The less program is regularly updated by its creator, Mark Nudelman. As of press time, under Mac OS X 10.3.4, the version of less included is 378, and the latest version available is 382. You can get the latest version at http://www.greenwoodsoftware.com/less/, if you want to compile it yourself.

To move to the next file, press : (colon) then press n. The less command displays the first screen of the next file, and the prompt at the bottom of the screen shows which file is displayed:

```
CivDis.txt (file 2 of 12)
```

If you press : (colon) then press e while viewing a group of files, the prompt changes to Examine:, and you can enter the name of a file here. Filename completion works here; you can type the first few letters of a filename and press Tab to complete its name. After typing the filename, or completing it with Tab, press Enter to view it. You can view any file in the group like this, whether it is before or after your current position in the group of files.

The less command offers a full range of keyboard shortcuts, or key bindings, to navigate files. Table 8.1 is a summary of some of the most useful shortcuts.

TABLE 8.1: KEYBOARD SHORTCUTS FOR *LESS*

SHORTCUT	FUNCTION
Space	Moves ahead one screen.
Return	Moves ahead one line.
d	Moves ahead one-half screen.
b	Moves back one screen.
u	Moves back one-half screen.
y	Moves back one line.
g	Moves to the beginning of the text.
G	Moves to the end of the text.
:n	Moves to the beginning of the next file (if several filenames are used as arguments to the command).
:e	Displays the Examine: prompt. Enter a filename to view that file (if several filenames are used as arguments to the command).
:p	Moves to the beginning of the previous file (if several filenames are used as arguments to the command).
/[string]	Searches forward for a search string. Press Return or Enter to search after entering your string.
?[string]	Searches backward for a search string. Press Return or Enter to search after entering your string.
n	Displays the next occurrence of the search string. This goes forward for a search run with /, and backward for a search run with ?.
N	Displays the previous occurrence of the search string. This goes backward for a search run with /, and forward for a search run with ?.
h	Displays help.
q	Quits less.

HANDS ON: PIPING DATA TO A PAGER

While pagers such as less or more are useful for viewing existing files, they are also excellent tools for viewing the results of commands in Terminal. Some commands may return very long results, and if this data is sent to Terminal as is, it will scroll on for a long time without you being able to find the salient information it contains.

By piping data to a pager, you can control the way you view it. In the following command:

```
$ ls -l ~/Library/Preferences | less
```

I want to see the contents of my Preferences directory, but I know it contains a couple hundred files. Using less to page the output of the ls command allows me to view this data screen by screen, making it much easier to find a specific file.

For more on pipes and redirection, see Interlude 3.

HANDS ON: PIPING OUTPUT TO A PAGER

As you saw above, in the sidebar "Viewing Macintosh Text Files with *less*," you can *pipe*, or send, output to the less command. You can naturally do this to any pager, and this is useful when you want to view the long results of other commands in a Terminal window.

For more on using pipes, see the section "Using Pipes" in Interlude 3.

Summing Up

This chapter has looked at some common and useful commands for viewing files in different ways: looking at the beginning or end of a file, or paging through longer files. These commands are practical for examining files because they are much faster than using a text editor or other program.

Chapter 9

Editing Text

The Unix part of Mac OS X includes many programs for working with text. In Chapter 8, "Viewing Files," we saw how to view files, and how specific programs let you view the beginning or the end of a file, while others let you page through files. There is another set of programs for editing and changing the text in files. Whether you want to edit text files that you have created or edit configuration files to change the way your Mac works, these programs are essential. There is also a wide range of single-use command-line tools for working with text: for formatting and sorting text files, counting the number of words or characters they contain, replacing certain characters with others, and making changes to text files.

In this chapter, I'll show you how to do lots of things with text files. I'll present some simple tools that do limited but valuable tasks, such as counting words. I'll look at other tools that format and sort text. I'll show you the basics of the text editors that work from the command line, and I'll look at how you can use graphical user interface text editors to work with the Unix files in your Mac.

But I won't go into a lot of detail on these commands. For the simple commands—those that carry out single tasks—it is important to know that they exist and what their basic functions are. For text editors, I'll give a brief introduction. These are complex programs that take some time to master; it's up to you to go further if you want to work with them regularly. I'll also show you how to edit text quickly and easily by combining the command line and graphical programs.

Counting Words, Lines, and Characters with *wc*

The wc (**w**ord **c**ount) command is a simple tool that counts the number of lines, words, characters, and bytes in a file. Its basic syntax is straightforward:

```
wc [filename]
```

Run the wc command on a text file and it returns, in this order, the number of lines, words, and bytes followed by the filename:

```
$ wc pepys_diary.txt
  129095 1301379 6796982 pepys_diary.txt
```

In the preceding example, the file `pepys_diary.txt` is 129,095 lines long, contains 1,301,379 words, and takes up 6,796,982 bytes.

Several options are available for the `wc` command, and they tell it to return only specific information. With the `-c` option, only the number of bytes is displayed. The `-l` option tells `wc` to display only the number of lines. The `-w` option displays only the number of words. And the `-m` option tells the command to show only the number of characters:

```
$ wc -m pepys_diary.txt
 6796982 pepys_diary.txt
```

Note that for text files the number of characters is the same as the number of bytes.

You can run the `wc` command on multiple files. If you do, the command returns the statistics for each file, plus a total for all the files examined:

```
$ wc pepys_diary.txt CivDis.txt
 129095 1301379 6796982 pepys_diary.txt
   1102    9372   51249 CivDis.txt
 130197 1310751 6848231 total
```

Using the `*` wildcard, you can have `wc` return data for all the files in a directory:

```
$ wc *
   1102    9372   51249 CivDis.txt
  17436  122066  711193 Leaves_of_Grass.txt
   8153  106718  580640 Walden.txt
 129095 1301379 6796982 pepys_diary.txt
 155786 1539535 8140064 total
```

See Interlude 6, "Wildcards and Globbing," for more on using wildcards.

Other than counting words or characters in text files, this command is useful for counting the number of entries in log files, or for counting the number of items in a directory without displaying its contents. If you run the command

```
$ ls | wc -l
       9
```

the output from the `ls` command is piped into the `wc` command. Since `ls` returns its output with one item per line, the `wc` command counts the number of lines in that output, which corresponds to the number of items in the directory.

This command only counts the *visible* items in the current working directory; it does not count hidden files whose names begin with . (dot). The `-a` option tells `ls` to display all files, including these hidden files. So, running the command with that option gives a higher number of files:

```
$ ls -a | wc -l
      34
```

You can find the total number of items in a directory and all its subdirectories using the following:

```
$ ls -R | wc -l
    5426
```

The -R option to the ls command is the recursive option, which tells ls to scan and list information on all subdirectories of the target directory. This command only tells you the number of visible items, those whose names do not begin with . (dot). You can add the -a option to the ls command to include hidden items; this will include items named both . and .., which appear in every directory and subdirectory beginning with the current working directory.

ON THE COMMAND LINE

Overview of the *wc* Command

COMMAND SYNTAX

```
wc [option(s)] [file ...]
```

FINDER EQUIVALENT

Word count function in a word processor or text editor.

OVERVIEW OF OPTIONS FOR *WC*

wc   The wc command displays the number of lines, words, characters, and bytes contained in a file.

-c   This option tells the wc command to display only the number of bytes with the filename.

-l   This option tells the wc command to display only the number of lines with the filename.

-m   This option tells the wc command to display only the number of characters with the filename.

-w   This option tells the wc command to display only the number of words with the filename.

GETTING MORE INFORMATION

To display the manual page and learn more about wc, type man wc in Terminal.

Sorting Lines with *sort*

The sort command sorts the lines in text files, and offers many options for both the way it sorts and the type of output it generates. In its basic form, it sorts lines in alphabetical order from a to z. Beginning with this list:

```
Thoreau, Henry David       555-1542
Emerson, Ralph Waldo       555-9210
Pepys, Samuel              555-2945
Bach, Johann Sebastian     555-1685
James, Henry               555-8307
Joyce, James               555-8844
Handel, Georg Friedrich    555-1699
Hume, Tobias               555-2498
```

running the `sort` command alone returns the following:

```
$ sort telephone.txt
Bach, Johann Sebastian    555-1685
Emerson, Ralph Waldo      555-9210
Handel, Georg Friedrich   555-1699
Hume, Tobias              555-2498
James, Henry              555-8307
Joyce, James              555-8844
Pepys, Samuel             555-2945
Thoreau, Henry David      555-1542
```

By default the `sort` command returns its output to Terminal. This is only useful if the file you are sorting is short and you want to see the output. To redirect this output to a file, run the command with the -o (output) option:

```
$ sort -o sorted_telephone.txt telephone.txt
```

Or, to overwrite the existing file, run the command like this:

```
$ sort -o telephone.txt telephone.txt
```

You can also sort anything in reverse order, running from z to a, by using the -r option.

```
$ sort -r telephone.txt
Thoreau, Henry David      555-1542
Pepys, Samuel             555-2945
Joyce, James              555-8844
James, Henry              555-8307
Hume, Tobias              555-2498
Handel, Georg Friedrich   555-1699
Emerson, Ralph Waldo      555-9210
Bach, Johann Sebastian    555-1685
```

Sometimes you want to sort files where certain lines begin with blank spaces. The -b option tells the `sort` command to ignore leading blank spaces when sorting:

```
$ sort -b telephone.txt
Bach, Johann Sebastian    555-1685
Emerson, Ralph Waldo      555-9210
Handel, Georg Friedrich   555-1699
  Hume, Tobias                555-2498
          James, Henry                  555-8307
    Joyce, James            555-8844
         Pepys, Samuel                555-2945
    Thoreau, Henry David    555-1542
```

The `sort` command displays the result with the spaces, but sorts only on the first character after the spaces.

The `sort` command has many options that allow you to specify the significance of input fields, which characters are used to separate fields, and much more.

Overview of the *sort* Command

COMMAND SYNTAX

```
sort [option(s)] [file ...]
```

FINDER EQUIVALENT

Sort function in a word processor, text editor, or spreadsheet.

OVERVIEW OF OPTIONS FOR *SORT*

sort   The sort command sorts the lines in a file.

-o   This option, followed by the name of a file, tells the sort command to save its output in the specified file.

-r   This option tells the sort command to sort in reverse order.

-b   This option tells the sort command to ignore leading spaces when sorting.

GETTING MORE INFORMATION

To display the manual page and learn more about sort, type man sort in Terminal.

Removing Repeated Lines with *uniq*

The uniq (**uniq**ue) command is a filter that removes any identical adjacent input lines. If you have, for example, a list of names, items or words, you can first sort it with sort, then filter it with uniq so only one occurrence of each line remains.

If you have a file containing this:

```
O
tell
me
all
about
Anna
Livia
I
want
to
hear
all
about
Anna
Livia
```

you can run the following command to sort it and then remove doubles:

```
$ sort list.txt | uniq
Anna
I
Livia
O
about
all
hear
me
tell
to
want
```

You can use the -c option to display each line, counting how many instances of each line are in the file:

```
$ sort list.txt | uniq -c
   2 Anna
   1 I
   2 Livia
   1 O
   2 about
   2 all
   1 hear
   1 me
   1 tell
   1 to
   1 want
```

Or you can use the -d option to print *only* duplicate lines:

```
$ sort list.txt | uniq -d
Anna
Livia
about
all
```

You can redirect the results of the uniq command to a file like this:

```
$ sort list.txt | uniq > new_list.txt
```

The uniq command is a very powerful tool for working with logs or databases. It offers an option that let you ignore the first *n* characters or fields of each line, allowing you to remove duplicate lines that appear, for example, at different times. In a file containing data like this:

```
10.0.1.201 - - [28/May/2004:16:42:23] "GET / HTTP/1.0" 304 -
10.0.1.201 - - [28/May/2004:16:42:32] "GET / HTTP/1.0" 304 -
10.0.1.201 - - [28/May/2004:16:42:33] "GET / HTTP/1.0" 304 -
10.0.1.201 - - [28/May/2004:16:42:33] "GET /apache_pb.gif HTTP/1.0" 304 -
10.0.1.201 - - [28/May/2004:16:42:33] "GET / HTTP/1.0" 304 -
10.0.1.201 - - [28/May/2004:16:44:05] "GET / HTTP/1.0" 304 -
```

```
10.0.1.201 - - [28/May/2004:16:45:21] "GET / HTTP/1.0" 304 -
10.0.1.202 - - [28/May/2004:16:46:26] "GET / HTTP/1.1" 200 1456
10.0.1.202 - - [28/May/2004:16:46:26] "GET /apache_pb.gif HTTP/1.1" 200 2326
10.0.1.201 - - [28/May/2004:16:47:41] "GET / HTTP/1.0" 304 -
10.0.1.201 - - [28/May/2004:16:47:42] "GET / HTTP/1.0" 304 -
10.0.1.201 - - [28/May/2004:16:48:13] "GET /~kirk HTTP/1.0" 301 293
10.0.1.201 - - [28/May/2004:16:48:17] "GET /~kirk/ HTTP/1.0" 200 647
```

you can run the uniq command with the +n option, entering the number of characters to ignore in the place of n. Here, I enter +38 to ignore the first 38 characters (the IP address of the server and the date and time) to weed out the duplicates regardless of date or time:

```
$ uniq +38 http_access_log
10.0.1.201 - - [28/May/2004:16:42:23] "GET / HTTP/1.0" 304 -
10.0.1.201 - - [28/May/2004:16:42:33] "GET /apache_pb.gif HTTP/1.0" 304 -
10.0.1.201 - - [28/May/2004:16:42:33] "GET / HTTP/1.0" 304 -
10.0.1.202 - - [28/May/2004:16:46:26] "GET / HTTP/1.1" 200 1456
10.0.1.202 - - [28/May/2004:16:46:26] "GET /apache_pb.gif HTTP/1.1" 200 2326
10.0.1.201 - - [28/May/2004:16:47:41] "GET / HTTP/1.0" 304 -
10.0.1.201 - - [28/May/2004:16:48:13] "GET /~kirk HTTP/1.0" 301 293
10.0.1.201 - - [28/May/2004:16:48:17] "GET /~kirk/ HTTP/1.0" 200 647
```

The uniq command offers many other options that can be useful when examining database and log files. See the program's man page for more.

Overview of the *uniq* Command

COMMAND SYNTAX

```
uniq [option(s)] [file ...]
```

FINDER EQUIVALENT

None.

OVERVIEW OF OPTIONS FOR *UNIQ*

uniq   The uniq command removes duplicate lines in a file.

-c   This option tells uniq to display each unique line once preceded by the number of occurrences of that line.

-d   This option tells uniq to display duplicate lines once each, but not unique lines.

+n   This option tells uniq to ignore the first n characters of each line when examining for duplicates.

GETTING MORE INFORMATION

To display the manual page and learn more about uniq, type man uniq in Terminal.

Comparing Files with *diff*

The diff (difference) command lets you compare two files or directories and find the differences between them. When comparing files, diff examines individual lines and returns the lines that contain differences—it doesn't highlight individual words or strings. The diff command is an excellent tool for comparing versions of files, such as an original and an edited version, but it only works on text files, and will not compare binary files in proprietary formats from word processors or other programs.

To use the diff command, you must specify a from-file (the original) and a to-file (the edited file). Here's an example of how to use diff:

```
$ diff Song_of_Myself.txt Song_of_Myself_edit.txt
4c4
< I celebrate myself, and sing myself,
---
> I celebrate myself, and sing of myself,
6c6
< For every atom belonging to me as good belongs to you.
---
> For every atom that belongs to me also belongs to you.
14c14
< I, now thirty-seven years old in perfect health begin,
---
> I, now thirty-seven years old, in perfect health begin,
51c51
< Have you practis'd so long to learn to read?
---
> Have you practiced so long to learn to read?
```

As you can see, the diff commands returns a list of lines that have changed. Let's look at the first of these and see what the output tells us.

```
4c4
< I celebrate myself, and sing myself,
---
> I celebrate myself, and sing of myself,
```

First, 4c4 tells us that line 4 of the second file has a change (c) when compared with line 4 of the first file. It then displays the line of the first file, beginning with a < symbol. After a separator (---) it displays the line in the second file, following a > symbol. Examining the two lines you can see that the text in the second file contains one added word: of.

If any lines were added or deleted, these would display as follows:

```
71a72
> The fault is not in your stars but in yourself.
84d84
< I and this mystery here we stand.
```

The first line (72) is added in the to-file (>); its text is shown following 71a72, which means that line 72 is added (a) following line 71. The second line is deleted (d) from line 84 of the from-file (<) and this is shown by 84d84.

Note that diff returns nothing if there are no differences between the two files.

The diff command has dozens of options to let you ignore spaces, blank lines or case, display additional context, or work with multiple files. See the command's man page for more. This is a difficult command to work with, and if you often need to compare files, you may prefer to use BBEdit's Find Differences function, which does the same thing more easily and more flexibly.

ON THE COMMAND LINE

Overview of the *diff* Command

COMMAND SYNTAX

```
diff [options] from-file to-file
```

FINDER EQUIVALENT

Compare file function in a word processor or text editor.

OVERVIEW OF OPTIONS FOR *DIFF*

diff   The diff command compares files and displays differences between them.

GETTING MORE INFORMATION

To display the manual page and learn more about diff, type man diff in Terminal.

Replacing Characters with *tr*

The tr (translate) command copies standard input to standard output after substituting or deleting selected characters. This works like a find/replace function on the character level; if you want to replace, for example, every occurrence of $ with %, you can run the following command:

```
$ tr '$' '%' < file
```

Since the tr command acts on standard input, you must use input redirection (< file) if you want it to act on a file. In addition, tr returns its changed text to standard output—Terminal by default—so, if you want the changes saved, you need to write it to a new file:

```
$ tr '$' '%' < file > file2
```

In addition to single characters, you can use character ranges with the tr command. One common use of this command is to change the case of characters. The following command changes all uppercase characters to lowercase:

```
$ tr 'A-Z' 'a-z' < file
```

Overview of the *tr* Command

COMMAND SYNTAX

```
tr [option(s)] string1 string2
```

FINDER EQUIVALENT

Find/replace function, for individual characters, in a word processor or text editor.

OVERVIEW OF OPTIONS FOR *TR*

tr   The tr command replaces specific characters by other characters.

-d   This option tells the tr command to delete the specified characters.

GETTING MORE INFORMATION

To display the manual page and learn more about tr, type man tr in Terminal.

You can use the tr command to change special characters, such as returns, tabs, etc. For example, if you have a text file formatted by a Mac, with Macintosh line breaks, and want to view it or edit it with Unix tools, you need to change these line breaks:

```
$ tr '\r' '\n' < fileMac > fileUnix
```

This translates the Mac line breaks (\r) to Unix line breaks (\n).

Other special characters are as follows:

```
\a    <alert character>
\b    <backspace>
\f    <form-feed>
\n    <newline>
\r    <carriage return>
\t    <tab>
\v    <vertical tab>
```

If you use the -d (delete) option, you can delete selected characters instead of replacing them. To delete all $ characters in a file, run this command:

```
$ tr -d '$' < file
```

You can also use *classes* in tr commands. Classes are predefined sets of characters; the following classes are available:

```
alnum    <alphanumeric characters>
alpha    <alphabetic characters>
blank    <blank characters>
cntrl    <control characters>
```

```
digit      <numeric characters>
graph      <graphic characters>
lower      <lowercase alphabetic characters>
print      <printable characters>
punct      <punctuation characters>
space      <space characters>
upper      <uppercase characters>
xdigit     <hexadecimal characters>
```

Make sure you specify class names as `'[:classname:]'`. For example, to remove all digits from a file, run this command:

```
$ tr -d '[:digit:]' < file
```

You can use these classes as both find and replace arguments. Another way to change case in files is to run this command:

```
$ tr '[:upper:]' '[:lower:]' < file
```

These classes give you a great deal of flexibility in using the `tr` command. They may provide some surprising results as well. Here's one example of what a class can change:

```
$ echo '0123456789' | tr '[:digit:]' '[:punct:]'
!"#$%&'()*
```

The second line shows the "equivalent" of the digits in the punctuation class. Here is the same thing using a string of all the letters of the alphabet, from a to z:

```
$ echo 'abcdefghijklmnopqrstuvwxyz' | tr '[:lower:]' '[:punct:]'
!"#$%&'()*+,-./:;<=>?@[\]^
```

You can see that the first 10 characters in the `punct` class are the same whether translated from digits or letters.

See the command's man page for more on using classes.

Formatting Files with *fmt*

The `fmt` (**format**) command reformats text files by realigning their lines as close to the *goal* length as possible without exceeding the maximum. This command is useful for reformatting running text to fit in windows of a certain width. If you have a text that is formatted in 80-character lines and try to read it in a 65-character window, it looks like this:

```
WALDEN Or Life In The Woods by Henry David Thoreau
ECONOMY
When I wrote the following pages, or rather the bulk of them, I l
ived alone,
in the woods, a mile from any neighbor, in a house which I had bu
ilt myself,
on the shore of Walden Pond, in Concord, Massachusetts, and earne
d my living
```

Overview of the *fmt* Command

COMMAND SYNTAX

```
fmt [goal [maximum]] filename...
```

FINDER EQUIVALENT

Wrap text command in some text editors.

OVERVIEW OF OPTIONS FOR *FMT*

fmt	The fmt command formats one or several files, producing a version of its input with lines as close to the goal length as possible without exceeding the maximum.
[goal [maximum]]	If you enter a goal length, the fmt command formats lines as close as possible to that length. If you enter a maximum length, the lines do not exceed that length.

GETTING MORE INFORMATION

To display the manual page and learn more about fmt, type man fmt in Terminal.

This is difficult to read. While you can change the width of your Terminal window, you may want to print the text, or you may need texts formatted to a certain width for other reasons.

The fmt command, by default, uses a goal length of 65 characters and a maximum of 75. If you run the command with no goal or maximum specified, as follows:

```
$ fmt Walden.txt > Waldenfmt.txt
```

it breaks lines so the text is between 65 and 75 characters long. If you want to be more precise, you can specify a goal and maximum length:

```
$ fmt 60 65 Walden.txt > Waldenfmt.txt
```

The resulting text looks like this:

```
WALDEN Or Life In The Woods by Henry David Thoreau

ECONOMY

When I wrote the following pages, or rather the bulk of them,
I lived alone, in the woods, a mile from any neighbor, in a
house which I had built myself, on the shore of Walden Pond,
in Concord, Massachusetts, and earned my living by the labor
```

The fmt command is mainly useful for formatting text to view in Terminal or in text editors. If you want to view text in a Macintosh word processor, you are better off removing line breaks to create paragraphs, either using a command such as `tr` to replace Unix line breaks with Mac line breaks or using a program such as BBEdit, whose Remove Line Breaks command does it in a jiffy. See the sidebar "Formatting Text Files" later in this chapter.

Editing Text with *sed*

The `sed` (stream **ed**itor) command is one of those command-line tools that shows just how much you can do from Terminal. Much more than a simple command, `sed` can carry out some of the most complex tasks on files. The principle behind `sed` is that it reads a stream of data from the input file (or standard input), processes it according to the commands or arguments specified, then writes the processed data to standard output. The `sed` command does not change the original file, and it can work on its own or in pipelines with other commands.

OTHER USEFUL TEXT EDITING COMMANDS

There are many other useful commands for editing and formatting text. Here is a list of some of them, with brief descriptions of what they do. See the individual commands' man pages for more. See also Chapter 8 for a presentation of commands for viewing files in Terminal.

`col`	Filters out reverse (and half reverse) line feeds and escape characters; useful for formatting man pages.
`colrm`	Removes columns from a file.
`column`	Formats input into multiple columns.
`cut`	Selects portions of each line of a file.
`enscript`	Converts files to PostScript so you can print or save as a `.ps` file.
`expand`	Converts tabs to spaces or vice versa.
`fold`	Like `fmt`, this command formats files to a certain line length, but `fold` breaks lines exactly at the specified length, even if it has to separate words.
`hexdump`	Displays a file as ASCII, decimal, hexadecimal, or octal.
`indent`	Formats C program source code.
`look`	Displays lines beginning with a specific string. By default this command searches in a dictionary file stored at `/usr/share/dict/words`.
`merge`	Merges files.
`paste`	Merges corresponding or subsequent lines of files.
`pr`	Formats files with headers, footers, and page numbers for printing.
`rev`	Reverses lines of a file.
`split`	Splits files to a given length.

All these commands perform limited operations, but combined with other commands through pipes or in scripts, they can help increase your command-line toolbox.

The `sed` command is a complex program, and entire books have been written on its use. I won't go into the many ways this command can be used, but I'll look at one of the most valuable functions it offers: that of finding and replacing text in a file.

As you have seen, the `tr` command can replace characters in a file. But `sed` can go much further and replace entire strings. When using `tr` to replace characters, you cannot specify whole words. Here's an example: if I want to replace the word "Walden" by the word "Goose" in a file containing Henry David Thoreau's Walden, I might think that `tr` can do the job and run this command:

```
$ tr 'Walden' 'Goose' < Walden.txt > Goose.txt
```

But the results are not what I wanted:

```
GALDEN Or Life Ie The Gooss by Heery Dovis Thoreou

ECONOMY

Ghee I wrote the foooowieg poges, or rother the buok of them,
I oives oooee, ie the wooss, o mioe from oey eeighbor, ie o
house which I hos buiot myseof, oe the shore of Goosee Poes,
ie Coecors, Mossochusetts, oes eorees my oivieg by the oobor
of my hoess oeoy. I oives there two yeors oes two moeths.
```

This is because `tr` sees the characters as a list of characters, not entire strings. So the "G" replaces the "W," the "o" replaces the "a," and so on.

With `sed` you can replace the words you want. Here's how you can replace "Walden" with "Goose":

```
$ sed 's/Walden/Goose/g' Walden.txt > Goose.txt
```

The results of this command are:

```
WALDEN Or Life In The Woods by Henry David Thoreau

ECONOMY

When I wrote the following pages, or rather the bulk of them,
I lived alone, in the woods, a mile from any neighbor, in a
house which I had built myself, on the shore of Goose Pond,
```

As you can see, the only change in the lines shown is "Goose Pond" in the last line; the title, WALDEN, was not changed because replacements with `sed` are case-sensitive. But if I look through the file I'll see that every occurrence of Walden has been changed to Goose (I've put these words in bold to make them stand out more easily):

```
dry tongue, who used to come to bathe in Goose once every year
when the water was warmest, and at such times looked in upon
me, told me that many years ago he took his gun one afternoon
and went out for a cruise in Goose Wood; and as he walked the
```

The syntax for replacing strings with `sed` is simple:

```
sed 's/string/replacement/g' file > output_file
```

If you don't use the trailing `g`, `sed` only replaces the string once on each line.

Overview of the *sed* Command

COMMAND SYNTAX

```
sed [option(s)] command [filename...]
```

FINDER EQUIVALENT

Powerful search and replace function in a word processor or text editor.

OVERVIEW OF OPTIONS FOR *SED*

`sed`	The sed command edits text input from standard input or from one or more files.
`sed 's/string/replacement/g'`	Using sed in this way replaces "string" by "replacement" in the entire input.

GETTING MORE INFORMATION

To display the manual page and learn more about sed, type `man sed` in Terminal. The standard book on sed is *sed & awk*, 2nd ed. by Dale Dougherty and Arnold Robbins (O'Reilly & Associates, 1997).

Text Editors

Sooner or later, if you work on the command line, you will need to edit text files. Whether these files contain text that you read or send to others, or whether they are configuration files that you need to add information to or change, text files are at the heart of every Unix system. All the files used to configure your system are text files, and for this reason can be edited from the command line. This includes the simplest file, such as `.bash_profile`, the file containing default settings and other information for the `bash` shell, as well as more complex files, such as those used to configure a web server or mail server.

In Chapter 8 I presented tools for viewing text files: commands such as `less`, `more`, and `cat` let you view the contents of text files but not change them. In this section, I'll look at text editors, programs that let you not only view text in files but also change their contents or create new text files.

The three main command-line text editors available on Mac OS X are Pico, vi, and Emacs. Each of these text editors has advantages and disadvantages:

Pico	Easy to use, easy to learn, but limited in its functions.
vi	More powerful and more complex than Pico, but available on almost every Unix system.
Emacs	Extremely complex, difficult to learn, yet by far the most powerful text editor. Not present on all Unix systems.

There are many other text editors available for Unix systems, and these include "improved" versions of vi and Emacs. (In fact, the version of vi included with Mac OS X Panther is vim, or Vi iMproved.) If you want to go further, check the Web for other programs, but start by checking out these three. They are installed on your Mac, and they represent the main types of programs available.

Text editors are different than most other command-line tools. They are complex applications, with multiple functions and commands, rather than single commands with options and arguments. They open files so you can edit their contents, they let you create text files from scratch, and they save these files. It is better to think of these programs as applications rather than command-line tools, which generally have more limited abilities.

For this reason, I will only give you a brief overview of how to use two of these text editors, Pico and vi. I won't try to tell you much about Emacs, since there is no way to do justice to this program in just a few pages. (See the sidebar "About Emacs" later in this chapter.)

Editing Text with Pico

The Pico (**pi**ne **co**mposer) text editor is one of the simplest to use. Unlike other text editors, such as vi and Emacs, it has a clear interface and should be unthreatening to users familiar with graphical text editors. The program's man page says it is "a simple, display-oriented text editor based on the Pine message system composer. As with Pine, commands are displayed at the bottom of the screen, and context-sensitive help is provided. As you type characters Pico immediately inserts them into the text. Editing commands are entered using control-key combinations."

The Pico text editor is the easiest to learn, thanks to its contextual help and on-screen commands. The version of Pico included with Mac OS X (as of press time, this was Mac OS X 10.2) is relatively old, version 2.5, but you can get a precompiled copy of a newer version for Mac OS X at http://www.osxgnu.org/software/Email/pine/. This comes as a package that installs both Pine and Pico, and uses the standard Mac OS X installer, so you don't even need to use the command line to set it up. You can also download the source code from http://www.washington.edu/pine/getpine/unix.html if you want to compile it yourself.

Editing Files with Pico

To open an existing file with Pico, use the following command:

```
$ pico filename
```

The Pico editor displays in Terminal, as shown in Figure 9.1.

GRAPHICAL TEXT EDITORS

I have a confession to make: with the exception of when I edit very short files, such as my .bash_profile file, I rarely use Terminal to edit text files. I don't see any reason to use command-line tools for editing text when there are so many good graphical tools available. Some users may think this is heresy, but in my opinion it's just logic. I work better with graphical tools for editing text.

However, you may not always have access to these tools. If your Mac won't start up correctly, and you have to boot in single-user mode, you may not have a choice but to use the command line. Or if you log on to another Mac with ssh, the only way you can edit files is from Terminal. But for most uses, graphical text editors are the way to go.

Even if you feel the same as I do, you should nevertheless become familiar with at least one command-line text editor. The best choice is Pico, since it is the easiest to use. You never know when you'll only be able to work from the command line.

Here are a few choices for good graphical text editors for Mac OS X. All of these tools can be used to edit files on your Mac, but you need to make sure of one thing: you need to check their preferences and set line breaks to Unix to make sure your files work. If the programs save files with Macintosh line breaks, the Unix underpinnings of your Mac may not be able to read them correctly.

TextEdit is Apple's simple text editor that is installed with Mac OS X—you'll find it in the Applications folder. It can save files in text, RTF, and .doc (Microsoft Word) formats, and can be used to edit text files on your Mac. With the open command (see Interlude 5, "The Versatile open Command"), you can open text files in TextEdit from the command line. It lets you use Unix line breaks so you can be sure that any files you edit with TextEdit are readable by other Unix tools.

BBEdit (http://www.barebones.com) is the Swiss-army knife of text editors. It is excellent for coding HTML or other languages (its built-in syntax coloring is a boon for developers), editing text files, searching for and replacing text in multiple files, and much more. This program has hundreds of features and takes a while to learn. Its little brother, TextWrangler, is a simplified version of the program, and BBEdit Lite is even simpler, but free. Both BBEdit and TextWrangler install command-line tools that let you open files in their programs.

TexEdit Plus (http://www.tex-edit.com) is a venerable program that has been popular on the Mac for many years. With strong Apple-scripting capabilities, and a powerful grep function built in, this inexpensive tool is perfect for those who want more than Apple's TextEdit but don't want to pay a lot.

Emacs (http://www.porkrind.org/emacs) is a graphical version of the Emacs command-line text editor. It opens in its own terminal-type window, and looks similar to Emacs on the command line, but it offers menus to access many of its commands.

FIGURE 9.1

The Pico text editor displayed in a Terminal window

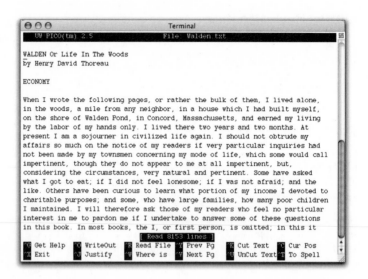

The top line of the screen shown in Figure 9.1 contains the version of Pico and the name of the file being edited. At the bottom is a list of commands available. The third line from the bottom—here "Read 8153 lines," showing how many lines the file contains—gives additional contextual information.

The main advantage to using Pico is that the available commands are displayed at the bottom of the screen. Each command is shown with its shortcut (such as ^G) and its name (Get Help). The ^ symbol means the Control key, so to get help you press Control+G. (Note: you don't need to press the Shift key with any Pico shortcuts, even though capital letters are shown for these shortcuts.)

You can move around the file with the arrow keys: press the Right arrow key to move to the right, press the Left arrow key to move to the left, press the Down arrow key to move down one line, and press the Up arrow key to move up one line. You can move forward or backward in your file by pressing Control+V to go to the next screen, or Control+Y to go to the previous screen. You'll notice the cursor changing position as it moves—you should use either a block cursor or underscore cursor (as in Figure 9.1, under the first letter in the file); they are easier to see than a bar cursor.

You can edit text in Pico just as you do in a word processor: start typing to add text, or press the backspace key to delete text. If you add or delete enough text to unbalance the lines in your file, you can justify the paragraphs by placing the cursor in the paragraph you want to justify (see Figure 9.2) and pressing Control+J. This moves the words around and adds new line breaks to balance the lines.

You can cut and paste text in files with Pico, but you cannot copy text. To cut text, move the cursor to the beginning or end of the text you want to cut then press Control+^. (This is a strange shortcut indeed; the ^ character is Shift+6 on a QWERTY keyboard.) The information line displays Mark Set (see Figure 9.3). Then use the arrow keys to select text. Figure 9.3 shows a word selected.

FIGURE 9.2

Text with a too-short first line

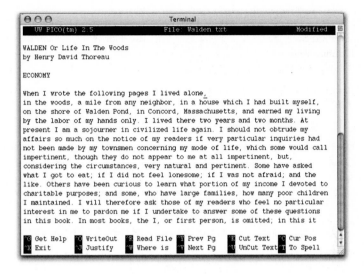

FIGURE 9.3

Text selected in Pico

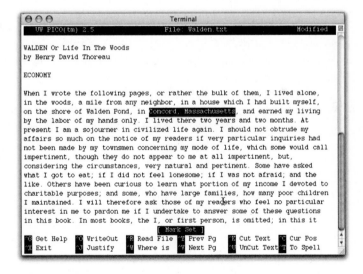

As you know, Mac OS X works with permissions for its files. Each user can access their own files, and administrators can access certain other files. When working on the command line, you can use the sudo command to access system files, or those owned by other users.

To edit system files with Pico, or any other text editor, such as vi or Emacs, you must prefix your command with sudo, like this:

```
$ sudo pico filename
```

The shell asks you to enter your administrator's password, then lets you access the file. Actually, you are allowed to view some system files without sudo, but if you make changes and try to save them, you won't be able to because you don't have write privileges. But make any such changes with care. One mistake, even one incorrect character, and you may not be able to restart or use your Mac.

To cut the selected text, press Control+K. Move the cursor to the new location, then press Control+U to paste the text (or UnCut it, in Pico lingo). To cut an entire line, move the cursor to the line you want to cut but don't select any text. Then press Control+K to cut it. You can paste it in another location using Control+U as earlier.

You can search for text in a file by pressing Control+W. The information line prompts you to enter your text. Press Enter to find the next occurrence of your string.

You cannot undo any operations in Pico, so you should make sure you save your files often. To do this, press Control+O (WriteOut). This displays `File Name to write:` in the information line, followed by the original filename (Figure 9.4). If you want to save the changes to this file, press Enter. If not, enter a new filename.

FIGURE 9.4

Saving a file in Pico

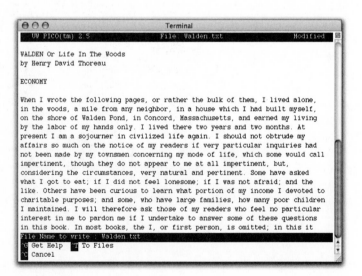

If you press Control+T from the save prompt, you enter the Pico file browser. (See Figure 9.5.) This lets you move around on your file system without quitting Pico.

Move around by pressing the arrow keys. When you want to enter a directory, press Enter. You'll be asked to confirm that you really want to enter that directory; press Enter again. In this manner you can move around easily, chose the location to save your file, and copy, rename, or delete files on your Mac.

When you have finished working with Pico, press Control+X to exit the program. If you haven't saved your file, Pico asks you if you want to. Follow the procedure given earlier to save the file.

Creating Files with Pico

There are two ways to create a new text file with Pico. The first is to simply open the Pico editor by running this command:

```
$ pico
```

The second is to run the `pico` command with the name of your file as an argument. If the file does not exist, Pico does not actually create it until you save it, but it does store the name of the file in its buffer (see Figure 9.6):

```
$ pico newfile
```

When you create a new file, as in Figure 9.6, your Terminal display looks like a blank page, just as in any word processor.

Just start typing your text in this file, then follow the instructions given earlier for cutting and pasting text and for saving files.

FIGURE 9.5
The Pico file browser lets you navigate your file system without quitting the editor.

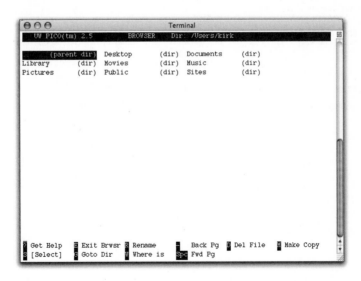

Overview of the *pico* Command

COMMAND SYNTAX

```
pico [option(s)] [file]
```

FINDER EQUIVALENT

Basic text editor such as TextEdit.

KEYBOARD SHORTCUTS FOR *PICO*

Shortcut	Command
Ctrl+F; Right arrow key	Move forward one character.
Ctrl+B; Left arrow key	Move backward one character.
Ctrl+P; Up arrow key	Move up one line.
Ctrl+N; Down arrow key	Move down one line.
Ctrl+A	Move to the beginning of the current line.
Ctrl+E	Move to the end of the current line.
Ctrl+V	Move forward one page.
Ctrl+Y	Move backward one page.
Ctrl+W	Search for text.
Ctrl+L	Refresh the display.
Ctrl+D	Delete the character at the cursor position.
Ctrl+^	Begin selecting text at the cursor.
Ctrl+K	Cut selected text or current line.
Ctrl+U	Paste last cut text at the cursor position.
Ctrl+I	Insert a tab at the current cursor position.
Ctrl+J	Justify the current paragraph.
Ctrl+T	Spell-check the text. (This does not work in the version supplied with Mac OS X 10.2.)
Ctrl+R	Insert a file at the cursor position.
Ctrl+O	Save a file.
Ctrl+G	View Pico's online help.
Ctrl+X	Exit Pico.

Continued on next page

Overview of the *pico* Command *(continued)*

GETTING MORE INFORMATION

To display the manual page and learn more about pico, type man pico in Terminal. The pico man page is not very helpful; if you search for "Pico tutorial" on the Web you'll find many documents that give more thorough explanations of the program.

Editing Text with vi

In the continuum of text editors, vi (visual interface to the **ex** editor), pronounced vee-eye, stands in the middle. More complex and with more functions than Pico, it has fewer functions than Emacs. But the advantage to learning vi is its ubiquity—you'll find it on just about every Unix or Linux system.

While it was possible to cover the majority of the functions available in Pico earlier in this chapter, I can only give you a brief introduction to vi. It has dozens of functions, and learning vi is similar to learning the command line; you need to learn a whole new set of commands that only work with vi. But if you want to edit text in Terminal, this steep learning curve will pay off. Using vi you can do just about anything you want to text files. (Note: the version of vi included with Mac OS X Panther is vim, or Vi iMproved, one of the many vi "clones" available, but I will refer to it as vi.)

FIGURE 9.6

A new file in Pico

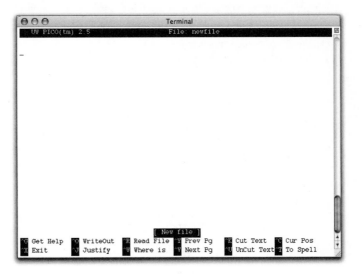

HANDS ON: SETTING A DEFAULT TEXT EDITOR

The tcsh shell, used by default under Mac OS X, has an environment variable called EDITOR. This variable tells the shell which text editor to use when another command or program wants to edit text files. When viewing files in less, for example, you can press v to move into your default text editor; this is vi, unless you choose a different editor by setting this variable.

To set this variable you must edit your .bash_profile or .tcshrc file (depending on which shell you use), found in your home directory. (See Chapter 16, "Configuring the Shell," for more on editing this file.)

If you are using the bash shell, you need to enter two lines in your .bash_profile file:

```
export FCEDIT=[name of editor]
export EDITOR=[name of editor]
```

So, to use Pico, you'd add the following:

```
export FCEDIT=/usr/bin/pico
export EDITOR=/usr/bin/pico
```

If you're using tcsh, you need to enter the following line to your .tcshrc file:

```
setenv EDITOR [name of editor]
```

If you want to use Pico, for example, add this:

```
setenv EDITOR pico
```

You can also set your default editor to use BBEdit, via its command-line tool. Add the following to your .bash_profile or .tcshrc file. For bash:

```
export FCEDIT=/usr/bin/bbedit
export EDITOR=/usr/bin/bbedit
```

For tcsh:

```
setenv EDITOR /usr/bin/bbedit
```

Finally, if you want to use TextEdit, you can add the following. For bash:

```
export FCEDIT=/Applications/TextEdit.app/Contents/MacOS/TextEdit
export EDITOR=/Applications/TextEdit.app/Contents/MacOS/TextEdit
```

For tcsh:

```
setenv EDITOR /Applications/TextEdit.app/Contents/MacOS/TextEdit
```

You must use the full path for TextEdit to work correctly. Make sure you quit TextEdit when you've finished working with your file.

One thing that's important to know about vi is that it is a *modal* editor. This means that it has different modes of usage, and you must be in one of these modes to issue the appropriate commands. The three modes of vi are:

Command Mode   In this mode you can issue commands instructing vi to do specific tasks in your files.

Insert Mode   In this mode you can insert or delete text in files.

ex Mode   In this mode you can send commands either to vi or to the shell.

A First Taste of vi

To start off, here's a brief tutorial that will show you the absolute basics of vi: launching vi, creating a new file, entering some text, saving it, and exiting vi.

To launch vi, run the following:

```
$ vi test
```

This displays the vi interface in the entire Terminal window, as shown in Figure 9.7. (I've used `test` as an example here, but you can enter any name you want to create a new, empty file.)

At the bottom of the window shown in Figure 9.7 you can see the name of the current temporary file that vi uses, then "new file," since the file hasn't yet been saved.

At this point, you are in the vi command mode. To enter text in vi, you must first enter insert mode by typing i. You can now enter text as you would in any text editor. Figure 9.8 shows the results of this.

As you can see in Figure 9.8, vi automatically wraps text at the end of a line (for display purposes only; it does not add line breaks), but does so without respecting word breaks.

FIGURE 9.7

What you see when you launch vi

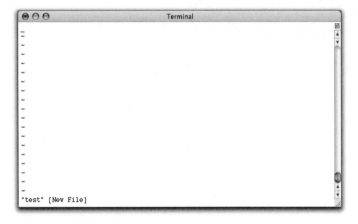

FIGURE 9.8

Entering text in the
vi editor

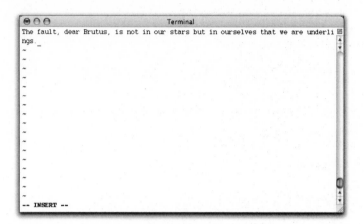

To save this file and exit vi, press Esc (Escape) to leave insert mode and return to command mode, then type : (colon) to enter ex mode. This tells vi that you are going to enter a command. The colon displays like a prompt. Type the following after the colon:

```
w test.txt
```

This tells vi to save the file as `test.txt`. Press Enter, and vi displays the name of the file at the bottom of the Terminal window along with the number of lines and characters it contains. (See Figure 9.9.)

To exit vi, type `:q`. Since you saved your file and have not made any more changes to it, vi exits and Terminal displays a shell prompt.

FIGURE 9.9

Saving a file with vi

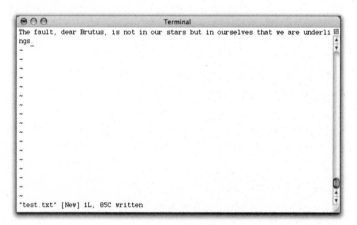

Editing Text Files with vi

To open a file with vi, run the following command:

```
$ vi filename
```

This opens your file in vi in a full Terminal window, as in Figure 9.10.

As you can see in Figure 9.10, vi displays as much of the file as it can in the Terminal window. A line at the bottom of the window shows the filename (`Walden.txt`), and the number of lines the file contains (here, 8153) as well as the number of characters (580640).

You can move around the file with the arrow keys: press the Right arrow key to move to the right, press the Left arrow key to move to the left, press the Down arrow key to move down one line, and press the Up arrow key to move up one line. You can move forward or backward in your file by pressing Control+F, to go to the next screen, or Control+B, to go to the previous screen.

You can move to the next word by pressing W, to the previous word by pressing B, to the end of the line by pressing $, and to the beginning of the line by pressing 0 (zero).

To edit a file in vi you must go into insert mode. Press I to enter this mode. The vi editor shows you, at the bottom of the window, that you are in insert mode. To add text to your file, position the cursor in the location where you want to add text, then begin typing, or move the cursor to the location where you want to delete text. The characters you type appear at the cursor location and the cursor moves forward with each one (see Figure 9.11), or they disappear as you delete them.

If you want to add a return, and continue typing from the next line, just press Return. Most operations to edit text are similar to what you're used to doing in graphical text editors.

After you have made changes to your file, press Escape to exit insert mode, then type :w, and press Enter. This saves your file. A line displays at the bottom of the Terminal window (Figure 9.12) showing the name of the file, the number of lines, and the number of characters as well as the word "written."

FIGURE 9.10

The vi text editor displaying a file in Terminal

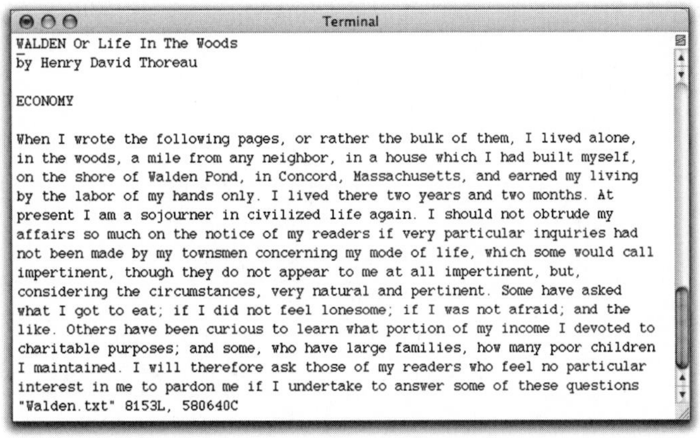

FIGURE 9.11

Adding text to a file with vi (the added text follows the heading "ECONOMY")

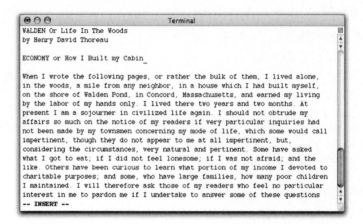

To quit vi, type :q, then press Enter. Terminal displays a normal shell prompt. If you wish to quit without saving changes, type :q!, then press Enter. (If you have already saved changes in your session by pressing :w, this will not undo those changes.)

Searching for Text with vi

Just like any good text editor or word processor, vi lets you search for text in files. Very often, when editing files, you need to find the exact text or string you want to change. You can do this easily with vi.

To search in vi you must be in command mode. If you're not sure, press Escape twice to make sure you are in this mode. Type / (slash), and vi displays a slash at the bottom of the Terminal window. Type the string you want to find, then press Enter. (Figure 9.13.)

FIGURE 9.12

Information at the bottom of the Terminal window for a file saved in vi

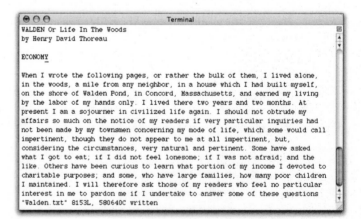

FIGURE 9.13

Entering a search string in vi

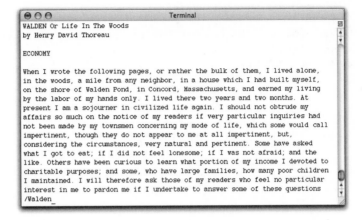

When you press Enter, vi searches for the next occurrence of the search string, and moves the cursor to the beginning of that string. You may want to set your cursor to flash, or to use a box cursor, if you search a lot; otherwise it might be difficult to spot the cursor. As you can see in Figure 9.14, the cursor is under the word "Walden" in the third line of the first paragraph.

To go to the next occurrence of the search string, press n. (You may recall that this is the same way you search with less. See Chapter 8.) To move to the previous occurrence, press N (that's Shift+n). When there are no more occurrences of the search string, vi returns to the beginning of the file and displays a message saying Search hit Bottom, continuing at TOP. If vi finds no occurrences of the search string, it displays Pattern not found.

FIGURE 9.14

The cursor in vi shows the location of the search string that it found.

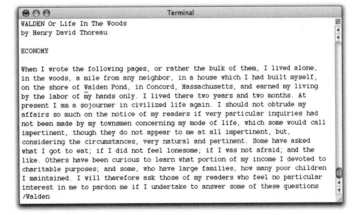

Overview of the *vi* Command

COMMAND SYNTAX

```
vi [option(s)] [file ...]
```

FINDER EQUIVALENT

Word processor or powerful text editor.

KEYBOARD SHORTCUTS FOR *VI*

Shortcut	Command
Escape	Enter command mode.
i	Enter insert mode.
h; Right arrow key	Move forward one character.
l; Left arrow key	Move backward one character.
k; Up arrow key	Move up one line.
j; Down arrow key	Move down one line.
0	Move to the beginning of the current line.
$	Move to the end of the current line.
Ctrl+F	Move forward one screen.
Ctrl+B	Move backward one screen.
o	Insert new line.
/	Search for text (in command mode).
?	Search for text backward (in command mode).
s/search_string/replacement_string/	Replace text in the current line.
1,$ s/search_string/replacement_string/g	Replace all.
x	Delete the character at the cursor position.
X	Delete the character to the left of the cursor.
:w filename	Save a file.
:q	Exit vi.
:q!	Exit vi without saving.

Continued on next page

ON THE COMMAND LINE

Overview of the *vi* Command *(continued)*

GETTING MORE INFORMATION

To display the manual page and learn more about vi, type man vi in Terminal. The vi man page is not very complete, and is at best an overview for users already familiar with the program. To find out more about vi, go to the VI LOVERS HOME PAGE (http://www.thomer.com/vi/vi.html), where you'll find everything you could ever want to know about vi, and more. You can also read the book *Learning the vi Editor*, 6th ed. by Linda Lamb and Arnold Robbins (O'Reilly & Associates, 1998).

Replacing Text with vi

In addition to searching for text, as explained in the preceding section, you may want to replace a specific string with vi. To do this, you must be in command mode. If you're not sure, press Escape twice to make sure you are in this mode.

To replace a search string, type the following:

:s/search_string/replacement_string/

Press Enter and vi replaces the first occurrence of the search string in the current line with the replacement string.

If you want to replace all the occurrences of your search string with the replacement string, type the following:

:%s/search_string/replacement_string/g

As you can see in Figure 9.15, vi makes the change then shows how many occurrences were changed at the bottom line of the Terminal window.

FIGURE 9.15

The number of changes made is shown in the bottom line of the Terminal window.

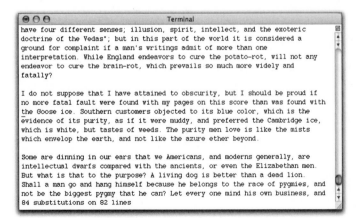

This introduction to vi is just the tip of the iceberg. This program has dozens of commands, and you've only gotten a glimpse of its abilities. If you are interested in exploring this program further, you'll find lots of interesting functions and capabilities.

Editing Text with Emacs

Depending on whom you ask, Emacs (**editor macros**) is either too complex or just right for their needs. Its commands are difficult to learn, its keyboard shortcuts complicated (they sometimes seem to have been designed for people with three hands), but it does things that other text editors cannot do. As the Emacs manual says, this program is "the extensible, customizable, self-documenting real-time display editor." To again quote the Emacs manual, this program is capable of the following: "controlling subprocesses; automatic indentation of programs; viewing two or more files at once; editing formatted text; and dealing in terms of characters, words, lines, sentences, paragraphs, and pages, as well as expressions and comments in several different programming languages."

A program like Emacs is an acquired taste, and can take a while to become comfortable with. Fortunately, Emacs offers a built-in tutorial, and this is the best place to start. Launch Emacs with the following command:

```
$ emacs
```

Terminal displays Emacs in its entire window (Figure 9.16).

EMACS FANS: BE KIND!

Please, dear reader who is a fan and regular user of Emacs, be kind to me. I haven't neglected to say more about your favorite text editor because of any personal opinion, but simply because it would take too long to truly do it justice. Entire books—and thick ones—have been written about Emacs, and the built-in tutorial gives a good overview of the program. For readers who do want to go further, see the section "Getting More Information" in the "Overview of the *emacs* Command" sidebar further on.

FIGURE 9.16
What you see when
you open Emacs

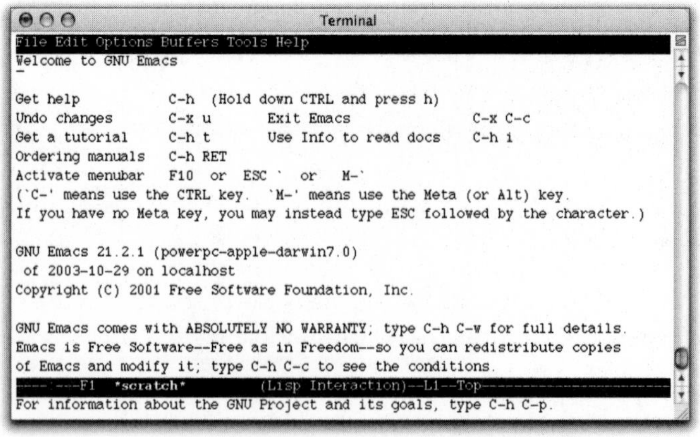

ON THE COMMAND LINE
Overview of the *emacs* Command

COMMAND SYNTAX

```
emacs [option(s)] [file ...]
```

FINDER EQUIVALENT

Word processor or powerful text editor.

OVERVIEW OF OPTIONS FOR *EMACS*

emacs   The Emacs program is a powerful text editor.

Control+H, T   Use this option to access the Emacs tutorial.

GETTING MORE INFORMATION

To display the manual page and learn more about Emacs, type man emacs in Terminal. To go further with Emacs, read the Emacs manual on-line (http://www.gnu.org/software/emacs/manual/), or download it in several formats (PDF, HTML, text, PostScript, etc.). Or you can look for one of the many books about Emacs, such as *Learning GNU Emacs*, 2nd ed. by Debra Cameron, Bill Rosenblatt and Eric S. Raymond (O'Reilly & Associates, 1996).

To access the on-line tutorial, press the following keys: Control+H, then T. Follow the tutorial to get a taste of Emacs and see if it fits your needs. Note: when Emacs tells you to press the Meta key, you must use the Escape key on your Mac. (Though if you use Emacs a lot, you should set the Use Option Key As Meta Key option in the Terminal emulation settings. See Chapter 2, "Using Terminal," for more on these settings.) But you don't press the Escape key at the same time as another key. To move forward one screen in Emacs, press Control+V at the same time. To move back one screen, press Escape then press V.

When you've finished working with the tutorial, or just want to quit Emacs, press Control+X, then Control+C.

HANDS ON: GETTING A LOAD OFF YOUR MIND WITH EMACS

Have you had a long day? Got problems? Annoyed trying to learn Emacs? Well, Emacs thoughtfully comes with a built-in psychotherapist program, eliza. To access eliza from Emacs, first press Escape. Then type **xdoctor** and press Return. The eliza program displays the following:

```
I am the psychotherapist.  Please, describe your problems.  Each time
you are finished talking, type RET twice.
```

Start by telling eliza what's wrong, then press Return twice. You can continue talking to your online shrink and answering the questions eliza asks. Just remember, it's not real.

Summing Up

This chapter has looked at the many ways you can edit and work with text from the command line. From simple commands to format text, count words, or replace characters to complex commands such as sed and awk, the command line gives you extraordinary power and flexibility.

The command line also provides several text editors, from the simple, user-friendly Pico through the more complex vi to the ultimate text editor Emacs. While graphical text editors such as TextEdit or BBEdit can do the same thing, and often do so more easily, it is useful to know how to use at least one command-line text editor, and Pico is a good choice for beginners.

Chapter 10

Printing

While you generally print from graphical interface applications, you may want to print from the command line for specific purposes; to print certain types of files or Terminal output. You can print to a printer connected directly to your Mac, or you can share a printer across a network with the Mac OS X built-in printer sharing.

In this chapter, I'll show you how to print certain types of files, how to manage printers and printer queues, and how to set custom printing parameters. While you can't print all types of files from the command line, you can save a lot of time using these commands with some kinds of files.

About Printing with Mac OS X

Mac OS X uses the Common Unix Printing System (CUPS), which is based on the Internet Printing Protocol (IPP). This system resides in the underbelly of Mac OS X; most users never see it, since Apple's Print Center utility provides a graphical interface to its setup and management functions. You can directly access the CUPS interface through a web browser by entering this URL:

```
http://localhost:631
```

The page that opens lets you add and remove printers, manage jobs and printers, and access the thorough online help for CUPS. The CUPS system works like a web server, and interfaces seamlessly with Mac OS X's printer sharing—if you have a printer shared on one Mac running OS X, CUPS sees this printer and lets you print to it from the command line, or via a GUI application.

But to be able to use your printer, you need drivers that work with Mac OS X. While Apple includes drivers for dozens of printers in Mac OS X, not all third-party printer manufacturers provide Mac OS X drivers for their printers. One solution, if your printer is not supported, is to use Gimp-Print, an open-source package of printer drivers for several hundred popular printers (http://gimp-print.sourceforge.net/MacOSX.php3).

Printing Files with *lp*

The lp (line print) command is part of the CUPS system, and is used to send files to the currently active printer. (There is an additional command, lpr, which is similar to lp but has fewer options. For most uses the two are equivalent.) You can use this command to print certain types of files: text files, graphics files (JPG, GIF, TIFF, PNG), PDF files, and PostScript files. You cannot, however, use it to print proprietary file formats such as .doc, .rtf, and others.

To print a file with lp, the syntax is simple:

```
$ lp filename
```

When running this command, Terminal displays a line of text confirming the currently active printer:

```
$ lp Walden.txt
request id is HL_1440_series-1 (1 file(s))
```

If there is no printer available, the lp command returns the following:

```
lp: unable to print file: client-error-bad-request
```

or, if there is no default printer set, the lp command returns this message:

```
lp: error - no default destination available.
```

You can print several files with the lp command by adding their names as arguments. To print three files named File1, File2, and File3, run the command as follows:

```
$ lp File1 File2 File3
```

If the files are not in the current working directory, you need to specify full paths for the files, either absolute or relative:

```
$ lp ~/Documents/File1 ../File2 /Applications/MyApp/File3
```

You can use shell wildcards to specify which files to print. Say your current working directory contains several other directories as well as a group of text files you want to print, all of which have the .txt extension; you can print them with this command:

```
$ lp *.txt
```

Or, if you use this command, you can print all the files in a directory that can be printed:

```
$ lp *
```

Terminal returns something similar to the following:

```
request id is HL_1440_series-1 (9 file(s))
```

In this example I have one file and eight directories in the current working directory. Even though the lp command tells me that it is printing nine files, it only prints one file; it cannot print the directories and they are ignored.

You can combine the lp command with other commands, such as the find command, which can allow you to tell lp what to print. For example, to print all the JPEG files in your home directory, or its subdirectories, run the following command:

```
$ lp `find ~ -name '*.jpg'`
```

This tells lp to print all files found by the command in single quotes. In this case, it finds all files whose names end with .jpg and sends them to the printer. For more on finding files, see Chapter 7, "Finding Files, Directories, and Everything Else"; for more on using pipes, see Interlude 3, "Redirecting Input and Output."

Advanced Printing Options with *lp*

There are many advanced options available for printing jobs with the lp command: you can choose the number of copies to print, you can direct your printing job to a specific printer, or you can change the layout or page size. You can do almost everything from the command line that you can in a normal Print dialog, though you cannot access printer-specific options with this command.

PRINTING MULTIPLE COPIES

The lp command only prints one copy of your files by default. To tell this command to print multiple copies, use the -n (number) option with the following syntax:

```
$ lp -n [number of copies] filename
```

HANDS ON: PRINTING PDF FILES MORE QUICKLY

If you often need to print PDF files, you know how time-consuming it can be: you need to open the files with Preview or Acrobat Reader, then tell each one to print. It takes these programs a long time to spool each file, and if you have more than just a couple of files you can spend a long time waiting for them to spool before being able to launch another one.

Using the lp command you can send as many PDF files as you want to your printer in just a couple of seconds. Make sure they are all in one directory, move to that directory in Terminal, then run the following command:

```
$ lp '*.pdf'
```

This tells the lp command to print all files whose names end with .pdf; if the files don't have the .pdf extension, or there are no other files in the directory, you can simply use this command, which tells lp to print all files in the current working directory:

```
$ lp *
```

The command launches the print job in seconds, and, while the actual printing is no faster than if you use a GUI application, you don't need to wait for each file to spool before sending the next one to the printer. If you have a lot of files to print, you can save a great deal of time this way.

The same is true for graphics files, such as TIFFs, JPGs, and GIFs. Using the lp command in this manner saves having to open each file and select the Print command.

This prints multiple copies one page at a time. If you want to collate documents, add the `-o Collate=True` option, as follows:

```
$ lp -n [number of copies] -o Collate=True filename
```

This prints one copy of the entire document, then another, and so on.

CHOOSING WHICH PAGES TO PRINT

You can use the `lp` command to select which pages of a document you want to print, but you need to first make sure that you know how the document's pages will be laid out when printing in this way. For documents such as PDF files this is easy, but for other text documents you may find it more useful to print from a GUI application.

To specify a page range for printing, use the `-o page-ranges=` option:

```
$ lp -o page-ranges=1-3,7,13-17 filename
```

You can specify individual pages, a range of pages, or a combination of both, with each page or range separated by commas.

You can also choose to print only odd or even pages, but you need to be aware of which pages will be odd and which will be even. To do this, use the `-o page-set=` option:

```
$ lp -o page-set=odd filename
$ lp -o page-set=even filename
```

SETTING MEDIA SIZE, TYPE, AND SOURCE

Just as you can choose different paper sizes from a Print dialog, the `lp` command has an option, the `-o media=` option, to let you choose media size, type, and source for your print jobs.

```
$ lp -o media=Letter,Upper,Transparency filename
```

You can string together several of these options, separated by commas, after `media=`; none of these options are case-sensitive. Table 10.1 shows the main media options available.

TABLE 10.1: MEDIA OPTIONS FOR THE *LP* COMMAND

OPTION	TYPE, SIZE, OR SOURCE
Letter	US Letter (8.5 × 11 inches, or 216 × 279mm)
Legal	US Legal (8.5 × 14 inches, or 216 × 356mm)
A4	ISO A4 (8.27 × 11.69 inches, or 210 × 297mm)
COM10	US #10 Envelope (9.5 × 4.125 inches, or 241 × 105mm)
DL	ISO DL Envelope (8.66 × 4.33 inches, or 220 × 110mm)
Transparency	Transparency media type or source
Upper	Upper paper tray
Lower	Lower paper tray

Continued on next page

TABLE 10.1: **TABLE 10.1:** MEDIA OPTIONS FOR THE *LP* COMMAND *(continued)*

OPTION	TYPE, SIZE, OR SOURCE
MultiPurpose	Multipurpose paper tray
LargeCapacity	Large capacity paper tray

Note that while not all printers support multiple paper trays or sources, these options work with many printers. Additionally, if a particular option, such as a source or paper tray, is not available, the job generally ignores the specific settings and falls back to whatever defaults the printer uses.

HANDS ON: GETTING MORE INFORMATION ABOUT YOUR PRINTER

There is a group of additional commands that provide information about your printer. The lpstat command gives you information about the current classes, jobs, and printers. If you want to find out which printers are available, run this command:

```
$ lpstat -p
printer AdobePDF is idle.  enabled since Jan 01 00:00
printer HL-1440_series is idle.  enabled since Jan 01 00:00
printer HL-1440_series@Kirks-iMac.local is idle.  enabled since Jan 01 00:00
printer Internal_Modem@Kirks-iMac.local is idle.  enabled since Jan 01 00:00
```

As you can see in this example, I have printers in two locations. The first two printers are local: one is the Adobe Acrobat print driver and the second a laser printer. The second two are connected to my iMac; one is the same as the second local printer and the other is my iMac's internal modem, which allows me to send faxes via the iMac. Curiously, all of these printers seem to have been enabled since Jan 1 at 00:00.

Going further, you can run this command to get more information about each printer:

```
$ lpstat -l -p
printer HL-1440_series is idle.  enabled since Jan 01 00:00
        Form mounted:
        Content types: any
        Printer types: unknown
        Description: HL-1440 series
        Alerts: none
        Location: Kirk's iBook
        Connection: direct
        Interface: /private/etc/cups/ppd/HL-1440_series.ppd
        On fault: no alert
        After fault: continue
        Users allowed:
                (all)
        Forms allowed:
                (none)
        Banner required
```

Continued on next page

```
Charset sets:
        (none)
Default pitch:
Default page size:
Default port settings:
```

I've displayed the information for only one printer in the previous example; you can see that many of the information fields are blank, because the printer does not provide this information. You'll see a different output if you have other types of printers. Note that, in the preceding command, you cannot use lpstat -lp; for this command, you need to specify each option with a preceding dash.

You can use another command to find out about options available for your printer:

```
$ lpoptions -l
PageSize/Media Size: *BrLetter BrLegal BrExecutive BrA4 BrA5 BrB5 BrJISB5 BrC5
BrCom10 BrDL BrA6 BrMonarch Br3x5 BrOrgJ BrOrgK BrOrgL BrHagaki BrYoukei4 BrYoukeiMax
PageRegion/PageRegion: BrLetter BrLegal BrExecutive BrA4 BrA5 BrB5 BrJISB5 BrC5
BrCom10 BrDL BrA6 BrMonarch Br3x5 BrOrgJ BrOrgK BrOrgL BrHagaki BrYoukei4 BrYoukeiMax
```

This command returns whatever options the printer offers, so each printer returns different information. In the previous example, my Brother laser printer only offers paper sizes and regions, but it offers a wide range of them. As a comparison, here are the options provided by another printer, a LaserWriter 360:

```
InstalledMemory/Memory Configuration: *7Meg 16Meg
OptionalCassette1/Cassette (250/500 Sheets): True *False Preferred
Resolution/Choose Resolution: *600dpi 300dpi
Smoothing/FinePrint(TM): True *False
TraySwitch/TraySwitch: True *False
PageSize/Media Size: *Letter Legal A4 B5 Executive A5 LetterSmall A4Small LegalSmall
Com10 Monarch C5 DL
 PageRegion/PageRegion: Letter Legal A4 B5 Executive A5 LetterSmall A4Small
LegalSmall Com10 Monarch C5 DL
 InputSlot/Media Source: *StandardCassette Multipurpose OptionalCassette
ManualFeed/Manual Feed: True *False
```

In most cases, printing from the command line is a stopgap solution; you have more options, and access them more easily, from the standard Print dialogs in Mac OS X. When you need to print anything using specific options, you'll probably find it easier to do so from the GUI.

SETTING PRINT ORIENTATION

By default, all jobs are printed in portrait orientation, where the top of the page is the shorter side of the paper. To change this and print in landscape orientation, use the -o landscape option:

```
$ lp -o landscape filename
```

You can combine this option with the previous ones for media size and type, or for multiple copies.

Overview of the *lp* Command

COMMAND SYNTAX

```
lp [option(s)] [file ...]
```

FINDER EQUIVALENT

Print files.

OVERVIEW OF OPTIONS FOR *LP*

`lp filename`	The `lp` command prints files to the default or selected printer.
`-n [number of copies]`	This option, followed by a number, tells the `lp` command to print that number of copies of your file(s).
`-o Collate=True`	This option tells the `lp` command to collate the copies of your print job.
`-o page-ranges=[pages]`	This option tells the `lp` command to print your file using the pages and ranges that you specify.
`-o page-set=even`	This option tells the `lp` command to print only even-numbered pages.
`-o page-set=odd`	This option tells the `lp` command to print only odd-numbered pages.
`-o media=[media]`	This option tells the `lp` command to print jobs using the specified media size, type, or source. See Table 10.1 for a list of media.
`-o landscape`	This option tells the `lp` command to print in landscape orientation.
`-d [printer name]`	This option tells the `lp` command to print using the specified printer.

GETTING MORE INFORMATION

To display the manual page and learn more about `lp`, type `man lp` in Terminal, or check the online CUPS help by entering `http://localhost:631/sum.html` in any web browser.

PRINTING TO A SPECIFIC PRINTER

If you have more than one printer available, either connected to your Mac or accessible on a network, you can use the `-d` option with the `lp` command to choose which printer to use:

```
$ lp -d [printer name] filename
```

To find out the names of printers available, run the `lpstat` command (see the sidebar "Getting More Information about Your Printer").

Checking the Printer Queue with *lpq*

Since the lp command doesn't give you any progress reports as you print, you may want to check the status of your print jobs, especially if you are printing to a network printer that is not near your Mac. The lpq (line printer queue) command shows all the jobs that have been sent to your printers, as well as a fair amount of information about them.

```
$ lpq
HL_1440_series@Walden2.local. is ready and printing
Rank      Owner      Job   File(s)        Total Size
active    kirk       1     Walden.txt       652785 bytes
1st       kirk       2     Report.pdf        37200 bytes
2nd       samuelpepys 3    Pepys_diary    1300048 bytes
3rd       kirk       4     server_log         2748 bytes
```

As you can see, the first line shows the name and location of the printer and tells whether it is ready and printing. (In this example, a printer called HL_1440_series is connected via a network; it is on a host called Walden2.local.) The next line is a series of column headers:

Rank   This shows the order in which the jobs will be printed.

Owner   This is the user who sent the print job.

Job   This is the job number.

File(s)   This is the name of the file or files being printed.

Total Size   This is the total size of the print job in bytes.

If you have more than one printer connected to your Mac or your network, you can use the -a (all) option with lpq to get information on all printers. In this case, the list will show each printer, followed by the active or queued jobs.

The lpq command has only a few options; one useful option is the +interval option, which tells the lpq command to refresh its display at the time interval you specify. If you run the following:

```
$ lpq +10
```

the lpq command refreshes its display every 10 seconds, updating its print job list until there are no more jobs to display. While this fills the Terminal screen with text, it lets you follow the progress of print jobs. To stop this command from returning information, press Control+C.

HANDS ON: FORMATTING TEXT FILES WITH PR

If you want to print long text files but want some control over how they are printed, the pr command is what you need. It is a formatting command that lets you convert text into pages with a fixed number of lines, add headers and footers, and choose precise multicolumn formats. Its plethora of options lets you adjust pretty much everything you need: tabs, spaces, columns, pages, and more.

For more on the pr command, read the command's man page by typing man pr in Terminal.

Overview of the *lpq* Command

COMMAND SYNTAX

```
lpq [option(s)] [+interval]
```

FINDER EQUIVALENT

Displays the contents of the print job queue.

OVERVIEW OF OPTIONS FOR *LPQ*

lpq   The lpq command displays the contents of the print job queue.

+interval   This option tells the lpq command to refresh its display every interval seconds until there are no more print jobs in the queue.

GETTING MORE INFORMATION

To display the manual page and learn more about lpq, type man   lpq in Terminal.

Canceling Print Jobs with *cancel*

After you have sent jobs to a printer with the lp command, you can use the cancel command if you want to stop those jobs from printing. The cancel command is very simple; its syntax is as follows:

```
cancel [job number]
```

There are two ways to find out the job number. The first is to look at the text returned when you run the lp command. Here's what Terminal displays when you send a job to the printer with lp:

```
$ lp test_file
request id is HL_1440_series-1 (1 file(s))
```

The job number is shown following the dash after the printer name; in the preceding example it is job number 1.

The other way to find out a job number is to run the lpq command (see the sidebar "Overview of the *lpq* Command"). This returns a list of all jobs waiting in the printer queue.

```
$ lpq
HL_1440_series is ready and printing
Rank    Owner        Job   File(s)       Total Size
active  kirk         1     Walden.txt     652785 bytes
1st     kirk         2     Report.pdf      37200 bytes
2nd     samuelpepys  3     Pepys_diary   1300048 bytes
3rd     kirk         4     server_log       2748 bytes
```

Here, the job number is shown in the job column.

Overview of the *cancel* Command

COMMAND SYNTAX

```
cancel [job number] [-a] [destination-id]
```

FINDER EQUIVALENT

Cancel print jobs using Print Center.

OVERVIEW OF OPTIONS FOR *CANCEL*

`cancel [job number]`	The cancel command cancels the specified print job.
`cancel [destination-id] [job number]`	This tells the cancel command to cancel the specified print job on the specified printer.
`-a`	This option tells the cancel command to cancel all jobs in the print queue sent by the user.

GETTING MORE INFORMATION

To display the manual page and learn more about cancel, type man cancel in Terminal. The lprm command offers the same function as the cancel command.

To cancel a print job, run the cancel command as follows, using the appropriate job number:

```
$ cancel 3
```

This cancels job number 3, but not the other jobs in the printer queue.

The cancel command returns no output, so if you want to make sure your job has been cancelled, run the lpq command again to see what jobs remain in the printer queue. If you want to cancel all jobs you have sent to the print queue, use the -a (all) option:

```
$ cancel -a
```

If you have more than one printer connected to your Mac or network, you can specify which printer's job you want to cancel when using the cancel command. The syntax for this is as follows:

```
cancel [destination-id] [job number]
```

```
$ cancel HL_1440_series@Walden2.local 21
```

In this example, the printer's destination-id is HL_1440_series@Walden2.local and the job number is 21.

Managing Printers from the Command Line

In addition to being able to print and manage print jobs from the command line, the CUPS system includes a suite of command-line tools to manage printers. There are three such commands:

lpadmin   This command configures CUPS printers and classes.

lpinfo   This command shows available devices or drivers.

lpoptions   This command lets you set printer options and defaults.

These commands provide similar results to what you can do from the Print Center application: you can add new printers, configure existing printers, and set options and defaults. For more information on these commands, see the online CUPS help file at `http://localhost:631/sum.html`.

Printing from Terminal

Terminal, like any other GUI application, lets you print its display. This can be used to print out lists of files, the results of commands, or texts such as man pages. There are two ways to print from Terminal: the first uses the `lp` command and the second uses the Print menu item in Terminal's File menu.

Printing with the *lp* Command

As I mentioned earlier in this chapter when discussing the `lp` command, you can pipe the results of any command into the `lp` command. This sends these results to your default printer. You might, for example, need to print a list of files in a certain directory. To print such a list, use the following:

```
$ ls - l ~/Documents | lp
```

In this example I asked for a long list (`ls -l`) of the `Documents` directory in my home directory (`~/Documents`) then piped the list (`|`) to the `lp` command, which sends it to the printer. Terminal does not display the results of the `ls -l` command, since output is directed to the `lp` command.

You can print the results of other commands as well. The following command prints out the results of the `vm_stat` command:

```
$ vm_stat | lp
```

This command gives you information on your computer's use of virtual memory. For more on `vm_stat`, see Chapter 14, "Managing Programs and Processes."

You may need to use special options to print the results of certain commands. The `top` command, for example, which gives a real-time view of your computer's process, can only be printed if a certain option (the `-l` option) is used. If you are unsuccessful when attempting to print the results of a command, see that command's man page; there may be special options available to allow the command's results to be printed. (For more on the `top` command, see Chapter 14.)

The CUPS system provides a web browser interface to manage and administer printers and print jobs. It can be much easier to use this point-and-click interface than to use the command line.

To access this web browser interface, just enter the following in your browser:

```
http://localhost:631
```

The following shows this page in Safari. Click any of the links in the banner at the top of the page, or click the text links below it to access the available functions. Any changes you make through this web interface are saved automatically.

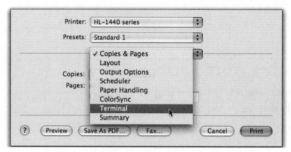

You can manage your printers, make some configuration changes to them, add new printers, and manage print jobs all from your browser. You can also access networked printers, if you have the appropriate privileges, by entering the corresponding address. On my network, when sending a print job to my networked printer, the address for the printer is:

```
HL_1440_series@Walden2.local.
```

To access the CUPS configuration page on that computer, I must enter this address in my browser:

```
http://walden2.local:631
```

This is a Rendezvous-based DNS name. This only works if the remote computer has been set up to allow remote administration. See the online help in the CUPS administration system for more on this.

Note: As of this writing, the CUPS system has a problem with Panther's shadowhash passwords, and many users will not be able to log in to the Administration section of CUPS using the links on the web page shown earlier in this sidebar. To resolve this—at least temporarily, until Apple fixes the problem—you need to do the following:

Edit the /etc/cups/cupsd.conf file with any text editor:

```
$ sudo pico /etc/cups/cupsd.conf
```

Go to the end of the file and look for this section:

```
#Encryption Required
<Limit GET>
AuthType Basic
```

Continued on next page

```
AuthClass System
</Limit>
</Location>
```

Comment out the part beginning with `<Limit GET>` and ending with `</Limit>`, so it looks like this:

```
#Encryption Required
#<Limit GET>
#AuthType Basic
#AuthClass System
#</Limit>
</Location>
```

Save this file, then restart the CUPS demon:

```
$ sudo killall -HUP cupsd
```

You will now be able to access the CUPS administration functions, but there will no longer be any password protection. This solution should only be used temporarily if you are on a network and want to prevent other users from accessing the CUPS administration functions.

Using the Print Menu Item

If you select File ➢ Print when in Terminal, you can print out the Terminal display. This works like almost any GUI application. However, several options are available so you can choose how much of the display gets printed.

If you merely click the Print button (or press Enter or Return) when the print sheet displays, Terminal sends the contents of its window to the printer. This is only what you see in Terminal; it does not include the scrollback buffer (text that is accessible by scrolling up in the window, but that is not visible in the window). To print more or less than what you see in the Terminal window, you must select Terminal from the pop-up menu in the print sheet. (See Figure 10.1.)

FIGURE 10.1

Select Terminal from the options pop-up menu to access Terminal print options.

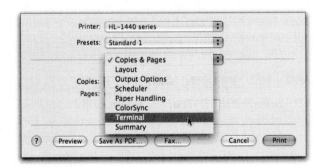

Three Terminal printing options are available (see Figure 10.2).

Print Visible Range   This is the default option, and prints only what is visible in the Terminal window.

Print Entire Scrollback Buffer   This prints the entire contents of the scrollback buffer. Be careful: this can be very long, especially if you have set the scrollback buffer to unlimited. You may find hundreds of pages spewing from your printer! If you want to print a long amount of Terminal output, a good idea is to clear the scrollback buffer first before running the command whose output you want to print. You can do this by selecting Scrollback ➤ Clear Scrollback in Terminal, or by pressing ⌘-K.

Print Selected Range   This prints only the text selected in the Terminal window. As you can see in Figure 10.2, one sentence is selected. If you click Print Selected Range, only that sentence is printed.

You can change any of the other options available in the print sheet, just as when you are printing from any GUI application.

As with other Mac OS X applications, Terminal allows you to save files as PDFs (by clicking Save As PDF on the Print sheet) or to fax documents. If you ever need to fax a man page to a friend or colleague, it's easy to do: just click the Fax button and enter the fax number and other information.

FIGURE 10.2
Terminal print options let you choose how much of its text is printed.

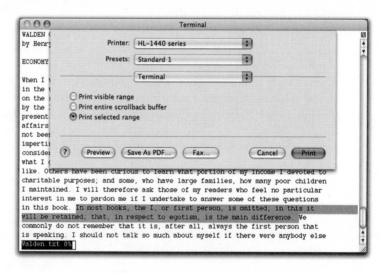

PRINTING MAN PAGES

The main documentation for the Unix commands of Mac OS X is in man pages. (See Chapter 3, "Getting Help while in Terminal," for more on man pages.) You can print out man pages if you want a hard copy of them for easier reading. Here's an example:

```
$ man lp | col -b | lp
```

This tells Terminal to take the man page for the lp command, pass it through the col command, which filters the text, and send it to the printer. Since man pages need special formatting to be displayed or printed—which the man command does when displaying these pages in Terminal—this is the best way to get printed copies of them. You cannot simply print out the man page from its text file, or by piping it directly to lp—well, you can, but you won't like what you see.

Summing Up

The group of commands to print and manage printers and print jobs lets you do almost everything from the command line that you can from Mac OS X's graphical interface. However, you cannot print all types of files with these commands: you are limited to nonproprietary formats that the Unix underpinnings of Mac OS X can understand. Terminal also offers printing options so you can make hard copies of the data returned by commands, printing out all or part of what Terminal displays.

Chapter 11

Compressing, Decompressing, and Archiving Files

Compressed files are very common: they are used to distribute software, to send attachments by e-mail, and to store infrequently used files to save space. Even though the price of hard disks has dropped greatly in recent years, everyone needs to compress files occasionally.

On Mac OS X, the standard for compressed files was long Aladdin's StuffIt; their free StuffIt Expander is included with the operating system, and this powerful program can decompress every common type of compressed file. But when Apple released Panther, they added a built-in zip archive tool. You can Control+click any file or folder and select Create Archive Of *Filename*, and the Finder zips up the file or folder. But there are other ways to do this, in zip and other formats, using the command line.

Mac OS X also includes several command-line tools for archiving files. You can back up some or all of your files, and you can even make a bootable backup (a clone) of your startup volume.

In this chapter, I'll look at the different command-line tools for compressing files and creating archives, for expanding archives, and for creating disk image files so you can archive your files and send compressed files over the Internet.

About Compressed Files

File compression can seem almost magical: programs can reduce the size of files, without losing any data, by exploiting repetitions in the files' internal bits and bytes. Compression can shrink some files by as much as 80 percent, while other files may only be compressed slightly. The difference in compression depends on the type of file: images tend to compress well, especially if they have large areas of colors where many pixels have the same values. Some kinds of text files compress well also, with the actual amount of compression depending on the type of text they contain.

There are two types of compression: *lossy* compression and *lossless* compression. These types of compression are used for different purposes. Some types of files, such as MP3 or JPEG files, use lossy compression, which allows them to contain the essential data in the files at a much smaller size. MP3 files can be very small compared with their originals, but only because some of the sound data is lost. This is acceptable for files such as music or images, where the loss is not generally noticed; there's a trade-off between file size and quality.

But when compressing files containing data that must remain intact—text files, applications, data-bases, etc.—you cannot use lossy compression; decompressing the files must result in the exact same data as the originals. Imagine the problems that you would have if every time you compressed then uncompressed a text file you lost a few words. Compression used for this kind of files is lossless compression, which ensures that the data you get out of an archive is the same as the data you put into it.

All the compression tools I present in this chapter use lossless compression, ensuring that your data remains the same.

Different compression tools result in different amounts of compression. To see the difference in how much compression you can expect from text files, I took a copy of Henry David Thoreau's *Walden* and compressed it using a half-dozen different formats. Of the formats I looked at, compress, gzip, and bzip2 are available via the command-line under Mac OS X; Zip is the standard Windows compression format; and StuffIt and StuffIt X are proprietary formats used by the StuffIt program. Table 11.1 shows the results of this test.

TABLE 11.1: COMPRESSION RESULTS FOR A TEXT FILE

FILENAME	COMPRESSION TYPE	SIZE	% SAVED
Walden.txt	None	568 kb	—
Walden.txt.Z	compress	232 kb	59%
Walden.txt.gz	gzip	228 kb	60%
Walden.txt.zip	Zip	220 kb	61%
Walden.txt.bz2	bzip2	180 kb	68%
Walden.txt.sit	StuffIt	176 kb	69%
Walden.txt.sitx	StuffIt X	152 kb	73%

As you can see in Table 11.1, the amount of savings ranges from 59 to 73 percent depending on the type of compression used. This was not a scientific study, because I only tried it on one file, and it was a text file; text files usually compress well. To really judge which compression algorithm is the most efficient, one should try it on all types of files: text files, graphics, applications, etc. But this gives an idea of the level of compression that can be expected from the different formats.

Compressing Files with *gzip*

The most common Unix compression tool is gzip (GNU **zip**), and both gzip and gunzip (the equivalent tool to decompress gzip files) are found on many types of Unix systems. If you need to distribute files to users on other Unix or Linux platforms, you can be pretty sure that they'll be able to work with gzip files. Even Mac OS 9 users will be able to decompress them if they have a recent version of StuffIt Expander. However, this is not the same as the Zip format used on Windows. Mac OS X does include zip and unzip command-line tools if you need to compress files to send to Windows users.

Compressing a file with gzip is easy. Use the following syntax:

```
gzip filename
```

The `gzip` command compresses the file, then, if compression is successful, deletes the original. If a problem occurs and the file can't be compressed (if you run out of disk space, for example) gzip won't delete the original file.

If I want to compress this file:

```
-rwxr-xr-x   1 kirk   staff   580640 Mar 28 16:09 Walden.txt
```

I run the following command:

```
$ gzip Walden.txt
```

Checking with `ls -l`, I see the results:

```
-rwxr-xr-x   1 kirk   staff   232522 Mar 28 16:09 Walden.txt.gz
```

As you can see, gzip compressed the file and added the `.gz` extension to the filename. You can see that the file size was reduced by more than half. To see how much the file was compressed, run the `gzip` command with the `-l` option:

```
$ gzip -l Walden.txt.gz
compressed   uncompr. ratio uncompressed_name
   232522    580640  59.9% Walden.txt
```

You can run `gzip` with several files as arguments, and the result is the same number of files in compressed versions. If you run this command:

```
$ gzip Walden.txt pepys_diary.txt
```

you end up with these two compressed files:

```
-rwxr-xr-x   1 kirk   staff   232522 Mar 28 16:09 Walden.txt.gz
-rw-r--r--   1 kirk   staff  2467675 Feb 14 22:04 pepys_diary.txt.gz
```

Note in this example that the time stamps for the two files are different, even though they were compressed at the same time: by default, gzip uses the original file's time stamp for the compressed file and maintains this time stamp when decompressing it.

Compressing several files at the same time does *not* result in a single compressed file, but if you use the `-c` (concatenate) option, you can include more than one file in an archive. However, the syntax is slightly different when using this option, because it sends the results of the command to standard output, which is, by default, Terminal. You therefore need to redirect the output into a new file:

```
$ gzip -c Walden.txt pepys_diary.txt > archive.gz
```

This file, `archive.gz`, contains the two files that were compressed. You can add files to it easily with the following syntax:

```
$ gzip -c filename >> archive.gz
```

This appends (>>) the output of the `gzip` command to the archive file (`archive.gz`), adding files to the archive.

Another way to combine several files into a single archive is to use the `tar` command (see the sidebar later in the chapter). This is more practical when you are archiving entire directories.

The `gzip` command has a wide range of options, including a choice of either faster or better compression. This is useful if you are compressing very large files and speed is more important than the final size.

HANDS ON: DECOMPRESSING ZIP ARCHIVES

As you saw earlier, the Finder offers a way to create zip archives by Control+clicking a file or folder and selecting Create Archive From *Filename*. This results in zip files that the Finder can open with a double-click.

If you ever need to decompress these archives from the command line, there are two ways to do so. The first uses the `unzip` command:

```
$ unzip archive.zip
```

The second is even easier: just use the open command:

```
$ open archive.zip
```

Since the open command is the equivalent of a double-click in the Finder, this unzips the archive immediately.

Decompressing gzip Archives with *gunzip*

Decompressing gzip archives is simple: the `gunzip` command restores files to their original form:

```
$ gunzip Walden.txt.gz
```

The `gunzip` command decompresses the resulting file to the same directory as the archive, then deletes the archive.

HANDS ON: DECOMPRESSING GZIP ARCHIVES WITH *GZIP*

While you can decompress gzip archives using `gunzip`, you can also use another command, `gzip -d`. There is no difference between the two commands.

HANDS ON: COMPRESSING FILES WITH RESOURCE FORKS

Some Macintosh files use resource forks, which contain metadata for the files. Just as when you copy files with `cp` or move them with `mv`, compressing files with any of the command-line tools presented in this chapter removes the resource forks.

There is one exception to this: StuffIt's stuff command-line tool, which is part of the StuffIt Deluxe program. The `stuff` command automatically saves resource forks if you use StuffIt compression (see the sidebar "Other Compression Commands" later in the chapter).

If you're sure that your files don't have resource forks, you don't need to worry. But it is best to test them before you discover that they don't work correctly. Try compressing a few files and decompressing them to make sure they work.

Overview of the *gzip* and *gunzip* Commands

COMMAND SYNTAX

```
gzip [option(s)] file...
gunzip [option(s)] file...
```

FINDER EQUIVALENT

The Create Archive command, in the File menu.

OVERVIEW OF OPTIONS FOR *GZIP* AND *GUNZIP*

gzip	The gzip command compresses the file(s) used as argument(s) into archives containing the .gz suffix.
-l	This tells the gzip command to list the contents of a .gz archive.
-c	This option tells the gzip command to concatenate multiple files into a single archive and sends the results to standard output. To create an archive file, these results must be redirected into a file.
-d	This option tells the gzip command to decompress a .gz archive. This is the equivalent of using gunzip.
gunzip	The gunzip command decompresses the archive(s) used as argument(s).

GETTING MORE INFORMATION

To display the manual page and learn more about gzip or gunzip, type man gzip in Terminal; the two programs share the same man page.

Compressing Files with *bzip2*

The bzip2 compression tool is becoming popular because of the level of compression it offers: this can be 10 to 20 percent better than gzip (see Table 11.1 for an example of this difference). However, not all Unix systems have bzip2 or bunzip2 installed to decompress these files. If you are planning to compress files only for your own usage, or if you are providing these files to people who have bzip2, then this may be a better solution.

You invoke bzip2 the same way as gzip:

```
bzip2 filename
```

Archives made with bzip2 have the .bz2 extension.

```
$ bzip2 Walden.txt

$ ls -l
-rwxr-xr-x  1 kirk    staff    176789 Mar 28 16:09 Walden.txt.bz2
```

The `bzip2` command uses many of the same options as `gzip`. See the `bzip2` man page for more on using these options.

Decompressing bzip2 Archives

Decompressing bzip2 archives is simple, and works just like gzip: the `bunzip2` command restores files to their original form:

```
$ bunzip2 Walden.txt.bz2
```

The `bunzip2` command decompresses the resulting file to the same directory as the archive, then deletes the archive.

HANDS ON: DECOMPRESSING BZIP2 ARCHIVES WITH *BZIP2*

While you can decompress bzip2 archives using bunzip2, you can also us the `bzip2 -d` command. There is no difference between the two commands.

ON THE COMMAND LINE

Overview of the *bzip2* and *bunzip2* Commands

COMMAND SYNTAX

```
bzip2 [option(s)] file...
bunzip2 [option(s)] file...
```

FINDER EQUIVALENT

The Create Archive command, in the File menu.

OVERVIEW OF OPTIONS FOR *BZIP2* AND *BUNZIP2*

bzip2	The `bzip2` command compresses the file(s) used as argument(s) into archives containing the `.bz2` suffix.
-d	This option tells the `bzip2` command to decompress a `.bz2` archive. This is the equivalent of using `bunzip2`.
bunzip2	The `bunzip2` command decompresses the archive(s) used as argument(s).

GETTING MORE INFORMATION

To display the manual page and learn more about `bzip2` or `bunzip2`, type `man bzip2` in Terminal; the two programs share the same man page.

While the previous compression commands (gzip and bzip2) work on single or multiple files, you can also use shell wildcards to compress files. Say you want to compress all the files in a directory. Move to that directory with cd, then run the following command:

```
$ gzip *
```

This makes individual compressed archives for each file.

If you only want to compress certain types of files, use the * wildcard with a file extension. To compress all the .tiff files in a directory, run this command:

```
$ gzip *.tiff
```

The same is true for decompressing archives. If you want to decompress all the archives in a directory, run this command:

```
$ gunzip *.gz
```

This only affects files that can be decompressed; gunzip ignores any files that it cannot process, and returns messages like this:

```
$ gunzip *
gunzip: Documents is a directory -- ignored
gunzip: Leaves_of_Grass.txt: unknown suffix -- ignored
```

In this manner, you can be sure that gunzip won't affect any files that are not compressed archives.

Creating Archives with *tar*

The tar (tape archive) command was designed, as its name suggests, to create archives on tape devices. It concatenates a group of files—a directory or directory tree—into a single file, which can then be copied or compressed. While compression commands, such as gzip and bzip2, only compress individual files (though you can use the concatenate option to add files to an archive), only tar allows you to retain a directory tree structure correctly.

Another advantage to using tar is that you can compress the resulting archive with gzip (or compress) in the same command. This saves time, and lets you save a compressed backup of an entire directory with a single command.

When using tar you must make sure to apply the correct options—this command is more complex than gzip, for example. Here's a tar command that backs up a directory in a tar archive and compresses it using gzip at the same time:

```
$ tar -czf Texts.tgz Texts
```

When run from my home directory, this command saves a tar gzip archive called Texts.tgz in the home directory. Here are the different parts of the command:

tar	The tar command.
-	The option indicator.

c	The create option. This tells tar that you are creating a new archive file. You must use one of five options: c (create a new archive), r (append to an existing archive), t (table of contents—this displays a list of the files in an existing archive), u (update—this updates new or modified files in an archive), or x (extract—this extracts files from an archive).
z	This tells tar to compress the archive with gzip.
f	This tells tar that you are specifying a filename for your archive. This must be the last option.
Texts.tgz	The name of the archive. The .tgz extension means that the archive is tarred and gzipped.
Texts	The directory being archived.

You can also use multiple directories with the tar command; this places all the directories in one archive:

```
$ tar -czf Archive.tgz Texts Files ~/Documents/Books
```

If you create a tar archive without compression, called a *tarball*, you can examine its contents using the -t (table of contents) and -v (verbose) options. Here's an example of this option:

```
$ tar -tvf texts.tar
drwxrwxrwx  2 kirk   staff         0 May  9 15:20 Texts
-rwxrwxrwx  1 kirk   staff      6148 May  9 15:20 Texts/.DS_Store
-rw-r--r--  1 kirk   staff     51249 Feb 28 16:40 Texts/CivDis.txt
-rw-r--r--  1 kirk   staff    711193 Mar 28 16:08 Texts/Leaves_of_Grass.txt
-rwxr-xr-x  1 kirk   staff   6796982 Feb 14 22:04 Texts/pepys_diary.txt
-rw-r--r--  1 kirk   staff       664 Mar 28 16:51 Texts/Song_of_Myself.txt
-rwxr-xr-x  1 kirk   staff    580640 Mar 28 16:09 Texts/Walden.txt
```

To extract files from a tar archive, use the x option. If the archive is compressed, run this command:

```
$ tar -xzf Texts.tgz
```

If the archive is compressed, run this command:

```
$ tar -xf Texts.tgz
```

The tar command decompresses or unpacks the archive and places it in the current working directory.

WARNING *If you already have a directory with the same name in the current working directory, the tar command overwrites existing files with those in the archive that have the same name. So, if you need to unpack or decompress a tar archive, use a separate directory to be safe.*

Overview of the *tar* Command

COMMAND SYNTAX

```
tar [-crtux] [option(s)] directory...
```

FINDER EQUIVALENT

No Finder equivalent.

OVERVIEW OF OPTIONS FOR *TAR*

tar [-crtux]	The tar command creates an archive (a single file) of the directory or directories used as arguments. You must use one of the following options: c (create a new archive), r (append to an existing archive), t (table of contents—this displays a list of the files in an existing archive), u (update—this updates new or modified files in an archive), or x (extract—this extracts files from an archive).
-f	This option (file) tells the tar command to create an archive in a file, as opposed to a device. You cannot create archives on tape devices currently with Mac OS X. When using this option, it must be the last option and must be followed by the name of the archive file to be created.
-v	This option (verbose) tells the tar command to display filenames as it operates.
-z	This option tells the tar command to compress the archive while creating it, using gzip. If you are extracting, listing, or verifying an archive, this option tells the tar command to first decompress it using gunzip.

GETTING MORE INFORMATION

The tar command has many options. To display the manual page and learn more about tar, type man tar in Terminal. You can also use gnutar, a GNU version of this command, which supports large files and very long filenames. See man gnutar for more on this command.

OTHER COMPRESSION COMMANDS

There are other compression commands available from the command line: the main command is compress. This command is not used very much these days, since a major computer manufacturer claimed a patent to the compression algorithm.

Another way to compress files from the command line is to use Aladdin's StuffIt command-line compression tools. If you purchase a copy of StuffIt Deluxe (http://www.stuffit.com), you can install two command-line programs: stuff and unstuff. The stuff command lets you create any of a dozen different types of archives and has a wide range of options for compression, encoding, encryption, and more. The unstuff command can decompress about two dozen different archive types, and offers several options concerning its behavior.

Managing Disk Image Archives with *hdiutil*

Another way to pack files together for archiving or for sending to other users is to use disk images. A disk image is a single file that mounts on the desktop as a virtual volume when double-clicked. Disk images can be encrypted, password protected, and/or compressed.

There are several advantages to using disk images to archive files or to send files to other users:

♦ Any Mac OS X user can open a disk image, even if it is compressed or encrypted and password protected (if they know the password). Double-clicking a disk image tells Mac OS X (actually a program called DiskImageMounter) to process the image and mount it.

♦ When you create a read-write disk image you can add or remove files from the archive easily, either from the Finder or from the command line. A disk image works exactly like any other type of volume.

♦ When you compress a disk image, users don't need any decompression tool to access the files. When Mac OS X mounts the disk image, it automatically decompresses the files.

♦ Files stored in a disk image can be copied individually. With other compression formats, you often need to decompress the entire compressed archive to access any of its contents (though some command-line or GUI tools let you extract individual files).

The easiest way to create and modify disk images is by using Disk Utility, which is located in /Applications/Utilities. This GUI tool is easy to use: you can create disk images by drag and drop. But there is also a way to access the DiskImages framework, which Disk Utility uses, from the command line. The hdiutil tool, which is an Apple command-line program, gives you access to every option and action that Disk Utility can perform. This is a complex program, with many options, but the basic tasks—creating, mounting, and unmounting disk images—are easy to accomplish.

The hdiutil program requires options for just about every action it performs. Here's an example of a command that creates a new 50MB read/write disk image on the desktop:

```
$ hdiutil create -size 50m -fs HFS+ -volname Test ~/Desktop/Test.dmg
.........................................................
Initialized /dev/rdisk3s2 as a 50 MB HFS Plus volume
/usr/bin/hdiutil: detach: "disk3s1" detached successfully.
/usr/bin/hdiutil: detach: "disk3s2" detached successfully.
/usr/bin/hdiutil: detach: "disk3" detached successfully.
```

The command returns several lines of text showing its progress.

Let's look at each of the different words in this command:

hdiutil	The name of the command.
create	This verb tells hdiutil to create a new disk image.

`-size 50m`	The `-size` option tells `hdiutil` the size of the new disk image. This can be any of the following: b, k, m, g, t, p, or e (respectively, 512-byte sectors, kilobytes, megabytes, gigabytes, terabytes, petabytes, or exabytes). If you are planning to compress the disk image, the size can be anything larger than the size required for the files you place in it. Compressing a disk image removes all empty space from the final disk image file; it gets compressed to almost nothing.
`-fs HFS+`	This tells `hdiutil` to format the disk image in HFS+ (the standard Mac OS file system). Other options are HFS, MS-DOS, or UFS.
`-volname Test`	This tells `hdiutil` to give the name "Test" to the volume. By default, if you don't add this option, volumes mounted on the desktop are called "Untitled."
`~/Desktop/Test.dmg`	This is the name of the disk image file. You should always use the `.dmg` extension, and this name can be relative or absolute.

There are many more options available for `hdiutil`. Type `man hdiutil` to see the program's man page.

ABOUT SPARSE DISK IMAGES

Sparse images are a special kind of disk image that are created at a given size, but that can grow if you add more files to them. When you create a sparse image, you set it to a logical volume size, which is the maximum size it can grow to. You can add files to the sparse image until it reaches that size, but no more.

You can create a sparse image that will grow to 50 MB using the following command:

```
$ hdiutil create -size 50m -fs HFS+ -volname Test ~/Desktop/test.sparseimage
```

You'll notice that this command differs from the first example only by the `.sparseimage` extension of the disk image's name. While there is a verb to use with `hdiutil` (`-type SPARSE`), adding the extension to the resulting disk image name is enough—this tells `hdiutil` to create a sparse image.

As you add files to a sparse image, it grows. But when you remove files, it does not shrink; to make a sparse image smaller, you must use a command like this:

```
$ hdiutil compact test.sparseimage
```

This removes any empty space from the sparse image, but if you add files to the sparse image it will grow again as necessary.

See `man hdiutil` for more on sparse images.

Mounting and Unmounting Disk Images

Once you have created the disk image, you need to mount it so you can copy files to it. You can either double-click the disk image or use this command to mount disk images:

```
$ hdiutil mount ~/Desktop/test.dmg
```

This is a simple command. You merely need to use the mount verb and add the name of the disk image as argument. The command returns information such as this:

```
/dev/disk2        Apple_partition_scheme
/dev/disk2s1      Apple_partition_map
/dev/disk2s2      Apple_HFS                    /Volumes/Test
```

This shows the different partitions in the volume. The first two are a partition scheme and partition map, which tell your computer how to read the volume, and the third one is the actual partition name. As you can see in the previous example, it is mounted at /Volumes/Test.

Once your disk image is mounted on the desktop, you can copy files to it. Again, this can be done in the Finder, with simple drag and drop, or via the command line. If you want to copy via the command line, you need to specify the volume. As you saw in the results of the hdiutil mount command, the disk image's volume is mounted in /Volumes/; here, it is /Volumes/Test.

When you are finished with the volume, you must unmount it to be able to copy or move the .dmg file. This command unmounts disk images; you must specify the path of the disk image volume:

```
$ hdiutil unmount /Volumes/Test
"disk2s2" unmounted successfully.
```

As you can see, you again use the volume name that the hdiutil mount command returned.

HANDS ON: CREATING A DISK IMAGE FROM A DIRECTORY

Apple's Disk Utility program, located in /Application/Utilities, lets you create a disk image from a folder by selecting Images ▷ New ▷ New Image From Folder. You can accomplish the same thing from the command line, in just one step, using an option to the hdiutil command.

Just run the command as follows:

```
$ hdiutil create -srcfolder Folder Folder.dmg
```

The -srcfolder option tells hdiutil to create a disk image from a folder, automatically finding the folder's size to know how big the disk image should be. Folder is the name of the source folder, and Folder.dmg is the name of the final disk image.

Note that this creates a compressed disk image, though the hdiutil man page does not specify this.

Compressing and Decompressing Disk Images

Once you have created a disk image file you can either use it as is or compress it. If you compress a disk image it becomes read-only; this means you can copy files from it but not add any to it. But the advantage of a compressed disk image file is that the decompression is automatic. You can use compressed disk images to send files to other Mac OS X users over the Internet and not worry about which compression tools they have, or even whether they know how to use them.

To create a compressed disk image, you must convert an existing disk image. Also, the disk image must not be mounted during conversion; if it is, `hdiutil` returns an error message. Use the following command to convert it to a compressed disk image (the following command should all be on one line in Terminal):

```
$ hdiutil convert -format UDZO test.dmg -o test_compressed.dmg
```

The command returns a few messages as it progresses:

```
Preparing imaging engine...
Reading DDM...
   (CRC32 $C2690752: DDM)
Reading Apple_partition_map (0)...
   (CRC32 $503FAC62: Apple_partition_map (0))
Reading Apple_HFS (1)...
............................................................
   (CRC32 $4580A89B: Apple_HFS (1))
Reading Apple_Free (2)...
............................................................
   (CRC32 $00000000: Apple_Free (2))
Terminating imaging engine...
Adding resources...
............................................................
Elapsed Time:  9.409s
 (1 task, weight 100)
File size: 7297347 bytes, Checksum: CRC32 $DD250A1C
Sectors processed: 102400, 37257 compressed
Speed: 1.9Mbytes/sec
Savings: 86.1%
created: test_compressed.dmg
```

These messages are not very useful, but if an error occurs they may help you understand its cause. In addition, the savings shown is purely theoretical; it is based on the size of the original disk image, not on the size of the files it contains. This example took a 50MB disk image, containing 17.3MB of files, and compressed it to 6.9MB. The compression process removes all the empty space, so, in this case, the actual saving was only about 40 percent.

When you mount a compressed disk image, Mac OS X decompresses it automatically. This means that a large disk image may take a while to mount, but when it does its files are all uncompressed. You can copy them to another location with no further processing.

If you want to convert a compressed disk image to a normal read/write disk image, you can do so with the following command:

```
$ hdiutil convert -format UDRW test_compressed.dmg -o test.dmg
```

This creates a read/write disk image that is the size of the original uncompressed disk image.

Overview of the *hdiutil* Command

COMMAND SYNTAX

```
hdiutil verb [options]
```

FINDER EQUIVALENT

The Disk Utility program.

OVERVIEW OF OPTIONS FOR *HDIUTIL*

hdiutil	The hdiutil command uses the DiskImages framework to create and manipulate disk image files. Different *verbs* tell the command to carry out different tasks.
create	This verb tells the hdiutil command to create a disk image. Several options are available to specify how the image is to be created.
-size	When used with the create verb, this option specifies the size of the disk image being created. It must begin with a number and be followed by b, k, m, g, t, p, or e (respectively, 512-byte sectors, kilobytes, megabytes, gigabytes, terabytes, petabytes or exabytes). Example: -size 50m tells hdiutil to create a 50MB disk image.
-fs	This option (file system) tells hdiutil to create a disk image with the specified type of file system. You can use HFS+ (the standard Mac OS file system), HFS, MS-DOS, or UFS.
-volname [name]	This option tells the hdiutil command to name the resulting disk image volume using the name specified as an argument.
-srcfolder [name]	This option tells the hdiutil command to create a disk image from a specified source folder.
mount [name]	This verb tells the hdiutil command to mount a disk image.
unmount [path]	This verb tells the hdiutil command to unmount a disk image.
convert [source] [destination]	This verb tells the hdiutil command to convert a disk image. There are several conversion formats available, such as compressed, encrypted, read-only, and read/write.
-format	When used with the convert verb, this option specifies the format of the disk image being converted. See the hdiutil man page for a list of formats.
internet-enable -yes [path]	This tells the hdiutil command to create an Internet-enabled disk image from the source disk image file specified as argument.

Continued on next page

Overview of the *hdiutil* Command *(continued)*

`internet-enable -no [path]`	This tells the `hdiutil` command to create a normal disk image file from an Internet-enabled disk image using the source disk image file specified as argument.
`internet-enable -query [path]`	This tells the `hdiutil` command to check the Internet-enabled status of a disk image file specified as argument. It returns `enabled` if the disk image file is Internet-enabled or `disabled` if not.

GETTING MORE INFORMATION

The `hdiutil` command has many options. To display the manual page and learn more about `hdiutil`, type `man hdiutil` in Terminal.

HANDS ON: CREATING INTERNET-ENABLED DISK IMAGES

There is a special kind of disk image, called an "Internet-enabled" disk image, that works somewhat like a self-extracting archive. When a user double-clicks these disk images, they automatically convert themselves into their contents, cleaning up after themselves and leaving nothing else behind. The original disk image is deleted and all the user sees is its contents, which may be a file, folder, or installation package. Apple designed Internet-enabled disk images for distributing software over the Internet, providing users with a simple way to download software and not get confused by the type of file they find on their computers.

The only way you can create an Internet-enabled disk image is from the command line. To do this, first create a disk image either as explained earlier or by using Disk Utility. (You can only convert read-only disk image files into Internet-enabled disk images. You cannot convert read-write disk images, nor can you convert older `.img` and `.smi` files.) Then run the following command:

```
$ hdiutil internet-enable -yes image.dmg
```

If the operation is successful, Terminal displays the following:

```
hdiutil: internet-enable: enable succeeded.
```

Now, check your disk image by double-clicking it in the Finder. If the conversion worked correctly, Disk Utility will change the disk image file into the files it contains, and move the original disk image file to the Trash (but this original file is no longer Internet-enabled, so you cannot remove it from the Trash and reuse it).

To convert an Internet-enabled disk image file to a normal disk image file, run this command:

```
$ hdiutil internet-enable -no image.dmg
```

And to check whether a disk image is Internet-enabled, use this command:

```
$ hdiutil internet-enable -query image.dmg
```

This is the only way to find out if a disk image file is Internet-enabled; there is no way to tell from the Finder.

Summing Up

Compressing files is useful for sending them over the Internet, providing them on FTP servers, or for backing up your data: the amount of disk space saved can be very large. The command-line tools included with Mac OS X make compression and decompression easy, but you must be careful not to use them on files with resource forks. You can use a command-line tool to create and manipulate disk images, using them for archives or to send files to other users.

Chapter 12

Working with Users, Groups, and Permissions

As you have surely discovered, Mac OS X is a multiuser operating system. While you could work without noticing this—when you install Mac OS X you create one user, and if you have no need for other user accounts you will never have to create any others—the underlying structure remains. In fact, even if you create only one user, your Mac has other user accounts that you never see.

Mac OS X offers simple graphical tools for creating, editing, managing, and deleting user accounts, and these are certainly easy to use and efficient. In fact, it is likely that you will never need to use the command line to manage user accounts, but the possibility exists, and, as with many other functions of Mac OS X, it can be useful to know how to do so in case other parts of your system do not work correctly.

In this chapter, I'll explain what user accounts are and how they work, what groups are, and what it means to belong to different groups. I'll show you the commands that give you information about users and groups and let you create and modify them. I'll also tell you about permissions, one of the key concepts of any multiuser operating system, and how they affect you and your files.

About Users

Unix systems were originally designed to accommodate users who were in different physical locations. A central system was used with users logging in from terminals, which could be in the same room, the same building, or a different country. Because of this, Unix systems were designed from the start as multiuser operating systems. What good would it be to offer first-come first-served access, when many users needed to run jobs and access files?

Not only can different users access a Unix computer, but they can do so simultaneously. In fact, when users begin remote sessions with a Unix system they don't see any difference between the way the computer reacts when they are alone and when one hundred other users are working at the same time (though system response may be slower). Sure, they know that other users have accounts, but they don't see these users.

The use of home folders or directories is one way of segregating users' files. On Mac OS X, your home folder contains several subfolders designed to hold specific types of files. You are not required to use these folders, nor are you required to use your home folder for anything other than preference files and other application support files—you can very well store your personal files in another folder or on another volume—but the existence of this home folder helps you understand the way the Mac is structured. (See Chapter 4, "Navigating the File System," for a description of the Mac OS X file system.)

Macintosh computers have offered multiple user functions for many years, through the Multiple Users and File Sharing control panels in previous versions of the Mac OS. But this implementation of multiple users was not an integral part of the system; it was a layer added on top of the basic Mac OS to allow file sharing.

In Mac OS X, every file belongs to a user. Unix systems use special information for all these files to record which user owns the files, which group the files belong to, and who can have access to the files. (For more on permissions, see the section "About Permissions" later in this chapter.)

While much of Mac OS X is based on the FreeBSD Unix operating system, its user and group management system is a heritage from NeXTStep, the operating system used for NeXT computers. This is a bit of a shame, since proven tools for managing users and groups exist in the Unix world, and the NetInfo system, used with Mac OS X, can be confusing.

User Account Types

Mac OS X offers three types of user accounts: normal user accounts, administrator accounts, and the root user. Each Mac OS X computer has at least one account, and there must be at least one administrator account. Other accounts can be either normal user accounts or administrators. The root user is a special user that has privileges to do anything and access all the files on your computer.

Normal user accounts have limited rights: these users can access the files in their home directories or folders, read files at the top level of any user's home directory, read and copy files from any user's Public folder, and add files to any user's Drop Box (located inside their Public folder). Normal users cannot access any other files, cannot change certain preferences that affect the entire computer, and cannot install software on their computer that is to be made available to all users. Some programs are off-limits to normal users: they cannot run Disk Utility or NetInfo Manager. Normal users generally cannot run the sudo (**substitute-user do**) command on the command line, unless an administrator grants them specific rights in the /etc/sudoers file. (See Interlude 7, "Using sudo," for more on sudo and the /etc/sudoers file.)

WHAT ARE ALL THESE TYPES OF ACCOUNTS?

I said that there are three types of user accounts: normal, administrator, and root. But this is not exactly true. If you look at the Accounts pane of your System Preferences, you may see other account types: managed and simplified. These two types of accounts are special types of normal accounts. A managed account is a normal account with limitations, and a simplified account is a normal account where the limitations are set so the user can only access a simple Finder. But other than these limitations, these two types of accounts are really just normal accounts with some extra blinders.

Administrators have greater rights. They can install software for all users and set all preferences, run programs such as Disk Utility and NetInfo Manager, create, edit, and delete user accounts, and, using sudo, run any command under Mac OS X. In fact, administrators can, after authenticating, access *any* file on a Mac running OS X.

Administrators can also limit normal users' access to their Macs using the Limitations tab in the Accounts preference pane. They can prevent users from changing their password, removing items from the Dock, and accessing the System Preferences, and can limit their use of applications and set certain user accounts to use a simple Finder.

The root user is a special user that exists on every Mac running OS X. This is the über-user who can do anything, access anyone's files, and run any command. It's not a good thing to log in as the root user, since any mistake can have disastrous effects. Under Mac OS X, the sudo command allows you to run any command as root, but prevents you from making mistakes when working in the GUI interface; if you log in as root, you won't get any warnings when changing or deleting key files.

If you want to be able to log in as root, you must first enable the root user. To do this, open NetInfo Manager, found in /Applications/Utilities. Click the lock and enter an administrator's user name and password. From the Security menu, select Enable Root User. If you haven't set a password for the root user, you'll see an alert saying "NetInfo Error," indicating that the password is blank. Click OK.

Enter a password for the root user, then click Set. Enter the password again to verify it and click Verify. The root user is now enabled. Note that enabling the root user can be a security risk, and is generally considered dangerous. Don't do this unless you really need to.

You can log in as root by clicking the Other button on the login screen and entering "root" as the user name, and the root password as the password. Do be careful, though; if you make any mistakes moving or deleting any files, or changing the settings in certain files, your Mac may become unusable.

Creating User Accounts

The principal way to create new users under Mac OS X is to use the Accounts pane of the System Preferences. You can access the System Preferences from the Apple menu; click the Accounts icon to access this preference pane. (See Figure 12.1.)

Creating a new user from the System Preferences is simple: the + button creates a new, blank user and displays the same screen as in Figure 12.1, but with all fields blank. You then enter the necessary information. This is the safest way to create new users, since you don't have to interact directly with the NetInfo database.

Another way to create users is through the NetInfo Manager. This program, found in /Applications/ Utilities/, is an interface to the NetInfo database. You can create new users through the NetInfo Manager, but you must be *very careful*—if you write incorrect information in your NetInfo database, you'll have difficulties ranging from problems using your Mac to an inability to start it up at all. Don't use this command if you're not sure of what you're typing.

FIGURE 12.1
The Accounts pane in the System Preferences shows all current user accounts.

Creating User Accounts from the Command Line

A third way of creating new users is via the command line. This should be your last resort—you should use the System Preferences to create users if possible, and only use the command line if you cannot access the GUI of a Mac.

There are many steps required to create a new user from the command line. This uses the `niload` (NetInfo **load**) command together with a few other commands to create the new user's account and all necessary settings. Here is how to do it, creating a new user named Ralph Waldo Emerson, with a short name of emerson.

First, you need to run a command to populate the NetInfo database with the appropriate information for a user account. The following command uses the `niload` command to load information directly into NetInfo. It uses the format of a standard `passwd` file, which is that of a series of fields separated by colons (this command must all be on one line):

```
$ echo 'emerson::512:512::0:0:Ralph Waldo Emerson:/Users/emerson:/bin/bash'
  | sudo niload -v passwd /
```

The shell asks for your password, since the second part of the command contains the `sudo` command, then displays information regarding the additions it has made to the NetInfo database:

```
1 items read from input
Netinfo /users contains 22 items

Processing input item:
_writers_passwd: emerson
change: 0
class:
```

```
expire: 0
gid: 512
home: /Users/emerson
name: test3
passwd:
realname: Ralph Waldo Emerson
shell: /bin/bash
uid: 512
```

```
writing new directory /users/emerson
```

Let's look at the different information you need to enter in the command shown in the example. Each "field" is a bit of text separated by colons. The command contains ten fields:

```
1:2:3:4:5:6:7:8:9:10
emerson::512:512::0:0:Ralph Waldo Emerson:/Users/emerson:/bin/bash
```

- ◆ Field 1: The user's short name—in this case, emerson.

- ◆ Field 2: The user's password; we'll set this later with another command.

- ◆ Field 3: The user ID number. See the sidebar "Choosing a User ID" later in the chapter for more on this.

- ◆ Field 4: The group ID number. For Panther, this is the same as the user ID number; for Jaguar, use 20 to put the user in the staff group.

- ◆ Field 5: A comment field; you don't need to enter anything here.

- ◆ Field 6: The user's class; not used by NetInfo.

- ◆ Field 7: The user's password change time; not used by NetInfo.

- ◆ Field 8: The user's full name.

- ◆ Field 9: The user's home directory path.

- ◆ Field 10: The user's default shell.

Next, you need to set the user's password. Run this command, then enter the password twice:

```
$ sudo passwd emerson
Changing password for emerson.
New password:
Retype new password:
```

Finally, you need to create a group for the user; Panther uses individual groups for each user, which have the same GID as the user's UID:

```
$ echo 'emerson:*:512:emerson' | sudo niload -v group /
```

HANDS ON: BACKING UP AND RESTORING YOUR NETINFO DATABASE

As I mentioned previously, the NetInfo database is a delicate file. Any mistakes in this database can have disastrous consequences. If you are planning to make any changes to this database—either with NetInfo Manager or from the command line—you should first back up the database just in case. In fact, it's a good idea to back it up regularly anyway.

The easiest way to back up your NetInfo database is by running the periodic daily command. (See Chapter 15, "System Maintenance from the Command Line," for more on the periodic command.) Unless your Mac is on 24 hours a day, this command does not get executed; the periodic daily command is set to run at 3:15 a.m. every day.

```
$ sudo periodic daily
```

This saves a backup of your NetInfo database to /var/backups and names it local.nidump. However, if the database was corrupted before periodic ran, then you'll be out of luck.

You can also back it up manually—if you often make changes to it, this might be the best choice. Your Net-Info database is this directory: /private/var/db/netinfo/local.nidb. Backing it up is as simple as just making a copy of it. Move to the /private/var/db/netinfo/ directory with cd, then copy the file with a new name:

```
$ cd /private/var/db/netinfo/
$ sudo cp -R local.nidb local.nidb.backup
```

If you back up this file regularly, you can number your backups such as .backup1, .backup2, etc. or you can add a date to them: .backup6_05.

Restoring your backup is a bit more complex. You first need to boot into single-user mode. To do this, start up your Mac while pressing ⌘-S until you see a black screen with text.

It is recommended that you run a file system check whenever you boot into single-user mode. Run this command (note that single-user mode assumes a U.S. English keyboard layout; if you are used to working with a different layout, you'll need to figure out which keys are which):

```
# /sbin/fsck -fy
```

(Note: This command assumes that your startup volume has journaling turned on. If this is not the case, use /sbin/fsck -y.)

After this has completed, run the following command to mount your file system:

```
# /sbin/mount -uw /
```

If you are restoring a NetInfo database backed up by the periodic command, use the following procedure;

first, run these commands:

```
# cd /var/db/netinfo
# mv local.nidb local.nidb.bad
# /usr/libexec/create_nidb
```

Continued on next page

HANDS ON: BACKING UP AND RESTORING YOUR NETINFO DATABASE *(continued)*

This makes a copy of your damaged NetInfo database. Then run these commands to load the database backed up by the periodic command:

```
# /usr/libexec/kextd
# /usr/sbin/configd
# /sbin/SystemStarter
# /usr/bin/niload -d -r -t / localhost/local < /var/backups/local.nidump
```

Then restart your Mac:

```
# reboot
```

If you are restoring a NetInfo database backed up manually, use the following procedure;

first, run these commands:

```
# cd /var/db/netinfo
# mv local.nidb local.nidb.bad
# mv local.nidb.backup local.nidb
```

In the third command, substitute the name of your backup for the first argument. Then restart your Mac:

```
# reboot
```

If nothing else works, you can restore from defaults.

If you have to get to this point, you either didn't back up your NetInfo database or your backup was corrupted. Running these commands tells your Mac to rebuild the database using default information—you'll need to reenter your user account info and start over.

```
# cd /var/db/netinfo
# mv local.nidb local.nidb.bad
# rm /var/db/.AppleSetupDone
# reboot
```

After rebooting, the Setup Assistant displays, just like when your Mac was brand new. Make sure to enter the same short user name in this assistant so you can recover access to your home directory and your files. You'll then need to recreate any user accounts you had before, and you'll need to reset a bunch of system preferences.

If, however, you still have problems after this procedure, your NetInfo database was not the cause and you can rename the .bad database to restore it when you find out what the problem was.

This command creates the group named "emerson," gives it the GID of 512, and adds emerson to the group, all in one step. (Don't run this command if you're using Jaguar.)

Finally, you may want to make the user a member of the admin group so they have administrative access. Run this command to add the user to the admin group:

```
$ sudo niutil -appendprop / /groups/admin users emerson
```

If you do this, your new user is an administrator and has all administrative rights. You can always change this later in the Accounts preference pane.

CHOOSING A USER ID

In the commands shown earlier, you create a user and give that user a user ID. But you must first make sure that this user ID has not already been given to another user. There are several ways to find which user IDs have been given; one way is to run the `nireport` command as follows:

```
$ nireport . /users name uid
nobody   -2
root     0
daemon   1
unknown  99
smmsp    25
lp       26
postfix  27
www      70
eppc     71
mysql    74
sshd     75
qtss     76
cyrus    77
mailman  78
appserver       79
perceval        503
mariefrance     504
henrydthoreau   506
samuelpepys     505
kirk     501
jsbach   507
```

This command returns a list of all users on your Mac. As you can see, the user IDs 501 and 503–507 have been used. You can therefore give Ralph Waldo Emerson the user ID 512, as in the example earlier.

At this point you have created the user account. You can check in the Accounts preference pane (Figure 12.2) to see whether the user has been created. (If the System Preferences are open, quit the application first, then relaunch it to see the new user.)

However, even though the account has been created, the new user does not yet have a home directory. All you need to do is log in under the user's account, and the system creates the actual home directory at first login. This directory is created from a directory template found in `/System/Library/User Template`.

Deleting User Accounts

While the easiest way to delete user accounts is through the Accounts preference pane, you can do this task from the command line:

```
$ sudo niutil -destroy . /Users/emerson
```

FIGURE 12.2
The new account created for Ralph Waldo Emerson appears in the Accounts preference pane.

This deletes the information about the user account in the NetInfo database, but it does not delete the user's home directory. When you delete a user through the Accounts preference pane, this creates a disk image of the user's home directory and places it in a `Deleted Users` directory in the `/Users` directory. But when running this command, you need to delete the user's home directory manually:

```
$ sudo rm -rf /Users/emerson
```

Make sure you enter the right user name. You can add the `-i` (interactive) option if you want as protection (see Chapter 5, "Moving, Copying, and Deleting Files and Folders," for more on running the `rm` command with the `-i` option), but you will then have to approve the deletion of each file, one by one.

HANDS ON: CHANGING THE SHORT USERNAME

Let's say you've got a user account, created using either the Accounts preference pane or the command line, and for some reason you want to change the short username. You might find it too long (when you create an account from the Accounts preference pane, the default short username is actually your first name and last name, which can be pretty long), or you just don't like it.

Changing the short username is not simple; you can't do it from the Accounts preference pane, and, while you can do it from the command line, it's a complex and risky process.

If you want to do this, check out a great script (a combination of a shell script and AppleScript Studio applet) that can do it for you easily. Dan Frakes, author of the great *Mac OS X Power Tools* book (2nd ed., Sybex, 2004) and James Bucanek, the technical editor for this book, wrote the script, and you can find it at http://www.macosxpowertools.com/. Look for ChangeShortName and follow the instructions carefully.

ON THE COMMAND LINE

Overview of the *niload* Command

COMMAND SYNTAX

```
niload verb [option(s)] domain
```

FINDER EQUIVALENT

Accounts preference pane for user account creation; NetInfo Manager for other tasks.

OVERVIEW OF OPTIONS FOR *NIUTIL*

niload   The niload command loads text or flat file format data into the NetInfo database.

GETTING MORE INFORMATION

To display the manual page and learn more about niload, type man niload in Terminal.

DIFFERENCES BETWEEN MAC OS X AND OTHER UNIX SYSTEMS

While much of Mac OS X is based on a FreeBSD Unix system, there are some important differences, one of which is the way user accounts are managed. In most Unix systems, accounts are managed via the /etc/passwd file. This is much simpler than the NetInfo database approach used by Mac OS X.

Mac OS X does have an /etc/passwd file, but this file is only used when you start up your computer in single-user mode (pressing ⌘-S at startup). The file contains an explanation:

```
$ cat /etc/passwd
##
# User Database
#
# Note that this file is consulted when the system is running in
# single-user mode.
# At other times this information is handled by one or more of:
# lookupd DirectoryServices
# By default, lookupd gets information from NetInfo, so this file will
# not be consulted unless you have changed lookupd's configuration.
# This file is used while in single user mode.
#
# To use this file for normal authentication, you may enable it with
# /Applications/Utilities/Directory Access.
##
nobody:*:-2:-2:Unprivileged User:/:/usr/bin/false
root:*:0:0:System Administrator:/var/root:/bin/sh
daemon:*:1:1:System Services:/var/root:/usr/bin/false
smmsp:*:25:25:Sendmail User:/private/etc/mail:/usr/bin/false
lp:*:26:26:Printing Services:/var/spool/cups:/usr/bin/false
```

Continued on next page

DIFFERENCES BETWEEN MAC OS X AND OTHER UNIX SYSTEMS *(continued)*

```
postfix:*:27:27:Postfix User:/var/spool/postfix:/usr/bin/false
www:*:70:70:World Wide Web Server:/Library/WebServer:/usr/bin/false
eppc:*:71:71:Apple Events User:/var/empty:/usr/bin/false
mysql:*:74:74:MySQL Server:/var/empty:/usr/bin/false
sshd:*:75:75:sshd Privilege separation:/var/empty:/usr/bin/false
qtss:*:76:76:QuickTime Streaming Server:/var/empty:/usr/bin/false
cyrus:*:77:6:Cyrus User:/var/imap:/usr/bin/false
mailman:*:78:78:Mailman user:/var/empty:/usr/bin/false
appserver:*:79:79:Application Server:/var/empty:/usr/bin/false
unknown:*:99:99:Unknown User:/var/empty:/usr/bin/false
```

As you can see, this file only contains information for a few system users. If you start up in single-user mode you cannot log in as any user whose account you have created.

HANDS ON: FINDING WHICH USERS ARE LOGGED IN

There are a few commands you can use to find which users are currently logged in to your Mac. These commands each show you the same thing in different ways, offering different amounts of information.

The simplest such command is users. It returns a line showing the current users separated by spaces:

```
$ users
emerson henrydth jsbach kirk
```

The who command tells you a bit more, showing the user names, which device they are connected on, and when they logged in:

```
$ who
kirk       console  Jun 10 15:37
kirk       ttyp1    Jun 10 19:33
henrydth   ttyp2    Jun 11 09:23
emerson    ttyp3    Jun 11 09:24
jsbach     ttyp4    Jun 11 09:30  (10.0.1.201)
```

Finally, the w command shows you the most information. It displays a summary of the current activity on the system, including what each user is doing if they are running jobs with Terminal. It also shows, in the first line, CPU load averages over 1, 5, and 15 minutes.

```
$ w
 9:30AM  up 17:55, 5 users, load averages: 0.65, 0.81, 0.73
USER     TTY FROM              LOGIN@  IDLE WHAT
kirk     co  -                Tue03PM 17:54 -
kirk     p1  -                Tue07PM     0 -
henrydth p2  -                 9:23AM     0 -
emerson  p3  -                 9:24AM     0 -
jsbach   p4 10.0.1.201         9:30AM     0 -
```

In addition, the who and w commands show you where users are logged in from, if they are working in remote sessions (here, 10.0.1.201 in both cases for user jsbach).

About Groups

On a multiuser operating system, user accounts allow you to segregate and protect the files belonging to each user, and groups allow you to share files among different users. File permissions (see later in this chapter) are applied to all files at three levels: for the files' owner, their group, and others.

By default, Mac OS X gives read-only privileges to the group that a file's owner belongs to, but these users can only access files that do not belong to them if these files are in directories they have permissions for. A user cannot enter another user's Documents folder, so any files it contains are off-limits, even if this user has read privileges for the files.

If you want to share files among a group, you have two options: use the Shared directory, located in the /Users directory, or create other directories at another location in the file system (you could create other directories in the /Users directory as well) or on other volumes. Say your hard disk has two partitions, a startup partition and a partition for files. This latter partition can be shared so your group can have access to its contents. To ensure that all of the correct users have this access, they must be in the same group.

To find out which groups a given user belongs to, run the groups command followed by a user name:

```
$ groups kirk
staff wheel admin
```

You can get more information with the id command, which returns both the user's ID and the names and IDs of the groups they belong to:

```
$ id kirk
uid=501(kirk) gid=20(staff) groups=20(staff) 0(wheel) 80(admin)
```

ON THE COMMAND LINE

Overview of the *groups* Command

COMMAND SYNTAX

```
groups [user]
```

FINDER EQUIVALENT

NetInfo Manager.

OVERVIEW OF OPTIONS FOR *GROUPS*

groups   The groups command returns a list of groups that the user, specified as argument, belongs to.

GETTING MORE INFORMATION

To display the manual page and learn more about groups, type man groups in Terminal.

Overview of the *id* Command

COMMAND SYNTAX

```
id [option(s)] [user]
```

FINDER EQUIVALENT

NetInfo Manager.

OVERVIEW OF OPTIONS FOR *ID*

id The id command returns a list of groups and group IDs that the user, specified as argument, belongs to.

GETTING MORE INFORMATION

To display the manual page and learn more about id, type man id in Terminal.

The default group for normal users under Mac OS X is "staff." In these examples, you can see that user kirk is a member of three groups: staff, wheel, and admin. To share files with other members of the staff group, you need simply ensure that this group has full privileges to the files in the Files partition. (See later in this chapter to learn how to set permissions from the command line.) But if you want to limit the users who can access these files, you can create a new group and add the users you want to this group.

Creating Groups

Unlike for user accounts, there is no way to create groups from the System Preferences. Apple obviously considers this a task that is beyond normal usage of Mac OS X. (Actually, they're right; it's something you do when administering a server, and Mac OS X, while it can function as a server, is not designed to be one. That's why they sell Mac OS X Server software.) You can create groups using NetInfo Manager, but you can also easily create groups from the command line. (Note: The same warning applies that I gave earlier about creating users and the risk this entails. Back up your NetInfo database to be safe.)

First, you want to find out which group IDs have been used. As with user IDs, which I presented earlier, you need to make sure that the group ID you give to a new group is not already applied to an existing group.

To see a list of groups and their IDs, run the following:

```
$ nireport . /groups name gid
nobody  -2
nogroup -1
wheel    0
daemon   1
```

```
kmem      2
sys       3
tty       4
operator        5
mail      6
bin       7
staff     20
smmsp     25
lp        26
postfix 27
postdrop        28
guest     31
utmp      45
uucp      66
dialer    68
network 69
www       70
mysql     74
sshd      75
qtss      76
mailman 78
appserverusr    79
admin     80
appserveradm    81
unknown 99
special 327
```

You can see all the groups and their IDs in the list that this displays. Another command shows you groups, their IDs, and the members of the groups:

```
$ nidump group .
nobody:*:-2:
nogroup:*:-1:
wheel:*:0:root,kirk
daemon:*:1:root
kmem:*:2:root
sys:*:3:root
tty:*:4:root
operator:*:5:root
mail:*:6:
bin:*:7:
staff:*:20:root
smmsp:*:25:
lp:*:26:
postfix:*:27:
postdrop:*:28:
guest:*:31:root
utmp:*:45:
```

```
uucp:*:66:
dialer:*:68:
network:*:69:
www:*:70:
mysql:*:74:
sshd:*:75:
qtss:*:76:
mailman:*:78:
appserverusr:*:79:
admin:*:80:root,kirk,samuelpepys,emerson
appserveradm:*:81:
unknown:*:99:
special:*:327:root,jsbach
```

This information is a bit incomplete. You saw earlier that group 20, the staff group, is the "normal" users' group. This command shows only root as a member of this group, even though all my normal users are in the group.

It may be practical to use group IDs in a certain range when you create groups, so you can remember that they are indeed groups you created rather than groups Mac OS X or other programs create. For this example, let's use group ID 499. Here's how to create a group called "concordians" with group ID 499:

```
$ sudo niutil -create / /groups/concordians
$ sudo niutil -createprop / /groups/concordians gid 499
$ sudo niutil -createprop . /groups/concordians passwd '*'
```

The first line creates the group; the second applies a group ID to the group; and the third line sets a null password for the group.

ON THE COMMAND LINE

Overview of the *nireport* Command

COMMAND SYNTAX

```
nireport [ -t ] domain directory [ property ...]
```

FINDER EQUIVALENT

NetInfo Manager.

OVERVIEW OF OPTIONS FOR *NIREPORT*

nireport   The nireport command returns information from the NetInfo database.

GETTING MORE INFORMATION

To display the manual page and learn more about nireport, type man nireport in Terminal.

ON THE COMMAND LINE

Overview of the *nidump* Command

COMMAND SYNTAX

```
nidump [-t ] {-r directory | format } domain
```

FINDER EQUIVALENT

NetInfo Manager.

OVERVIEW OF OPTIONS FOR *NIDUMP*

nidump   The nidump command returns information from the NetInfo database.

GETTING MORE INFORMATION

To display the manual page and learn more about nidump, type man nidump in Terminal.

Adding Users to a Group

Once you have created a group, you'll want to be able to add users to it. Here's how to add two users to the new group that I created in the previous example:

```
$ sudo niutil -appendprop / /groups/concordians users emerson
$ sudo niutil -appendprop / /groups/concordians users henrydthoreau
```

You can check to see that these changes were made by running the groups command as follows:

```
$ groups henrydthoreau
staff concordians
$ groups emerson
staff concordians
```

Henry David Thoreau and Ralph Waldo Emerson are now members of the "concordians" group.

Removing Users from a Group

To remove a user from a group and no longer allow them to access the files that the given group has permissions for, use the niutil command in this way:

```
$ sudo niutil -destroyval . /groups/concordians users emerson
```

The user emerson will no longer have access to any files that have permissions for the transcendentalists group that belong to other users. He will, however, still have access to all the files that belong to him, even those that have permissions for the transcendentalists group.

Deleting Groups

If you want to delete a group, run the `niutil` command as follows:

```
$ sudo niutil -destroy . /groups/concordians
```

This removes the group from the NetInfo database. If you have set permissions for any files to allow this group access, the files then belong to no group at all (since the group no longer exists). However, if you create a new group with the same GID, this group will have access to files that were previously owned by the group with the same GID, regardless of the new group's name. You'll need to change permissions manually for all the files to allow another group to access them.

About Permissions

As I mentioned earlier in this chapter, Mac OS X is a multiuser operating system; one advantage of this is the ability to segregate files, allowing certain users access to files and preventing others from viewing, reading, copying, or changing them. The mechanism used to provide and block access is that of *permissions* (or *privileges*), which tell the operating system that a given file belongs to a specific user, and also tell which other users can access the file and what kind of access they can have.

You see the permissions for files when running the `ls -l` command:

```
$ ls -l
total 1136
drwxrwxrwt   8 root      wheel       272   6 May 16:57 Shared
-rwxrwxr--   1 kirk      admin    580640  19 May 13:24 Walden.txt
drwxr-xr-x  11 emerson   staff       374  27 Sep  2003 emerson
drwxr-xr-x  16 henrydth  staff       544  19 May 15:36 henrydthoreau
drwxr-xr-x  12 jsbach    staff       408  29 Jul  2003 jsbach
drwxr-xr-x  36 kirk      staff      1224  24 May 16:28 kirk
drwxr-xr-x  15 mariefra  staff       510   6 Mar 15:30 mariefrance
drwxr-xr-x  13 perceval  staff       442   7 Feb 11:39 perceval
drwxr-xr-x  12 samuelpe  staff       408  29 Jul  2003 samuelpepys
```

The first column in the listing is the permissions column. This combination of letters and dashes tells the operating system who can do what to each file, directory, or application.

HANDS ON: SOLVING PERMISSION PROBLEMS

While permissions are essential for any Unix-based operating system, they can lead to problems. Users may change permissions for certain files, denying you access or preventing you from running certain programs, because support files are not available. Or permissions can get corrupted if you have disk problems; after all, permission settings each represent just a few bytes, and if one or more bytes gets written incorrectly it can change the access you have to files or directories.

It's pretty difficult to find out whether faulty permissions are the cause of your problems. If you try to open a specific file and you get an alert in the Finder, telling you "You do not have sufficient access privileges," or if Terminal tells you Permission denied, then the cause is clear. If you think you should have access to the files or directories in question, try examining their permissions and change them if necessary, making sure not to block any other users. If you do not have an administrator account, check with someone who does.

Other permission problems are more difficult to detect. If you cannot open or run a program or application, there may be a permission problem. For graphical applications that depend on dozens or even hundreds of files, you may not be able to find out if the permissions for one file are incorrect. The best way to resolve that kind of problem is to reinstall the application.

At the system level, permissions can be problematic as well, and for this reason Apple includes a Repair Disk Permissions tool in the Disk Utility program. Open this program, which is found in /Applications/ Utilities, click the First Aid tab, then click your startup volume in the left-hand column to select it. Click the Repair Disk Permissions button to repair permissions. This checks all the system files on your startup volume and compares them to a permissions database, correcting any permissions that diverge from this database. Curiously, no matter how often you repair permissions, the program always finds something to fix. It displays information like this as it makes changes:

```
User differs on ./private/var/db/locate.database,
    should be 0, owner is -2
Permissions differ on ./private/var/db/locate.database,
    should be -rw-r--r-- , they are -r--r--r--
Owner and group corrected on ./private/var/db/locate.database
Permissions corrected on ./private/var/db/locate.database
```

Naturally, there is a command-line equivalent for the Repair Disk Permissions tool. Run this command:

```
$ sudo diskutil repairPermissions /
```

Many people run this tool regularly, at least after every system update, and even more often. It can solve many unexplained system problems and should be a part of any regular maintenance routine.

If you're curious about the erroneous and harmless error messages you see when repairing permissions, or wonder why certain permissions get repaired every time you do this, check this Apple technical note: http://docs.info.apple.com/article.html?artnum=106712. It covers many of these issues.

Let's look closely at one line of the example:

```
-rwxrwxr--   1 kirk     admin  580640 19 May 13:24 Walden.txt
```

This file, `Walden.txt`, belongs to user `kirk` and group `staff`. Its permissions are:

```
-rwxrwx---
```

These 10 characters can be broken down as in Figure 12.3.

FIGURE 12.3

The permission bits of a file and what they represent.

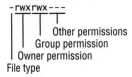

These 10 characters are read in four groups: first the file type, then the permissions for the owner of the file, the group, and others. The different letters in the permissions list represent the following:

r   read permission

w   write permission

x   execute permission

File Types

There are several types of files on a Unix system, but you'll usually only encounter two: files and directories. Files are indicated by a - (dash) in the file type character and directories by a d.

```
drwxr-xr-x  8 kirk  staff    272 24 Feb 16:15 Sites
-rwxrwx---  1 kirk  staff 580640 19 May 13:24 Walden.txt
```

In this listing, the first line is a directory and the second a file.
But what about something like this:

```
-r-xr-xr-x  1 root  wheel  348068 16 Mar 12:56 /bin/tcsh
```

This is the `tcsh` shell; it shows as a file. Well, in a Unix system, even executables, or applications, are files, and are differentiated only by the executable bit (the x that appears three times in the permissions for `tcsh`) and the code they contain. While text files can have executable bits:

```
-rwxrwx---   1 kirk   staff  580640 19 May 13:24 Walden.txt
```

they contain no code, and cannot be run. In fact, the executable bit means something different for files.
Table 12.1 shows the different types of files you may find on a Unix system.
You won't often see anything other than d, l, or -.

TABLE 12.1: FILE TYPE INDICATORS

LETTER	FILE TYPE
d	Directory
b	Block-type special file
c	Character-type special file
l	Symbolic link
p	Pipe
s	Socket
–	File

What File Permissions Mean

There are three types of file permissions: read, write, and execute. Here's a brief explanation of what these three types of permissions allow or prohibit:

Read Permission   When you have read permission for a **file**, you are allowed to view the file or open it in an application. You can also copy a file if you have read permission. If you have read permission for a file but not write permission, you can copy the file to a directory you own, and this process gives you ownership. You can then write to the file, make changes, or delete it. If it is a **directory**, you can *enter* the directory and list the files it contains, as well as copy files *from* it if you have read permissions for those files. If it is an **application**, you can read it, and therefore run the application.

Write Permission   When you have write permission for a **file**, you can make changes to it and save it. If it is a **directory**, you can copy files *to* it and delete and rename files it contains. You can also change the permissions of any files you own.

Execute Permission   When you have execute permission for an **application** or command, that means you can run that application or command. The same is the case for script **files**, such as shell scripts or Perl scripts. If it is a **directory**, you can enter the directory with the `cd` command and you can also specify or do things with files in the directory, if you have the appropriate permissions for the files.

Changing the Owner of a File

To provide access to certain files or directories, you may want to change their ownership instead of changing permissions. The `chown` (**ch**ange **own**er) command lets you do this. When you change the owner of a file or directory, the new owner and group inherit the current permission settings of that file or directory. You can change the group on any files you own to a group you belong to, but to change the owner or to change to any groups you are not a member of, you must preface the `chown` command with `sudo`. Here's a file that is owned by `kirk` and group `staff`:

```
-rwxrwx---  1 kirk  staff  580640 19 May 13:24 Walden.txt
```

When you create new files, they get a default set of permissions. Here's what a file looks like when I create it:

```
-rw-r--r--   1 kirk  staff       0 24 May 18:41 file
```

This file is owned by me (kirk) and my group (staff) and it grants me read-write permission and grants read permission to my group and to others. This default permission is based on a umask value that is hard-wired into Mac OS X. To view the umask value, run this command:

```
$ umask
0022
```

The umask number is subtracted from 666 (for files) or 777 (for directories); these numbers are the octal representation of the maximal permission settings, or read, write, and execute permissions for the user, group, and others. (See the section "Changing File Permissions with Absolute Mode" later in this chapter for an explanation of octal permissions representations.) To figure out which umask number to use, subtract the octal value of the permissions you want for new files from 666 or 777. You can change the umask value temporarily if you want to create new files or directories with specific permissions by running this command; in this case, the permissions for new files would be 600 (666 − 66), which gives full access to the user and no access to the group or others:

```
$ umask 066
```

Or if you want to change it permanently, you can add a line to your ~/.bash_profile file (see Chapter 16, "Configuring the Shell," for more on this file):

```
umask 066
```

Since Mac OS X lets all others read your files, you might want to change this value. Using 066 means that you have full privileges but neither your group nor others have *any* access to files you create; and for directories it means that you have full permissions and the group and others only have execute or search permission. But this umask only affects files created from the command line; any files you create with graphical applications are created with standard permissions, as in the preceding example, which allow your group and others to read them.

If I run the following command I can change both the owner and group:

```
$ sudo chown henrydthoreau:concordians Walden.txt
```

Checking the file information, I can see that the change is made:

```
-rwxr-xr-x   1 henrydth  concordi  580640 19 May 13:24 Walden.txt
```

To use the chown command, you must enter the command name, then one of the following:

```
owner
owner:group
:group
```

then the name of the file(s) or directory(ies) you are changing. In this example I changed both the owner (henrydthoreau) and the group (concordians).

Overview of the *chown* Command

COMMAND SYNTAX

```
chown [option(s)] owner [:group] file ...
chown [option(s)] :group file ...
```

FINDER EQUIVALENT

Ownership & Permissions section of the Info window.

OVERVIEW OF OPTIONS FOR *CHOWN*

chown   The chown command changes the owner of files, directories, or applications. It can change the user, the group, or both.

-R   The -R (recursive) option changes ownership of the specified directory as well as its contents and all subdirectories and their contents.

GETTING MORE INFORMATION

To display the manual page and learn more about chown, type man chown in Terminal. Many options are available that allow you to change the owner of multiple files in a hierarchy, follow symbolic links, and more.

You can use shell wildcards with the chown command. The command

```
$ sudo chown henrydthoreau *.txt
```

changes all files ending with txt to belong to the user henrydthoreau.

Changing Ownership Recursively

The chown command offers a useful option, -R (recursive), which changes the ownership of all files and directories below the specified directory. If you want to change the ownership of the directory Transcendentalists, as well as all the files and subdirectories it contains, run the chown command as follows (you'll need to preface this command with sudo):

```
$ sudo chown -R henrydthoreau Concordians
```

This lets you quickly change ownership for both the directory and all its contents.

Changing File Permissions

As you saw earlier in this chapter, file permissions are shown when listing directory contents, and they consist of nine characters: three for the file's owner, three for the group the file's owner belongs to, and three for others (see Figure 12.3). These permissions are of three types: read, write, and execute.

You can change the permissions of any files that belong to you (or with the sudo command if you are an administrator) using the chmod (change file **mod**es) command.

There are two ways to use this command: with either *absolute* or *symbolic* mode. Absolute mode uses octal numbers that represent the different permissions. Each permission has a value, and the permissions set for each group of three bits are added. Symbolic mode uses letters for the permissions, and also uses letters to represent the owner, group, and others. I'll look at both of these modes of changing file permissions.

Changing File Permissions with Symbolic Mode

Symbolic mode uses letters to indicate permissions, and the basic syntax of the chmod command in symbolic mode is as follows:

```
chmod who operator permissions filename
```

Following the chmod command you must specify whose permissions you are changing (user, group, or others), what the new permissions are, and the name(s) of the file(s) you are changing. Table 12.2 shows the letters used with the chmod command.

Running the chmod command in symbolic mode involves combining one item from each of these columns. This is best understood by looking at a few examples using the following file:

```
-rwxr-xr-x  1 kirk  staff  580640 19 May 13:24 Walden.txt
```

This file, Walden.txt, gives the user read-write-execute permission, gives the user's group read-execute permission, and gives all other users read-execute permission. First, let's see how to change this so only the user has access to this file:

```
$ chmod go-rx Walden.txt
```

This results in the following (in subsequent examples I won't show the line with the ls -l command):

```
$ ls -l Walden.txt
-rwx------  1 kirk  staff  580640 19 May 13:24 Walden.txt
```

TABLE 12.2: SYMBOLIC MODE VALUES FOR THE *CHMOD* COMMAND

WHO		OPERATOR		PERMISSION	
u	User	+	Add some permissions	r	Read permission
g	Group	–	Remove some permissions	w	Write permission
o	Others	=	Set all three permissions	x	Execute permission
a	All			u	User's current permission
				g	Group's current permission
				o	Others' current permission

The chmod go-rx command states that for the group and others (go) it is to remove (-) read and execute permissions (rx).

To add read and write permissions for this file for my group, I can run this command:

```
$ chmod g+rw Walden.txt
-rwxrw----  1 kirk  staff  580640 19 May 13:24 Walden.txt
```

To give the user, group, and others full permissions, the command is as follows:

```
$ chmod a=rw Walden.txt
-rwxrwxrwx 1 kirk  staff  580640 Jun 10 14:39 Walden.txt
```

Here, a is a shortcut for all (you could also use ugo), = tells chmod to set permissions rather than remove or add, and rw grants read and write permissions.

The next example uses the = operator to set all permissions to off for the group and others:

```
$ chomod go= Walden.txt
-rwx------  1 kirk  staff  580640 19 May 13:24 Walden.txt
```

In this example, you can see that putting nothing after the = operator is the same as removing permissions.

Using chmod in symbolic mode is relatively simple: you don't need to calculate anything (as with absolute mode; see the next section), and you can either add, remove, or set permissions. In many cases you can set permissions, instead of adding or removing them: if the new permissions differ, they are changed; if not, they remain the same.

Changing File Permissions with Absolute Mode

Absolute mode uses numbers to indicate permissions, and the basic syntax of the chmod command in absolute mode is as follows:

```
chmod permissions filename
```

The permissions part of the chmod command is a three-digit number, where the first digit represents user permissions, the second represents group permissions, and the third represents others' permissions.

These digits are octal (base-eight) numbers created by adding up the decimal equivalents of the binary numbers that represent the different permissions. Execute permission equals 1, write permission equals 2, and read permission equals 4. Table 12.3 shows the octal numbers and their equivalent permissions.

It's important to understand the different levels of abstraction that come into play here. Permissions are indicated by bits: these binary markers have two settings, on and off, or 1 and 0. Each group of three bits represents one octal digit, and the decimal values of the three bits are added together to create the octal number shown in Table 12.3.

Let's use the same file as in the previous examples and make changes to permissions using absolute mode:

```
-rwxr-xr-x 1 kirk  staff  580640 19 May 13:24 Walden.txt
```

TABLE 12.3: ABSOLUTE MODE VALUES FOR THE *CHMOD* COMMAND

NUMBER	BINARY EQUIVALENT			PERMISSION
	R	W	X	
0	0	0	0	None (the equivalent of a dash)
1	0	0	1	Execute permission only
2	0	1	0	Write permission only
3	0	1	1	Write and execute permission
4	1	0	0	Read permission only
5	1	0	1	Read and execute permission
6	1	1	0	Read and write permission
7	1	1	1	Read, write, and execute permission

One thing to remember about absolute mode is that you never add or remove permissions; you only set them. So, to set permissions to allow only the user to have access, and to give the group and others no access, you run this command:

```
$ chmod 700 Walden.txt
-rwx------  1 kirk  staff  580640 19 May 13:24 Walden.txt
```

To grant read and write permissions to the group and others, and to grant all permissions to the user, run this command:

```
$ chmod 766 Walden.txt
-rwxrw-rw-  1 kirk  staff  580640 19 May 13:24 Walden.txt
```

And to provide read-write-execute permissions to the user and group, and nothing to others, use this command:

```
$ chmod 770 Walden.txt
-rwxrwx---  1 kirk  staff  580640 19 May 13:24 Walden.txt
```

While absolute mode may be a bit more difficult to get a handle on at first, you'll find that you often change permissions to only a handful of settings, and it could be easier, in this case, to memorize (or write down) the three-digit numbers for the permissions you use regularly.

Changing Permissions Recursively

The chmod command offers a useful option, -R (recursive), which changes permissions to all files and directories below the specified directory. You can set any permissions recursively using this option, but if you change permissions on files and directories, you may run into problems. While you want execute permissions for directories, you don't want these permissions for files.

ON THE COMMAND LINE

Overview of the *chmod* Command

COMMAND SYNTAX

```
chmod [option(s)] mode file ...
```

FINDER EQUIVALENT

Ownership & Permissions section of the Info window.

OVERVIEW OF OPTIONS FOR *CHMOD*

chmod   The chmod command changes the permissions for files, directories, or applications. It can change permissions for the user, the group, and others.

-R   The -R (recursive) option changes the permissions for the specified directory as well as its contents and all subdirectories and their contents.

GETTING MORE INFORMATION

To display the manual page and learn more about chmod, type man   chmod in Terminal. Many options are available that allow you to change the owner of multiple files in a hierarchy, follow symbolic links, and more.

If you want to change the permissions for the directory Concordians, as well as all the files and subdirectories it contains, run the chmod command as follows:

```
$ chmod -R u+rwX Concordians
```

This uses a special execute bit that sets execute permissions for directories only (this doesn't affect files) so you can correctly access these directories. Using the special +X execute bit, you can set execute permissions for directories and *not* files, and you can even do this recursively.

The command in this example sets read, write, and execute permissions for all files and directories within the Concordians directory and its subdirectories. But it only sets the executable bit to execute for directories, not files.

HANDS ON: HOW THE FINDER WORKS WITH PERMISSIONS

While you can change file owners, groups, and permissions from the Finder, you cannot set the full range of permissions in this way. To change ownership and permissions, click any file in the Finder to select it, then select File ➤ Get Info, or press ⌘-I. Click the disclosure triangle next to Ownership & Permissions. You need to be an administrator to make changes here; click the lock icon and enter your password if necessary.

Continued on next page

HANDS ON: HOW THE FINDER WORKS WITH PERMISSIONS *(continued)*

As you can see in the following graphic, you can only set permissions to Read & Write, Read Only, or No Access.

You can change any file's owner or group from the Info window, and set some permissions, but you cannot set execute permission for any file, which means you cannot set read-execute permission, a common permission setting for shell scripts and Unix executables.

The permissions settings are a bit different for folders. As the next graphic shows, you have an additional option, Write Only (Drop Box), and a button lets you apply permissions to all the items contained in the folder.

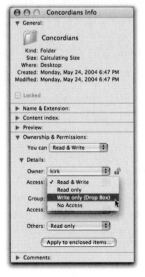

Continued on next page

HANDS ON: HOW THE FINDER WORKS WITH PERMISSIONS *(continued)*

After setting permissions for a folder, you can click Apply To Enclosed Items to apply those permissions to all the contents of the folder; this is the equivalent of the recursive option with chown and chmod. Permissions set through these info windows are applied immediately; you don't need to close the info window for them to take effect.

While you cannot apply the full range of permissions with these info windows, it can be a quicker, simpler way to change permissions for files and folders.

Setting a Directory's Sticky Bit

When examining permissions, we saw that there are 10 characters that indicate, in a list displayed in Terminal, which permissions are applied to files or directories. There is an additional permission available called the *sticky bit*: if the sticky bit is set on a directory, users cannot delete or rename files belonging to other users in that directory even if they have write access to the directory. Any user can set the sticky bit on a directory for which they are the owner or have the appropriate permissions. Since write access to a directory allows both writing *and* deleting, the sticky bit is an extra protection.

There are two ways to set the sticky bit on a directory: using symbolic mode or using absolute mode. Symbolic mode is easier to use, since you merely add the sticky bit to the directory's permissions:

```
$ chmod +t Concordians
```

You can see the change by running ls -l:

```
drwxr-xr-t   2 kirk  staff        68 24 May 18:47 Concordians
```

The t in the final position of the directory's permissions indicates that the sticky bit has been set. If execute permission had not been granted before setting the sticky bit, this would show as a T.

To set the sticky bit using absolute mode, you must first calculate the octal equivalent of the directory's permissions, then set the permissions by adding a 1 before the three-digit permissions value:

```
$ chmod 1777 Concordians
```

To remove the sticky bit using symbolic mode, run this command:

```
$ chmod -t Concordians
```

And to remove the sticky bit using absolute mode, reset the permissions without the preceding 1:

```
$ chmod 777 Concordians
```

You can use directories with the sticky bit set as drop boxes or FTP directories when you are sure that files will only be added or deleted by their owners. This protects unauthorized users from deleting or renaming files that belong to other users, ensuring the integrity of files added to these directories.

Summing Up

Users, groups and permissions are key elements of any multiuser operating system, especially Unix or Unix-based systems. Mac OS X offers the same robustness as other Unix systems, allowing you to create as many user accounts and groups as you need, and offering the security of file permissions that prevent users from accessing files they are not authorized to use. Mac OS X offers both graphical and command-line alternatives for working with user accounts, groups, and permissions, and these tools are essential for managing your user accounts and files.

Interlude 7: Using *sudo*

As you have certainly noticed, unless you've just started reading this book in this section, I have often said things like "Run this command with **sudo**" or "Use **sudo** with this command." The **sudo** (**sub**stitute-user **do**) command is a useful command to allow you to access files and run commands that are otherwise off-limits. In fact, it gives you the ultimate power over your Mac—that of running commands as root.

To understand **sudo**, you must first understand the concept of the root user. In Unix systems, including Mac OS X, there are several types of users who have permissions to access files and run commands according to their status (see Chapter 12, "Working with Users, Groups, and Permissions," for more on users and permissions). The root user is almighty on a Unix computer and can do anything they want with no restrictions, but also with no safeguards. Using the **sudo** command, you temporarily become root and have the same powers, but also the same risks.

Not all users can run the **sudo** command. By default under Mac OS X, all users who are part of the admin group (administrators) can run commands using **sudo**. This is both practical and dangerous. It is practical because any administrator can accomplish tasks such as changing permissions for files and directories, removing files that don't belong to them, or installing software; it is dangerous because any of these users can potentially disable a computer by making a false move. One small typing mistake when running an **rm** command, for example, can have disastrous consequences.

By default, if you are not an administrator, you cannot use **sudo**. However, an administrator *can* grant users the right to run commands with **sudo** by editing the /etc/sudoers file (see the "Configuring the */etc/sudoers* File" section later in this Interlude). This should be done with care, however, since any user with full **sudo** rights can effectively become root. This is not a problem when you have a Mac at home and just a few users, but any Mac on a network that is accessible to many users, or that is connected to the Internet, could be a potential security risk if too many users have **sudo** rights. All it takes for someone to "get root," or total access to your Mac, is a user name and password for any account with **sudo** rights.

How to Use *sudo*

The **sudo** command is very easy to use—you merely prefix other commands with it:

```
$ sudo periodic daily
```

The first time you use **sudo** on your Mac, the command displays the following warning:

```
We trust you have received the usual lecture from the local System
Administrator. It usually boils down to these two things:

        #1) Respect the privacy of others.
        #2) Think before you type.
```

It then asks for your password:

```
Password:
```

Type your password, then press Enter or Return to execute the command. If you enter your password incorrectly, sudo gives you a total of three tries before exiting:

```
Password:
Sorry, try again.
Password:
Sorry, try again.
Password:
Sorry, try again.
sudo: 3 incorrect password attempts
```

The system logs all uses of sudo in /var/log/system.log. You can check this file to see if any users have run commands with sudo by issuing this command:

```
$ sudo less /var/log/system.log
```

The system also logs all failed attempts to use sudo, and you can check this in /var/log/system.log or in the console.log file using the Console application to see if anyone attempted to run commands with sudo:

```
May 30 12:22:24 Walden sudo: kirk : 3 incorrect password attempts ;
TTY=ttyp3 ; PWD=/Users/kirk ; USER=root ;
COMMAND=/usr/sbin/periodic daily
```

The sudo command sets a timestamp each time you run it, and after you correctly enter your password you can run sudo again for five minutes without having to enter your password again. (You can change this time period; see the sudo man page for more on this.)

WHEN TO USE *SUDO*

You need to use sudo for certain types of commands, especially those involving files belonging to other users or commands used to configure the system. Over time, you'll learn which commands require sudo, but the shell will always inform you if this is the case; if you run such a command without sudo, the shell returns the following message:

```
Permission denied
```

Many types of commands may return this message. You may get this message when running a find command, especially if you start the search at the root level (/) of the file system:

```
$ find / -name Walden
/: /.Trashes: Permission denied
/: /private/etc/cups/certs: Permission denied
/: /private/var/backups: Permission denied
/: /private/var/cron: Permission denied
/: /private/var/db/dhcpclient: Permission denied
[etc.]
```

You need to use sudo to run certain system or maintenance commands, such as the periodic command, which performs maintenance routines:

```
$ periodic daily
/usr/sbin/periodic: /var/log/daily.out: Permission denied
```

You must use sudo to install or uninstall files from the command line. If you want to remove the Mac OS X Developer Tools, for example, you can only run this command if you have sudo rights:

```
$ sudo /Developer/Tools/uninstall-devtools.pl
```

And you need to run sudo to edit system files or files in directories where you do not have write permissions. While you can open these files, text editors cannot save your changes and will return messages like this one when you attempt to do so:

```
[Cannot open file for writing ]
```

You need to use sudo to copy volumes, such as when cloning your startup volume (see Interlude 4, "Cloning Your Mac OS X Startup Volume"), to ensure that all files are copied:

```
$ sudo ditto -rsrcFork /Applications /Volumes/Backup/Applications
$ sudo ditto -rsrcFork /Developer /Volumes/Backup/Developer
$ sudo ditto -rsrcFork /Library /Volumes/Backup/Library
$ sudo ditto -rsrcFork /System /Volumes/Backup/System
$ sudo ditto -rsrcFork /Users /Volumes/Backup/Users
[etc.]
```

HANDS ON: USING *SUDO* TO EDIT SYSTEM FILES

One thing you may need to use sudo for is to edit system files. You can use sudo as a prefix to any text editor command, and run the text editor as root. For example, to create or edit the configuration file for the Apache web server, run this command:

```
$ sudo pico /etc/httpd/httpd.conf
```

The Pico text editor opens the file, and you are allowed to make changes and save the file. Without using sudo you can open the file in Pico, but you cannot save your changes.

If you want to edit system files in a graphical text editor, such as TextEdit, you can do so if you launch the program the correct way. To edit the Apache configuration file with TextEdit, you might think that using sudo with the open -e or open -a TextEdit commands would do the trick, but this is not the case. You must call the actual executable of the program (the following should all be on one line):

```
$ sudo "/Applications/TextEdit.app/Contents/MacOS/TextEdit" /etc/httpd/httpd.conf
```

You will notice that when running this command TextEdit opens in the background, and that the shell does not give you a prompt until you quit TextEdit.

TextEdit does not give you much feedback when you do this—it neither asks you to confirm that you are working on a file owned by root, nor does it ask for your password when writing the changed file. But if you want to avoid using command-line text editors, this is an easy way to edit any file you need to change.

If you don't use sudo in these commands, you cannot copy all the files in the different directories.

You also need to use sudo if you want to list or access files in directories belonging to other users for which you do not have read permissions:

```
$ less /Users/henrydthoreau/Walden.txt
Documents/: Permission denied.
```

You also need sudo to run any commands that set or change user privileges, such as chmod, chown, and others. You need sudo for just about every command that affects the configuration of your Mac.

WHAT *SUDO* CAN'T DO

The sudo command only works with other independent commands—it has no effect on any commands built into the shell you use. If you try to use sudo with the cd command, for example, you get the following message:

```
$ sudo cd /Users/henrydthoreau /Documents
Password:
sudo: cd: command not found
```

The sudo command first asks for your password, then looks for the cd command, which it does not find. While you can list files in another user's directories, or even open them, you cannot move to their directories, at least not in the usual way.

There are two ways around this: the first is to run the cd command in a subshell, such as in the following command:

```
$ sudo sh -c "cd /Users/henrydthoreau ; du -s * | sort -rn"
3360    Library
1136    Public
64      Sites
0       Pictures
0       Music
0       Movies
0       Documents
0       Desktop
```

This command is shown as an example of using a subshell. You can substitute any command or series of commands after the ; or |.

BECOMING ROOT

Another way to access shell commands is to become root by running sudo with the -s (shell) option. Warning: This is dangerous and you should handle Terminal with great care when doing this. Running the command

```
$ sudo -s
Password:
```

opens a new shell as root after you enter your password. You can see this by the prompt that displays:

```
root#
```

LOGGING IN AS ANOTHER USER

In the earlier section "What sudo Can't Do," you saw that sudo cannot execute commands that are built into a shell. While running a root shell is one workaround, another way is to simply log in as the user whom you want to run the command. If you are an administrator you should know your users' passwords, so this is easy.

To log in as another user, run the login command:

```
$ login
login: henrydthoreau
Password:
Last login: Wed May 19 15:40:38 on ttyp4
Welcome to Darwin!
Walden:~ henrydthoreau$
```

Enter the user's name at the login: prompt, then their password. Terminal displays the usual welcome message, but if the user is set to use the tcsh shell, Terminal tells you that the shell is "using dumb terminal settings." (If the user has bash as their default shell, this won't happen.) This occurs because Terminal cannot access the appropriate files. In this case, you can't use shell history and auto-completion, for example, but you can execute any commands you want as this user.

There is another way to log in as a different user and retain that user's environment settings:

```
$ su perceval
Password:
perceval%
```

As you can see from the prompts in both of these examples, you are logged in as the other user and can access any of their files or directories. You also have the same rights they have regarding the use of sudo or other commands—if the user does not have administrative access or sudo access, you'll be limited in the commands you can run.

If you run the su command with no user name, you log in as root, if you have enabled the root account (see the sidebar "Enabling the root Account"). This is the same as the sudo -s command (see the earlier section "Becoming root").

When you are finished, run the exit command to close the session.

If you run commands as root, make sure to use the exit command to shut down the shell as soon as you are finished.

```
root# exit
exit
kirk$
```

As you can see, the exit command returns you to the previous shell in its user account. Whenever you see the # prompt, you are acting as root, so beware.

ENABLING THE ROOT ACCOUNT

When you install Mac OS X, the root account is disabled by default. If you've heeded my warnings in this Interlude, you'll understand why: logging in as root, or even running individual commands as root, can be dangerous.

While you can use the `sudo` command if the root account is disabled, you cannot "become" root, use the `su` command, or log in as root unless you enable this account. You can, however, become root by running the `sudo -s` command.

Here's what you need to do to enable root. **(Warning: root is dangerous. Use this at your own risk.)**

First, open NetInfo Manager, located in your `/Applications/Utilities` folder. Then select Security ➤ Enable Root User. NetInfo Manager asks you to enter your password; only administrators can activate the root account.

Enter a password for the root user in the next dialog; you might want to enter a different password than your administrator's password, just to make sure you are aware that you are using root. Click Set, then enter the password again and click Verify.

If you want to disable the root account, select Security ➤ Disable Root User in NetInfo Manager. Enter your administrator's password, then click OK. The root user is disabled.

You can also log in as root from the Login screen of your Mac. Either at startup, if you have not set your Mac to log in automatically with a specific user, or after selecting the Apple menu ➤ Log Out, or after selecting Login Window from the Fast User Switching menu, this screen displays. Click the Other button, then enter **root** as the user name and the root password in the password field. This logs you in as root not only in Terminal, as when you use the `sudo -s` command, but also in the Finder—all actions you make are run as root, and you can view, move, or delete any files you want. Again, be careful; any false moves could have disastrous consequences.

FINDING OUT WHAT YOU CAN DO WITH *SUDO*

While administrators can run all commands as root using `sudo` by default under Mac OS X, you can configure the `/etc/sudoers` file so specific users can or cannot run certain commands with `sudo`. To find out what you can do with `sudo`, run this command:

```
kirk$ sudo -l
Password:
User kirk may run the following commands on this host:
    (ALL) ALL
```

Some users may not be allowed to run `sudo` at all:

```
perceval$ sudo -l
Sorry, user perceval may not run sudo on Walden.
```

ON THE COMMAND LINE

Overview of the *sudo* Command

COMMAND SYNTAX

```
sudo [option(s)] command
```

FINDER EQUIVALENT

Performing actions logged in as root.

OVERVIEW OF OPTIONS FOR *SUDO*

sudo   The sudo command runs the command(s) that follow it as root, or as another user.

-s   This option tells the sudo command to open a root shell.

-u user   This option tells the sudo command to execute the command included as argument as the user specified by user name or user ID.

-l   This option tells the sudo command to display a list of commands that the current user can access with sudo.

GETTING MORE INFORMATION

To display the manual page and learn more about sudo, type man sudo in Terminal.

But other users may only be allowed to run certain commands:

```
henrydthoreau$ sudo -l
Password:
User henrydthoreau may run the following commands on this host:
    (root) /sbin/periodic
```

In this example, user henrydthoreau is only allowed to run the periodic command as sudo. See the section "Configuring the */etc/sudoers* File" further on in this interlude for more on setting user restrictions for sudo.

RUNNING *SUDO* AS A DIFFERENT USER

The sudo command runs as root by default, but if you want to run a command as another user you can invoke the sudo command with the -u option:

```
$ sudo -u user command
```

You can enter either the user's name or their user ID. With this option, if you want to launch a print job as another user, you could use the following:

```
$ sudo -u henrydthoreau lp /Users/henrydthoreau/Documents/Walden.txt
```

You could launch the job as your own user, but this lets you run it as henrydthoreau.

Configuring the */etc/sudoers* File

By default, all users with administrators' accounts can run sudo under Mac OS X, which gives them the equivalent of root access. This is not a problem for home users, but for users in professional or academic environments this could be a source of worry. Fortunately, you can limit this access to the sudo command, blocking access to certain users, and even giving individual users the right to only use sudo with specific commands.

The sudo command reads the /etc/sudoers file each time it is run and uses the configuration set in this file to determine whether the current user can or cannot use sudo in connection with specific commands.

To configure the /etc/sudoers file you can use a special command, visudo, as follows:

```
$ sudo visudo
```

The visudo command opens the /etc/sudoers file with the vi text editor by default, but if you have set your shell's EDITOR variable to another text editor, visudo will use this editor if possible. (The visudo command contains a hard-coded list of text editors that it can use.)

The visudo command has built-in checks and protections: only one user can edit the file at a time, and when you save an edited /etc/sudoers file, visudo checks its syntax to make sure there are no errors. This is a safety net, since a small mistake in the /etc/sudoers file can prevent *any* user from accessing sudo, and therefore editing this file. (Note: Some versions of Unix include a man page for the sudoers file; this is not the case in Mac OS X 10.2, but 10.3 does contain one. You can see this man page at http://www.courtesan.com/sudo/man/sudoers.html. There is also a sample sudoers file on this site, which shows you many different ways to configure users' sudo access.)

The sudoers file allows you to configure many options. I'm including the entire list here to show the extent of detail you can use when configuring sudo (you can display this list by running sudo -L in Terminal):

LISTING INT. 7.1: AVAILABLE OPTIONS IN A *SUDOERS* "DEFAULTS" LINE

```
always_set_home: Always set $HOME to the target user's home directory
authenticate: Require users to authenticate by default
badpass_message: Incorrect password message
editor: Path to the editor for use by visudo
env_check: Environment variables to check for sanity
env_delete: Environment variables to remove
env_editor: Visudo will honor the EDITOR environment variable
env_keep: Environment variables to preserve
env_reset: Reset the environment to a default set of variables
exempt_group: Users in this group are exempt from password and PATH requirements
fqdn: Require fully-qualified hostnames in the sudoers file
ignore_dot: Ignore '.' in $PATH
insults: Insult the user when they enter an incorrect password
lecture: Lecture user the first time they run sudo
listpw: When to require a password for 'list' pseudocommand
log_host: Log the hostname in the (non-syslog) log file
log_year: Log the year in the (non-syslog) log file
```

```
logfile: Path to log file
loglinelen: Length at which to wrap log file lines (0 for no wrap)
long_otp_prompt: Put OTP prompt on its own line
mail_always: Always send mail when sudo is run
mail_badpass: Send mail if user authentication fails
mail_no_host: Send mail if the user is not in sudoers for this host
mail_no_perms: Send mail if the user is not allowed to run a command
mail_no_user: Send mail if the user is not in sudoers
mailerflags: Flags for mail program
mailerpath: Path to mail program
mailsub: Subject line for mail messages
mailto: Address to send mail to
passprompt: Default password prompt
passwd_timeout: Password prompt timeout
passwd_tries: Number of tries to enter a password
path_info: Allow some information gathering to give useful error messages
preserve_groups: Don't initialize the group vector to that of the target user
requiretty: Only allow the user to run sudo if they have a tty
root_sudo: Root may run sudo
rootpw: Prompt for root's password, not the users's
runas_default: Default user to run commands as
runaspw: Prompt for the runas_default user's password, not the users's
set_home: Set $HOME to the target user when starting a shell with -s
set_logname: Set the LOGNAME and USER environment variables
shell_noargs: If sudo is invoked with no arguments, start a shell
stay_setuid: Only set the effective uid to the target user, not the real uid
syslog: Syslog facility if syslog is being used for logging
syslog_badpri: Syslog priority to use when user authenticates unsuccessfully
syslog_goodpri: Syslog priority to use when user authenticates successfully
targetpw: Prompt for the target user's password, not the users's
timestamp_timeout: Authentication timestamp timeout
timestampdir: Path to authentication timestamp dir
tty_tickets: Use a separate timestamp for each user/tty combo
umask: Umask to use or 0777 to use user's
use_loginclass: Apply defaults in the target user's login class if there is one
verifypw: When to require a password for 'verify' pseudocommand
```

As you can see in Listing Int. 7.1, you have a great deal of latitude when configuring sudo. Since sudo is such a sensitive command—any user who has full sudo access has the equivalent of root access—the level of configuration depends on your need for security. I'll only go over the basics here; if you need to go further, you should carefully read the sudoers man page on your Mac or at http://www.courtesan.com/sudo/man/sudoers.html.

THE DEFAULT /ETC/SUDOERS FILE

Mac OS X provides the following default /etc/sudoers file:

```
# sudoers file.
#
# This file MUST be edited with the 'visudo' command as root.
#
# See the sudoers man page for the details on how to write a sudoers file.
#

# Host alias specification

# User alias specification

# Cmnd alias specification

# Defaults specification

# User privilege specification
root    ALL=(ALL) ALL
%admin  ALL=(ALL) ALL
```

As you can see, the User privilege specification contains two lines: the first grants access to all commands for the root user; the second grants access to all commands for the admin group.

Lines beginning with # are comments; any lines in this file beginning with # are not read by sudo, so you can add your own comments if you need to. Several headings are included as comments to show you the basic structure of the file:

```
# Host alias specification

# User alias specification

# Cmnd alias specification

# Defaults specification

# User privilege specification
```

You can enter your own *aliases* under any of these headings, though the actual headings are here merely as a guide.

CONFIGURING USER ALIASES

You can add any number of user aliases to the /etc/sudoers file. The basic form of a user alias is the following:

```
username/%group MACHINE = (RunAs) Command(s)
```

For example, if you want to allow user henrydthoreau to only be able to run the **reboot** command, from any machine, add the following line:

```
henrydthoreau  ALL=(ALL) /sbin/reboot
```

This gives henrydthoreau access from any machine (in case he has to log in remotely) *only* to the **reboot** command. If this user tries to run any other command with **sudo**, he sees the following message:

```
henrydthoreau$ sudo visudo
Password:
Sorry, user henrydthoreau is not allowed to execute
'/usr/sbin/periodic' as root on Walden.local..
```

To allow user henrydthoreau to only be able to run commands in a specific directory, you can add this line:

```
henrydthoreau  ALL=(ALL) /sbin/
```

If you want to limit the users who can run commands as **sudo**, you can change this line in the default **sudoers** file:

```
%admin  ALL=(ALL) ALL
```

Instead of allowing anyone in the admin group to have unlimited access, you could change it to one or several users:

```
kirk,henrydthoreau  ALL=(ALL)  ALL
```

You can also set a group to have this access:

```
%staff  ALL=(ALL)  ALL
```

See the **sudoers** man page for more on user aliases.

ADDITIONAL *SUDOERS* CONFIGURATION

There are many things you can configure in the /etc/sudoers file. In addition to specifying which users can run which commands, you can configure some of the behavior of the **sudo** command.

By default, the **sudo** command has a password timestamp that asks you to enter your password every five minutes. If you want to change this timeout, add the following line to the /etc/sudoers file:

```
Defaults timestamp_timeout = 10
```

This tells **sudo** to allow ten minutes before asking for a password. If you want **sudo** to ask users for their password each time they run the command, add the following line:

```
Defaults timestamp_timeout = 0
```

If you want to have **sudo** save a separate log file (instead of writing **sudo** usage to /var/log/system.log), add the following line:

```
Defaults  logfile = /var/log/sudo.log
```

You can change the name or location of this file as you wish.

Several defaults allow you to have e-mail messages sent when users attempt to use sudo, use it, or enter incorrect passwords:

```
mail_always: Always send mail when sudo is run
mail_badpass: Send mail if user authentication fails
mail_no_host: Send mail if the user is not in sudoers for this host
mail_no_perms: Send mail if the user is not allowed to run a command
mail_no_user: Send mail if the user is not in sudoers
mailerflags: Flags for mail program
mailerpath: Path to mail program
mailsub: Subject line for mail messages
mailto: Address to send mail to
```

To have an e-mail message sent when user authentication fails, enter the following line:

```
Defaults  mail_badpass = "name@domain.com"
```

You also need to specify the path to the mailer:

```
Defaults  mailerpath = "/usr/sbin/sendmail"
```

This assumes that you are running Sendmail.

Chapter 13

Using the Network

Mac OS X is designed to connect to several types of networks out of the box. Using the Internet is a cinch; setting up file sharing on a local network is as easy as clicking the mouse; and sharing files with Windows or Linux or Unix computers is simple. "The network is the computer," says one major computer vendor, and this is certainly the case today: computers are designed to connect to each other, and—to paraphrase Robert Metcalfe—their value increases exponentially when they work together over a network.

Unix-based operating systems have long been ideal for connecting to other computers. Originally designed to allow remote access for users, Unix systems are the most robust network computers around. With such powerful tools as mail servers, FTP servers, and the Apache web server, any computer running a Unix-based system can be a server. With strong capabilities for connecting to other computers, using the ubiquitous TCP/IP networking protocol, these computers can act as clients just as easily.

Mac OS X has brought powerful networking tools to the desktop, and the graphical interfaces to these tools make such tasks as web serving as easy as clicking a button. Naturally, to fully exploit the power of these networking tools you need to dig deeper, and many Unix tools available only on the command line let you unleash the full capabilities of your network.

In this chapter, I'll talk about how to use your Mac on a network, how to use the command line to control and configure networking tools, and how command-line tools can help you better understand your network. I'll talk about how you can access the Internet from the command line, getting web pages and downloading files from FTP servers with simple commands. And I'll look at some of the basics of network security and configuring a firewall from the command line.

Local Network Tools

The old distinction between local networks and wide-area networks has faded away in recent years, thanks to the omnipresence of the Internet. You can connect to any computer that is on the Internet—as long as you know its IP address—just as if it were next door. But I'll retain that distinction in this chapter for simplicity's sake. In this section, I'll talk about tools that let you connect directly to another computer and copy files across a network. In the next section, "Internet Tools," I'll talk about connecting to FTP servers (even though you can use FTP on a local network) and using commands to retrieve web pages and other data. In the final section, "Networking Tools," I'll look at tools to diagnose network problems and get information on other hosts.

Connecting to Other Computers

Mac OS X offers you many ways to connect to other computers: you can mount remote volumes on your desktop using the AppleShare protocol; you can mount volumes on Windows computers using the Samba protocol; you can mount volumes on Unix computers with a variety of file systems; and you can even mount an iDisk from the command line.

There are two ways to connect to a remote computer. The first is to mount a volume from the remote computer on your Mac. This allows you to copy files that you have permission to access. The second way is to open a session on a remote computer. This is the same as logging in to a user account through Terminal. You can carry out most of the same tasks in a remote session as you can when actually working on the computer itself, as long as they run from the command line.

MOUNTING A REMOTE APPLESHARE VOLUME FROM THE COMMAND LINE

While it is certainly easy to mount a remote AppleShare volume from the Finder, there is a way—albeit complex—to do so from the command line. The mount command mounts an AFP volume specified by this URL:

```
afp://[user[;AUTH=uamname][:password]@]host[:port]/node
```

at the mount point indicated by node.

The full syntax is as follows:

```
mount [-o options] -t afp afp_url node
```

But first, in order to be able to mount an AppleShare volume in this manner, you must create a node, or an empty directory, which functions as a mount point. Run this command to create an empty directory:

```
$ mkdir /temp
```

This can be any name, and it can be at any location. Next, give full permissions to the directory:

```
$ chmod 777 temp
```

Then run the mount command as follows:

```
$ mount -t afp afp://kirk:password@10.0.1.201/Files /temp
```

In this example, I connect to a remote computer, specified by its IP address (10.0.1.201), and mount the volume Files. Replace user with the user name and password with the actual user's password. The volume name can be either a volume on the remote computer or a user name. In the latter case the user's home directory is mounted.

When you mount a remote volume in this way, it appears in the Finder window sidebar, or on the desktop, the same as a volume mounted through one of the Finder's methods for connecting to an AFP server (using the Network icon or the Connect To Server dialog). You can access the volume through the Finder or through Terminal if you prefer.

When you have finished working with this volume, you need to unmount it. Use the following:

```
$ umount /temp
```

When you unmount the node, you delete the directory.

You should be aware that this procedure is inherently insecure. You have to enter your password in clear text, which means that anyone who can access your history file can see your password. See the section "Logging in to a Remote Computer Securely with *ssh*," later in this chapter for a more secure way to access remote volumes.

MOUNTING A SAMBA VOLUME FROM THE COMMAND LINE

Mac OS X includes the Samba protocol for networking with Windows computers; some Linux and Unix systems can also share files with this protocol as well. You can easily mount a shared Samba volume using the `mount` command. To mount a Windows shared folder, first follow the procedure for creating a mount point. Then run the command as follows:

```
$ mount -t smbfs //kirk@kirkspc/shareddocs /temp
```

In this command, `kirk` is my user name, `kirkspc` the name of my Windows computer, and `shareddocs` the name of the shared folder. The mount point, `/temp`, is a directory that must exist for the shared folder to be mounted. This directory can be anywhere on your file system. (See the earlier section "Mounting a Remote AppleShare Volume from the Command Line" for more on setting up the `/temp` directory.)

When you run the command, Terminal will ask you to enter your password. If you have no password set on the Windows computer, just press Enter or Return. If there is a password, enter it and press Enter.

To unmount a Windows shared folder, run the following:

```
$ umount /temp
```

You can also use the `mount` command to mount volumes running other file systems, such as UFS. See the `mount` man page for more.

MOUNTING AN IDISK FROM THE COMMAND LINE

An iDisk is a network volume like any other. Apple has integrated the iDisk into Mac OS X, so you can mount an iDisk from any Mac as long as you have your user name and password. You can easily mount your iDisk from the Finder, but here's how to do it from the command line.

As in the preceding examples, you must have a directory ready to serve as a mount point. Then run this command:

```
$ mount -t afp afp://username:password@idisk.mac.com/kirkmc /temp
```

In this command, `username` is my user name and `password` is my password (you enter your actual password here). The iDisk mounts at `/temp`, and also mounts on your desktop. To unmount your iDisk, run this command:

```
$ umount /temp
```

As with mounting AppleShare volumes, this procedure is intrinsically insecure, because you must type your password in the command.

Overview of the *mount* Commands

COMMAND SYNTAX

```
mount [option(s)] [-t type] remote_volume node
umount [option(s)] node
```

FINDER EQUIVALENT

Mounting network volumes by selecting Go ➢ Connect to Server.

OVERVIEW OF OPTIONS FOR *MOUNT* COMMANDS

mount   The mount command mounts a file system.

umount   The umount command unmounts a file system.

GETTING MORE INFORMATION

To display the manual page and learn more about mount or umount, type man mount or man umount in Terminal.

Logging in to a Remote Computer Securely with *ssh*

If you want to run commands on a remote computer running Mac OS X or another Unix-based operating system, you must log in to a user account on that computer. When you log in to a remote computer, it is as if you open a session in Terminal on that computer; distance makes no difference. You can run just about every command from the remote Terminal, regardless of which operating system it is running. (You must, of course, be aware of any differences in commands if it is a different Unix-based system.)

First, however, remote login must be enabled on the host computer. Under Mac OS X, this is done by checking Remote Login in the Sharing preference pane. This allows users to access your Mac using the ssh (secure shell) program, which provides secure encrypted communications between two hosts over a network. In addition, you must not have a firewall blocking port 22 to use this login method.

The ssh command is simple to use. Its syntax is the following:

```
ssh username@host
```

where username is the name of a user account on the host machine and host is the IP address or host name of the remote computer.

To log in to a Mac with an IP address of 10.0.1.201, run the following command:

```
Walden:~ kirk$ ssh kirk@10.0.1.201
```

Terminal displays this warning:

```
The authenticity of host '10.0.1.201 (10.0.1.201)' can't be established.
RSA key fingerprint is 58:35:46:c9:de:c6:81:17:d2:97:d1:83:f5:b6:9a:02.
Are you sure you want to continue connecting (yes/no)?
```

HANDS ON: OPENING GRAPHICAL APPLICATIONS ON A REMOTE MAC

When you log in to a remote Mac via ssh, you have access via the command line and can run any commands from Terminal as if you were sitting in front of that computer. You cannot, however, do anything with graphical interface applications.

But you can open applications on a remote Mac from the command line. The open command lets you do this. Say you want to open iTunes on a Mac on your network to allow MP3 files to be shared on your local network. After connecting with ssh, just run this command:

```
$ open -a iTunes
```

You can open any other graphical application you want from the command line using the open command, though this is not always very useful; this is only interesting if the application in question can do something on its own, as soon as it's run, or if it can accept connections or commands from the Mac you are using.

For more on using the open command, see Interlude 5, "The Versatile open Command."

Type yes to allow access or no to stop the connection. Terminal then displays the following:

```
Warning: Permanently added '10.0.1.201' (RSA) to the list of known hosts.
kirk@10.0.1.201's password:
```

Enter your password, then Terminal shows the standard welcome message you see when opening a new Terminal session:

```
Last login: Fri Jun 13 12:17:42 2004 from 10.0.1.202
Welcome to Darwin!
Walden2:~ kirk$
```

As you can see, the prompt shows the name of the computer I have connected to (Walden2), and the Last Login shows that I have connected from 10.0.1.202.

By default, ssh connects on port 22. If for any reason you need to connect using a different port, you can use the -p option with ssh and specify the port number:

```
$ ssh -p 2000 kirk@10.0.1.201
```

While connected to another Mac like this, you can run commands from Terminal as if you were sitting in front of it. This is very useful for troubleshooting or system management. Say you have a stuck process on one Mac and you cannot force-quit it. You can log on to that Mac and find out what the process is, using the top command, and shut it down using the kill command. (See Chapter 14, "Managing Programs and Processes," for more on managing processes.)

You can also connect to a remote computer, then connect *back* to the computer you are on. This may seem strange, but it can be useful to diagnose network problems. Look at the following:

```
Walden:~ kirk$ ssh 10.0.1.201
kirk@10.0.1.201's password:
Last login: Fri Jun 13 12:23:03 2004 from 10.0.1.202
Welcome to Darwin!
Walden2:~ kirk$ ssh 10.0.1.202
kirk@10.0.1.202's password:
```

```
Last login: Fri Jun 13 12:16:15 2004
Welcome to Darwin!
Walden:~ kirk$
```

In this example I connected from Walden to Walden2, then opened a connection, in the same session, back to Walden. If I'm having network problems in just one direction—say, from Walden2 to Walden—I can run tools such as Ping and Traceroute to try and solve them.

To end an ssh session, just type exit.

ON THE COMMAND LINE

Overview of the *ssh* Command

COMMAND SYNTAX

```
ssh username@host [command]
```

FINDER EQUIVALENT

None.

OVERVIEW OF OPTIONS FOR *SSH*

ssh	The ssh command creates a secure (encrypted) shell session with a remote computer.
-p [port_number]	This option tells the ssh command to connect using the specified port.

GETTING MORE INFORMATION

To display the manual page and learn more about ssh, type man ssh in Terminal.

RUNNING SINGLE COMMANDS REMOTELY

With ssh you can also run single commands on a remote computer. Instead of opening a session, you merely tell the computer to execute the command and return its output to you. This can be any type of command you can run from Terminal. For example, to see which user accounts exist on a remote computer, run this command:

```
$ ssh kirk@10.0.1.201 nireport . /users name uid
kirk@10.0.1.201's password:
nobody   -2
root     0
daemon   1
unknown  99
smmsp    25
lp       26
postfix  27
www      70
eppc     71
```

```
mysql     74
sshd      75
qtss      76
cyrus     77
mailman   78
appserver       79
kirk      501
thoreau   502
samuelpepys     503
bach      504
```

After you type the command and press Return or Enter, there may be a bit of a delay while the remote computer checks that you are authorized to access it. Then you must enter your password, and the command is run, with its output sent to standard output.

Logging in to a Remote Computer with *telnet*

The Telnet protocol (according to the original specifications cited in RFC 854) is an older protocol designed to "allow a standard method of interfacing terminal devices and terminal-oriented processes to each other." Unlike ssh, Telnet is not encrypted, and therefore is much less secure. In the past, Telnet was used for bulletin board servers (BBSs), game servers, and other types of servers where security is not essential. It is not often used today, because it is not secure, but some servers do provide services via Telnet.

To connect to a server with Telnet, use the following syntax:

```
$ telnet hostname
```

ON THE COMMAND LINE

Overview of the *telnet* Command

COMMAND SYNTAX

```
telnet hostname [port]
```

FINDER EQUIVALENT

None.

OVERVIEW OF OPTIONS FOR *TELNET*

telnet	The telnet command creates a shell session with a remote computer.
telnet port_number	Specifying a port number tells the telnet command to connect using that port instead of the default port.

GETTING MORE INFORMATION

To display the manual page and learn more about telnet, type man telnet in Terminal.

This attempts to connect to the server via the default Telnet port, which is port 23. If you need to connect via Telnet to another port, use this syntax:

```
$ telnet hostname port
```

Here's an example of a Telnet session beginning. In this example, I connect to `nngs.cosmic.org` (the NNGS Internet Go server) using a special port, number 9696:

```
$ telnet nngs.cosmic.org 9696
Trying 198.36.217.60...
Connected to nngs.cosmic.org.
Escape character is '^]'.
```

```
        Copyright 1995-2001 by Erik H. Van Riper, all rights reserved.
```

```
        /~~~~~~~~~~~~~~~~~~~~~~~~~~~~~~~~~~~~/~~\     Invented in China some 4000
       | Welcome to the No Name Go Server! |___|      years ago, known there as
       |                                   |         "WeiQi," as "Baduk" in Korea,
       |  Glad you could visit to play or  |           and as "Go" in Japan, this
       |  watch some Go and meet with      |        delightful game combines simple
       |  friends.                         |          forms with an amazing depth of
       /~~~~~~~~~~~~~~~~~~~~~~~~~~~~~~~~~~~~/     |        strategy. Now you too can enjoy
       _____/      playing it live on the Internet.
```

```
We enjoy getting your email questions/comments at wgc@nngs.cosmic.org
To connect as a guest, please log in with an unusual name that is probably
not being used by another player.
```

```
Login:
```

The server asks for a login; after you enter this login and press Return, it asks for a password. Since playing Go does not require any special security, this is relatively safe. But the password is sent as clear text, making it simple for anyone packet-sniffing to find out what it is.

Copying Files Remotely with *scp*

When you are connected to a remote computer, the way you copy files across the network depends on the connection method. If you have simply mounted a network volume, you can use the standard copy commands, `cp` and `ditto`; see Chapter 5, "Working with Files and Directories," for more on these commands.

To copy a file from a mounted network volume into my home directory, I just run this command:

```
$ cp /Volumes/Files/Walden.txt ~/Walden.txt
```

Regardless of where the volume is located, the command works in the same manner.

If, however, you want to copy files from a network volume securely, you can use a special command called `scp` (secure copy). But to use this, you must make sure that Remote Login is turned on on the remote computer.

HANDS ON: ENABLING TELNET

When you enable Remote Login in the Sharing preference pane, only ssh is turned on. You may want to also run Telnet on your Mac to provide Telnet access to others. (You can still run Telnet as a client to connect to other computers running it without enabling it on your Mac.)

To enable these services, you must edit the /etc/xinetd.d/telnet file as root. You can do this with Pico by running the following command:

```
$ sudo pico /etc/xinetd.d/telnet
```

This file contains information for the Telnet service. To turn on Telnet, change the disable = yes line to disable = no.

```
{
        disable         = yes
        socket_type     = stream
        wait            = no
        user            = root
        server          = /usr/libexec/telnetd
        groups          = yes
        flags           = REUSE
}
```

Next, restart xinetd:

```
$ sudo kill -HUP `cat /var/run/xinetd.pid`
```

Remember that Telnet is not encrypted, and therefore is not secure.

You can enable other services, which you'll see in the /etc/xinetd.d directory, using the same technique as that described here.

The syntax for the scp command is similar to the cp command:

```
scp source destination
```

However, since scp copies from one computer to another, you need to specify both the user name and the host in the source or the destination, depending on which computer you are logged in on:

```
scp [user@host:]source [user@host:]destination
```

Here's an example of the scp command:

```
$ scp kirk@10.0.1.201:~/Walden.txt ~/Walden.txt
kirk@10.0.1.201's password:
Walden.txt              100% |************************|    567 KB     00:01
```

This copies the file Walden.txt from user kirk's home directory on 10.0.1.201 and places the file in my home directory on the computer I'm logged in on. After asking for my password, the command runs; the line of asterisks acts as a progress bar. At the end of the line, the total size of the file copied and the amount of time the copy took are displayed.

The scp command creates an encrypted connection using ssh, and sends files encrypted as well. If you are already logged in on the remote computer using ssh, then you run the command differently:

```
$ scp Walden.txt kirk@10.0.1.202:~/Walden.txt
kirk@10.0.1.202's password:
Walden.txt              100% |***********************|   567 KB    00:00
```

In this case, I am actually *on* the remote computer, having initiated a connection with ssh, so I *send* the file to the computer where I am physically located, which is 10.0.1.202.

If you want to copy a directory from one computer to another with scp, you must use the -r (recursive) option. Here's an example:

```
$ scp -r Texts kirk@10.0.1.202:~/Desktop/
kirk@10.0.1.202's password:
A Week                  100% |***********************|   655 KB    00:01
Cape Cod                100% |***********************|   422 KB    00:00
Civil_Disobedience.h    100% |***********************| 52310       00:00
Dispersion of Seeds     100% |***********************|   312 KB    00:00
Life_without_Princip    100% |***********************| 44883       00:00
Walden                  100% |***********************|   567 KB    00:01
Walking.htm             100% |***********************| 69301       00:00
```

The command executes, and displays one line for each file with its progress, its size, and the amount of time it took.

ON THE COMMAND LINE
Overview of the *scp* Command

COMMAND SYNTAX

```
scp [user@host:]source [user@host:]destination
```

FINDER EQUIVALENT

Copy to a network volume, though scp offers a secure (encrypted) copy.

OVERVIEW OF OPTIONS FOR SCP

scp   The ssh command copies files securely to a remote computer.

-r   This option tells the scp command to copy directories and all their contents.

GETTING MORE INFORMATION

To display the manual page and learn more about scp, type man scp in Terminal.

HANDS ON: ANOTHER WAY TO COPY FILES REMOTELY

There is another way to copy files from a remote computer, though it's not always useful. Remember that you can run commands on a remote computer, either after initiating an ssh connection or by running one-liners with ssh. If you run a one-liner, and your command involves output redirection, you can redirect output to the computer you are working on very simply.

Here's an example. This simple command uses cat to read a file and redirect its output to my computer:

```
$ ssh kirk@10.0.1.201 cat Walden.txt > ~/Desktop/Walden.txt
```

As you can see, the command starts with ssh kirk@10.0.1.201, which is required for a one-liner with ssh. It then issues the cat command for Walden.txt. Since this command is being issued to the remote computer, the cat command on that computer reads the file, then redirects output (>). But since this is a one-liner—I haven't actually opened an ssh session with the remote computer—any output redirection is sent to my computer. If I ran cat on this file without redirection it would go to standard output, my Terminal, but I can redirect it to a file anywhere on my computer.

So, when is this useful? It can save you a step in complex commands sent to a remote computer where you may otherwise have to save a file then copy it. Or you can use it to examine the latest entries in a log file, such as this command:

```
$ ssh user@server.com grep ssh /var/log/system.log > ~/Desktop/RemoteLog.txt
```

Using scp is best for most copies, but this tip can provide another way to get data across the network.

Synchronizing Files and Directories with *rsync*

The rsync (remote **sync**hronization) command lets you copy directories and their contents from one computer to another over a network (you can also use it locally, copying to another directory on your computer). You don't need to mount any network volumes, and it can create a secure connection, encrypting the file transfer. It goes much further than the scp command (see the sidebar "Overview of the *scp* Command"), which merely copies files; rsync compares the contents of the source and destination directories and only copies files from the source directory that are new or have been updated. It also lets you delete files on the destination directory that are no longer in the source directory, allowing you to create a mirror image of one directory on a remote computer. Since rsync only copies new or changed files, the copy procedure is much faster than if you copied an entire directory.

There are two reasons to use rysnc:

◆ To back up files and directories to a remote computer, maintaining the exact same files on both sides.

◆ To synchronize files and directories across computers.

However, rsync does not synchronize files the same way as some commercial backup programs—if files have been changed on both sides, rsync deletes those in the destination (if you use the --delete option; see the sidebar "Overview of the *rsync* Command") and replaces them with files from the source. Some programs can keep both copies, renaming them, so you can be sure not to lose any updated files. For this reason, you should only use rsync for unidirectional backups or synchronizations. For example, you can back up your files regularly to a backup directory on another computer, or you can update a directory containing HTML files from a development computer to a production computer. If you want to put the latest versions of files in a directory on another computer, you can run rsync in that direction, where the source is a remote directory and the destination a local directory, but rsync will overwrite any local files that have changed in the source.

One other note: in all cases, at least one of the source or destination directories must be a local directory. You cannot use rsync to copy from one remote computer to another. However, if you initiate an ssh session on a remote computer you *can* run rysnc from that computer to another remote computer.

Here's an example of how to use rsync to copy the contents of a directory to a remote directory:

```
$ rsync -e ssh -avz Concordians kirk@10.0.1.201:Public
rsync: open connection using ssh -l kirk 10.0.1.201 rsync
    --server -vlogDtpr . Public
kirk@10.0.1.201's password:
rsync: building file list...
rsync: 3 files to consider.
Concordians/
Concordians/Walking.txt
Concordians/Walden.txt
wrote 587084 bytes  read 52 bytes  35584.00 bytes/sec
total size is 586788  speedup is 1.00
```

As you can see, there are a lot of options with this command. The -e ssh option tells rysnc to use a secure shell connection; the -a (archive) option tells rsync to use a preset group of options (-vlogDtpr) to preserve file information such as permissions, owner and group; the -v option is the verbose option, which tells rsync to return detailed information about the copy process; and the -z option tells rysnc to compress files using gzip during the transfer.

Since this command uses the verbose option, rysnc displays all the files it copies, as well as a summary at the end, with the amount of data transferred and the throughput. In this example, there were only two files in the Concordians directory: Walking.txt and Walden.txt. (The directory counts as a file as well, which is why rsync said "3 files to consider".

If I add two files to this local directory then run the rsync command again, here's what happens:

```
$ rsync -e ssh -avz Concordians kirk@10.0.1.201:Public
rsync: open connection using ssh -l kirk 10.0.1.201 rsync
    --server -vlogDtpr . Public
kirk@10.0.1.201's password:
rsync: building file list...
rsync: 5 files to consider.
Concordians/
Concordians/CivDis.txt
Concordians/Song_of_Myself.txt
wrote 139500 bytes  read 52 bytes  9003.35 bytes/sec
total size is 725978  speedup is 5.20
```

Overview of the *rsync* Command

COMMAND SYNTAX

```
rsync [option(s)] [user@host:]source [user@host:]destination
```

FINDER EQUIVALENT

None. Some third-party backup programs have similar functions.

OVERVIEW OF OPTIONS FOR *RSYNC*

rsync	The rsync command synchronizes a directory and its contents between a source and destination. It can work locally or between a local and remote computer.
-e ssh	This option tells the rsync command to make a secure connection with ssh.
-a	This option tells the rsync command to use a set of defaults that retain owner, group, permissions, and more. This is equal to using the -vlogDtpr options.
-v	This option tells the rsync command to be verbose and provide detailed information about what it copies.
-z	This option tells the rsync command to compress files with gzip during the copy process.
--delete	This option tells the rsync command to delete any files in the destination that are not in the source.

GETTING MORE INFORMATION

To display the manual page and learn more about rsync, type man rsync in Terminal. The rysnc command is extremely powerful, and has dozens of options allowing you to exclude files, delete files, ignore files updated in the destination, add specific suffixes to files copied, and much more. The preceding examples show merely the basics of using rysnc; a visit to the rysnc man page will be very useful if you plan to work with this command.

In this example, rsync examines five files, compares them with the destination, and copies only the two new files.

But since Walt Whitman, the author of "Song of Myself," didn't live in Concord, and was therefore not a Concordian, this file doesn't belong. If I remove it from the source directory, then run rsync again, adding the --delete option, here's what happens:

```
$ rsync -e ssh -avz --delete Concordians kirk@10.0.1.201:Public
rsync: open connection using ssh -l kirk 10.0.1.201 rsync --server -vlogDtpr --
delete . Public
kirk@10.0.1.201's password:
```

```
rsync: building file list...
rsync: 4 files to consider.
deleting Concordians/Song_of_Myself.txt
Concordians/
wrote 181 bytes   read 20 bytes   17.48 bytes/sec
total size is 638037   speedup is 3174.31
```

The `rysnc` command here checks four files and deletes the file that was removed from the source directory.

Internet Tools

As I mentioned at the beginning of this chapter, the tools in this section are not limited to use over the Internet; most of them can be used on local networks as well. But they are more commonly used with Internet servers, and this separation helps group the different commands logically. Tools for transferring files by FTP, for example, can be just as practical on a local network, but more users work with FTP programs to upload and download files between computers on the Internet and their Macs.

Downloading Data from the Internet with *curl*

While you probably won't want to browse the web with Terminal tools (though you can; see the sidebar "Using a Text-Based Browser"), you often need to download data from the web or other Internet sites. Using Terminal for this can be both faster and easier than using some browsers. The `curl` (client for **URLs**) command is a powerful tool that can download anything that can be referenced by a URL. The `curl` command covers a wide range of protocols, such as FTP, TELNET, LDAP, GOPHER, DICT, FILE, HTTP and HTTPS. While `curl` is not a substitute for web browsing, it is an easy way to download files or web pages.

The `curl` command also provides "a busload of useful tricks like proxy support, user authentication, FTP upload, HTTP post, SSL connections, cookies, file transfer resume and more," as the program's man page says. This command is truly a Swiss-army knife for using the Internet.

The `curl` command's syntax is simple:

```
curl [option(s)] URL
```

In its most basic form, `curl` gets a URL and returns it to standard output. So if I run this command:

```
$ curl http://www.mysite.com/index.html
```

I'll see a lot of text displayed in Terminal:

```
<!DOCTYPE HTML PUBLIC "-//W3C//DTD HTML 4.0 Transitional//EN">
<HTML>
<head>
<title>Title</title>
[etc.]
```

This is because `curl` gets the data that resides at that URL, and does nothing with it; `curl` is not an interpreter. For this to be useful, you must save the data as a file. There are two ways to do this. The first is to use the -O (output; this is a capital letter O) option with `curl`:

```
$ curl -O http://www.mysite.com/index.html
  %   Total % Received % Xferd Average Speed          Time              Curr.
                              Dload Upload Total   Current Left      Speed
  100 18291 0 18291     0 0    13260  0    --:--:--  0:00:01 --:--:--  8532
```

As `curl` downloads the file, it displays dynamic information about the percentage of the file received, the time, the speed, and more, and saves the file in your current working directory.

The other way to save a file is to simply redirect the output to a file in the location you want:

```
$ curl http://www.mysite.com/index.html > ~/index.html
```

You can do this with any type of file, so if you want to download an archive or disk image file, for example, you just need to know its exact URL:

```
$ curl http://www.mysite.com/archive.gz > archive.gz
```

The `curl` command can be useful for getting parts of a page as well. If you know there is, say, a JPEG graphic embedded in a page, you can find its exact URL using `grep`, then download it:

```
$ curl http://www.mysite.com/ | grep jpg
```

ON THE COMMAND LINE

Overview of the *curl* Command

COMMAND SYNTAX

```
curl [option(s)]URL
```

FINDER EQUIVALENT

None. Reproduces functions found in web browsers, FTP programs, and more.

OVERVIEW OF OPTIONS FOR *CURL*

curl   The curl command retrieves URLs and files accessible with a URL.

-O   This option tells the curl command to save the data as a file, with the same name as the remote file.

-s   This option tells the curl command to not display progress meters or error messages.

GETTING MORE INFORMATION

To display the manual page and learn more about the many features of curl, type man curl in Terminal.

This returns each line of the page that contains the text jpg. You can look at these URLs and, when you find the one you want to download, use curl to get just that file:

```
$ curl http://www.mysite.com/graphic.jpg
```

The curl command is an excellent tool for getting files from FTP servers. If I want to download a copy of Henry David Thoreau's *Walden* from Gutenberg.org's FTP server, I merely go to their website and find the exact URL for the text. Then, using curl, I can download it from their FTP server, decompress the archive, and save it as a text file on my desktop:

```
$ curl ftp://sailor.gutenberg.org/pub/gutenberg/etext95/waldn10.gz
  | gunzip > ~/Desktop/Walden.txt
```

The curl command allows you to resume FTP downloads that were cut off, making it an excellent tool for that type of file transfer. That busload of useful tricks includes cookie control for HTTP servers, form fill options, proxy use, and even the ability to upload files. You can also use curl for transferring files on a local network. See the program's man page for information on these options.

HANDS ON: GOING FURTHER WITH *CURL*

In the preceding example, I used a web browser to find the URL I wanted to download from the Gutenberg.org FTP server. But I could do all of this without a web browser. Combining the curl command with grep, I can limit the amount of text I have to search through to find what I want. Here's how:

First, go to the main page of the site with curl. Since I know there is a link to a listing by author, I can get that URL with the following command:

```
$ curl -s http://www.gutenberg.org | grep author
        <LI><A HREF="/index/by-author.html">Listings by Author</A>
```

(In these examples I use the -s (silent) option to prevent the display of progress information and statistics.) This first command shows me the address of the Listings By Author page; this is a relative URL, so I have to append this to the site name when I run the next command, which looks for the name Thoreau in that page:

```
$ curl -s http://www.gutenberg.org/index/by-author.html | grep Thoreau
    <li><strong><A href="by-author/th4.html">Henry David Thoreau</a></strong>
```

Now that I have found the page with Thoreau's works, I can look at what that page contains:

```
$ curl -s http://www.gutenberg.org/index/by-author/th4.html    <head>
<title>Books by Henry David Thoreau</title>
</head>
<body>
Author: <strong>Henry David Thoreau</strong>
    <ul>
        <li> Entry: 1022
      <strong>Walking</strong><br>
            note: [Thoreau #3]<br>
        <ul>
        <li><a href="ftp://sailor.gutenberg.org/pub/gutenberg/etext97/wlkng10.txt">
```

Continued on next page

HANDS ON: GOING FURTHER WITH *CURL* *(continued)*

```
                 plain text format</a>
            <li><a href="ftp://sailor.gutenberg.org/pub/gutenberg/etext97/wlkng10.gz">
                 Gnu gzip format</a>
            <li><a href="ftp://sailor.gutenberg.org/pub/gutenberg/etext97/wlkng10.Z">
                 Unix Compress format</a>
            <li><a href="ftp://sailor.gutenberg.org/pub/gutenberg/etext97/wlkng10.zip">
                 info-zip/pkzip format</a>
            </ul>
            <li> Entry: 205
        <strong>Walden</strong><br>
                 note: [Thoreau #2]<br>
            <ul>
            <li><a href="ftp://sailor.gutenberg.org/pub/gutenberg/etext95/waldn10.txt">
                 plain text format</a>
            <li><a href="ftp://sailor.gutenberg.org/pub/gutenberg/etext95/waldn10.gz">
                 Gnu gzip format</a>
            <li><a href="ftp://sailor.gutenberg.org/pub/gutenberg/etext95/waldn10.Z">
                 Unix Compress format</a>
            <li><a href="ftp://sailor.gutenberg.org/pub/gutenberg/etext95/waldn10.zip">
                 info-zip/pkzip format</a>
            </ul>
    [etc.]
```

This command returned a lot of information, including the URLs for four different types of files of *Walden*. Note that if I had used the grep command to display only lines containing "Walden" I would have seen only this line:

```
<strong>Walden</strong><br>
```

Now, to download the file, I can use this command:

```
$ curl ftp://sailor.gutenberg.org/pub/gutenberg/etext95/waldn10.gz > walden.gz
```

I could download any of the four types of files, and, if I wanted to read the file directly, could even just download the text file and pipe it into a pager or text editor.

Admittedly, this is a bit more work than clicking links in a web browser, but if you don't have access to a browser it can be a lifesaver when you need to get a file and can only use the command line.

USING A TEXT-BASED BROWSER OR E-MAIL PROGRAM

In the old days, before graphics were prevalent and when you could only connect to the Internet with a 9600-baud modem, a text-based browser could be useful. If you merely wanted to find simple information, you could use a browser such as Lynx to view pages and get what you needed.

But those days are gone. Fortunately, not many of us have to connect at 9600 bauds. Unfortunately, many websites are so graphic-laden that even with broadband it may take a while to view pages.

Continued on next page

> ### USING A TEXT-BASED BROWSER OR E-MAIL PROGRAM *(continued)*
>
> So, why would you need to use a text-based browser today? The only reason I can see is to access technical information if your Mac's graphical interface isn't working. If you want to have a backup tool for this purpose, you can download and install Lynx. One place to get it is from the GNU Mac OS X Public Archive (http://www.osxgnu.org), where you can download a precompiled package that you install using the Mac OS X installer. (And if your Aqua interface is dead, you can *still* install this package from the command line using the installer command. See Chapter 15, "System Maintenance from the Command Line," for more on installing packages from the command line.)
>
> Another text-only browser is Links (not the homonym), available from http://links.source-forge.net. Some people find this easier to use, since you can navigate HTML links to other pages using the arrow keys on your keyboard.
>
> The same comments apply to text-based e-mail programs, such as Pine. These programs are much more limited than graphical programs in their ability to manage e-mail. Sure, they work fine, and if you're used to using an e-mail program like Pine in Terminal, continue doing so. But the vast majority of users find a graphical program simpler and more attuned to their needs.

Transferring Files with *ftp*

FTP (File Transfer Protocol) is a widely used protocol for transferring files both locally and across the Internet. FTP servers let both registered users and guests access files for download, and offer the possibility of accepting files for upload as well. You can use any Mac running Mac OS X as an FTP server; just turn on FTP Access in the Sharing preference pane. The ftp command is easy to use, and offers every imaginable option for transferring files.

I'll use a local server here for my examples, but the procedure is the same when using ftp to download or upload files to servers on the Internet. The syntax for the ftp command is as follows:

```
ftp server
```

where server is either an IP address or a domain name. When you connect to an FTP server, the ftp command "takes over" the Terminal window, and remains active until you close the connection or the remote server does so.

Here's an example of opening an FTP session with a local server:

```
$ ftp 10.0.1.201
Connected to 10.0.1.201.
220 Kirks-iMac.local FTP server (lukemftpd 1.1) ready.
Name (10.0.1.201:kirk): kirk
331 Password required for kirk.
Password:
230-
    Welcome to Darwin!
230 User kirk logged in.
Remote system type is UNIX.
Using binary mode to transfer files.
ftp>
```

In this example, I connected to another Mac on my network. The server asked for my name and password, then opened a session.

Getting information from an FTP server is simple: you can use many of the same commands you are familiar with for navigating the server and listing its contents. The ls command lists contents, the cd command changes directories, and so on. You can also use other commands, such as dir to list directories; the FTP protocol offers compatibility with both Unix- and DOS-type commands.

The FTP prompt is ftp>; when you see this, you can enter commands.

```
ftp> ls
229 Entering Extended Passive Mode (|||49162|)
150 Opening ASCII mode data connection for '/bin/ls'.
total 2
drwx------  11 kirk  kirk   374 Jun  2 09:11 Desktop
drwx------  27 kirk  kirk   918 Apr 13 11:30 Documents
drwx------  35 kirk  kirk  1190 May 10 09:35 Library
drwx------   5 kirk  kirk   170 Mar 17 14:16 Movies
drwx------   5 kirk  kirk   170 May 13 10:50 Music
drwx------   8 kirk  kirk   272 Mar 17 12:20 Pictures
drwxr-xr-x   5 kirk  kirk   170 Nov 10  2003 Public
drwxr-xr-x   5 kirk  kirk   170 Oct 30  2003 Sites
226 Transfer complete.
```

In this example, I sent the ls command to list the contents of the current directory; since I've logged in to my home directory on another Mac, you can see there are familiar directories. (I've not displayed all the other files that appear in this list; unlike when you run ls in a normal Terminal session, the ls command when in ftp returns a list of all files, even those that are normally invisible since their names are preceded by a dot [.]. This command is therefore the equivalent of ls -a.)

To change to another directory, I can use the cd command:

```
ftp> cd Texts
250 CWD command successful.
```

Then I can list its contents with ls:

```
ftp> ls
229 Entering Extended Passive Mode (|||49163|)
150 Opening ASCII mode data connection for '/bin/ls'.
total 1
drwxrwxrwx 22 kirk  staff   748 Jan 28  2002 Thoreau, Henry David
226 Transfer complete.
```

Since I want to get a text from the Thoreau directory, I move into that directory, then list its contents:

```
ftp> cd Thoreau,\ Henry\ David
250 CWD command successful.
ftp> ls
229 Entering Extended Passive Mode (|||49165|)
150 Opening ASCII mode data connection for '/bin/ls'.
total 7
```

```
-rwxrwxrwx  1 kirk  staff   671100 May 21   2000 A Week
-rwxrwxrwx  1 kirk  staff   433002 May 21   2000 Cape Cod
-rwxrwxrwx  1 kirk  staff    52310 Jun 18   1999 Civil_Disobedience.htm
-rwxrwxrwx  1 kirk  staff    44883 May 21   2000 Life_without_Principle.htm
-rwxrwxrwx  1 kirk  staff   578298 May 21   2000 Maine Woods
-rwxrwxrwx  1 kirk  staff   580650 Nov 17   2002 Walden.txt
-rwxrwxrwx  1 kirk  staff    69301 May 21   2000 Walking.htm
226 Transfer complete.
```

The command to retrieve a file is get; to retrieve the file Walden.txt, I run the following command:

```
ftp> get Walden.txt
local: Walden.txt remote: Walden.txt
229 Entering Extended Passive Mode (|||49167|)
150 Opening BINARY mode data connection for 'Walden.txt' (580650 bytes).
100% |**************************|   567 KB  589.17 KB/s    00:00 ETA
226 Transfer complete.
580650 bytes received in 00:00 (579.45 KB/s)
```

The ftp command displays a "progress bar" as the transfer occurs, and shows statistics, such as the file's size, the transfer speed, and the time remaining. When the transfer is completed, it shows a summary of this information.

Uploading a file is just as simple. The put command lets you send files to an FTP server. Here's how it works:

```
ftp> put ~/Journal.txt
local: /Users/kirk/Journal.txt remote: /Users/kirk/Journal.txt
229 Entering Extended Passive Mode (|||49169|)
150 Opening BINARY mode data connection for '/Users/kirk/Journal.txt'.
100% |**************************| 11340 KB  534.12 KB/s    00:00 ETA
226 Transfer complete.
11613001 bytes sent in 00:21 (531.91 KB/s)
```

Just use put followed by the path of the file you want to send; or type put, then drag the file from the Finder into Terminal, and Terminal automatically enters its full path. Again, the ftp command displays a progress bar and statistics.

If you want to either download or upload multiple files, ftp uses different commands: mput lets you upload several files at once, and mget lets you download several files. Here's an example:

```
ftp> mget Walden.txt Maine\ Woods Walking.htm
mget Walden.txt [anpqy?]? y
229 Entering Extended Passive Mode (|||49173|)
150 Opening BINARY mode data connection for 'Walden.txt' (580650 bytes).
100% |**************************|   567 KB  539.47 KB/s    00:00 ETA
226 Transfer complete.
580650 bytes received in 00:01 (533.76 KB/s)
mget Maine Woods [anpqy?]? y
229 Entering Extended Passive Mode (|||49174|)
```

```
150 Opening BINARY mode data connection for 'Maine Woods' (578298 bytes).
100% |***************************|    564 KB   511.33 KB/s     00:00 ETA
226 Transfer complete.
578298 bytes received in 00:01 (471.23 KB/s)
mget Walking.htm [anpqy?]? y
229 Entering Extended Passive Mode (|||49175|)
150 Opening BINARY mode data connection for 'Walking.htm' (69301 bytes).
100% |***************************| 69301       336.05 KB/s     00:00 ETA
226 Transfer complete.
69301 bytes received in 00:00 (332.60 KB/s)
```

I entered `mget` followed by three file names. The `ftp` command asked me to confirm that I wanted to get the first file; I typed y to say yes (I could have typed a to answer yes for all files, or no to answer no). It then downloaded the file, and did the same for the two other files.

To find out which commands are available within the `ftp` command, type a ? at the prompt. The `ftp` command returns this list:

```
ftp> ?
Commands may be abbreviated.  Commands are:

!               get             nmap            rstatus
$               glob            ntrans          runique
account         hash            open            send
append          help            page            sendport
ascii           idle            passive         set
bell            image           pdir            site
binary          lcd             pls             size
bye             less            pmlsd           sndbuf
case            lpage           preserve        status
cd              lpwd            progress        struct
cdup            ls              prompt          sunique
chmod           macdef          proxy           system
close           mdelete         put             tenex
cr              mdir            pwd             throttle
debug           mget            quit            trace
delete          mkdir           quote           type
dir             mls             rate            umask
disconnect      mlsd            rcvbuf          unset
edit            mlst            recv            usage
epsv4           mode            reget           user
exit            modtime         remopts         verbose
features        more            rename          xferbuf
fget            mput            reset           ?
form            msend           restart
ftp             newer           rhelp
gate            nlist           rmdir
```

ON THE COMMAND LINE

Overview of the *ftp* Command

COMMAND SYNTAX

```
ftp server
```

FINDER EQUIVALENT

The Finder can mount FTP servers as volumes on the desktop, and transfer files by drag and drop, but these volumes are read-only. The ftp command has many more options and lets you both read and write files.

OVERVIEW OF COMMANDS FOR *FTP*

ftp	The ftp command opens a session with an FTP server.
ls	The ls command lists the contents of the current working directory.
cd directory	The cd command changes the current working directory to that specified as argument.
get file	The get command retrieves the specified file from the FTP server.
put file	The put command sends the specified file to the FTP server.
mget file1 file2 ...	The mget command retrieves the specified files from the FTP server.
mput file1 file2 ...	The mput command sends the specified files to the FTP server.
quit	The quit command ends the session with the FTP server.

GETTING MORE INFORMATION

To display the manual page and learn more about ftp, type man ftp in Terminal. If you want to know more about the FTP protocol, you can read the RFC document defining this protocol: http://www.ietf.org/rfc/rfc959.txt.

The message Commands may be abbreviated means that you can just type the first few letters of any command to run it. For example, rm is the equivalent of rmdir; you need only type enough letters for the command to be unique. For help on a given command, type ? followed by the command:

```
ftp> ? mdelete
mdelete         delete multiple files
```

The ftp command gives a succinct description of what the command does.

To end an ftp session, type quit. This may give you some information, such as the amount of traffic or a goodbye message, then returns you to the shell prompt.

```
ftp> quit
221-
    Data traffic for this session was 13421900 bytes in 5 files.
    Total traffic for this session was 13429933 bytes in 14 transfers.
221 Thank you for using the FTP service on 10.0.1.201.
[Walden:~] kirk$
```

The `ftp` command offers many options, such as the ability to choose file transfer mode (ASCII or binary), the use of filename expansion and globbing with some servers, and the ability to resume interrupted downloads (depending on the server). You can also create and delete directories on the remote server, if you have the appropriate permissions, and rename and delete files.

FTP is not a secure protocol, however, and other programs exist, such as `sftp`, which accomplish the same tasks but do so through a secure connection. If you need this security, use `sftp`, which works in a similar way but has fewer commands.

Network Utilities

Mac OS X comes with a set of network utilities that are useful for diagnosing problems with networks or that provide specific information about network hosts. Apple put a graphical interface around several command-line tools to create their Network Utility program (see Figure 13.1), found in `/Applications/Utilities`.

Each of the tabs in the Network Utility corresponds to a command-line tool that you can use to get network information. While you can use the Network Utility to get all this information, it can be helpful to know how to use the command-line equivalents. I'll go over these tools briefly here, and also mention some other commands useful for getting information on your network.

FIGURE 13.1
Apple's Network Utility gives you graphical access to a number of command-line tools useful for network diagnosis and information.

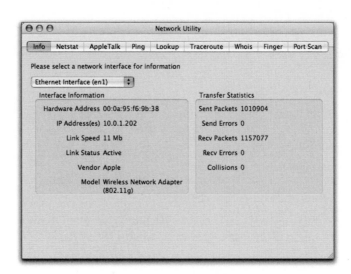

Getting Network Information with *ifconfig*

The ifconfig (interface **configure**) command is used on most Unix-based systems to configure a network interface, such as an Ethernet card or other interface. Under Mac OS X, other tools are used for this purpose, and it is best not to attempt to use ifconfig to make changes to network interface settings.

But you can use the ifconfig command to get information on your network interfaces. Run ifconfig -a (the -a option returns information for all available interfaces); it returns information similar to this:

```
$ ifconfig -a
lo0: flags=8049<UP,LOOPBACK,RUNNING,MULTICAST> mtu 16384
        inet6 ::1 prefixlen 128
        inet6 fe80::1 prefixlen 64 scopeid 0x1
        inet 127.0.0.1 netmask 0xff000000
gif0: flags=8010<POINTOPOINT,MULTICAST> mtu 1280
stf0: flags=0<> mtu 1280
en0: flags=8822<BROADCAST,SMART,SIMPLEX,MULTICAST> mtu 1500
        ether 00:0a:95:bc:06:84
en1: flags=8863<UP,BROADCAST,SMART,RUNNING,SIMPLEX,MULTICAST> mtu 1500
        inet6 fe80::20a:95ff:fef6:9b38 prefixlen 64 scopeid 0x5
        inet 10.0.1.202 netmask 0xffffff00 broadcast 10.0.1.255
        ether 00:0a:95:f6:9b:38
        media: autoselect status: active
        supported media: autoselect
fw1: flags=8822<BROADCAST,SMART,SIMPLEX,MULTICAST> mtu 2030
        lladdr 00:0a:95:ff:fe:bc:06:84
        media: autoselect <full-duplex> status: inactive
        supported media: autoselect <full-duplex>
```

ON THE COMMAND LINE

Overview of the *ifconfig* Command

COMMAND SYNTAX

```
ifconfig [option(s)] interface
```

FINDER EQUIVALENT

The Info tab of the Network Utility.

OVERVIEW OF OPTIONS FOR *IFCONFIG*

ifconfig   The ifconfig command returns information about your network interfaces and allows you to configure some aspects of these interfaces.

-a   This option tells the ifconfig command to return information on all available interfaces.

GETTING MORE INFORMATION

To display the manual page and learn more about ifconfig, type man ifconfig in Terminal.

As you can see in this example, I have two network interfaces: en0 is an Ethernet card and is off; en1 is an AirPort card and is active. You can see information such as the MAC addresses of the different interfaces, the IP address of the computer (inet 10.0.1.202), and more. The remainder of the information presented here is beyond the scope of this book; the ifconfig man page will explain most of it.

Getting Network Status Information with *netstat*

The netstat (**net**work **stat**us) command provides a wealth of information about your network, network traffic, and routing tables. The most useful part of what netstat returns is the first part of its output:

```
$ netstat
Active Internet connections
Proto Recv-Q Send-Q  Local Address           Foreign Address        (state)
tcp4       0      0  10.0.1.202.56018        idisk.mac.com.http     CLOSE_WAIT
tcp4       0      0  10.0.1.202.55980        205.188.8.42.aol       ESTABLISHED
tcp4       0      0  10.0.1.202.55702        idisk.mac.com.http     CLOSE_WAIT
tcp4       0      0  10.0.1.202.55701        idisk.mac.com.http     CLOSE_WAIT
tcp4       0      0  10.0.1.202.55544        10.0.1.201.ipp         CLOSE_WAIT
tcp4       0      0  localhost.55543         localhost.ipp          CLOSE_WAIT
tcp4       0      0  localhost.netinfo-loca  localhost.925          ESTABLISHED
tcp4       0      0  localhost.925           localhost.netinfo-loca ESTABLISHED
udp4       0      0  localhost.63052         localhost.63052
udp4       0      0  *.svrloc                *.*
udp4       0      0  *.mdns                  *.*
udp4       0      0  10.0.1.202.netbios-dgm  *.*
udp4       0      0  10.0.1.202.netbios-ns   *.*
udp4       0      0  *.netbios-dgm           *.*
udp4       0      0  localhost.49167         localhost.1023
udp4       0      0  *.ipp                   *.*
udp4       0      0  *.netbios-ns            *.*
udp4       0      0  localhost.49158         localhost.1022
udp4       0      0  localhost.49157         localhost.1022 [etc.]
```

As you can see, there are a lot of connections open. Many of them are to localhost, and represent local services, but the first line shows a connection to my iDisk, the second a connection to an address that ends with .aol; that's iChat connecting to the AIM service. This command will tell you who is connected to your Mac, if you are running it as a server, and you can use it to find out which connections are open locally as well.

Following this information is a long list of lines showing the active sockets for each protocol used.

If you run netstat -s, you'll see a long list of network statistics for each protocol. This tells you how many packets were sent, how many were dropped, and much more:

```
$ netstat -s
tcp:
    1378093 packets sent
        564773 data packets (327385740 bytes)
        1122 data packets (395496 bytes) retransmitted
        0 resends initiated by MTU discovery
        418464 ack-only packets (128218 delayed)
```

```
        0 URG only packets
       15 window probe packets
   238155 window update packets
   155597 control packets
1574689 packets received
   452360 acks (for 327253504 bytes)
    53868 duplicate acks
        0 acks for unsent data
  1091904 packets (883106867 bytes) received in-sequence
    17906 completely duplicate packets (5229078 bytes)
       21 old duplicate packets
      398 packets with some dup. data (250813 bytes duped)
    67829 out-of-order packets (84649026 bytes)
       89 packets (121794 bytes) of data after window
        0 window probes
      700 window update packets
      785 packets received after close
       30 discarded for bad checksums
        0 discarded for bad header offset fields
        0 discarded because packet too short
    74491 connection requests
    30372 connection accepts
        8 bad connection attempts
        0 listen queue overflows
    96361 connections established (including accepts)
   106946 connections closed (including 21228 drops)
      642 connections updated cached RTT on close
      642 connections updated cached RTT variance on close
       87 connections updated cached ssthresh on close
     5209 embryonic connections dropped
   451626 segments updated rtt (of 443920 attempts)
    13917 retransmit timeouts
       95 connections dropped by rexmit timeout
       16 persist timeouts
        1 connection dropped by persist timeout
       90 keepalive timeouts
        6 keepalive probes sent
       15 connections dropped by keepalive
    99636 correct ACK header predictions
   883499 correct data packet header predictions
```

I've left the full display of TCP data here to show you the level of detail this command returns. Not all protocols return this much data.

If you run netstat -r, you'll see the routing tables for your Mac:

```
$ netstat -r
Routing tables
```

```
Internet:
Destination    Gateway          Flags  Refs     Use  Netif Expire
default        10.0.1.1         UGSc      6     434   en1
10.0.1/24      link#5           UCS       3       0   en1
10.0.1.1       0:3:93:21:76:1d  UHLW      6    2427   en1    889
10.0.1.201     0:a:27:b1:9b:74  UHLW      2    5358   en1    203
10.0.1.202     localhost        UHS       0     530   lo0
10.0.1.255     link#5           UHLWb     1      34   en1
127            localhost        UCS       0       0   lo0
localhost      localhost        UH       58  479613   lo0
169.254        link#5           UCS       0       0   en1

Internet6:
Destination        Gateway          Flags  Netif Expire
localhost          localhost        UH     lo0
fe80::%lo0         fe80::1%lo0      Uc     lo0
fe80::1%lo0        link#1           UHL    lo0
fe80::%en1         link#5           UC     en1
fe80::20a:95ff:fef 0:a:95:f6:9b:38  UHL    lo0
ff01::             localhost        U      lo0
ff02::%lo0         localhost        UC     lo0
ff02::%en1         link#5           UC     en1
```

ON THE COMMAND LINE

Overview of the *netstat* Command

COMMAND SYNTAX

```
netstat [option(s)] ...
```

FINDER EQUIVALENT

The Netstat tab of the Network Utility.

OVERVIEW OF OPTIONS FOR *NETSTAT*

netstat   The netstat command returns information about your network activity.

-s   This option returns statistics for each active network protocol.

-r   This option returns routing tables for your Mac.

GETTING MORE INFORMATION

To display the manual page and learn more about netstat, type man netstat in Terminal.

You can also use `netstat` to check on the number of packets moving through a specific network interface, and see how many errors occur.

```
$ netstat -I en1 -w 5
          input       (en1)        output
    packets errs    bytes  packets errs    bytes colls
          6    0      841        5    0      230     0
        104    0    92428       93    0    15901     0
        141    0    79194      147    0    43021     0
         93    0    78730       80    0     8223     0
        148    0    84388      161    0    19096     0
         51    0    59966       32    0     2006     0
```

In this command, the `-I` option is used to specify the network interface (here `en1`), and the `-w` option is used to indicate a wait period, here five seconds. The display is updated every five seconds with a new line.

The `netstat` command can give you lots of information, some general and some very specific. The command's man page gives you a good overview of the many things it can do.

Checking Machine Availability with *ping*

The `ping` command is very simple: it sends ICMP ECHO_REQUEST packets to the specified network host, in order to verify its availability. You can use it to check whether a specific machine—a computer, printer, router, firewall, etc.—is on and working.

The basic syntax is the following:

```
ping host
```

where `host` is an IP address or domain name. For example, you can send a command like this:

```
$ ping 10.0.1.201
PING 10.0.1.201 (10.0.1.201): 56 data bytes
64 bytes from 10.0.1.201: icmp_seq=0 ttl=64 time=9.204 ms
64 bytes from 10.0.1.201: icmp_seq=1 ttl=64 time=3.051 ms
64 bytes from 10.0.1.201: icmp_seq=2 ttl=64 time=2.856 ms
[etc.]
--- 10.0.1.201 ping statistics ---
20 packets transmitted, 20 packets received, 0% packet loss
round-trip min/avg/max = 2.81/3.289/9.204 ms
```

This checks the machine at 10.0.1.201 by sending a series of packets and informs you how long it takes to get a response. By default, the `ping` command keeps on sending these packets until you stop it. When you stop the command, by pressing Control+C, the last three lines in the previous example display. This shows you overall statistics.

If you want to only send a certain number of packets, you can use the `-c` (count) option and specify how many packets to send:

```
$   ping -c 5 www.apple.com
PING www.apple.com.akadns.net (17.112.152.32): 56 data bytes
```

Overview of the *ping* Command

COMMAND SYNTAX

```
ping [option(s)] host
```

FINDER EQUIVALENT

The Ping tab of the Network Utility.

OVERVIEW OF OPTIONS FOR *PING*

ping   The ping command sends packets to a specified host and waits for their return.

-c count   This option tells the ping command to only send the number of packets specified as argument.

GETTING MORE INFORMATION

To display the manual page and learn more about ping, type man ping in Terminal.

```
64 bytes from 17.112.152.32: icmp_seq=0 ttl=48 time=224.506 ms
64 bytes from 17.112.152.32: icmp_seq=1 ttl=48 time=222.435 ms
64 bytes from 17.112.152.32: icmp_seq=2 ttl=48 time=223.476 ms
64 bytes from 17.112.152.32: icmp_seq=3 ttl=48 time=224.212 ms
64 bytes from 17.112.152.32: icmp_seq=4 ttl=48 time=231.774 ms

--- www.apple.com.akadns.net ping statistics ---
5 packets transmitted, 5 packets received, 0% packet loss
round-trip min/avg/max = 222.435/225.28/231.774 ms
```

In this example, I sent five packets to www.apple.com. As you can see, the command resolved the IP address for this host and then began sending packets.

There are several options available for ping that let you determine the size of packets, their time-to-live, and more.

Checking Domain Information with *nslookup*

The nslookup (**n**ame **s**erver **lookup**) command checks the DNS server you have set in your Network preferences and looks up the IP address for the domain name you specify. First it displays your DNS server and its IP address, then it displays the DNS information for the host you check.

```
$ nslookup www.apple.com
Note:  nslookup is deprecated and may be removed from future
releases. Consider using the `dig' or `host' programs instead.
```

```
Run nslookup with the `-sil[ent]' option to prevent this message
from appearing.
Server:         193.252.19.3
Address:        193.252.19.3#53

Non-authoritative answer:
www.apple.com    canonical name = www.apple.com.akadns.net.
Name:   www.apple.com.akadns.net
Address: 17.112.152.32
```

As you can see, the nslookup command returns a warning, saying that it may be removed from future releases. The Network Utility program offers a check box so you can use dig instead of nslookup; running that command returns more information:

$ dig apple.com

```
; <<>> DiG 8.3 <<>> apple.com
;; res options: init recurs defnam dnsrch
;; got answer:
;; ->>HEADER<<- opcode: QUERY, status: NOERROR, id: 2
;; flags: qr rd ra; QUERY: 1, ANSWER: 1, AUTHORITY: 6, ADDITIONAL: 6
;; QUERY SECTION:
;;      apple.com, type = A, class = IN

;; ANSWER SECTION:
apple.com.           54m26s IN A      17.254.3.183

;; AUTHORITY SECTION:
apple.com.      1d23h59m11s IN NS  nserver4.apple.com.
apple.com.      1d23h59m11s IN NS  nserver.asia.apple.com.
apple.com.      1d23h59m11s IN NS  nserver.euro.apple.com.
apple.com.      1d23h59m11s IN NS  nserver.apple.com.
apple.com.      1d23h59m11s IN NS  nserver2.apple.com.
apple.com.      1d23h59m11s IN NS  nserver3.apple.com.

;; ADDITIONAL SECTION:
nserver.asia.apple.com.  23h59m11s IN A  203.120.14.5
nserver.euro.apple.com.  23h59m11s IN A  17.72.133.64
nserver.apple.com.       4d23h59m11s IN A  17.254.0.50
nserver2.apple.com.      4d23h59m11s IN A  17.254.0.59
nserver3.apple.com.      4d23h59m11s IN A  17.112.144.50
nserver4.apple.com.      4d23h59m11s IN A  17.112.144.59
```

```
;; Total query time: 221 msec
;; FROM: Walden.local. to SERVER: default -- 193.252.19.3
;; WHEN: Thu Jun 19 19:07:39 2003
;; MSG SIZE  sent: 27  rcvd: 284
```

This command returns the domain's IP address and its name servers and their IP addresses. The main reason for using these commands is to find whether a host you are trying to connect to is unavailable for DNS reasons—either they didn't renew their registration (it happens) or your DNS server cannot find them.

The host command is more concise, and gives you merely the IP address for the domain you are checking, as well as any aliases:

```
$ host www.apple.com
www.apple.com is an alias for www.apple.com.akadns.net.
www.apple.com.akadns.net has address 17.112.152.32
```

As with the other network utilities, these commands have many options, including the possibility to search for specific types of information. See the nslookup man page for more.

ON THE COMMAND LINE

Overview of the *nslookup* Command

COMMAND SYNTAX

```
nslookup [option(s)] host
dig [option(s)] host
host [option(s)] host
```

FINDER EQUIVALENT

The Lookup tab of the Network Utility.

OVERVIEW OF OPTIONS FOR *NSLOOKUP*

nslookup	The nslookup command returns DNS information about the specified host.
dig	The dig command returns DNS information about the specified host.
host	The host command returns DNS information about the specified host.

GETTING MORE INFORMATION

To display the manual page and learn more about these commands, type man command_name in Terminal.

Following the Trail of Your Packets with *traceroute*

Another useful tool for diagnosing network problems is `traceroute`. This command sends packets to every hop between your computer and the selected host, and returns the IP address and time it takes for each of these machines to respond. Here's an example:

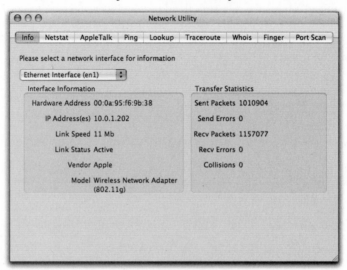

In this example I ran a `traceroute` for www.google.com. Each hop along the way replies, but the final one does not—this is probably because there is a firewall set to not respond to `traceroute` packets.

The `traceroute` command can be very useful for finding where a network problem is occurring. If you cannot get data beyond a certain point, there is obviously a problem at that location. This is useful for diagnosing problems with the Internet and with local networks.

ON THE COMMAND LINE

Overview of the *traceroute* Command

COMMAND SYNTAX

    traceroute [option(s)] host

FINDER EQUIVALENT

The Traceroute tab of the Network Utility.

OVERVIEW OF OPTIONS FOR *TRACEROUTE*

    traceroute   The traceroute command returns information about the path data takes between two hosts.

GETTING MORE INFORMATION

To display the manual page and learn more about `traceroute`, type `man traceroute` in Terminal.

Getting Domain Information with *whois*

The whois command lets you find information about a host, such as who owns a domain name, what their name servers are, and more. The whois command is very simple and returns limited information.

Here's an example of the whois command in action:

```
$ whois apple.com

Whois Server Version 1.3

[...]

Domain Name: APPLE.COM
    Registrar: EMARKMONITOR INC. DBA MARKMONITOR
    Whois Server: whois.markmonitor.com
    Referral URL: http://www.markmonitor.com
    Name Server: NSERVER2.APPLE.COM
    Name Server: NSERVER.EURO.APPLE.COM
    Name Server: NSERVER.APPLE.COM
    Name Server: NSERVER.ASIA.APPLE.COM
    Name Server: NSERVER3.APPLE.COM
    Name Server: NSERVER4.APPLE.COM
    Status: REGISTRAR-LOCK
    Updated Date: 20-may-2004
    Creation Date: 19-feb-1987
    Expiration Date: 20-feb-2007
[etc.]
```

ON THE COMMAND LINE

Overview of the *whois* Command

COMMAND SYNTAX

```
whois [option(s)] host
```

FINDER EQUIVALENT

The Whois tab of the Network Utility.

OVERVIEW OF OPTIONS FOR *WHOIS*

whois   The whois command returns domain name registration information for the specified host.

GETTING MORE INFORMATION

To display the manual page and learn more about whois, type man whois in Terminal.

As you can see, this tells you little more than the date that the domain was registered (Apple's had their domain for a long time!), updated and the expiration date, as well as the registrar and the domain's name servers. The data returned by whois goes on to provide more specific information, such as IP addresses for name servers and more.

Getting User Information with *finger*

The finger command provides basic information about users who have accounts on your system. Its syntax is:

```
finger user
```

Here's what it says about me:

```
$ finger kirk
Login: kirk                        Name: Kirk McElhearn
Directory: /Users/kirk             Shell: /bin/bash
On since Mon 31 May 13:23 (CEST) on console, idle 1 day 21:17 (messages off)
On since Wed  2 Jun 08:58 (CEST) on ttyp1
Last login Wed  2 Jun 10:32 (CEST) on ttyp2
No Mail.
No Plan.
```

You can get similar information for any other user on your system, or, if a finger server is running on a remote host, about a user of another computer. To get information on a remote user, run the command like this:

```
finger user@host
```

Most organizations turn off the finger server, so you'll not often be able to get remote information on users like this. This is the case for Mac OS X. If you want to turn it on, see the sidebar "Enabling Telnet" earlier in this chapter. You can enable finger using the same technique described in that sidebar.

ON THE COMMAND LINE

Overview of the *finger* Command

COMMAND SYNTAX

```
finger user@host
```

FINDER EQUIVALENT

The Finger tab of the Network Utility.

OVERVIEW OF OPTIONS FOR *FINGER*

finger   The finger command returns information about the specified user.

GETTING MORE INFORMATION

To display the manual page and learn more about finger, type man finger in Terminal.

Scanning Ports with *stroke*

Apple includes a port scan tool with their Network Utility—this is surprising, because this kind of tool is often used by hackers to find which ports are open on computers so they can attempt to connect through these open ports. But port scanning can be useful for two reasons. First, you can find what vulnerabilities exist on your computer. Under Mac OS X you don't have to worry too much, since most ports are closed by default, but some applications may open ports for their own use without telling you. The second use is to check whether a computer on your network is available for remote connections, such as `ssh`, or for `ftp` or `http` services.

Just like all the other command-line tools presented in this chapter that correspond to tabs in Network Utility, there is a port scan tool. However, Apple has hidden it from normal view. It is called `stroke`, and is located inside the Network Utility program at this location:

```
$ /Applications/Utilities/Network\ Utility.app/Contents/Resources/stroke
```

To use this tool to scan ports from the command line, you must use the following syntax:

```
stroke host start_port end_port
```

Here's an example (the following command must all be on one line):

```
$ /Applications/Utilities/Network\ Utility.app/Contents/Resources/stroke
    10.0.1.201 1 3000
Port Scanning host: 10.0.1.201

         Open Port:      21              ftp
         Open Port:      22              ssh
         Open Port:      139             netbios-ssn
         Open Port:      515             printer
         Open Port:      548             afpovertcp
         Open Port:      631             ipp
```

As you can see, this shows the ports open between port 1 and port 3000.

HANDS ON: USING *NETSTAT* TO CHECK FOR OPEN PORTS

If you want to scan the ports of another computer on your network, the easiest way is to use Network Utility or the `stroke` command (see the sidebar "Overview of the *stroke* Command"). This will tell you which ports are open and which services are available. But this only tells you some of the ports that are open. If you want to check your own computer, or if you can connect to another computer via `ssh` and want to check it, you can use the `netstat -a` command to look for open ports:

```
$ netstat -a
Active Internet connections (including servers)
Proto Recv-Q Send-Q Local Address          Foreign Address        (state)
tcp4      0      0 10.0.1.202.56018       idisk.mac.com.http     CLOSE_WAIT
tcp4      0      0 10.0.1.202.55980       205.188.8.42.aol       ESTABLISHED
tcp4      0      0 *.5298                 *.*                    LISTEN
tcp4      0      0 10.0.1.202.55702       idisk.mac.com.http     CLOSE_WAIT
```

Continued on next page

HANDS ON: USING *NETSTAT* TO CHECK FOR OPEN PORTS *(continued)*

tcp4	0	0	10.0.1.202.55701	idisk.mac.com.http	CLOSE_WAIT
tcp4	0	0	10.0.1.202.55544	10.0.1.201.ipp	CLOSE_WAIT
tcp4	0	0	localhost.55543	localhost.ipp	CLOSE_WAIT
tcp4	0	0	*.3791	*.*	LISTEN
tcp4	0	0	*.svrloc	*.*	LISTEN
tcp4	0	0	*.afpovertcp	*.*	LISTEN
tcp46	0	0	*.afpovertcp	*.*	LISTEN
tcp46	0	0	*.ssh	*.*	LISTEN
tcp46	0	0	*.ftp	*.*	LISTEN

This is the beginning of the results that netstat returns. We're interested in those connections that are listed as LISTEN or ESTABLISHED. In this example you can see that several services are running and are open: svrloc (Server Location), afpovertcp (AppleShare over TCP), ftp (file transfer), and ssh (secure shell).

One interesting thing you can see in this example is that port 3791 is open. This port is opened by Microsoft Word, and the program is listening to see if another copy of Word is active on the local network. This could, in fact, be a security risk, especially if you have Microsoft Office v. X and have not updated it since it was released (a security update fixes a potential danger). Neither the Network Utility Scan Port tool nor stroke sees this port as open, though, because this is a UDP port.

Many ports have standard uses, though some Trojan horses (especially on Windows) try to use common ports. You can find out what many of these ports are by examining the /etc/services file with a pager such as less or more.

ON THE COMMAND LINE
Overview of the *stroke* Command

COMMAND SYNTAX

```
stroke host start_port end_port
```

FINDER EQUIVALENT

The Port Scan tab of the Network Utility.

OVERVIEW OF OPTIONS FOR *STROKE*

stroke   The stroke command lets you scan the ports of a host finding which ports are open.

GETTING MORE INFORMATION

There is no man page for stroke.

Securing Your Mac with the *ipfw* Firewall

Computer security is a key issue today, with so many computers connected via the Internet with always-on connections. These computers are accessible to the rest of the world, and not protecting your computer with a firewall is like not locking your front door. We'd all like to live like that, but the reality is that there are always people who want to come in that door, out of either curiosity or malice.

Macintosh computers are inherently safer than certain platforms, and the basic security policy of Mac OS X is relatively effective: no services are activated out of the box; you must turn on any services (such as file sharing) that you want to make accessible. It has been said that no computer can be fully secure unless it is in a locked vault, protected by armed guards, and, especially, never turned on. But without going that far—after all, you do want to *use* your Mac—there are precautions you can take to make it safer.

The main risk with a computer is that services are activated or ports are open without your knowledge. You can check which services are on fairly easily; under Mac OS X you turn on most services from the Sharing preference pane, though there are ways to turn on services from the command line, or even from within malicious applications. But some applications may open ports, without your awareness, for the purpose of communicating with other applications or for piracy prevention. For full security, you need to make sure that no traffic can go through any ports that you do not want to use.

Apple includes an industrial-strength firewall, `ipfw` (Internet protocol firewall) with Mac OS X. This firewall is based on a relatively simple principle: traffic is either allowed or denied according to certain rules. These rules cover ports, IP addresses, address ranges and more. Unfortunately, `ipfw` is a complex tool to configure; this is why Apple includes basic configuration tools in the Sharing preference pane. The Firewall tab of this preference pane (see Figure 13.2) lets you turn on or off firewall protection by port or service; it does not let you set addresses or address ranges, but for most users this is sufficient. If you click Start, the firewall becomes active and blocks all services and ports other than those enabled in the list.

FIGURE 13.2

The Firewall tab of the Sharing preference pane.

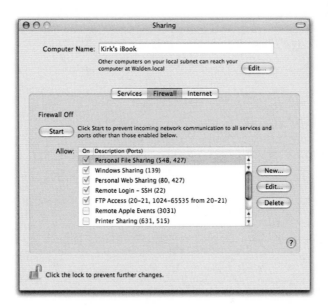

HANDS ON: LISTENING IN ON YOUR NETWORK TRAFFIC

Do you want to see what really goes on between your Mac and the network? Run the `tcpdump` command:

```
$ sudo tcpdump
```

This command shows you every packet that comes in and goes out over your network. Admittedly, the data it returns is a bit hard to sift through, but if you're curious and want to see all the activity on your network, this is the only way to go.

See the `tcpdump` man page for more on using this command.

To get customized protection from `ipfw`, you must configure the firewall from the command line. The `ipfw` firewall is loaded as a kernel extension when you start up your Mac; this means that it is actually always on, and when you turn it off from the Sharing preference pane you merely flush its rules, creating a single rule that allows all traffic to enter and leave your Mac. You can see this rule by running the following command with the firewall off:

```
$ sudo ipfw list
65535 allow ip from any to any
```

Whenever you turn the firewall off in the Sharing preference pane, it runs this command:

```
$ sudo ipfw flush
```

which deletes all rules and replaces them with the default rule, the one shown in the above example, which allows all traffic to enter and leave your Mac. Whenever you want to reset your firewall rules, run that command.

The syntax for firewall rules is the following (all the parts of a rule should be on one line):

```
[rule number 1-65535] action [log [logamount number]] protocol
from source to destination [interface] [options]
```

As you can see in this example, the contents of the rule are as follows:

`65535`	The rule number
`allow`	The action
`ip`	The protocol
`from any to any`	The `from` source and the `to` destination

Now look at what you see if you turn on the firewall with all services off in the Sharing preference pane:

```
$ sudo ipfw list
02000 allow ip from any to any via lo*
02010 deny ip from 127.0.0.0/8 to any in
02020 deny ip from any to 127.0.0.0/8 in
02030 deny ip from 224.0.0.0/3 to any in
02040 deny tcp from any to 224.0.0.0/3 in
```

```
02050 allow tcp from any to any out
02060 allow tcp from any to any established
12190 deny tcp from any to any
65535 allow ip from any to any
```

You can see that the system has added a set of rules, some allowing traffic and some denying traffic. If I turn on file sharing, remote login, and FTP access, I can see that different rules are active:

```
$ sudo ipfw list
02000 allow ip from any to any via lo*
02010 deny ip from 127.0.0.0/8 to any in
02020 deny ip from any to 127.0.0.0/8 in
02030 deny ip from 224.0.0.0/3 to any in
02040 deny tcp from any to 224.0.0.0/3 in
02050 allow tcp from any to any out
02060 allow tcp from any to any established
02070 allow tcp from any to any 548 in
02080 allow tcp from any to any 427 in
02090 allow tcp from any to any 20-21 in
02100 allow tcp from any 20,21 to any 1024-65535 in
02110 allow tcp from any to any 22 in
12190 deny tcp from any to any
65535 allow ip from any to any
```

Here are some of the rules—the first two are present in both examples:

02050	This lets you send outgoing traffic. If this were not here, you could not connect to any remote servers.
02060	This is an important rule: it allows incoming traffic in response to any outgoing connections you initiate.
02070	This allows incoming activity to port 548, the AppleShare port, so other Macs can access your network volumes.
02080	This port, 427, is also used by AppleShare.
02090	Ports 20 and 21 are used for FTP.
02100	This range of ports is also used for FTP.
02110	Port 22 is used for `ssh` connections (remote login).

If you want to configure the firewall manually, you must remember several things:

◆ You should not combine use of the firewall in the Sharing preference pane and manual rule configuration. This can only cause confusion, especially if you have to diagnose network problems. If you set rules with one and change them with the other, you may lose all your rules (turning off the firewall in the Sharing preference pane flushes all active rules).

◆ Manually configured firewall rules are not persistent; if you want to use them after rebooting, you need to reconfigure them. One way to do this is to set up a startup script. You can find a good example of a startup script here: `http://www3.sympatico.ca/dccote/firewall.html`.

◆ If you go to a lot of trouble setting up firewall rules, save them in a file so you don't have to retype them each time you reset the firewall. You can load rules from a file by running `sudo ipfw filename`.

◆ Incorrect configuration of your firewall can block your network traffic. If you have network problems and think this is the cause, run `sudo ipfw flush`.

Creating Firewall Rules

Let's look at a few examples of creating firewall rules. Say you use Timbuktu to transfer files and communicate on a network. Timbuktu uses port 407, so you need to allow traffic to enter and leave via that port. Here's the command you want to run to create that rule:

```
$ sudo ipfw add allow tcp from any to any 407 in
```

This adds a rule allowing TCP traffic from any source to any destination via port 407 incoming only. You also need to allow the same traffic to go out of your Mac; the easiest way is to create a rule like this:

```
$ sudo ipfw add allow tcp from any to any out
```

This should be one of the first rules in your list, since rules are read sequentially. This rule will let you run any kind of TCP traffic out of your computer; you need this for any network activity.

THIRD-PARTY TOOLS FOR MANAGING *IPFW*

Managing ipfw from the command line is no mean feat. For this reason, several developers have released freeware or shareware programs that provide a graphical interface to rule creation and management.

sunShield (`http://www.sunprotectingfactory.com`) is a free program that installs as a preference pane. It lets you view and create rules, provides network interface information, and installs a startup item so your firewall settings are loaded at each boot. It can also export your settings as a shell script so you can create a configuration on one computer and easily apply it to another. Even if you want to use the command line to configure ipfw, this free tool can save you time in setting up your rules.

Impasse (`http://www.glu.com/products/impasse/index.html`) is a shareware program that also installs as a preference pane and lets you create rules and view logs. It installs a startup item to automatically apply your rules on boot, and offers two modes: Easy and Advanced.

BrickHouse (`http://personalpages.tds.net/~brian_hill/brickhouse.html`) is a shareware application that provides the most powerful control over ipfw. Its Quick and Expert modes let you create rules either via its graphical interface or by writing them in text. It also has an assistant that lets you choose the services you want active in a jiffy. And, like the first two programs, it installs a startup item to activate your rules each time you boot your Mac.

Overview of the *ipfw* Command

COMMAND SYNTAX

```
ipfw [option(s)] command(s)
```

FINDER EQUIVALENT

The Firewall tab of the Sharing preference pane.

OVERVIEW OF OPTIONS FOR *IPFW*

ipfw   The ipfw command lets you set rules for the internal firewall in Mac OS X.

flush   This option resets all firewall rules.

GETTING MORE INFORMATION

To display the manual page and learn more about ipfw, type man ipfw in Terminal. Since the ipfw command comes from FreeBSD, you can find several tutorials and how-to documents on the Web. Here are two such documents:

```
http://www.freebsd-howto.com/HOWTO/Ipfw-HOWTO
http://www.freebsd-howto.com/HOWTO/Ipfw-Advanced-Supplement-HOWTO
```

Note that Apple's implementation of ipfw is not exactly the same as the FreeBSD version; for example, FreeBSD reads an rc.conf file on startup. This file gives information as to where the firewall rules are stored, but Mac OS X doesn't use this file. Nevertheless, these how-to documents give you detailed information on how to create rules.

For a comprehensive book on security issues with Mac OS X, see *Mac OS X Maximum Security*, by John Ray and William C. Ray (Sams, 2003).

Rolling your own firewall is a difficult and risky procedure; most users will never need to do this, and will be sufficiently protected with Apple's built-in firewall. If you really want to create your own rules, see the section "Getting More Information" in the sidebar "Overview of the *ipfw* Command" for some tutorials and how-tos on using ipfw.

Summing Up

Mac OS X's networking capabilities are as powerful as any operating system's, and there is a full range of command-line tools that let you use the network, get network information, diagnose problems, and manage network interfaces. Security is a key issue in any connected computer, and the Mac OS X built-in firewall is a powerful tool to protect your Mac. With all these commands in your toolkit, you'll have full control over networking activities.

Chapter 14

Managing Programs and Processes

Mac OS X offers preemptive multitasking, which lets the operating system dynamically adjust processing priorities among tasks, processes, and applications. Unlike earlier versions of Mac OS, which used cooperative multitasking, this makes the user experience much smoother and more efficient. Each application, process, and task gets its share of processor time, and the system makes sure that this is shared correctly.

Your Mac runs dozens of processes at all times. In addition to the applications you use, the system runs many daemons and services that you never see (at least not in the Aqua interface). Many of these processes merely wait for actions to occur—one example is the cupsd process, which is a background daemon for the CUPS printing system. While you are working on your Mac, this process waits for you to call it to work, which occurs whenever you print a file. But the rest of the time it lies in the shadows, just watching to see if it is needed, and this passive activity uses very little processor time or memory.

Looking at my Mac as I write these words, I can see that there are 64 processes running: 29 of these are user processes, which are launched when I log in or open applications. These may be programs, support processes for programs, or background processes for hardware devices or other programs. The remaining 35 processes are administrator processes, which are launched by the system; most of these are truly system processes (such as cupsd, other processes required for sharing files, and processes needed for networking), and the remainder are processes started by other programs.

You don't need to know what all these processes are, but it is useful to have an idea of the most important processes and how to manage them. An understanding of these processes will help you better manage your Mac, find potential problems, and shut down processes that either hog your processor or slow down your computer. In this chapter, I'll present tools for managing programs and processes, getting information on processes, and shutting down processes. I'll also tell you how to change the processor time allocated to processes and programs.

Getting System Information with *top*

Of all the commands you can use to get information on your system and its operations, the `top` command is the most useful and practical. Whenever you want to see what's happening on your Mac, `top` gives you a quick overview, which can be either a snapshot of activity at a given moment or a real-time picture of what your Mac is doing, updated regularly.

Running the `top` command is simple:

```
$ top
```

The `top` command gives you a lot of information, and its display takes up the entire Terminal window, as you can see in Figure 14.1.

When you run `top` in this way, the display is live, and is updated once every second. You'll see the figures changing in Terminal as CPU usage varies, memory usage changes, and the numbers of processes and threads at the top of the window change. Here is an explanation of what you see in the `top` display. The first six lines give you general system information:

◆ **Processes:** This is the number of total processes, the number that are active (`running`), the number that are waiting in the background (`sleeping`), and the number that are stuck or that are zombies, if any. `Threads` are the number of actual memory threads being used. The last data on this line is the current time, or the time that `top` ran.

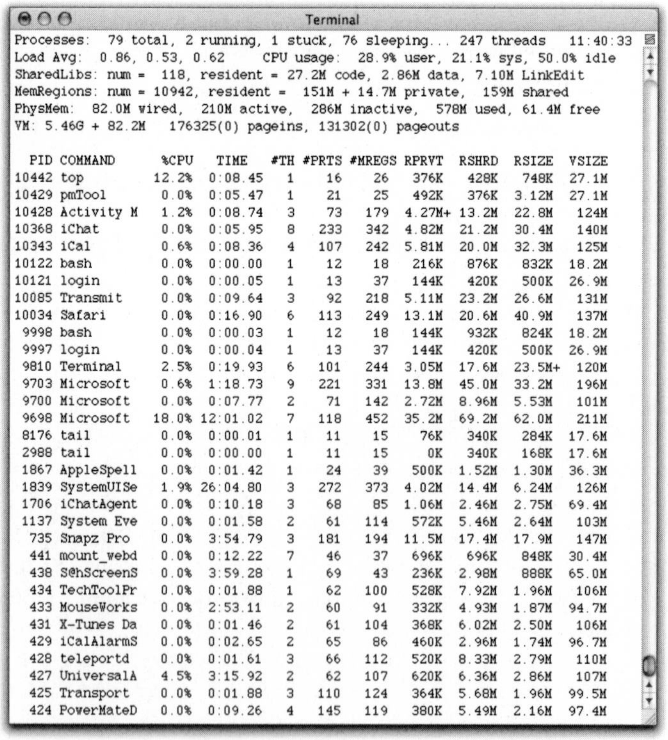

FIGURE 14.1

The `top` command shows you the processes currently running on your Mac.

```
●○○                            Terminal
Processes:  79 total, 2 running, 1 stuck, 76 sleeping... 247 threads   11:40:33
Load Avg:  0.86, 0.53, 0.62     CPU usage:  28.9% user, 21.1% sys, 50.0% idle
SharedLibs: num =  118, resident = 27.2M code, 2.86M data, 7.10M LinkEdit
MemRegions: num = 10942, resident =  151M + 14.7M private,  159M shared
PhysMem:  82.0M wired,  210M active,  286M inactive,  578M used, 61.4M free
VM:  5.46G + 82.2M  176325(0) pageins, 131302(0) pageouts

  PID COMMAND      %CPU   TIME   #TH #PRTS #MREGS RPRVT  RSHRD  RSIZE  VSIZE
10442 top         12.2%  0:08.45  1    16     26   376K   428K   748K  27.1M
10429 pmTool       0.0%  0:05.47  1    21     25   492K   376K  3.12M  27.1M
10428 Activity M   1.2%  0:08.74  3    73    179  4.27M+ 13.2M  22.8M   124M
10368 iChat        0.0%  0:05.95  8   233    342  4.82M  21.2M  30.4M   140M
10343 iCal         0.6%  0:08.36  4   107    242  5.81M  20.0M  32.3M   125M
10122 bash         0.0%  0:00.00  1    12     18   216K   876K   832K  18.2M
10121 login        0.0%  0:00.05  1    13     37   144K   420K   500K  26.9M
10085 Transmit     0.0%  0:09.64  3    92    218  5.11M  23.2M  26.6M   131M
10034 Safari       0.0%  0:16.90  6   113    249  13.1M  20.6M  40.9M   137M
 9998 bash         0.0%  0:00.03  1    12     18   144K   932K   824K  18.2M
 9997 login        0.0%  0:00.04  1    13     37   144K   420K   500K  26.9M
 9810 Terminal     2.5%  0:19.93  6   101    244  3.05M  17.6M  23.5M+  120M
 9703 Microsoft    0.6%  1:18.73  9   221    331  13.8M  45.0M  33.2M   196M
 9700 Microsoft    0.0%  0:07.77  2    71    142  2.72M  8.96M  5.53M   101M
 9698 Microsoft   18.0% 12:01.02  7   118    452  35.2M  69.2M  62.0M   211M
 8176 tail         0.0%  0:00.01  1    11     15    76K   340K   284K  17.6M
 2988 tail         0.0%  0:00.00  1    11     15     0K   340K   168K  17.6M
 1867 AppleSpell   0.0%  0:01.42  1    24     39   500K  1.52M  1.30M  36.3M
 1839 SystemUISe   1.9% 26:04.80  3   272    373  4.02M  14.4M  6.24M   126M
 1706 iChatAgent   0.0%  0:10.18  3    68     85  1.06M  2.46M  2.75M  69.4M
 1137 System Eve   0.0%  0:01.58  2    61    114   572K  5.46M  2.64M   103M
  735 Snapz Pro    0.0%  3:54.79  3   181    194  11.5M  17.4M  17.9M   147M
  441 mount_webd   0.0%  0:12.22  7    46     37   696K   696K   848K  30.4M
  438 S@hScreenS   0.0%  3:59.28  1    69     43   236K  2.98M   888K  65.0M
  434 TechToolPr   0.0%  0:01.88  1    62    100   528K  7.92M  1.96M   106M
  433 MouseWorks   0.0%  2:53.11  2    60     91   332K  4.93M  1.87M  94.7M
  431 X-Tunes Da   0.0%  0:01.46  2    61    104   368K  6.02M  2.50M   106M
  429 iCalAlarms   0.0%  0:02.65  2    65     86   460K  2.96M  1.74M  96.7M
  428 teleportd    0.0%  0:01.61  3    66    112   520K  8.33M  2.79M   110M
  427 UniversalA   4.5%  3:15.92  2    62    107   620K  6.36M  2.86M   107M
  425 Transport    0.0%  0:01.88  3   110    124   364K  5.68M  1.96M  99.5M
  424 PowerMateD   0.0%  0:09.26  4   145    119   380K  5.49M  2.16M  97.4M
```

◆ `Load Avg`: This is the average system load over the past 1, 5, and 15 minutes. This is a global measurement of how your system is working; it is based on the number of processes that are ready to run, or active, at any instant in time. Running processor-intensive activities will raise this figure drastically: this includes such tasks as displaying complex video or ripping MP3 files. There is no standard amount of load average that is *good* or *bad*; suffice it to say that if your Mac slows down, it's working hard and your load average is high. If you're not running many applications, your most recent load average may be around 1; if you run several applications that are very active it may go as high as 4 or 5.

◆ `CPU usage`: This is the percentage of CPU usage that is currently being used by user processes (`user`), being used by system processes (`sys`), and unused (`idle`). If you see that your CPU usage stays high, you are either running too many applications or one of your applications is using too much CPU time. This is the most valuable reason to run `top`: if your Mac slows down, you can find out which program is hogging the CPU and slowing you down. See `%CPU` below.

◆ `SharedLibs`: The number of shared libraries your system is using, and the amount of memory they use.

◆ `MemRegions`: The number of virtual memory regions being used, and the amount of memory they use.

◆ `PhysMem`: The amount of physical memory being used. This is broken down into several types:

  ◆ `Wired` memory cannot be written to the swap file, and is generally used by core system processes.

  ◆ `Active` memory is currently being used by programs and processes.

  ◆ `Inactive` memory is in a "holding pattern" waiting to be used; it contains something (application code and data) that has not been recently accessed, or cached data (recently accessed disk blocks) that is being held for possible reuse at a later time.

  ◆ `Used` memory is the total amount of memory used, the sum of `wired`, `active`, and `inactive` memory.

  ◆ `Free` memory is the amount of unused memory.

  Unlike under previous versions of Mac OS, such as Mac OS 9, you don't need to worry if you see that all your physical memory is being used. In many cases most of it will be used, and due to the way Mac OS X uses virtual memory, this is not a problem.

◆ `VM`: This is virtual memory. Mac OS X uses an advanced virtual memory system to allow you to use more memory than you have. It's like a free lunch, but it has its limits. Data from memory is *paged*, or written, to swap files when it's not being used, and is paged in to active memory when needed. This is normal. But when you need more memory than you have, data is paged out from the swap file to physical memory. This causes your Mac to read data from a swap file on your hard disk instead of from your RAM, slowing down performance drastically.

The pageins and pageouts statistics show how virtual memory is working. The first numbers are cumulative figures since the last startup and the numbers in parentheses are the current numbers (pageins or pageouts in the last second, or the last refresh period if you run **top** with a different refresh period). If the numbers in parentheses remain high over a period of time, you should install more RAM. This means that you are doing more than your RAM can handle, and your Mac has to use hard disk space for memory. Unfortunately for your bank account, Mac OS X runs best with a lot of RAM, and the ideal amount is generally the maximum that your Mac can handle. Fortunately, RAM prices have dropped in recent years, though its price fluctuates even more than the NASDAQ.

When you get to the stage that virtual memory writes a lot of pageouts, your Mac writes additional swap files. A first file is created at startup and other files are created as needed. If you use an older Mac that is not capable of using Quartz Extreme graphics, your CPU and RAM do a lot of the graphics rendering. In this situation, your Mac may open quite a few swap files if you carry out any graphically-intense operations.

The second part of the output from the **top** command is a series of columns and rows. Each row represents a process, or program, and each column gives specific information about it.

◆ PID: the Unix process id.

◆ COMMAND: the Unix command name or the name of the program; this column only displays 10 characters, and abbreviates longer names.

◆ %CPU: the percentage of CPU consumed (kernel and user). If this is consistently high, the program or process is slowing down your Mac. This could be normal—say, with a graphics rendering program or a process that is compiling source code—but it could be a sign of an application that's not written well, using more CPU time than it should.

◆ TIME: the absolute CPU consumption (mins:secs.hundreths).

◆ #TH: the number of threads in the process.

◆ #PRTS: the number of Mach ports.

◆ #MREGS: the number of memory registers.

◆ RPRVT: the amount of resident private memory; the amount of memory used by this process.

◆ RSHRD: the amount of shared private memory; the amount of memory shared by this process with others. This figure is not very useful since you have no way of knowing which other processes are sharing this memory.

◆ RSIZE: the amount of resident memory; the total amount of physical memory used by the process. This figure may sometimes show a + or − following it; this means that the amount has increased (+) or decreased (−) since the last update.

◆ VSIZE: the amount of virtual memory used, or the total address space an application uses or requests. If this figure is very high, it can indicate an application with a memory leak.

When you want to quit **top**, just press Q; Terminal displays a normal shell prompt.

HOW MANY SWAP FILES?

As I mentioned above, one reason why your Mac may slow down is because it has too many swap files open. When your Mac boots, it creates one swap file and stores it in /var/vm. You can check this directory to find how many swap files are open:

```
$ ls -l /var/vm
total 1048576
drwx--x--x  12 root   wheel        408 20 Apr 10:15 app_profile
-rw------T   1 root   wheel   67108864 21 Apr 10:22 swapfile0
-rw------T   1 root   wheel   67108864 21 Apr 11:22 swapfile1
-rw------T   1 root   wheel  134217728 21 Apr 14:29 swapfile2
-rw------T   1 root   wheel  268435456 21 Apr 15:10 swapfile3
```

If you see more than a few files whose names contain swapfile, your Mac is using a lot of virtual memory on disk. In some cases poorly written applications with memory leaks can cause your Mac to open swap files until you have no more disk space. The only solution is to restart to get rid of them, or to quit and relaunch the application that's using all the memory, if you know which it is.

In some cases, your Mac will reclaim virtual memory and shut swap files, but there is no hard and fast rule as to when or how often this happens. I regularly find up to five swap files open on my G4 iBook, and they only tend to close when I've quit a lot of applications. (One culprit I've found that uses lots of virtual memory is Safari. If you use this browser, you might want to quit it every now and then to free up memory.)

Another way to monitor swap files is by using Matt Neuberg's freeware MemoryStick (found at http://www.tidbits.com/matt). This small, unobtrusive program shows you a graphical representation of your memory usage, and can give you either visual or audible indication of when your Mac is paging memory to disk and how many swap files are open.

Other Ways to Run *top*

When you run top as explained above, it displays as many processes as it can fit in your Terminal window and refreshes its display once every second, with the top processes displayed in reverse ID number order. Here are several other ways to run top.

SORTING BY CPU USAGE

You can run the top command so its displays shows processes in reverse order by CPU usage, with the process using the most CPU time at the top of the list. To do this, run top as follows:

```
$ top -u
```

This is useful because it shows you which processes are the most demanding. But since the display changes every second and CPU usage is dynamic and changes frequently, you'll find it difficult to read; the processes keep changing lines as their CPU usage changes, so the highest usage is always at the top. When you press Q to exit top, however, the display remains, so you can run the command then exit it immediately to see processes in CPU order at a given time.

MORE INFORMATION ABOUT VIRTUAL MEMORY

While the top command gives you some information about virtual memory, another command, vm_stat, gives you cumulative statistics on virtual memory usage since system startup. There are two ways to run this command. The first, running the command with no arguments, gives you a summary of virtual memory statistics:

```
$ vm_stat
Mach Virtual Memory Statistics: (page size of 4096 bytes)
Pages free:                    15931.
Pages active:                  53144.
Pages inactive:                73687.
Pages wired down:              21078.
"Translation faults":          57469857.
Pages copy-on-write:           1061441.
Pages zero filled:             45109196.
Pages reactivated:             671521.
Pageins:                       176421.
Pageouts:                      131421.
Object cache: 164264 hits of 355476 lookups (46% hit rate)
```

The second, running vm_stat with a number as argument, tells the command to update its display every *n* seconds. The first display is a cumulative display and subsequent lines show activity over the past *n* seconds, as shown here.

The vm_stat command will continue displaying a new line every five seconds until you press Control+C to exit it.

For information on the data returned by vm_stat, see the vm_stat man page.

CHANGING THE UPDATE INTERVAL

By default, top updates its display every second. You can use the -s option to set your own interval; this is especially useful combined with the -u option (see above), so you have more time to view the display before it changes. Run this command:

```
$ top -s 5
```

The `top` command updates every five seconds. To have `top` display its output sorted by CPU usage, and updated every five seconds, run this command:

```
$ top -s 5 -u
```

When you run `top` in this way, you may see the first display showing only 0.0% in the CPU usage column; it sorts immediately according to usage but does not display a percentage in its first display. Wait for it to refresh to see the CPU usage in percent.

DISPLAYING FULL PROCESS INFORMATION

The `top` command only displays as much information as it can in your Terminal window. If you have very small fonts and a very large screen, you might be able to see all your processes in the list. Another way to get a full list of processes is to use the -l option:

```
$ top -l 1
```

(That's a lower-case L followed by the digit 1.) This tells `top` to run once in logging mode, return all its information, then exit. You can set the number of times you want `top` to run by changing the number following -l; this is most useful if you want to monitor system activity over a period of time. You can also redirect output into a file, running the command like this:

```
$ top -l 20 > top_log.txt
```

This lets you save the output of the `top` command to check later.

MONITORING A SINGLE PROCESS

You may want to monitor the activity of a single process without needing to see the entire output from the `top` command. You can use `top` in conjunction with `grep` to do this. First you need to know the name or process ID of the process you want to monitor. Run the `top` command once to find this.
Say you want to monitor the activity of the Window Manager. Run this command:

```
$ top -l 20 | grep Window
```

Figure 14.2 shows what this command returns.

ACTIVITY MONITOR: A GRAPHICAL WAY TO VIEW PROCESSES

Apple includes a graphical tool that gives you much of the same information as top or ps, but which does not give you all the statistics that top shows in its first six lines. Activity Monitor, found in /Applications/ Utilities, is an easy-to-use tool that displays information about all your processes and lets you quit processes (by clicking a process to select it then clicking the Quit Process button) if you need to. This does the same thing as the kill command.

Activity Monitor offers additional features, and you may find it more useful than working on the command line. In addition to the information you see in the top command, Activity Monitor lets you monitor disk activity, disk usage, and network activity.

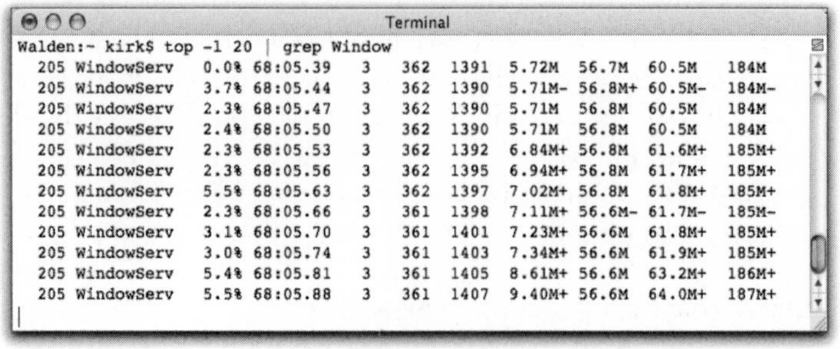

FIGURE 14.2

The top command showing only one process—here, the Window Manager

```
● ○ ○                          Terminal
Walden:~ kirk$ top -1 20 | grep Window
   205 WindowServ  0.0% 68:05.39  3   362  1391  5.72M  56.7M  60.5M   184M
   205 WindowServ  3.7% 68:05.44  3   362  1390  5.71M- 56.8M+ 60.5M-  184M-
   205 WindowServ  2.3% 68:05.47  3   362  1390  5.71M  56.8M  60.5M   184M
   205 WindowServ  2.4% 68:05.50  3   362  1390  5.71M  56.8M  60.5M   184M
   205 WindowServ  2.3% 68:05.53  3   362  1392  6.84M+ 56.8M  61.6M+  185M+
   205 WindowServ  2.3% 68:05.56  3   362  1395  6.94M+ 56.8M  61.7M+  185M+
   205 WindowServ  5.5% 68:05.63  3   362  1397  7.02M+ 56.8M  61.8M+  185M+
   205 WindowServ  2.3% 68:05.66  3   361  1398  7.11M+ 56.6M- 61.7M-  185M-
   205 WindowServ  3.1% 68:05.70  3   361  1401  7.23M+ 56.6M  61.8M+  185M+
   205 WindowServ  3.0% 68:05.74  3   361  1403  7.34M+ 56.6M  61.9M+  185M+
   205 WindowServ  5.4% 68:05.81  3   361  1405  8.61M+ 56.6M  63.2M+  186M+
   205 WindowServ  5.5% 68:05.88  3   361  1407  9.40M+ 56.6M  64.0M+  187M+
```

This tells top to run 20 times, and pipes its results through grep, which searches for lines containing Window, then displays them. You'll have this line displayed once per second, and you'll be able to see the changes in activity for the Window Manager process.

ON THE COMMAND LINE

Overview of the *top* Command

COMMAND SYNTAX

    top [option(s)]

FINDER EQUIVALENT

Process Viewer.

OVERVIEW OF OPTIONS FOR *TOP*

top	The top command displays information on processes and their activity.
-u	The -u option tells the top command to display its results sorted by CPU activity in decreasing order.
-s [number]	The -s option tells the top command to update its display every *number* seconds.
-l [number]	The -l option tells the top command to return a full display of all processes, *number* times, then exit.

GETTING MORE INFORMATION

To display the manual page and learn more about top, type man top in Terminal.

Getting System Information with *ps*

Just as the top command gives you an overview of your system's activity—its currently running processes and programs—the ps (process status) command gives you detailed information on all the processes running on your Mac. The two commands overlap, providing much similar information, and the top command is easier to use since it offers real-time, dynamic output. But the ps command goes much further and displays more detailed information about your active processes. For many users the ps command may be overkill; it displays many columns of information, and offers a vast number of possibilities for the data it returns. But for others it is exactly what is needed, because of its granularity and detail.

To display all the active processes on your Mac, run this command:

```
$ ps -ax
```

The -a option tells ps to display all running processes, not just those that you initiated, and the -x option tells it to include processes that are not controlled by a terminal. This command returns the following:

```
  PID  TT  STAT      TIME COMMAND
    1  ??  Ss     0:00.02 /sbin/init
    2  ??  Ss     0:10.69 /sbin/mach_init
   51  ??  Ss     0:02.77 kextd
   77  ??  Ss     0:07.64 update
   81  ??  Ss     0:00.00 dynamic_pager -H 40000000
  111  ??  Ss     4:04.03 configd
  141  ??  Ss     0:03.89 /System/Library/CoreServices/Security
  189  ??  Ss     2:57.70 /System/Library/Frameworks/Applicatio
  194  ??  Ss    18:54.13 /System/Library/CoreServices/WindowSe
  233  ??  Ss     0:10.37 /sbin/autodiskmount -va
  289  ??  Ss     0:00.35 syslogd
  300  ??  Ss     0:00.00 /usr/libexec/crashreporterd
[etc.]
```

I've only shown the first dozen lines of its output in the above example. I have also shortened the lines: some of them are very long, since they contain the full path for the command, program, or process they represent. As you can see in this example, the ps command shows the process ID number (PID), together with other information about the process, the time it has been running, and the full path of the command.

If you add the -c option, ps returns the actual executable name, rather than its full path:

```
$ ps -acx
  PID  TT  STAT      TIME COMMAND
    1  ??  Ss     0:00.03 init
    2  ??  Ss     0:20.66 mach_init
   51  ??  Ss     0:03.20 kextd
   77  ??  Ss     0:14.09 update
   81  ??  Ss     0:00.00 dynamic_pager
  111  ??  Ss     8:33.07 configd
  141  ??  Ss     0:06.41 SecurityServer
  189  ??  Ss     5:13.94 ATSServer
  194  ??  Ss    31:58.81 Window Manager
```

These examples show the simple level of output from ps. If you add the -u option to the command, you get much more information. Figure 14.3 shows output from the ps -aux command.

FIGURE 14.3
The ps -aux command gives you detailed information on your active processes.

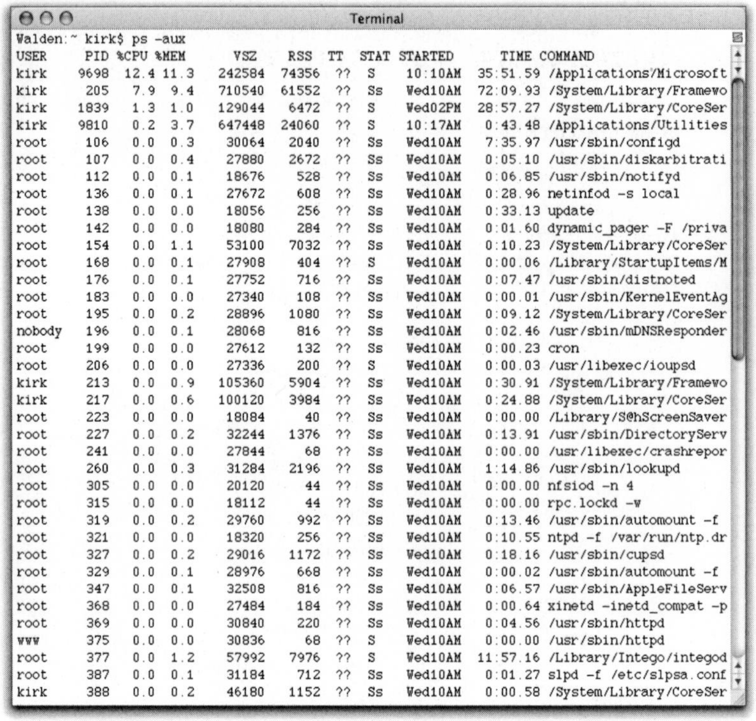

```
Walden:~ kirk$ ps -aux
USER       PID %CPU %MEM      VSZ    RSS  TT  STAT STARTED       TIME COMMAND
kirk      9698 12.4 11.3   242584  74356  ??  S    10:10AM   35:51.59 /Applications/Microsoft
kirk       205  7.9  9.4   710540  61552  ??  Ss   Wed10AM   72:09.93 /System/Library/Framewo
kirk      1839  1.3  1.0   129044   6472  ??  S    Wed02PM   28:57.27 /System/Library/CoreSer
kirk      9810  0.2  3.7   647448  24060  ??  S    10:17AM    0:43.48 /Applications/Utilities
root       106  0.0  0.3    30064   2040  ??  Ss   Wed10AM    7:35.97 /usr/sbin/configd
root       107  0.0  0.4    27880   2672  ??  Ss   Wed10AM    0:05.10 /usr/sbin/diskarbitrati
root       112  0.0  0.1    18676    528  ??  Ss   Wed10AM    0:06.85 /usr/sbin/notifyd
root       136  0.0  0.1    27672    608  ??  Ss   Wed10AM    0:28.96 netinfod -s local
root       138  0.0  0.0    18056    256  ??  Ss   Wed10AM    0:33.13 update
root       142  0.0  0.0    18080    284  ??  Ss   Wed10AM    0:01.60 dynamic_pager -F /priva
root       154  0.0  1.1    53100   7032  ??  Ss   Wed10AM    0:10.23 /System/Library/CoreSer
root       168  0.0  0.1    27908    404  ??  S    Wed10AM    0:00.06 /Library/StartupItems/M
root       176  0.0  0.1    27752    716  ??  Ss   Wed10AM    0:07.47 /usr/sbin/distnoted
root       183  0.0  0.0    27340    108  ??  Ss   Wed10AM    0:00.01 /usr/sbin/KernelEventAg
root       195  0.0  0.2    28896   1080  ??  Ss   Wed10AM    0:09.12 /System/Library/CoreSer
nobody     196  0.0  0.1    28068    816  ??  Ss   Wed10AM    0:02.46 /usr/sbin/mDNSResponder
root       199  0.0  0.0    27612    132  ??  Ss   Wed10AM    0:00.23 cron
root       206  0.0  0.0    27336    200  ??  S    Wed10AM    0:00.03 /usr/libexec/ioupsd
kirk       213  0.0  0.9   105360   5904  ??  Ss   Wed10AM    0:30.91 /System/Library/Framewo
kirk       217  0.0  0.6   100120   3984  ??  Ss   Wed10AM    0:24.88 /System/Library/CoreSer
root       223  0.0  0.0    18084     40  ??  Ss   Wed10AM    0:00.00 /Library/S@hScreenSaver
root       227  0.0  0.2    32244   1376  ??  Ss   Wed10AM    0:13.91 /usr/sbin/DirectoryServ
root       241  0.0  0.0    27844     68  ??  Ss   Wed10AM    0:00.00 /usr/libexec/crashrepor
root       260  0.0  0.3    31284   2196  ??  Ss   Wed10AM    1:14.86 /usr/sbin/lookupd
root       305  0.0  0.0    20120     44  ??  Ss   Wed10AM    0:00.00 nfsiod -n 4
root       315  0.0  0.0    18112     44  ??  Ss   Wed10AM    0:00.00 rpc.lockd -w
root       319  0.0  0.2    29760    992  ??  Ss   Wed10AM    0:13.46 /usr/sbin/automount -f
root       321  0.0  0.0    18320    256  ??  Ss   Wed10AM    0:10.55 ntpd -f /var/run/ntp.dr
root       327  0.0  0.2    29016   1172  ??  Ss   Wed10AM    0:18.16 /usr/sbin/cupsd
root       329  0.0  0.1    28976    668  ??  Ss   Wed10AM    0:00.02 /usr/sbin/automount -f
root       347  0.0  0.1    32508    816  ??  Ss   Wed10AM    0:06.57 /usr/sbin/AppleFileServ
root       368  0.0  0.0    27484    184  ??  Ss   Wed10AM    0:00.64 xinetd -inetd_compat -p
root       369  0.0  0.0    30840    220  ??  Ss   Wed10AM    0:04.56 /usr/sbin/httpd
www        375  0.0  0.0    30836     68  ??  S    Wed10AM    0:00.00 /usr/sbin/httpd
root       377  0.0  1.2    57992   7976  ??  S    Wed10AM   11:57.16 /Library/Intego/integod
root       387  0.0  0.1    31184    712  ??  Ss   Wed10AM    0:01.27 slpd -f /etc/slpsa.conf
kirk       388  0.0  0.2    46180   1152  ??  Ss   Wed10AM    0:00.58 /System/Library/CoreSer
```

In Figure 4.3, I have cut off both the line length and the number of lines. This display shows many things, including CPU usage, memory usage, and much more. The length of the lines depends on the width of your Terminal window, up to a maximum of 132 characters. If you want to see as much as possible of the commands' paths, widen your Terminal window to this width—but it still might not be enough for some commands if they have very long paths.

As with the `top` command, you can use `ps` in conjunction with `grep` to search for specific processes or programs. For example, to find whether iChat is running and, if so, which process ID it has, run this command:

```
$ ps -acx | grep iChat
 1706  ??  Ss     0:10.41 iChatAgent
10368  ??  S      0:08.21 iChat
```

You can see that the command returns two lines: the first is iChatAgent, the iChat background process, and the second is the iChat application itself. This information is most useful when you want to quit a process from the command line; you need to know its process ID to run the `kill` command. See the next page for more on quitting processes using the `kill` command.

ON THE COMMAND LINE

Overview of the *ps* Command

COMMAND SYNTAX

```
ps [option(s)]
```

FINDER EQUIVALENT

Process Viewer.

OVERVIEW OF OPTIONS FOR *PS*

ps   The ps command displays information on processes and their activity.

-a   The -a option tells the ps command to display information about all active processes.

-u   The -u option tells the ps command to display the following for each process: user, pid, %cpu, %mem, vsz, rss, tt, state, start, time, and command.

-x   The -x option tells the ps command to display information about processes without controlling terminals.

-c   The -c option tells the ps command to display the actual executable names of processes rather than their full paths.

GETTING MORE INFORMATION

To display the manual page and learn more about ps, type man ps in Terminal. This command offers many other useful options.

Shutting Down Processes with *kill*

This ominous-sounding command, kill, does what its name suggests: it shuts down processes and programs, just as you quit or force-quit a program from the Finder. The kill command offers several ways to quit applications.

To run the kill command, you need to know the PID of the process you want to shut down. To find this out, use either the **top** or **ps** command, as explained earlier in this chapter. Once you know this PID, you can run the kill command as follows to quit a process:

```
$ kill PID
```

The kill command gives you no feedback; it just sends you to the shell prompt, whether it has worked or not. This way of running the kill command issues a SIGTERM signal. This means that the process should terminate "gracefully," if possible. Note that if you have any unsaved files open in an application and run the kill command, you'll lose your work; that's why the kill command should be a last resort.

ANOTHER WAY TO KILL PROCESSES

In addition to the `kill` command, there is another command that lets you shut down processes. The `killall` command (which, as its name suggests, will kill all processes at once if you run it without an argument) shuts down processes by name rather than by PID. But you still need to know the exact name of the process; for this you need to run `ps -acx` (see above for more on the `ps` command) to find the correct name.

To kill a process with the `killall` command, run the following:

```
$ killall process_name
```

So, to shut down TextEdit, I would need to run this command:

```
$ killall TextEdit
```

If no processes are found with the name you use following the `killall` command, the command returns a message telling you that no matching processes were found. See the `killall` man page for more on using this command.

Using the normal quit, as above, the `kill` command does not always work: with some processes, usually applications, it may work, but with others it won't. For this reason there is another way to use the `kill` command. Using the -9 option with the `kill` command gives it extra power, issuing a KILL signal and nuking the process, shutting down even the most recalcitrant processes:

```
$ kill -9 PID
```

You can run the `kill` command like this for any process that you have launched; for system processes you must preface the command with **sudo**. (For more on **sudo**, see Interlude 7, "Using **sudo**.")

The `kill` command is useful when you have a process that is stuck, or that is relentlessly hogging CPU cycles because of a memory leak. You can usually spot this kind of process by running **top** and looking for something that has constantly high CPU usage. If it is not an application—which you could force-quit from the Finder by selecting the Apple menu ➤ Force Quit or by selecting Force Quit from the application's Dock icon menu—then the only way to shut it down is from the command line. I have seen problems force-quitting the Finder from the Finder's Force Quit dialog; the only way to do so is sometimes from Terminal.

Another reason for using the `kill` command is because your Mac is totally frozen. If you have another Mac on your network and have enabled Remote Login, you can connect to the frozen Mac using **ssh**. (See Chapter 13, "Using the Network," for more on **ssh** and remote login.) If you can connect, you can run **top** and find which processes might be the culprits, then try and shut them down using the `kill` command. Again, this has worked for me many times when running alpha or beta software that has taken over one of my Macs.

You can also use the `kill` command with other signals, such as STOP to pause a process and CONT to resume it. To see the full list of signals, run this command:

```
$ kill -l
 1) SIGHUP       2) SIGINT      3) SIGQUIT     4) SIGILL
 5) SIGTRAP      6) SIGABRT     7) SIGEMT      8) SIGFPE
 9) SIGKILL     10) SIGBUS     11) SIGSEGV    12) SIGSYS
13) SIGPIPE     14) SIGALRM    15) SIGTERM    16) SIGURG
```

17) SIGSTOP	18) SIGTSTP	19) SIGCONT	20) SIGCHLD
21) SIGTTIN	22) SIGTTOU	23) SIGIO	24) SIGXCPU
25) SIGXFSZ	26) SIGVTALRM	27) SIGPROF	28) SIGWINCH
29) SIGINFO	30) SIGUSR1	31) SIGUSR2	

For more on these signals (though not all of them are listed), type man sigaction in Terminal.

On The Command Line
Overview of the *kill* Command

COMMAND SYNTAX

```
kill [option(s)] PID
```

FINDER EQUIVALENT

Force Quit.

OVERVIEW OF OPTIONS FOR *KILL*

kill   The kill command shuts down processes and programs.

-9   The -9 option tells the kill command to forcibly shut down the specified process.

GETTING MORE INFORMATION

To display the manual page and learn more about kill, type man kill in Terminal.

HANDS ON: STARTING AND STOPPING CLASSIC FROM THE COMMAND LINE

In Interlude 5, "The Versatile *open* Command", I showed you how to open the Classic environment from the command line with this command:

```
$ open -a "Classic Startup"
```

You can also stop the Classic environment from the command line, using the tools presented in this chapter. This is less useful in Panther than it was in previous versions of Mac OS X, where the only other way to shut down Classic was via the Classic preference pane. But even if you are running Panther, you may need to kill Classic if it gets frozen.

When Classic is running, you'll notice that no process called "Classic" is listed when you run top or ps. That's because the process is not called Classic, but TruBlueEnvironment:

```
$ ps -acx | grep TruBlue
   824 ??  R      0:12.50 TruBlueEnvironme
```

So, to shut down Classic, find the TruBlueEnvironment process ID using top or ps, then send a kill command as explained above.

Summing Up

The ability to manage the programs and processes running on your Mac allows you to know if any of them are eating up CPU time, and also to shut down any that are blocking your Mac. The tools presented in this chapter let you find out what your Mac is doing and let you change priorities and shut down processes whenever you need to.

Chapter 15

System Maintenance from the Command Line

Just as Mac OS X comes with graphical utilities to maintain your computer and perform certain tasks—such as update its software, install software, and manage hard disks—it also includes a set of command-line tools to carry out these essential operations. Some of these are standard Unix tools, which also exist on other flavors of Unix, but many of them are Apple programs, specific to Mac OS X. In this chapter, I'll present the most useful tools to perform system maintenance operations: you'll learn how to update Mac OS X from the command line by downloading software updates and installing them; you'll learn how to manage hard disks and perform disk maintenance operations; and you'll see how to get information about your system from the command line.

Getting System Information

Part of any system maintenance operation involves analyzing information. This can be specific information regarding your computer's hardware, information about its software, or information about its actual operation. Mac OS X includes tools that provide much of this information for you.

Getting Hardware Information with *system_profiler*

One of the graphical tools Apple provides is System Profiler, an application found in /Applications/ Utilities. This tool is very useful for troubleshooting hardware problems: for example, you can check whether a USB or FireWire peripheral is recognized, or you can find how much RAM your Mac sees. If you cannot use the graphical version of this program, a command-line alternative exists: system_profiler. However, if the graphical program is not installed, or is not working, the command-line tool will not function.

This command does only one thing: it generates a report of your Mac's hardware, software, and logs. If you run the command like this:

```
$ system_profiler
```

it displays a full report on your computer and its operating system in Terminal. This report begins as follows:

```
Hardware:

    Hardware Overview:

        Machine Model: iBook G4
        CPU Type: PowerPC G4  (3.3)
        Number Of CPUs: 1
        CPU Speed: 933 MHz
        L2 Cache (per CPU): 256 KB
        Memory: 640 MB
        Bus Speed: 133 MHz
        Boot ROM Version: 4.7.7f0
        Serial Number: UV34632QQE

Software:

    System Software Overview:

        System Version: Mac OS X 10.3.4 (7H63)
        Kernel Version: Darwin 7.4.0
        Boot Volume: Mac OS X
        Computer Name: Kirk's iBook
        User Name: Kirk McElhearn (kirk)
[etc.]
```

The report includes a number of different sections:

Hardware   This tells which model Mac you have, its speed, the amount of cache memory, and more.

Software   This tells which version of Mac OS X you are running, the name of your boot volume, the kernel version, and your username.

Network   This tells what your currently active network interface is, including its hardware address.

Memory   This tells how much RAM you have and what type of DIMMs it is.

PCI/AGP Cards, ATA, SCSI, USB, FireWire, etc.   These sections give a list of all active internal and external devices and volumes, including PCI cards, USB devices, and FireWire devices. It also tells you the type, model, and size of your hard disk(s), and information on each volume, if your hard disk is partitioned.

Applications   This is a list of all applications (other than Classic applications) installed on your Mac. Note that this only lists applications installed in your `Applications` folder; if you have applications elsewhere they are not included.

Frameworks   This is a list of software frameworks available.

Extensions   This is a list of kernel extensions available.

Logs   These are logs for the system and individual applications. The crash logs shown here are generally only useful to developers, providing them with details on when an application crashed and what occurred at that moment. You can also view these logs in the Console, found in /Applications/ Utilities.

If you want to save the system_profiler report, you can redirect the command's output like this:

```
$ system_profiler > report.txt
```

This saves a text file with the contents of the report, the same as what displays in Terminal.

You can also save this report in XML format, which results in a special file with an .spx extension. If you double-click this file in the Finder it will open with the System Profiler application, providing an easier-to-read report. To do this, run the command as follows:

```
$ system_profiler -xml > report.spx
```

ON THE COMMAND LINE

Overview of the *system_profiler* Command

COMMAND SYNTAX

```
system_profiler [option(s)]
```

FINDER EQUIVALENT

The System Profiler utility.

OVERVIEW OF OPTIONS FOR *SYSTEM_PROFILER*

system_profiler	The system_profiler command returns a report of information on your hardware and software.
-xml	This tells the system_profiler command to save its output in XML format. This should then be redirected into a file with an .spx extension, so the resulting report can be read by the graphical System Profiler application.
-detailLevel	This can be -2, -1, 0, or 1, with each level generating different amounts of information in its report. With level 1, the command returns a full report; this is the same as running the command with no specified level of detail.

GETTING MORE INFORMATION

To find out more about the system_profiler command, type man system_profiler in Terminal.

The system_profiler command offers several levels of detail, which allow you to generate shorter reports, covering just the most essential information. For example, if you run the following command, only the first two sections (as shown in the first example earlier) display:

```
$ system_profiler -detailLevel -2
```

The next level of detail returns complete hardware information for your Mac, but nothing about its software:

```
$ system_profiler -detailLevel -1
```

Finally, the "short report," as the command's man page calls it, returns complete hardware information and a list of applications (this is shorter than the full report, which also includes frameworks and logs):

```
$ system_profiler -detailLevel 0
```

You can save any of these reports as text or XML files as necessary.

Getting Disk Usage Information with *du*

The du (disk usage) command tells how much disk space a given directory uses (though if the directory contains files with resource forks, it won't include the resource forks). Here's one example:

```
$ du -sk ~
1309800 /Users/kirk
```

I've used two options in this example: the -s option tells du to display only the total space used for the directories and its subdirectories; if I hadn't used that option, the command would have returned a long list of all the subdirectories and their space used. The -k option tells du to display its results in kilobytes.

As you can see in this example, my home directory takes up over 1.3 GB of disk space. To get more detailed information on this directory and its immediate subdirectories, I can run the command as follows:

```
$ du -sk ~/*
81000    /Users/kirk/Desktop
421592   /Users/kirk/Documents
251808   /Users/kirk/Library
309364   /Users/kirk/Movies
33916    /Users/kirk/Music
192620   /Users/kirk/Pictures
32       /Users/kirk/Public
5216     /Users/kirk/Sites
```

Again, using the -s option tells the command to display only totals. The * wildcard tells du to return information on every directory and file in my home directory.

You can use the du command prefaced by sudo to get disk usage information for your entire file system, or for directories belonging to other users. If you run this command:

```
$ sudo du -sk /
20226798      /
```

the command traverses all the directories in your file system and returns the total space used. This can take a few minutes, and it includes any volumes that are mounted, whether they are external volumes or network volumes. You can limit the results to the current file system by using the -x option.

The du command has several options allowing you to choose whether or not to follow symbolic links and to vary the level of detail of the information it returns.

ON THE COMMAND LINE

Overview of the *du* Command

COMMAND SYNTAX

```
du [option(s)] directory(ies)
```

FINDER EQUIVALENT

Size section of the Info window.

OVERVIEW OF OPTIONS FOR *DU*

du   The du command returns the amount of disk space used by a directory or file.

-s   This option tells the du command to display only totals for the specified directories.

-k   This option tells the du command to display its results in kilobytes.

-x   This option tells the du command to examine only the current file system.

GETTING MORE INFORMATION

To find out more about the du command, type man du in Terminal.

Getting Free Disk Space Information with *df*

Just as the du command gives you information on the amount of disk space used by given directories, the df (disk space free) command tells you how much free space is on your disk. When you run this command, it tells you the free space on the disks available on your file system:

```
$ df -k
Filesystem         1K-blocks      Used     Avail Capacity Mounted on
/dev/disk0s10      15596160  11768992   3671208     76%   /
devfs                    95        95         0    100%   /dev
fdesc                     1         1         0    100%   /dev
<volfs>                 512       512         0    100%   /.vol
/dev/disk0s12      42741024  40237256   2503768     94%    /Volumes/Backup
```

The three lines beginning with devfs, fdesc, and <volfs> are special pseudo partitions used by Mac OS X. The other two lines show the actual partitions on my Mac. The startup partition, mounted on /, is 76 percent full, and my Backup partition is 94 percent full.

You can also run the df command specifying a directory:

```
$ df -k ~
Filesystem     1K-blocks     Used   Avail Capacity  Mounted on
/dev/disk0s10  15596160 11769012 3671188    76%    /
```

In this case, df returns only information for the disk containing the specified directory.

In these examples, I used the -k option to tell df to display its results in kilobytes. The df command offers additional options that let you select specific file systems or types of file systems.

ON THE COMMAND LINE

Overview of the *df* Command

COMMAND SYNTAX

```
df [option(s)] [file system(s)]
```

FINDER EQUIVALENT

Available section of the Info window.

OVERVIEW OF OPTIONS FOR DF

df The df command returns the amount of free disk space for the specified file system(s).

-k This option tells the df command to display its results in kilobytes.

GETTING MORE INFORMATION

To find out more about the df command, type man df in the Terminal.

Managing Disks and Volumes with *diskutil*

Apple's Disk Utility, located in /Applications/Utilities, is a tool for managing disks and volumes. This graphical program lets you format, erase, and partition disks, mount and unmount volumes, repair disks and privileges, work with disk images, and manage RAID volumes. Its command-line equivalent, diskutil, lets you do all these operations from the Terminal.

To see what diskutil can do, run the command with no arguments. It returns a list of its options and their functions:

```
$ diskutil
```

Syntax for diskutil is as follows:

```
diskutil verb [option(s)]
```

Most of the commands require the use of sudo. Table 15.1 shows the commands available with diskutil.

Getting Disk Info with *diskutil*

To get information on a disk, run diskutil info with the disk's mount point; this is / for your Mac OS X startup volume or /Volumes/volume_name for other volumes.

```
$ diskutil info /
Device Node:        /dev/disk0s10
   Device Identifier: disk0s10
   Mount Point:      /
   Volume Name:      Mac OS X

   File System:      Journaled HFS+
                     Journal size 8192 k at offset 0x1a8000
   Permissions:      Enabled
   Partition Type:   Apple_HFS
   Bootable:         Is bootable
   Media Type:       Generic
   Protocol:         ATA

   Total Size:       14.9 GB
   Free Space:       3.5 GB

   Read Only:        No
   Ejectable:        No
```

An you can see, this tells you basic information about the disk, including its mount point, volume name, the type of file system and partition, the protocol, its size and free space, and whether the disk is read only or ejectable. It also tells you if its permissions are enabled (they can be disabled for non-startup volumes), whether the disk is bootable, and whether journaling is turned on.

Getting a List of Mounted Disks with *diskutil*

The diskutil command can return a list of all mounted disks, which can help you when using diskutil by showing you what kinds of disks are mounted and where. Run this command:

```
$ diskutil list
/dev/disk0
   #:                  type name         size       identifier
   0: Apple_partition_scheme           *55.9 GB    disk0
   1:    Apple_partition_map            31.5 KB    disk0s1
   2:        Apple_Driver43             28.0 KB    disk0s2
   3:        Apple_Driver43             28.0 KB    disk0s3
   4:    Apple_Driver_ATA               28.0 KB    disk0s4
   5:    Apple_Driver_ATA               28.0 KB    disk0s5
   6:      Apple_FWDriver               256.0 KB   disk0s6
   7:  Apple_Driver_IOKit              256.0 KB   disk0s7
   8:      Apple_Patches               256.0 KB   disk0s8
   9:        Apple_HFS Mac OS X         14.9 GB    disk0s10
  10:        Apple_HFS Backup           40.8 GB    disk0s12
```

```
/dev/disk3
   #:                   type name          size       identifier
   0: Apple_partition_scheme              *153.4 GB  disk3
   1:      Apple_partition_map             31.5 KB   disk3s1
   2:         Apple_Driver43               28.0 KB   disk3s2
   3:         Apple_Driver43               28.0 KB   disk3s3
   4:     Apple_Driver_ATA                 28.0 KB   disk3s4
   5:     Apple_Driver_ATA                 28.0 KB   disk3s5
   6:        Apple_FWDriver               256.0 KB   disk3s6
   7:    Apple_Driver_IOKit              256.0 KB   disk3s7
   8:         Apple_Patches               256.0 KB   disk3s8
   9:            Apple_HFS FW160          153.2 GB   disk3s10
/dev/disk4
   #:                   type name          size       identifier
   0: Apple_partition_scheme              *124.0 MB  disk4
   1:      Apple_partition_map             31.5 KB   disk4s1
   2:            Apple_HFS KeyDrive       123.9 MB   disk4s2
```

As you can see, there are three disks mounted. The first one, an internal hard disk, has two partitions: Mac OS X and Backup. The second, an external FireWire disk, has only one partition. And the third is a USB key drive, again with just one partition.

But all these disks have multiple partitions, even if you don't see them when examining the disks themselves: these partitions hold drivers and mapping information. The partitions that you can mount are the ones with names in the Name column.

Using *diskutil*

As you can see in Table 15.1 below, diskutil lets you do a lot to your disks and volumes. But be forewarned: diskutil can be dangerous. Partitioning a disk deletes all its data; using the eraseDisk or eraseVolume options and making a mistake in the disk's name or device node can have serious consequences. Make sure you know what you are doing with this command.

The diskutil command lets you handle many disk maintenance operations from the command line. You can verify and repair disk structure, and you can verify and repair permissions. Running disk structure repairs is a good thing to do from time to time, even though Mac OS X does this automatically on startup. As for repairing permissions, this can solve many problems with Mac OS X, and many people do it every time they run a system upgrade.

To repair permissions on your startup volume, run this command:

```
$ sudo diskutil repairPermissions /
```

You'll notice that this command finds something to fix almost every time it runs.

To repair a disk's structure, run this command:

```
$ sudo diskutil repairDisk /Volumes/Backup
```

In this example, I ran diskutil on a volume called Backup.

The `diskutil` command lets you do everything that you can do using Disk Utility, as long as you use it correctly. Be careful before erasing or partitioning disks, though, since there is no safety net. Make sure you've got a full backup of all your disks before you perform any such operations.

TABLE 15.1: VERBS FOR USE WITH *DISKUTIL*

VERB	FUNCTION
list	List the partitions of a disk.
info | information	Get information on a disk or volume.
unmount	Unmount a single volume.
unmountDisk	Unmount an entire disk, all volumes.
eject	Eject a disk.
mount	Mount a single volume.
mountDisk	Mount an entire disk, all mountable volumes.
rename	Rename a volume.
enableJournal	Enable HFS+ journaling on a mounted HFS+ volume.
disableJournal	Disable HFS+ journaling on a mounted HFS+ volume.
verifyDisk	Verify the structure of a volume.
repairDisk	Repair the structure of a volume.
verifyPermissions	Verify the permissions of a volume.
repairPermissions	Repair the permissions of a volume.
repairOS9Permissions	Repair the permissions of the selected Classic System Folder and Applications folder.
eraseDisk	Erase an existing disk, removing all volumes.
eraseVolume	Erase an existing volume
eraseOptical	Erase an optical media CD/RW, DVD/RW, etc.
zeroDisk	Erase a disk writing zeroes to its media.
randomDisk	Erase a disk writing random data to its media.
partitionDisk	Repartition a disk, removing all volumes.
createRAID	Create a RAID set on multiple disks.
destroyRAID	Destroy an existing RAID set.
checkRAID	Check a RAID set for errors.
enableRAID	Convert a disk to an unpaired mirror RAID set.
repairMirror	Repair a damaged RAID mirror set.

ON THE COMMAND LINE

Overview of the *diskutil* Command

COMMAND SYNTAX

```
diskutil verb [option(s)]
```

FINDER EQUIVALENT

Disk Utility.

OVERVIEW OF OPTIONS FOR *DISKUTIL*

diskutil   The diskutil command lets you manage disks and volumes. See Table 15.1 for a list of verbs and functions.

GETTING MORE INFORMATION

To find out more about the df command, type man diskutil in Terminal.

Repairing Disk Problems with *fsck*

While hard disks are mechanically reliable, up to a certain point, it is not uncommon for them to become corrupted. Disks use directories, which store the names and locations of files on disk. If a disk's directory gets corrupted, your disk can no longer find its files; if corruption is serious, you may lose access to all your files.

Each time you start up your Mac, the boot process includes a file system check, which may repair small problems with the directory if your computer has crashed or been shut down incorrectly, or if you disconnected an external drive without first ejecting it. In addition, if you have a kernel panic (a crash requiring you to restart your Mac), the boot process is longer as fsck runs a more thorough check and repair. (While Mac OS X can run for a long time without reboots, this alone is a good reason to restart from time to time.)

But if you have more serious problems, your best bet is to boot from a Mac OS X Install CD first, and run Disk Utility by selecting it from the Installer menu. Naturally, you may not always have an Install CD handy; in this case, you can run the fsck (file system check) command to repair them. While this command cannot repair all disk corruption, it does a good job with basic directory problems.

MANAGING DISKS WITH *DISKTOOL*

In addition to diskutil, another command lets you manage disks: disktool lets you mount and unmount, rename, and eject disks and control certain disk parameters. But disktool has fewer options than diskutil, and can be more complicated to use.

The disktool command has no man page; to find out what it can do, just type disktool in Terminal with no arguments: the command returns a summary of its functions and options.

To run this command, you first need to boot your Mac in "single user" mode. This starts up your Mac in the simplest possible manner, with no graphical interface; all you see is a black screen with white text. This is like the Terminal, without the window and menus.

To book in single user mode, press 2 ⌘-S at startup. You will quickly see the minimal console interface. Some messages display, then you see a # prompt. (Note: if you use a non-QWERTY keyboard, you'll be a bit confused; in this interface, your Mac reads keys *as if* you were typing on a QWERTY keyboard, so it may take some time for you to find which keys are which.)

Start by typing the following:

```
# /sbin/fsck -y
```

The -y option tells `fsck` that you are answering "yes" to all its questions. As `fsck` runs, the command displays a few messages. When it has completed, it says "The volume [*volume name*] appears to be OK." If, however, it finds problems, `fsck` returns "FILE SYSTEM WAS MODIFIED"; in this case, it is best to run `fsck` again, until this message no longer displays.

If you are using a journaled file system, you need to run `fsck` with the -f (force) option for it to check the file system.

If `fsck` fixes anything, restart your Mac by running this command:

```
# restart -n
```

If not, type `exit` and press Enter; your Mac will continue booting and display the graphical interface at the end of the boot process.

ON THE COMMAND LINE

Overview of the *fsck* Command

COMMAND SYNTAX

```
fsck [option(s)]
```

FINDER EQUIVALENT

Disk Utility's disk repair function.

OVERVIEW OF OPTIONS FOR *FSCK*

fsck   The `fsck` command lets you check the consistency of file systems, and makes repairs if possible.

-y   This option tells `fsck` that you are answering "yes" to all its questions.

-f   This option forces a file system check; you need to use this if you are running a journaled file system.

GETTING MORE INFORMATION

To find out more about the `fsck` command, type `man fsck` in Terminal.

In some cases, your disk problems may be too severe for `fsck` to repair them. If so, you'll need to run a third-party disk repair tool, such as Alsoft DiskWarrior or Micromat TechTool. As of this writing, TechTool is included with AppleCare contracts, so, if you have AppleCare protection, try running that program to fix any disk problems you encounter.

Blessing a System Folder with *bless*

Volumes on Macintosh computers must be "blessed," or set to be bootable, so you can start up your computer with them. If you have several volumes on your Mac and move your Classic System Folder, you may find that the Classic preference pane does not see it, or that the Startup preference pane does not allow you to select it. The same may occur with Mac OS X volumes. To enable booting for a volume or System Folder, you can use the `bless` command.

This command works in three modes: folder mode, device mode, and info mode. In folder mode you select a System Folder (yes, even under Mac OS X) and bless it for startup. You usually use device mode only when formatting and setting up a volume for the first time. And info mode tells you which volumes or folders are blessed.

In my case, I have my Classic System Folder on a separate partition. Running `bless` in info mode on both partitions shows me the following:

```
$ bless -info /
finderinfo[0]: 104794 => Blessed System Folder is /System/Library/CoreServices
finderinfo[1]:      0 => No Startup App folder (ignored anyway)
finderinfo[2]:      0 => Open-folder linked list empty
finderinfo[3]:      0 => No OS 9 + X blessed 9 folder
finderinfo[4]:      0 => Unused field unset
finderinfo[5]: 104794 => OS X blessed folder is /System/Library/CoreServices
64-bit VSDB volume id:  0x4762A70348707693

$ bless -info /Volumes/Backup/
finderinfo[0]:      0 => No Blessed System Folder
finderinfo[1]:      0 => No Startup App folder (ignored anyway)
finderinfo[2]:      0 => Open-folder linked list empty
finderinfo[3]:     21 => OS 9 blessed folder is /Volumes/Backup/System Folder
finderinfo[4]:      0 => Unused field unset
finderinfo[5]:      0 => No OS 9 + X blessed X folder
64-bit VSDB volume id:  0x48B0F1B788BAB952
```

The first case shows the blessed System Folder on my startup volume, and the second shows me the blessed Classic (OS 9) System Folder.

To bless a Mac OS 9 volume, to boot in OS 9 only, run this command, replacing `vol_name` with the name of your volume:

```
$ bless -folder9 "/Volumes/Mac OS 9/System Folder" -bootBlockFile
         "/usr/share/misc/bootblockdata"
```

ON THE COMMAND LINE

Overview of the *bless* Command

COMMAND SYNTAX

```
bless [option(s)] directory
```

FINDER EQUIVALENT

None.

OVERVIEW OF OPTIONS FOR *BLESS*

bless   The bless command lets you make volumes and System Folders bootable.

GETTING MORE INFORMATION

To find out more about the bless command, type man bless in Terminal. This is a complex command, and can be dangerous, so read this man page carefully.

To bless a Mac OS X volume, to boot only into OS X, run this command, replacing *vol_name* with the name of your volume (this should all be one line):

```
$ bless -folder "/Volumes/vol_name/System/Library/CoreServices"
-bootinfo "/Volumes/vol_name/usr/standalone/ppc/bootx.bootinfo"
```

To bless a volume containing either Mac OS X or OS 9, run this command:

```
$ bless -mount "/Volumes/Mac OS" -setBoot
```

Use this command with care; if you make a mistake, you may not be able to boot your Mac.

Running Periodic Maintenance Routines with *periodic*

Your Mac regularly runs a set of maintenance routines, using the periodic command, archiving logs, deleting old logs, and updating the locate database. Or does it? Since Unix computers are designed to be on 24 hours a day, these routines are run in the wee hours; if you turn your Mac off at night, they will never be run.

The periodic command is set to run at specific times as a cron task. You can change the times this is run by editing the crontab file, (for more on cron, see Interlude 9, "Automating Commands") or you can run the periodic command manually.

Since the periodic weekly command creates and updates the locate database, it is important to run it at least once to be able to use the locate command; running it regularly ensures that the database is up to date. (See Chapter 7, "Finding Files, Directories and Everything Else" for more on locate.)

Overview of the *periodic* Command

COMMAND SYNTAX

```
periodic [daily | weekly | monthly]
```

FINDER EQUIVALENT

None.

OVERVIEW OF OPTIONS FOR *PERIODIC*

periodic   The periodic command runs daily, weekly, and monthly maintenance routines.

GETTING MORE INFORMATION

To find out more about the periodic command, type man periodic in Terminal.

You can run the periodic command as follows:

```
$ sudo periodic daily weekly monthly
```

You can run any or all of the three periodic tasks (daily, weekly, monthly). The weekly task is the longest, and may take several minutes to update the locate database, depending on the size of your hard disk(s).

HOW IMPORTANT ARE THESE MAINTENANCE TASKS?

A great deal of pixels get used on the Internet as Mac users tell each other how important it is to run these tasks, and how much not doing so can slow down their Macs. Unfortunately, the received wisdom on this issue is incorrect.

While these tasks are important, they are far from essential; if they were essential, Apple would have set them to run at other times. In fact, by setting them to run in the wee hours of the morning and on weekends, Apple has clearly shown that they are only important for computers that run 24/7.

Why is this so, even though many developers have created applications to run these tasks? Quite simply because for most users they do nothing important. When you look at the scripts that the periodic command runs, you can see that they do little more than rotate log files and update the locate database. The latter is useful only if you use the locate command, and the former if you need to examine your logs. Sure, if your logs get long they can be a hassle to check, but since log information is merely appended to text files, they can be any length and not slow down your system.

The only truly useful thing these maintenance tasks do is back up your NetInfo database; as for the rest, you can live without them.

If it makes you feel better, you can run these tasks occasionally, especially the daily maintenance routine (which backs up the NetInfo database). But if you're not using your Mac as a server (where you would want to examine your logs from time to time), they really won't make any difference.

Updating and Installing Software

Apple releases regular updates to Mac OS X, and to other Apple software, and makes them available through its Software Update application. This application can automatically check Apple's servers at regular intervals and inform you of any new updates. You can then choose whether you want to install the available updates.

Other software you add or update uses Apple's Installer application. This program installs software, optimizes your hard disk, and restarts your Mac if necessary.

Naturally, there are command-line tools that can do both of these operations. This is especially useful if you administer a group of Macs; you can initiate remote connections to them and download and install updates or install new software easily.

Installing Software with *installer*

The `installer` command provides the same functions as Apple's Installer application, allowing you to easily install software from the command line. This command can install non-system software on any volume, or it can install system software on a non-booted volume. To run this command you need to be an administrator, and run it as root or using `sudo`.

Since many installation packages are in disk images, you need to mount the disk image first to be able to install the software. Here's an example of installing a version of Apple's Backup on a remote Mac.

First, the remote computer must have Remote Login turned on in the Sharing preference pane.

Next, if the software you want to install is not present on the remote computer, and you have it in the form of a disk image or package, you need to copy it to that computer. You can use the `scp` command (see Chapter 13, "Using the Network," for more on this command):

```
$ scp /Volumes/Backup/Backup_2.0.1.dmg kirk@10.0.1.201:/Users/Shared
Backup_2.0.1.dmg      100% |*****************|  1524 KB     00:00
```

The `scp` command shows the progress of the copy and when the copy is complete returns you to the prompt.

Then, use `ssh` to connect to the remote computer. (See Chapter 13 for more on `ssh`.)

```
$ ssh kirk@10.0.1.201
```

Next, mount the disk image you just copied:

```
$ hdiutil mount /Users/Shared/Backup_2.0.1.dmg
Verification completed...
verified   CRC32 $5D02223D
Attaching...
Finishing...
/dev/disk3              Apple_partition_scheme
/dev/disk3s1            Apple_partition_map
/dev/disk3s2            Apple_HFS              /Volumes/Backup 2.0.1
```

The last line shows you the name of the disk image volume. List this volume's contents to find the name of the package you want to install:

```
$ ls /Volumes/Backup\ 2.0.1/
About Backup    Backup.pkg
```

ON THE COMMAND LINE

Overview of the *installer* Command

COMMAND SYNTAX

```
installer [option(s)] -pkg <pathToPackage> -target <pathToTarget>
```

FINDER EQUIVALENT

Installer utility.

OVERVIEW OF OPTIONS FOR *INSTALLER*

installer   The installer command installs software from .pkg or .mpkg files.

-pkginfo   The -pkginfo option lists the contents of the specified .mpkg file.

GETTING MORE INFORMATION

To find out more about the installer command and its many options, type man installer in the Terminal.

Now, run the installer command. You need to specify -pkg followed by the name of the package, and -target followed by the target location.

```
$ sudo installer -pkg /Volumes/Backup\ 2.0.1/Backup.pkg -target /
installer: Package name is Backup Software
installer: Upgrading volume mounted at /.
installer: The upgrade was successful.
```

The installer command tells you the results of its operation. In the preceding example, I upgraded existing software. In other cases, the installer command will tell you that the installation was successful. Next, unmount the disk image.

```
$ hdiutil unmount /Volumes/Backup\ 2.0.1/
"disk3s2" unmounted successfully.
```

Then type exit to end the remote ssh connection.

```
$ exit
```

In some cases you will want to install .mpkg files, which contain multiple packages. To find out which packages they contain, run the installer command like this:

```
$ installer -pkginfo -pkg /Volumes/Developer\ Tools/Developer.mpkg
DevSDK.pkg
DevDocumentation.pkg
DevExamples.pkg
BSDSDK.pkg
MacOSX10.1.pkg
```

```
MacOSX10.2.pkg
MacOSX10.3.pkg
gcc2.95.2.pkg
X11SDK.pkg
```

You can then specify which packages you want to install by listing them after the `-pkg` option.

One thing the `installer` command does not tell you is whether you need to restart the computer after installing software. It's best to try out the installation using the graphical installer to know if this is necessary. If it is, restart the remote computer using the `reboot` command:

```
$ sudo reboot
```

But first make sure that no users are going to be affected by this restart.

Updating Mac OS X with *softwareupdate*

The `softwareupdate` command is the command-line equivalent of Apple's Software Update program, which checks Apple's servers for updates to Mac OS X and other Apple programs. The command-line tool offers less flexibility and fewer functions than the graphical program, but it can be useful for updating software on remote computers.

The main differences are that you cannot set the `softwareupdate` command to make periodic checks of Apple's servers (though you could create a `cron` task that does this; see Interlude 9 for more on `cron`), and you cannot save updates from the command line, you can only install them. You can also ignore specific updates; this is useful if you don't need to install a certain update and don't want it to display each time you run the `softwareupdate` command.

The `softwareupdate` command is very easy to use. Just run the command like this to find out what updates are available:

```
$ softwareupdate -l
Software Update Tool
Copyright 2002-2003 Apple Computer, Inc.

Software Update found the following new or updated software:
   ! ARDClient124Update-1.2.4
        Apple Remote Desktop Client, 1.2.4, 832K [required]
   ! iCal-1.5.2
        iCal, 1.5.2, 7852K [required]
   ! iChatAV21-2.1
        iChat Update, 2.1, 5040K [required] [restart]
   ! iPodWeb2004-04-28-3.0
        iPod Update 2004-04-28, 3.0, 8112K [required]
   ! iTunes4-4.5
        iTunes, 4.5, 8372K [required]
   ! MacOSXUpdateCombo10.3.4-10.3.4
        Mac OS X Update Combined, 10.3.4, 83412K [required] [restart]
   * AirPortSW-3.4.1
        AirPort Software, 3.4.1, 9152K [restart]
```

As you can see in this output, the command lists the updates that are available and tells you which are required (though this seems to not always be the case, as in the Apple Remote Desktop Client, which is not essential for Mac OS X) and which require a restart. Using sudo, which you need in order to install any software from the command line, run a command like the following to install one of the available updates:

```
$ sudo softwareupdate -i iTunes4-4.5
Software Update Tool
Copyright 2002-2003 Apple Computer, Inc.

iTunes: 0...10...20...30...
```

As the softwareupdate command downloads and installs the update, it displays a line such as this one, showing the progress of the update. When it has finished it displays the following:

```
Optimizing system performance.  This may take a while...
Done.
```

Depending on the update, the "optimizing system performance" part may take from a few seconds to quite a while. For major updates it can take over 15 minutes.

ON THE COMMAND LINE

Overview of the *softwareupdate* Command

COMMAND SYNTAX

```
softwareupdate [item]
```

FINDER EQUIVALENT

Software Update utility.

OVERVIEW OF OPTIONS FOR *SOFTWAREUPDATE*

softwareupdate	The softwareupdate command checks for updates to Mac OS X or other Apple software and installs them.
-l	This option tells the softwareupdate command to list available updates.
-i	This option, followed by the name of an update, tells the softwareupdate command to install the selected update. This requires the use of sudo.

GETTING MORE INFORMATION

To find out more about the softwareupdate command, type man softwareupdate in Terminal.

If you wish to install more than one update, just add the names of all the updates you want to install as arguments. You can simplify this by running the software update command with the -a option, to install all available updates, or the -r option, which installs all required updates.

If the update in question requires that you restart the Mac you've installed the software on, you'll see the following:

```
You have installed one or more updates that requires that you restart your
computer.  Please restart immediately.
```

If this is the case, you can restart the remote computer using the reboot command:

```
$ sudo reboot
```

But first make sure that no users are going to be affected by this restart.

Summing Up

Mac OS X comes with many tools that allow you to manage your system. From getting hardware and software information to installing and updating your system software, the command-line tools at your disposal are powerful and efficient. In many cases they do the same things as Apple's utilities, such as Disk Utility, Software Update, and Installer. These tools offer extra advantages to those administering many Macs, since you can use them to manage their systems remotely.

OTHER USEFUL SYSTEM MANAGEMENT COMMANDS

Here is a selection of other commands that can be useful for system administration:

The asr (Apple Software Restore) command copies disk images onto volumes and restores software from disk images. It is the command-line equivalent of the Apple Software Restore program.

The pmset (Power Manager set) command reads and changes power management settings such as idle sleep timing, wake on administrative access, automatic restart on power loss, etc. It is the command-line equivalent of the Energy Saver preference pane.

The nvram (non-volatile RAM) command manipulates Open Firmware NVRAM variables. It can be used to print a list of variables or set variables.

The shutdown command provides an automated shutdown procedure for superusers to nicely notify users who are working in Terminal on their computers when the system is shutting down. It won't say anything to users working in the GUI, however.

The halt and reboot commands flush the file system cache to disk, send all running processes a SIG-TERM (and subsequently a SIGKILL), and, respectively, halt or restart the system.

The screencapture command lets you take screen shots from the command line.

Interlude 8: Using the Developer Tools

Mac OS X comes with a set of Developer Tools—programs, templates, and documentation for use by developers who create software for Mac OS X. These tools are available on a separate CD, if you purchased Mac OS X in a box, or on one of the installation CDs, if you got Mac OS X with a new computer.

You can also get the Developer Tools, and updates to these tools, by joining the Apple Developer Connection (`http://developer.apple.com`). Basic membership is free, and lets you download the Developer Tools over the Internet, but to get regular CDs containing updates and other tools and documentation, you must subscribe to one of Apple's fee-based services.

While these tools are most useful for those developing software, some of the command-line tools they install are very practical for other users as well. If you haven't installed the Developer Tools yet, you might want to do so to access certain commands they offer. In addition, check the Apple web site for updates to the Developer Tools; since the Panther release, there was one major update, Apple updates these Developer Tools from time to time.

Command-Line Developer Tools

When you install the Developer Tools, a `Developer` directory is created at the root level of your file system. This directory contains several subdirectories, and includes applications, documentation, samples, and much more. The command-line tools are installed in `/Developer/Tools`:

```
% ls /Developer/Tools/
BuildStrings      RezWack         cvswrappers
CpMac             SetFile         pbhelpindexer
DeRez             SplitForks      pbprojectdump
GetFileInfo       UnRezWack       pbutil
MergePef          WSMakeStubs     pbxcp
MvMac             agvtool         pbxhmapdump
ResMerger         cvs-unwrap      sdp
Rez               cvs-wrap        uninstall-devtools.pl
```

To use these tools, you should first add `/Developer/Tools` to your shell's path variable. (See Chapter 16, "Configuring the Shell," for more on this.) If you do this, you'll be able to invoke these commands by using just their names; you won't need to type their full paths.

I won't look at all of these tools, which are useful mainly to developers, but will examine the following commands, which can be helpful to anyone using the Mac OS X command line:

- ◆ `CpMac`: This command works like the `cp` (copy) command, but preserves resource forks.

- ◆ `GetFileInfo`: This command returns file information, such as creator and type, and other file attributes.

◆ **MvMac:** This command works like the mv (move) command, but preserves resource forks.

◆ **SetFile:** This command sets HFS+ file attributes.

Copying Files with *CpMac*

The CpMac (copy Macintosh file) command works like the cp command, with one exception: it retains resource forks and file metadata that the cp command ignores. When you copy a file with cp, this metadata is lost, which means that you cannot use cp to correctly copy files used by older Macintosh applications.

Mac OS has historically used a unique way of saving files: many files are in two parts, called the data fork and the resource fork. Back in the days of Mac OS 9 and earlier, the data fork contained data (the contents of a file, or code for applications) and the resource fork contained settings, icons, and other information. Since Mac OS didn't use filename extensions (such as .txt), this information is what told the Finder what type a certain file was, and what application could open it. Most files used this two-part system, and if you have ever copied files to a PC disk and looked on a Windows computer, you have seen additional folders copied together with your files; these are the resource forks.

ON THE COMMAND LINE

Overview of the *CpMac* Command

COMMAND SYNTAX

    CpMac [-p] [-r] source   destination

FINDER EQUIVALENT

Copy and Paste, or drag and drop copy.

OVERVIEW OF OPTIONS FOR *CPMAC*

CpMac   This command copies the source argument to the destination, retaining resource forks. You can use multiple sources or wildcards. You can specify a directory as the destination, or specify a path containing a filename, if you wish to change the name of the file being copied.

-p   This option causes CpMac to preserve in the copy as many of the file attributes as allowed by permissions such as modification time, access time, file flags, file mode, user ID, and group ID as allowed by permissions.

-r   If the source is a directory, CpMac copies the directory and all its subdirectories.

GETTING MORE INFORMATION

To display the manual page and learn more about CpMac and the options available, type man CpMac in Terminal.

For this reason, Apple includes in the Developer Tools a special command to copy files with this information. To copy files with the CpMac command, use the following syntax:

```
$ CpMac source destination
```

This is exactly like the cp command (see Chapter 6, "Moving, Copying and Deleting Files and Folders") with two exceptions: the first is that the command name is case-sensitive; you must type CpMac with the correct upper- and lower-case letters. The second exception is that CpMac has fewer options.

Moving Files with *MvMac*

The MvMac (move **Mac**intosh file) command works like the mv command, but it retains resource forks and file metadata that the mv command does not understand. When you move a file with mv, this metadata is lost, which means that you cannot use mv to correctly copy files used by older Macintosh applications.

For this reason, Apple includes in the Developer Tools a special command to move files with this information. To move files with the MvMac command, use the following syntax:

```
$ MvMac source destination
```

This is exactly like the mv command (see Chapter 6) with two exceptions. The first exception is that the command name is case-sensitive; you must type MvMac with the correct upper- and lowercase letters. The second exception is that MvMac has no options.

ON THE COMMAND LINE

Overview of the *MvMac* Command

COMMAND SYNTAX

```
MvMac source destination
```

FINDER EQUIVALENT

Drag and drop move.

OVERVIEW OF OPTIONS FOR *MVMAC*

MvMac   This command moves the source argument to the destination, retaining resource forks. You can use multiple sources or wildcards. You can specify a directory as the destination, or specify a path containing a filename, if you wish to change the name of the file being moved.

GETTING MORE INFORMATION

To display the manual page and learn more about MvMac, type man MvMac in Terminal.

Getting File Info with *GetFileInfo*

Many files on an HFS+ file system contain a set of flags, called Finder flags, which indicate whether certain settings are on or off. While this information is used less often under Mac OS X than previous versions of Mac OS, some of these attributes are still common: whether a file is invisible, whether it is an alias, whether it is a stationery file, and more.

The GetFileInfo tool returns the specific attributes for any file or files, showing which flags are on and which are off. It can also return the type and creator of a file, if this information exists, and the file's creation and modification dates.

The syntax for this command is as follows:

```
GetFileInfo [option] file ...
```

To get a list of attributes for a file, run the command like this:

```
% GetFileInfo  ~/Walden.txt
file: "/Users/kirk/Walden.txt"
type: ""
creator: ""
attributes: avbstclinmed
created: 03/15/2003 15:53:45
modified: 05/30/2003 15:24:37
```

As you can see, the command displays, by default, all the information it can return.

The attributes section of the list shows, for each attribute, whether the flag is on or off. Lowercase letters indicate attributes that are off, and uppercase letters indicate attributes that are on. The attributes are shown in Table Int. 8.1:

TABLE INT. 8.1: ATTRIBUTES SHOWN BY THE *GETFILEINFO* COMMAND

SET	UNSET	ATTRIBUTE
A	a	Alias file
B	b	Has bundle
C	c	Custom icon (allowed on folders)
D	d	Located on the desktop (allowed on folders)
E	e	Extension is hidden (allowed on folders)
I	i	Inited—Finder is aware of this file and has given it a location in a window (allowed on folders)
L	l	Locked
M	m	Shared (can run multiple times)
N	n	File has no INIT resource
S	s	System file (name locked)
T	t	Stationary file
V	v	Invisible (allowed on folders)

You can also use the `GetFileInfo` command with five options to return only specific information:

- ◆ `-a`: returns only attribute information
- ◆ `-c`: returns only creator information
- ◆ `-d`: returns only the file's creation date
- ◆ `-m`: returns only the file's modification date
- ◆ `-t`: returns only the file type

For example, to return just the file's creation date, run the command like this:

```
% GetFileInfo -d ~/Walden.txt
03/15/2003 15:53:45
```

Note that you cannot combine options with the `GetFileInfo` command; you must run it either with no options, to return all of its information, or with a single option. You can, however, run it so it returns only an indication for a specific attribute. Use the -a option followed by the letter representing the attribute. Here's an example:

```
% GetFileInfo -aE ~/Walden.txt
1
```

This command checks to find whether the Extension (E) attribute is set; the command returns 1, which shows that the attribute is indeed set. If the `GetFileInfo` command returns 0, this shows that the attribute is not set.

Setting File Info with *SetFile*

Just as the `GetFileInfo` command returns HFS+ file attributes, the `SetFile` command allows you to set any of these attributes. The syntax and options for the command are the same:

```
SetFile [option] file ...
```

You can use the `SetFile` command to set any of the attributes shown in Table Int. 8.1:

```
% SetFile -a L ~/Walden.txt
```

This command locks the file `Walden.txt` in the Finder. To unlock the same file, run this command:

```
% SetFile -a l ~/Walden.txt
```

You can set multiple attributes for a file in a single command:

```
% SetFile -a LVE ~/Walden.txt
```

You can also use the `SetFile` command with five options to set specific information:

- ◆ `-a attribute`: sets the specified attribute
- ◆ `-c creator`: sets the creator code

Overview of the *GetFileInfo* Command

COMMAND SYNTAX

```
GetFileInfo [option] file
```

FINDER EQUIVALENT

None, though some of this information is displayed in Finder Info windows.

OVERVIEW OF OPTIONS FOR *GETFILEINFO*

GetFileInfo	The GetFileInfo command returns HFS+ file attributes for the specified file.
-a	This option returns only attribute information for the specified file.
-c	This option returns only creator information for the specified file.
-d	This option returns only the file's creation date.
-m	This option returns only the file's modification date.
-t	This option returns only the file type.

GETTING MORE INFORMATION

To display the manual page and learn more about GetFileInfo and the options available, type man GetFileInfo in Terminal.

- ◆ -d date: sets the file's creation date
- ◆ -m date: sets the file's modification date
- ◆ -t type: sets the file type

For example, to set the file's creation date, run the command like this:

```
% SetFile -d "6/4/2003 16:00" ~/Walden.txt
```

Unlike with GetFileInfo, which can only use one option at a time, you can set as many options as you want with SetFile. For example, to change an individual PDF file so it opens with Preview, run this command:

```
% SetFile -t "PDF " -c PREV Walden.pdf
```

Note the use of quotes around PDF; the type is PDF followed by a space, and the quotes are needed to set the correct type including that space.

Chapter 16

Configuring the Shell

In Chapter 2, "Using Terminal," I explained how the Terminal application is "the gateway to the command line in Mac OS X." Terminal provides an interface to a shell, which is the actual program that you send commands to, that interprets them and that returns the results of those commands to the Terminal window, passes them on to other commands, or redirects them to files or other output.

While Mac OS X Panther (10.3) comes with several shells installed, it uses the bash shell by default. You can use this shell, or you can choose to launch a different shell when you open Terminal, such as tcsh, which was the default shell before Panther. In this chapter, I'll look at how you can configure both the bash and tcsh shells: how to define shell variables and environment variables, how to create and use shell aliases, and how to configure other shell functions, such as command history, filename completion, and more.

Working with the Shell

In Chapter 2, I explained how you can set preferences and display settings for the Terminal application. You set all these preferences in windows by checking radio buttons, by selecting items from pop-up menus, or from other user interface controls.

The shell you use lets you set other preferences and settings, all of which are made from the command line or by editing a special file. Since Mac OS X uses the bash shell by default, I'll look at how to configure this shell. But since the default shell before Panther was tcsh, and many users still work with this shell, I'll look at tcsh as well. For more on which shell you are using, and how to change shells, see the sidebar "Which Is Your Default Shell?" in Chapter 2.

You can naturally use other shells with Mac OS X: you can use any of the shells that are included with the operating system or other shells that you install. (See the sidebar "Using Different Shells" later in the chapter.) You configure other shells in a manner similar to the way you configure bash or tcsh; see the shell's man page for information on this.

When working on the command line, the shell is the single most important tool you use. You issue all commands through the shell, and the shell manages the output of those commands.

HANDS ON: SAVING OR PRINTING THE MAN PAGE FOR YOUR SHELL

As I mentioned, it's a good idea to save the man page for your shell as a text file so you can search it more easily, or even print it. Since man pages have special formatting, you cannot simply save them as text files without doing a bit of manipulation. To save the bash man page to a text file, run the following command:

```
$ man bash | col -b > bash.txt
```

This reformats the man page correctly so the text it displays is human-readable. You'll find that there are some extra spaces throughout the file, but nothing that gets in the way of understanding the page. To print the bash man page, open a new Terminal window and run the following command:

```
$ man bash | col -b
```

Then choose File ➢ Print, and click the unnamed pop-up menu in the Print sheet. (It says Copies & Pages by default.) Select Terminal and check Print Entire Scrollback Buffer. To print the entire text as it is displayed in the Terminal window, click Print. You can save it as a PDF file by clicking Save As PDF; this might be better, since the bash man page is quite long. (You can find out about other ways to view man pages in Chapter 3, "Getting Help while in Terminal.")

Finally, there is an even easier way: download a copy of the tcsh manual in PDF format from the program's web site: http://mirrors.tcsh.org/tcsh-book/tcsh.pdf.

You can download a copy of the *Bash Reference Manual*, written by Chet Ramey and Brian Fox, the original developers of GNU Bash, in PDF format (or purchase a paper copy) from http://www.network-theory.co.uk/bash/manual/.

Note, however, that the versions of the shells installed by Mac OS X may be slightly different than the version documented at these URLs; there may therefore be minor differences in the documentation.

For more on getting help and viewing man pages, see Chapter 3.

While it may come to seem transparent after a while, the shell is always there, and the way you configure it affects your work and productivity. For this reason, it is important to get to know your shell. One way to do this is by reading its man page, though this can often be a daunting experience. The bash man page, for example, is more than 33,000 words long. This length makes it more difficult to read in Terminal than most commands, and you may find it useful to save a copy of it to search with your word processor or text editor, or to print out the file.

The *bash* Shell Startup Process

Configuring the bash shell requires an understanding of how the shell works when it starts up. The bash shell reads specific files on your computer, looking for information on which settings and variables to use, and whether it is a login or non-login shell.

When bash starts up, it reads certain files, and does so in a specific order:

First, bash reads the /etc/profile file, which contains systemwide environment and startup commands and variables, including the important PATH variable. This file contains the following (in Mac OS X 10.3):

```
# System-wide .profile for sh(1)

PATH="/bin:/sbin:/usr/bin:/usr/sbin"
```

LOGIN VS. NON-LOGIN SHELLS

When you invoke a shell, it is either a login or non-login shell. A login shell is, simply, a shell that you use to log in as a specific user. Under Mac OS X this is not related to the login process, which you carry out in the login window when starting up your Mac. Login shells are "normal" shells, as you see when you open a Terminal window or log in to a remote machine with ssh or telnet.

A non-login shell is either a subshell (invoked by running the shell within another shell, such as typing tcsh at the bash prompt in Terminal), or shells invoked by shell scripts. Login shells read different files than non-login shells to find out what settings to use and variables to set.

```
export PATH

[ -r /etc/bashrc ] && source /etc/bashrc
```

The information in this file tells bash what the default PATH is, then tells bash to export PATH (which makes this variable available to other processes you start from the current session), then tells bash to source, or read, the /etc/bashrc file, if it exists (which is the case in the default Panther installation).

The bash shell then reads the /etc/bashrc file, which contains a number of systemwide functions and aliases as well as the default prompt that bash displays in Terminal. This file, under Mac OS X 10.3, contains the following:

```
# System-wide .bashrc file for interactive bash(1) shells.
PS1='\h:\w \u\$ '
# Make bash check its window size after a process completes
shopt -s checkwinsize
```

The prompt is set on the line beginning with PS1; then, as the comments explain, bash checks its window size after a process completes.

Next, bash reads one of three files, in the following order:

```
~/.bash_profile
~/.bash_login
~/.profile
```

When bash finds and reads one of these files, it stops looking for the other, so it's important to be aware of this order and to not place aliases or other settings in multiple files unless you're sure you want to do so.

You can use any of these files for your environment and configuration settings and aliases, but it's best to just use one of them. My recommendation is that you use ~/.bash_profile, since it's the first one bash looks for. Also, putting your settings and aliases in this file rather than in ~/.profile prevents potential problems with shell scripts that use sh, since sh reads ~/.profile. If, by chance, you use ~/.profile and for some reason a ~/.bash_profile file were to be added to your home folder, bash wouldn't read your settings.

The bash shell reads one other file, but only if you launch it as a non-login shell: ~/.bashrc. If you plan to use bash in this manner, you may need to duplicate some of your settings and aliases in this file.

The *bash* Shell Shutdown Process

While bash reads many files when starting up, it only reads one file when shutting down, and only if it's a login shell: ~/.bash_logout. If that file exists, bash executes the commands it contains. You can create this file and add any commands you would like bash to run on shutdown.

Non-login shells exit without reading or writing any files.

The *tcsh* Shell Startup Process

Like the bash shell, the tcsh shell reads a certain number of files, in a specific order, and these files tell it which settings and variables are to be applied, depending on whether it starts up as a login shell or a non-login shell.

When tcsh starts up as a login shell, it first reads the following files:

```
/etc/csh.cshrc
/etc/csh.login
```

These files provide systemwide settings, since the tcsh shell reads them no matter which user runs the shell. If you examine the contents of these files, you can see the type of information they contain. The /etc/csh.cshrc contains this:

```
# System-wide .cshrc file for csh(1).

if ($?prompt) then
        set promptchars = "%#"
        if ($?tcsh) then
                set prompt = "[%m:%c3] %n%# "
        else
                set prompt = "[%m:%c3] `id -nu`%# "
        endif
endif
```

This file is used to set the prompt for the tcsh shell when run as a login shell, but can also be used for the csh shell—this is why there is an if statement checking to see if the shell is tcsh.

SHELL CONFIGURATION BEFORE JAGUAR

In Mac OS X before Jaguar, or Mac OS X 10.2, Apple used a nonstandard way of configuring the tcsh shell. This was very confusing for some users who were familiar with Unix, and the changeover became even more confusing for Mac users who suddenly found things working differently in Terminal.

The /usr/share/tcsh/examples directory contains a group of files used for this configuration, and if you have continued to use these files according to Apple's pre-Jaguar configuration method, you need to be aware that the files I describe in this chapter do not work the same way.

The README file in the /usr/share/tcsh/examples directory explains how these files are set up. It is probably a good idea to abandon this system, since it does not correspond with the normal Unix way of configuring your shell.

The /etc/csh.login file contains the following:

```
# System-wide .login file for csh(1).

setenv PATH "/bin:/sbin:/usr/bin:/usr/sbin"
```

This sets the PATH variable so the login shell knows where to look for commands.

You can add configuration information to the /etc/csh.cshrc file if you wish. The main reason to use this file for shell configuration is if you administer a system with many users and want to maintain the same settings for all the users.

After reading the two files located in /etc, the tcsh shell then reads the following files:

~/.tcshrc (or if ~/.tcshrc is not found, ~/.cshrc)

~/.history (or the value of the histfile shell variable)

~/.login

~/.cshdirs (or the value of the dirsfile shell variable)

As you can see from these paths, the files are in the user's home (~) directory and all information in these files is user-specific.

- ◆ The .tcshrc file contains configuration information, shell variables, shell aliases, and more. This is the main file to use for all your custom settings. While this file can get long if you add a lot of variables and aliases to it, it has the advantage of keeping all your configuration information in a single file.

- ◆ The .history file contains your command history, if you have set the savehist shell variable to save your command history across sessions. See Setting Shell Variables for more on setting the savehist variable.

- ◆ The .login file contains any settings you want to apply only to login shells.

- ◆ The .cshdirs file contains your directory stack, if you have set the savedirs shell variable. See Setting Shell Variables for more on setting the savedirs variable.

Non-login shells read only /etc/csh.cshrc and ~/.tcshrc or ~/.cshrc on startup.

The *tcsh* Shell Shutdown Process

While there are many files involved in the tcsh startup process, the shutdown process is simpler. The tcsh shell reads ~/.logout, if it exists, to look for any commands that must be performed on logout. It writes ~/.history, if the savehist shell variable is set, and writes ~/.chsdirs if the savedirs shell variable is set.

Non-login shells exit without reading or writing any files.

HANDS ON: USING DIFFERENT SHELLS

While Apple has chosen the bash shell as the default for Mac OS X, you can use other shells if you wish: you can use tcsh, if you became comfortable with it under Jaguar or earlier, or you can use one of the other available shells, or install your own.

If you want to change your shell, just run this command:

```
$ chsh -s /bin/tcsh username
```

where you would replace /bin/tcsh with the path of the shell you want to use, and *username* by the name of the user whose shell you want to change.

Configuring the Shell

As you saw in the "Working with the Shell" section, your shell reads certain files when it starts up looking for configuration information. The main file used is either the ~/.bash_profile file or the ~/.tcshrc file (hereinafter referred to simply as the .bash_profile file or .tcshrc file). While there are other ways to configure your shell (see the sidebar "Shell Configuration before Jaguar"), using one of these files is probably the best way to set user-related configurations.

You can add all kinds of configuration information to these files: shell variables, environment variables, aliases, and more. You can even put shell scripts in this file if you want them to run each time you open a shell—but bear in mind that they will run *each* time you invoke your shell.

Configuring these files is simple: they are merely text files, and you create and edit them with any text editor. You can use a command-line text editor, such as Pico, vi, or Emacs, or you can use a graphical editor such as TextEdit, BBEdit, or others. For more on editing text files, see Chapter 10, "Editing Text."

One thing to note is that you will not find these files in your home directory by default. You must create the file you want using your text editor.

Setting Environment Variables for *bash*

There are two types of variables that you can set for your shell: environment variables and shell variables. When you configure a shell variable, it is only available to the shell itself; when you configure environment variables, they are also available to processes that the shell invokes. There are fewer environment variables than shell variables, though you could create your own environment variables to use in your own programs.

I've recommended earlier that you use your .bash_profile file for any personal configurations, so I'll look at what you can put in this file and how to correctly set variables.

The bash shell uses two different commands to turn variables and options on or off, and to set their values. Each of these commands—set and shopt—works with different variables, and you'll generally find that you need to use both if you want to personalize your bash environment.

To find which environment variables have been set, run the set command alone:

```
$ set
BASH=/bin/bash
BASH_VERSINFO=([0]="2" [1]="05b" [2]="0" [3]="1" [4]="release"
```

```
[5]="powerpc-apple-darwin7.0")
BASH_VERSION='2.05b.0(1)-release'
CLICOLOR=1
COLUMNS=80
DIRSTACK=()
EDITOR=/usr/bin/pico
EUID=501
FCEDIT=/usr/bin/pico
GROUPS=()
HISTCONTROL=ignoredups
HISTFILE=/Users/kirk/.bash_history
HISTFILESIZE=500
HISTSIZE=500
HOME=/Users/kirk
HOSTNAME=Walden.local
HOSTTYPE=powerpc
IFS=$' \t\n'
LINES=39
LOGNAME=kirk
LSCOLORS=ExFxCxDxBxegedabagacad
MACHTYPE=powerpc-apple-darwin7.0
MAILCHECK=60
OPTERR=1
OPTIND=1
OSTYPE=darwin7.0
PATH='/bin:/sbin:/usr/bin:/usr/sbin:/Developer/Tools'
PIPESTATUS=([0]="0")
PPID=16777
PS1='\h:\w \u\$ '
PS2='> '
PS4='+ '
PWD=/Users/kirk
SECURITYSESSIONID=213ef0
SHELL=/bin/bash
SHELLOPTS=braceexpand:emacs:hashall:histexpand:history:interactive-comments:monitor
SHLVL=1
TERM=vt100
TERM_PROGRAM=Apple_Terminal
TERM_PROGRAM_VERSION=100
UID=501
USER=kirk
_=.bash_profile
__CF_USER_TEXT_ENCODING=0x1F5:0:0
```

As you can see in the previous example, the **set** command returns a long list of variables, most of which are set by the system, or by Terminal preferences, and that you don't need to change. Some of these include your username, your home directory path, your default shell, your user ID, and others.

While the set command returns a list of environment variables when run alone, it also lets you set specific options that affect the way the bash shell works. To find out which options you can change with the set command, run the following:

```
$ set -o
allexport          off
braceexpand        on
emacs              on
errexit            off
hashall            on
histexpand         on
history            on
ignoreeof          off
interactive-comments     on
keyword            off
monitor            on
noclobber          off
noexec             off
noglob             off
nolog              off
notify             off
nounset            off
onecmd             off
physical           off
posix              off
privileged         off
verbose            off
vi                 off
xtrace             off
```

You can find out about all of these options in the bash man page. To set any of these variables, use the following syntax:

```
set -o option
```

To unset a variable, use this syntax:

```
set +o option
```

This may seem a bit counterintuitive; it would probably be more logical to set something with the +o and unset with the -o, but that's just the way it works.

Here's one example. To set the noclobber option, which tells your shell to not overwrite existing files with the same name when redirecting output to a file, add this line to your .bash_profile file:

```
set -o noclobber
```

Adding this line to your `.bash_profile` file tells `bash` to activate the option each time you start a session with the shell (as a login shell). You can also run this as a command if you only want to set it temporarily:

```
$ set -o noclobber
```

Then turn it off with this command:

```
$ set +o noclobber
```

The second type of options you set using the `shopt` command. This command turns on or off other options that affect the way the `bash` shell works. You can run the following to see a list of available options:

```
$ shopt -p
shopt -u cdable_vars
shopt -u cdspell
shopt -u checkhash
shopt -s checkwinsize
shopt -s cmdhist
shopt -u dotglob
shopt -u execfail
shopt -s expand_aliases
shopt -u extglob
shopt -u histreedit
shopt -u histappend
shopt -u histverify
shopt -s hostcomplete
shopt -u huponexit
shopt -s interactive_comments
shopt -u lithist
shopt -s login_shell
shopt -u mailwarn
shopt -u no_empty_cmd_completion
shopt -u nocaseglob
shopt -u nullglob
shopt -s progcomp
shopt -s promptvars
shopt -u restricted_shell
shopt -u shift_verbose
shopt -s sourcepath
shopt -u xpg_echo
```

In the previous example, options preceded by `-u` are unset (or off) and options preceded by `-s` are set. To change these options, use the following syntax. To set an option:

```
shopt -s option
```

SETTING THE *PATH* VARIABLE FOR *BASH*

One important variable to set is the PATH variable. This variable tells the shell where to look for command names you type in Terminal. In most cases, the default is sufficient, but if you want to use commands in nonstandard directories without typing their full paths, you should add these directories here.

One useful change you can make to your PATH variable is to add the path for the command-line developer tools, if you have installed Apple's Xcode developer software. These commands are found in /Developer/ Tools. Add the following line to your .bash_profile file so bash can find these tools:

```
export PATH="$PATH:/Developer/Tools"
```

This adds the /Developer/Tools directory to the PATH variable that has already been declared ($PATH).

You can add as many directories as you need to the PATH variable, so if you have command-line tools in other locations, add the paths of their enclosing directories here.

To unset an option:

```
shopt -u option
```

As with options set by the **set** command, you can run these as commands or simply add the lines to your .bash_profile file so they are activated when you start a bash session.

Finally, you can set environment variables for your bash sessions using the **export** command. With bash, you must declare your variables and then export them, so other processes can use them. Here's an example, using the EDITOR variable, which tells the shell what your default text editor is:

```
export EDITOR=/usr/bin/pico
```

In this example, the **export** command exports the declaration that follows. Here, EDITOR is declared as being /usr/bin/pico; hence all processes know that the default text editor is pico.

You'll find a full list of options and variables in the bash man page. Check these out; you'll find that some of them are useful.

Setting Environment Variables for *tcsh*

As with bash, there are two types of variables that you can configure in your .tcshrc file: environment variables and shell variables. The tcsh shell uses two different commands for the different types of variables.

To see which environment variables are set, run this command:

```
% setenv
HOME=/Users/kirk
SHELL=/bin/tcsh
USER=kirk
LANG=en
PATH=/bin:/sbin:/usr/bin:/usr/sbin:/usr/local/bin:
/Developer/Tools:/Users/kirk/Documents/bin
__CF_USER_TEXT_ENCODING=0x1F5:0:0
TERM=vt100
TERMCAP=\277\377\330
```

```
TERM_PROGRAM=Apple_Terminal
TERM_PROGRAM_VERSION=81
LOGNAME=kirk
HOSTTYPE=macintosh
VENDOR=apple
OSTYPE=darwin
MACHTYPE=powerpc
SHLVL=1
PWD=/Users/kirk
GROUP=staff
HOST=Walden.local.
EDITOR=pico
```

As you can see, there are many environment variables set, but not all of them are set from the .tcshrc file. My .tcshrc file contains the following (note that the PATH variable line is one line without a break):

```
#environment variables
setenv EDITOR pico

#shell variables

set history = 500
set savehist = (500 merge)
set autolist
set path = ( $path
/Developer/Tools ~/Documents/bin )

#aliases
alias note 'touch ~/Desktop/\!$'
alias rm 'rm -i'
alias safari 'open -a Safari'
```

I have separated my .tcshrc file into three sections: environment variables, shell variables, and aliases. Using the # symbol marks lines as comments, so the text of these three headers is not read. You can comment your .tcshrc file as much as you want; this can be helpful to make sure you remember why you added a certain line to it.

To set environment variables, add a line like this to your .tcshrc file:

```
setenv NAME value
```

As you can see in the preceding example, I have the EDITOR variable set to pico; if a command such as a pager calls an editor to make changes to a file, Pico opens automatically.

To set any environment variable, simply add a line to your .tcshrc file and it will be set when you invoke the tcsh shell. While there are a couple of dozen environment variables (see the tcsh man page), you'll probably only need to consider setting the EDITOR variable, since the system takes care of setting most of the others. You should avoid making changes to other variables, unless you are sure what they affect; the changes you make only apply when running tcsh, and they may lead to unexpected consequences.

HANDS ON: SETTING THE *PATH* VARIABLE FOR *TCSH*

As you saw in the sidebar "Setting the PATH Variable for bash," the PATH variable is very important, since it tells the shell where to look for your commands. Here's how to set it for tcsh.

Again using my `~/.tcshrc` file as an example, note that I have two additional entries in my PATH variable:

```
/Developer/Tools
/Users/kirk/Documents/bin
```

The first is the location of the command-line tools included with the Mac OS X Developer Tools (see Interlude 8, "Using the Developer Tools," for more on these tools), and the second is a directory where I store shell scripts.

To set your path variable, add a line to your `~./tcshrc` file with this syntax:

```
set path = ( $path directory1 directory2 etc.)
```

You can add as many directories as you need to the path variable.

Since the environment variables set in the `.tcshrc` file only affect operations that run through the shell, any changes you make will have no effect on programs run from the Finder. If you need to set other environment variables (and if you're sure you know what you are doing), you can do so by creating a `~/.MacOSX/environment.plist` file. See `http://developer.apple.com/qa/qa2001/qa1067.html` for information on creating and setting up this file.

Setting Shell Variables

There are far more shell variables than environment variables, and setting shell variables is similar to setting preferences in a graphical application. To see which ones are set, run this command:

```
% set
_
addsuffix
argv    ()
autolist
cwd     /Users/kirk
dirstack        /Users/kirk
echo_style      bsd
edit
gid     20
group   staff
history 500
home    /Users/kirk
loginsh
owd
path    (/bin /sbin /usr/bin /usr/sbin /usr/local/bin
/Developer/Tools /Users/kirk/Documents/bin)
```

```
prompt    [%m:%c3] %n%#
prompt2 %R?
prompt3 CORRECT>%R (y|n|e|a)?
promptchars    %#
savehist       (500 merge)
shell   /bin/tcsh
shlvl   1
status  0
tcsh    6.10.00
term    vt100
tty     ttyp1
uid     501
user    kirk
version tcsh 6.10.00 (Astron) 2000-11-19
    (powerpc-apple-darwin) options 8b,nls,dl,al,sm,rh,color
```

As you can see in this example, many of the shell variables come from system information, provided through the NetInfo system: these include gid, group, home, uid, user, and shell. But other variables, such as autolist, path, and savehist, are defined in my .tcshrc file.

There are three ways to set shell variables, depending on the type of variable:

```
set variable
set variable = value
set variable = (value1, value2, etc.)
```

HANDS ON: SETTING AND UNSETTING VARIABLES TEMPORARILY

As you saw earlier, you can set environment and shell variables by adding lines to your .bash_profile or .tcshrc file. When you open Terminal, the shell reads these files and executes these lines as commands.

For some of these variables or shell options, you may want to try them out before adding them to your initialization files, or you may want to turn them on or off temporarily. This is very simple, because the commands you use to set and unset variables are commands that you can run in Terminal. For example, to temporarily turn on or off the noclobber variable, just run one of these commands. In bash:

```
$ set -o noclobber
$ set +o noclobber
```

The first command turns the option on; the second turns it off.

In tcsh:

```
% set noclobber
% unset noclobber
```

The first command turns the option on; the second turns it off.

Setting and unsetting variables in this way lets you not only try out their results, but also means you don't need to open a new shell session to see their effects.

You use the first example to set variables that have on/off values. The second sets variables that have values that you can choose. And the third is for variables that take multiple values. Here are some examples:

```
set autolist
set history = 500
set path = (/bin /sbin /usr/bin /usr/sbin /usr/local/bin
/Developer/Tools /Users/kirk/Documents/bin)
```

These three examples show the three different ways of setting variables. In the first, the autolist variable has an on/off condition; using the set autolist line turns it on. In the second example, the history variable takes a value; using set history = 500 sets the variable to that value. The third example shows a variable that takes multiple values. Here, the values are separated only by spaces. You can add as many directories as you wish to your search path.

You can find a full list of shell variables in the tcsh man page; there are dozens of them, listed in the Special Shell Variables section, and many of them are good to know about.

Setting Shell Aliases

Shell aliases are nothing like Macintosh Finder aliases. They are command shortcuts—similar, perhaps, to keyboard shortcuts or abbreviations. With shell aliases you can invoke long, complex commands by typing very short commands.

You can set shell aliases in your .bash_profile or .tcshrc file so they are available all the time, or you can set one temporarily, just as you set shell variables, from the command line. To set an alias, use the following syntax. For bash:

```
alias aliasname=command
alias aliasname='command argument(s)'
```

And for tcsh:

```
alias aliasname command
alias aliasname 'command argument (s)'
```

As you can see, the methods of declaring aliases are very similar between the two shells; the only difference is the use of the = character instead of a space.

For simple commands, you can use the first forms in the example—you would do this to set a long command name to a short one. For example, to set an alias to the softwareupdate command, use one of these (remember, the first one, with =, is for bash and the second one is for tcsh):

```
alias sw=softwareupdate
alias sw softwareupdate
```

This works as an abbreviation for the longer command name.

To set an alias for a more complex command, or even a group of commands, use this form:

```
alias rm='rm -i'
alias rm 'rm -i'
```

This alias is a safety net for the rm command. Each time I run the rm command with this alias active, it runs the rm -i command, which asks me to confirm the deletion of each file.

A similar safety net is the following:

```
alias rm='mv \!* ~/.Trash/'
alias rm 'mv \!* ~/.Trash/'
```

This moves files to the Trash, rather than deleting them. You can then empty the Trash from the Finder.

When you set aliases, you may, at times, want to use the original, unaliased version of the command. If you set one of the preceding aliases for rm, you can use the *real* version of rm by running the command like this:

```
$ \rm
```

The backslash tells the shell to turn off aliasing.

HANDS ON: CHECKING ALIASES AND COMMANDS

While you can check which aliases are active by running the alias command, as previously explained, you can also check an individual alias to find what it refers to. The which command tells you which command an alias refers to in tcsh:

```
% which rm
rm:       aliased to rm -i
```

If the command you specify as argument for which is not an alias, it returns the full path for the command:

```
% which ls
/bin/ls
```

And if the command is a built-in shell command, which tells you this as well:

```
% which cd
cd: shell built-in command.
```

The equivalent command for bash is type; it shows whether the argument you run after the command is an alias:

```
$ type rm
rm is aliased to 'rm -I'
```

While the which command works in bash for commands other than aliases, the type command will also tell you where other commands are to be found:

```
$ type which
which is hashed (/usr/bin/which)
```

For more on the which command, see the command's man page. For more on the type command, see the bash man page.

VIEWING ALIASES

To view a list of all the aliases you have set, either in your `.bash_profile` or `~/.tcshrc` file or manually, run the alias command. This works in both `bash` and `tcsh`:

```
$ alias
note     touch ~/Desktop/!$
rm       rm -i
safari   open -a Safari
```

This list shows all your active aliases.

REMOVING ALIASES

While the easiest way to remove an alias is to delete it from your `.bash_profile` or `~/.tcshrc` file, you may also want to turn certain aliases off temporarily, or you may want to remove aliases you have set manually without quitting your shell session. To do this, use the `unalias` command:

```
$ unalias aliasname
```

ON THE COMMAND LINE

Overview of the *alias* and *unalias* Commands

COMMAND SYNTAX

```
alias
unalias
```

FINDER EQUIVALENT

None.

OVERVIEW OF OPTIONS FOR *ALIAS* AND *UNALIAS*

`alias`	The `alias` command returns a list of active shell aliases.
`alias aliasname=command`	
`alias aliasname command`	To set an alias, run the `alias` command followed by an `aliasname` and a command; the command must be in single quotes if it contains more than one argument. For bash, use the = character between the alias name and the command; for tcsh, use a space.
`unalias`	The `unalias` command removes an alias.

GETTING MORE INFORMATION

To find out more about the `alias` and `unalias` commands, type `man tcsh` or `man bash` in Terminal. These commands are built into the respective shells.

This works with both `bash` and `tcsh`, and removes whatever alias you have manually set for the alias `aliasname`, or temporarily turns off an alias you have set in your `.bash_profile` or `.tcshrc` file.

Summing Up

The shell you use is a powerful program that offers many types of customization, from shell variables to aliases. It depends on certain files that you can edit to set customizations when the shell launches. To go beyond basic command-line tasks, a good understanding of how you can configure the shell can not only save you time, but also make the shell better adapted to the way you work.

Interlude 9:
Automating Commands

In the many chapters of this book you have seen how to run commands manually, from Terminal, one at a time. Now it's time to take a brief look at how you can combine commands and run them automatically. The Unix underpinnings of Mac OS X feature several ways you can group commands, run them at specified times, and, using other parts of Mac OS X, make double-clickable commands that even those with no command-line experience can use.

From automating commands with cron, to combining commands in shell scripts, to using AppleScript, the Mac OS X systemwide scripting language, you have many ways to extend your use of the commands I've presented in this book. In this interlude, I'll show you how you can do all these things to increase the reach and flexibility of your work with the command line.

Automating Command Execution with *cron*

As you saw in Chapter 15, "System Maintenance from the Command Line," there are several maintenance commands that run at regular times. The `periodic` command runs a set of clean-up scripts, and its execution is regulated by the `cron` daemon, a process that runs in the background, checking certain files once per minute to see if it should run preset commands.

The `cron` command checks in several places to run commands automatically: the first is the `/etc/crontab` file, which is owned by root and which contains entries for commands that are generally run for the entire system. Here's what the default Mac OS X `/etc/crontab` file looks like:

```
# /etc/crontab
SHELL=/bin/sh
PATH=/etc:/bin:/sbin:/usr/bin:/usr/sbin
HOME=/var/log
#
#minute hour   mday   month  wday   who      command
#
#*/5     *      *      *      *      root     /usr/libexec/atrun
#
# Run daily/weekly/monthly jobs.
15       3      *      *      *      root     periodic daily
30       4      *      *      6      root     periodic weekly
30       5      1      *      *      root     periodic monthly
```

The lines beginning with # are comments, and are not read; they help you understand the file. As you can see, there are headers showing what the different fields are before the first command line:

◆ minute: from 1 to 60

◆ hour: from 1 to 24

- ◆ mday: the day of the month, from 1 to 31

- ◆ month: from 1 to 12

- ◆ wday: the day of the week, from 1 to 7

- ◆ who: the user running the command

- ◆ command: the command to run

An asterisk in any of these columns is a wildcard that represents all valid values for that field. If you were to put asterisks in every column, the cron job would run once every minute.

When discussing the periodic command in Chapter 15, I mentioned that this command runs automatically during the wee hours and that if your Mac is not running, it will not execute. As you can see, in the /etc/crontab file, the periodic command is set to run at the following times:

- ◆ daily: 3:15 a.m.

- ◆ weekly: Saturday at 4:30 a.m.

- ◆ monthly: the 1st of the month at 5:30 a.m.

You can change these times by editing this file with any text editor. You must use sudo to do this; run this command to edit /etc/crontab with Pico:

$ sudo pico /etc/crontab

(If you don't use sudo, you can view the file, but not edit it.) Make any changes you want in your text editor and save the file. Here's how I've set my /etc/crontab file:

```
15      16      *       *       *       root    periodic daily
30      10      *       *       5       root    periodic weekly
30      11      1       *       *       root    periodic monthly
```

This ensures that the periodic command runs when my computer is on: daily at 4:15 p.m., weekly on Fridays at 10:30 a.m., and monthly at 11:30 a.m. on the 1st of the month.

If you are an administrator, you can add commands to /etc/crontab to run them automatically. All you need to do is follow the template shown in the file: set up the date and time information, the user and the command name (if you are running a shell script, enter its full path, unless you are sure that it is in a directory included in your PATH variable; see Chapter 16, "Configuring the Shell," for more on the PATH variable).

For example, to add an automatic command that runs a shell script called backup, located in /Users/kirk/bin, every day at 6 p.m:

```
*       18      *       *       *       root    /Users/kirk/bin/backup
```

As long as the computer is on at that time, cron will run the script. But if the computer is off, the script is not run at a later time.

SETTING USER CRON TASKS

The /etc/crontab file is a systemwide file, and should only be used for settings that affect the entire computer. Each user can also have a crontab file, setting any commands they want to run automatically under their user accounts.

By default, users have no crontab files; they must create them and load them into the crontab system. Each user can check to see if there is a crontab file for them by running the following:

```
henrydthoreau$ crontab -l
crontab: no crontab for henrydthoreau
```

In this example, user henrydthoreau checked to see if he had a crontab file; as you can see, he didn't. To create this file, use any text editor and save the file with any name you want.

```
$ pico hdt_crontab
```

You'll find it easiest to type in these headers to help you place your data in the right place:

```
#minute hour   mday   month   wday   command
```

Add any tasks you want to run to this file:

```
#minute hour   mday   month   wday   command
#
*       12     *      *       *      ~/bin/backup
```

In this example, a shell script called backup is set to run every day at noon.

Save the file with the text editor, then run this command to add it to the crontab system:

```
$ crontab hdt_crontab
```

You don't need to keep the file you saved, since loading it into the crontab system copies it to /var/cron/tabs. If you look in this directory, you'll see a list of crontab files for each user who has set one:

```
$ sudo ls /var/cron/tabs
henrydthoreau   jsbach   kirk   root
```

If you are an administrator, you can edit any of these files by running a command like this:

```
$ sudo crontab -u username -e
```

You can check what your users have set and make any changes you want.

Combining Commands

There are several ways you can combine commands to run them together as a single command. Shell scripting is one such way (see About Shell Scripting), but another way is to simply use the built-in shell functions that allow you to run more than one command on a line in Terminal, then set an alias to a complex command.

Say you often want to get a list of the contents of some of your users' Documents directories and save them to a file. This involves, for each user, a command like the following:

```
$ sudo ls /Users/username/Documents > files.txt
```

You can put several commands together, separating them with semicolons (the following must be all on one line in Terminal):

```
$ sudo ls /Users/henrydthoreau/Documents > files.txt ;
sudo ls /Users/jsbach/Documents >> files.txt ;
sudo ls /Users/emerson/Documents >> files.txt
```

This gets a list of the specified user's Documents directory, then, for the first user, writes it (>) to a file, and, for the other users, appends it (>>) to the same file.

But to go even further, you can create an alias to that complex command, so when you need to run it you merely type a short name. You could add the following alias to your .bash_profile file (all the text must be on one line):

```
alias list_files='sudo ls /Users/henrydthoreau/Documents >
files.txt ; sudo ls /Users/jsbach/Documents >> files.txt ;
sudo ls /Users/emerson/Documents >> files.txt'
```

With this alias, you can run this complex command with just the following:

```
$ list_files
```

This saves you a lot of time having to retype the commands. You can string together as many commands as you want in this manner.

For more on setting shell aliases, see Chapter 16.

Creating Double-Clickable Command Files

There is a very simple way to create command files that you can double-click in the Finder to run complex commands, such as the list_files command in the previous section, or shell scripts. All you need to do is save the command or script in a text file, and add the .command extension to it.

For example, if I save the list_files command, to create a list of files in my users' Documents directory, as list_files.command, all I need to do is double-click this file to run the command. Terminal opens, if it is not already open, or comes to the front if it is open; the command runs; and the process exits, logging out from the Terminal session:

```
$ /Users/kirk/Desktop/list_files.command; exit
logout
[Process completed]
```

If you have a sudo command in this file, Terminal will ask you to enter your password.

This is an excellent way to provide commands to users who are unfamiliar with the command line. For example, you may want them to copy a specific file to a location, such as their Preferences folder; you can use a .command file to execute this command easily. It's also a good way for you to save commands that you want to use repeatedly. You can either double-click the .command file in the Finder or invoke it from the command line like any other command (as long as you give its full path, or it is in a directory in your PATH variable).

Automating Commands with AppleScript

AppleScript is a system-level scripting language used in Mac OS X. With AppleScript you can automate tasks in the Finder or in scriptable applications. AppleScript has been around for many years; it was introduced with System 7, back in the early 1990s. With Mac OS X, Apple has ensured that AppleScript and the command line can work together, and in both ways: you can invoke command-line commands from within AppleScripts and you can invoke AppleScripts from the command line.

USING APPLESCRIPTS FROM THE COMMAND LINE

The osascript command (OSA means Open Scripting Architecture) provides a bridge between the command line and AppleScript. With this command you can run AppleScripts from the command line, either in Terminal or in shell scripts.

When using the osascript command, you can either put the AppleScript in the command (if so, you must use the -e option) or run it from a file. Here's an example of running an AppleScript to tell a user that you are going to shut down the computer they are on (this command must be all on one line):

```
$ osascript -e 'tell Application "Finder" to display dialog
"Please save your work. This computer must be shut down."'
```

If this AppleScript were in a script file, I could run it with this command:

```
$ osascript script_file
```

For one-line AppleScripts, you can easily run them from Terminal, but for longer scripts it's better to use a script file.

RUNNING COMMAND-LINE COMMANDS FROM WITHIN APPLESCRIPTS

Just as you can run AppleScripts from the command line, you can run command-line commands and shell scripts from within AppleScripts. To do this, you use the do shell script command in Apple-Script, telling Terminal to execute the desired command:

```
do shell script "ls"
```

You can enter a simple command in quotes following do shell script, or a more complex command, or the name of a shell script. If you save the script as an application, users can run it by simply double-clicking it.

COMPILING APPLESCRIPTS FROM THE COMMAND LINE

In addition to running AppleScripts from the command line, you can also compile them, using the osacompile command. But Script Editor is much better for this purpose, especially since it has syntax checking.

However, if you're used to using a text editor such as BBEdit to write AppleScripts, you may find it easier to compile them from the command line. See the osacompile man page for more on this command.

Overview of the *osascript* Command

COMMAND SYNTAX

```
osascript
```

FINDER EQUIVALENT

AppleScripts run in the Script Editor or as double-clickable applications.

OVERVIEW OF OPTIONS FOR *OSASCRIPT*

`osascript`   The `osascript` command lets you run AppleScripts from the command line.

GETTING MORE INFORMATION

To find out more about the `osascript` command, type `man osascript` in Terminal.

You can learn more about AppleScript by reading the documentation included with the Developer Tools, if you have installed this documentation, at `/Developer/Documentation/AppleScript`. Or you can check out Apple's AppleScript website at `http://www.apple.com/applescript/` and The AppleScript Sourcebook at `http://www.applescriptsourcebook.com`.

About Shell Scripting

One of the most common ways of automating command-line commands is via shell scripting, or shell programming. This involves writing scripts using the wide range of commands accessible in Terminal, which may or may not include commands in other languages, such as Perl. Given the vast number of commands you can use, as well as the possibilities of integrating such languages as Perl or other scripting languages, you have an unlimited toolkit.

Naturally, shell scripting can range from very simple, with one-line scripts or simple combinations of basic commands, to very complex, with long scripts that work with data arrays, variables, if-then statements, and more. The advantage of using shell scripts lies in their scalability: you can begin with simple commands and build on them as you learn more about working with the command line. The disadvantage, however, is that when writing shell scripts you are not working in a "language" and have no borders. It may be a bit more complicated to figure out how to do something when you have a nearly unlimited fount of commands.

Shell scripts allow both beginners and experienced programmers to write scripts that meet their needs. Whether you merely paste together a few simple commands to create, delete, and copy files or use `awk`, `sed`, and `perl` to write complex database management scripts, you can do a lot with shell scripts.

While it is beyond the scope of this book to look at shell scripting in depth, I'll give a brief overview of how you can use shell scripts with Mac OS X.

USING SHELL SCRIPTS

Shell scripts can be as brief as one-line commands. The purpose of saving such commands as scripts is to save time: if you are planning to reuse the same commands, you don't have to type them over. For example, to use the command from earlier in this interlude, you could make a shell script that lists the contents of certain users' Documents directories. To do so, create a text file and enter the following:

```
#!/bin/bash
sudo ls /Users/henrydthoreau/Documents > ~/files.txt
sudo ls /Users/jsbach/Documents >> ~/files.txt
sudo ls /Users/emerson/Documents >> ~/files.txt
```

The first line of this script, #!/bin/bash, is called the *shebang*. This line is essential, for it tells your computer which program is interpreting the script. In this example I use /bin/bash, which tells the computer to use the bash shell. Which shell to use for scripting is a very controversial question, and arguments and flame wars can break out when people begin defending their choices. Many people have criticized the tcsh shell for scripting; some people find fault with other shells. The bash shell is a good shell for scripting, but for most scripts you can use whichever shell you are most comfortable with.

Once you have entered this text in a new file, you must save it. Give it any name you want, but make sure it is not the same name as any other command accessible from the command line. After you have saved the file, you must make it executable by running the chmod command:

```
$ chmod +x script_file
```

Your script is ready to run. To invoke it, either call it by its full path or put the file in a directory that is in your PATH variable. If you add it to a directory that is in your PATH variable, you must then run the hash -r command (bash) or the rehash command (tcsh) so your shell updates its internal command list and can find it quickly:

```
$ hash -r
% rehash
```

I have a bin directory inside my Documents directory; I use this directory to store shell scripts, and have added this to my PATH variable in my .bash_profile file (see Chapter 16 for more on the PATH variable.) You can put shell scripts anywhere, but if you are going to use them often, it's best to keep them in a specific directory.

You can create and edit shell scripts with any text editor, either a command-line editor or a graphical editor. I personally use BBEdit to write shell scripts, because of its syntax coloring and other useful features. One thing to make sure of if you use a graphical editor is that it uses Unix line breaks when saving files:. See Chapter 10, "Editing Text," for more on line breaks.)

LEARNING MORE ABOUT SHELL SCRIPTING

Shell scripting is a huge subject, and many books have been written about it. If you want to look into shell scripting, see the Appendix, "Further Reading," for a few books that will help you write even the most complex scripts.

While shell scripting uses the basic commands you have seen throughout this book, you can write scripts with other languages, such as Perl, Python, and Ruby, which are included with Mac OS X. These languages use their own internal commands, but you can combine them with other commands in shell scripts.

Appendix A

Further Reading

No book can cover every aspect of a subject as vast as Mac OS X, or even cover all the commands accessible from the Terminal. The following is a list of books I recommend if you want to delve more deeply into the various subjects I have explored in this book.

Mac OS X

Mastering Mac OS X, 3rd ed. by Todd Stauffer and Kirk McElhearn (Sybex, 2003) is a thorough coverage of the GUI side of Mac OS X. This comprehensive book covers things from the Finder to web serving, from networks to security.

Mac OS X Power Tools, 2nd ed. by Dan Frakes (Sybex, 2004) is a collection of tips, tricks, and troubleshooting techniques for Mac OS X. Many of the techniques in this book use the command line.

Mac OS X Power Hound by Rob Griffiths (O'Reilly, 2004) is a collection of hints from Rob's web site, http://www.macosxhints.com. A lot of these hints show how you can hack your Mac with the command line.

General Unix Books

Teach Yourself Unix in 24 Hours, 3rd ed. (Sams, 2001) and *Teach Yourself Unix System Administration in 24 Hours* (Sams, 2002), both by Dave Taylor, give a good introduction to Unix in general. Dave's a Mac user as well as a Unix geek, and the system administration book gives clear explanations of the differences between Mac OS X and other Unix flavors.

FreeBSD Unleashed, 2nd ed. by Michael Urban and Brian Tiemann (Sams, 2003) covers FreeBSD, which is at the heart of Mac OS X. There are many differences between the two operating systems, but you'll find some good explanations of some of the finer points in this book.

Unix Power Tools, 3rd ed. by Shelley Powers, Jerry Peek, Tim O'Reilly, and Mike Loukides (O'Reilly, 2002) is a huge book of tips and tricks for all types of Unix systems. Most of the information in this book applies to the commands available in Mac OS X. This is a gold mine of information.

Shell Scripting

Unix Shells by Example, 3rd ed. by Ellie Quigley (Prentice Hall PTR, 2001) not only gives you an overview of the five main Unix shells (C, Bourne, Korn, bash, and tcsh), but also gives a good introduction to shell scripting with bash.

Linux Shell Scripting with Bash by Ken O. Burtch (Sams, 2004) looks at shell scripting with bash, the default shell under Mac OS X 10.3.

Wicked Cool Shell Scripts by Dave Taylor (No Starch Press, 2004) is a compendium of ready-made scripts, with explanations that will help you better understand scripting. While most of the scripts are for any flavor of Unix, the book has a chapter on scripts written specifically for Mac OS X.

Teach Yourself Perl in 21 Days by Laura Lemay (Sams, 1999) is an excellent book on Perl for beginners.

Books on Specific Unix Tools

Using csh & tcsh by Paul DuBois (O'Reilly, 1995) is the only book that focuses entirely on the tcsh shell, and tells you just about everything about how to get the most out of this shell.

Learning the bash Shell, 2nd ed. by Cameron Newham and Bill Rosenblatt (O'Reilly, 1998) focuses on configuring and using the bash shell.

Mastering Regular Expressions, 2nd ed. by Jeffrey E. F. Friedl (O'Reilly, 2002) is the most complete book on this complex subject.

sed & awk, 2nd ed. by Dale Dougherty and Arnold Robbins (O'Reilly, 1997) is a thorough examination of these two essential tools for shell scripting and advanced command-line usage.

Learning the vi Editor, 6th ed. by Linda Lamb and Arnold Robbins (O'Reilly, 1998) tells you everything you need to know about this command-line text editor.

Learning GNU Emacs, 2nd ed. by Debra Cameron, Bill Rosenblatt, and Eric S. Raymond (O'Reilly, 1996) gives you the lowdown on Emacs, a complex yet awesomely powerful text editor.

Index

Note to the reader: Throughout this index **boldfaced** page numbers indicate primary discussions of a topic. *Italicized* page numbers indicate illustrations.